The Evolution of Desire

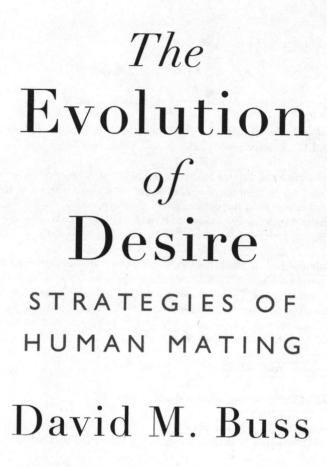

The
Evolution
of
Desire

STRATEGIES OF
HUMAN MATING

David M. Buss

REVISED AND UPDATED EDITION

BASIC BOOKS
New York

Published in the United States by Basic Books, an imprint of Perseus Books, LLC, a subsidiary of Hachette Book Group, Inc.

Books published by Basic Books are available at special discounts for bulk purchases in the United States by corporations, institutions, and other organizations. For more information, please contact the Special Markets Department at Perseus Books, 2300 Chestnut Street, Suite 200, Philadelphia, PA 19103, or call (800) 810-4145, ext. 5000, or e-mail special.markets@perseusbooks.com.

Designed by Trish Wilkinson

Library of Congress Cataloging-in-Publication Data

Names: Buss, David M., author.
Title: The evolution of desire : strategies of human mating / David M.
    Buss.
Description: Revised and Updated edition. | New York : Basic Books,
    [2016] |
Includes bibliographical references and index.
Identifiers: LCCN 2016036547 (print) | LCCN 2016044407 (ebook) |
    ISBN 9780465097760 (paperback) | ISBN 9780465093304 (ebook)
Subjects: LCSH: Sex. | Sex (Psychology) | Sexual attraction.
Classification: LCC HQ21 .B95 2016 (print) | LCC HQ21 (ebook) |
    DDC 306.7—dc23
LC record available at https://lccn.loc.gov/2016036547
LSC-C
Printing 8, 2021

Contents

Preface to the Revised and Updated Edition

SINCE THE PUBLICATION of the first edition of *The Evolution of Desire* in 1994, the field has witnessed an explosion of new scientific research on human mating. Although neglected within mainstream psychology for decades, mating is beginning to command the attention it properly deserves. Nothing lies closer to the reproductive engine of the evolutionary process. Those who fail to mate do not become ancestors. Each living human, therefore, has descended from a long and unbroken line of successful mateships stretching back millions of years. If any one of our ancestors had failed to traverse the complex hurdles posed by mating, we would not be alive to ponder these improbable feats. Our mating minds—the glory of romance, the flush of passion, the triumph of love—are fortunate products of this evolutionary process.

The original publication of *Desire* was greeted with a gratifying amount of attention, but it also provoked some strong emotions. The intensity of sentiment probably reflects the importance of the topic. Humans don't seem well designed for dispassionate in-tellectual discourse about domains that have profound personal relevance. Some readers told me before the book was even pub-lished that the information it contained might be so damaging if it became widely known that it should be suppressed. Some refused to believe that gender differences in mating strategies exist, since the dominant dogma in social science for decades has contended that women and men are essentially identical in basic sexual psychology. Others acknowledged the formidable body of scien-tific findings, but refused to believe that gender differences have evolutionary origins. Many like to think that humans have been magically exempt from the processes of natural selection and sex-ual selection. It is encouraging that the hostility to this work has largely, although certainly not entirely, subsided. Mating research has entered the mainstream and is now known throughout the world; the first edition of *The Evolution of Desire* was translated into ten languages.

The original publication of *The Evolution of Desire* shed some light on previous mysteries of human mating, but it also pointed to gaps in knowledge, notably those surrounding the complexi-ties of female sexuality. These are now covered in greater depth. The new edition also deals with some enduring mysteries of mat-ing. Why does homosexuality exist? Can men and women be "just friends"? How do people who pursue short-term mating strategies avoid entangling commitments? Do women have evolved anti-rape defenses? Are men and women hopelessly biased in reading each other's minds? Some of these topics were briefly discussed in the original edition and addressed at greater length in two supplemen-tal chapters added to the 2003 paperback edition. Now this ma-terial has been integrated throughout the book, which has been fully revised and updated from beginning to end to reflect the past twenty-two years of theory and research.

Although I am aware of the cliché that if you give someone a hammer everything looks like a nail, I've come to believe that human mating strategies permeate nearly every human endeavor. I see them everywhere. They shape status hierarchies among women and foster sexual treachery among men. They delay male puberty early in life while causing premature death at the other end—both products of mate competition. They unite people in love's embrace and drive mates apart with jealous rages and sexual infidelity. Human sexual psychology is deeply embedded in the fabric of our social endeavors, in all of its glorious and disturbing manifestations.

1

Origins of Mating

We are walking archives of ancestral wisdom.
—HELENA CRONIN, *The Ant and the Peacock*

HUMAN MATING DELIGHTS and amuses us and galvanizes our gossip. In all cultures, few domains of human activity generate as much discussion, as many laws, or such elaborate rituals. Yet the elements of human mating seem to defy understanding. Women and men sometimes find themselves choosing mates who make them unhappy. Some abuse them psychologically and physically. Some live mating lives of quiet desperation. Efforts to attract new mates often backfire. Conflicts erupt within couples, producing downward spirals of blame and despair. Despite their best intentions and vows of lifelong love, nearly half of all married couples end up divorcing.

Pain, betrayal, and loss contrast sharply with the usual romantic notions of love. We grow up believing in true love, in finding our "one and only." We assume that once we do, we will marry in bliss and live happily ever after. But reality rarely coincides with our beliefs. Even a cursory look at the divorce rate, the 30 to 50 percent incidence of extramarital affairs, and the jealous rages that rack so many relationships shatters these illusions.

Discord and dissolution in mating relationships are typically seen as signs of failure. Regarded as distortions or perversions of the natural state of mating life, they are thought to signal personal inadequacy, immaturity, neurosis, failure of will, or simply poor judgment in the choice of a mate. This view is radically wrong. Conflict in mating is the norm and not the exception. It ranges from a man's anger at a woman who declines his advances to a wife's frustration with a husband who fails to listen or help in the home. These pervasive patterns defy easy explanation. Something deeper and more telling about human nature is involved— something we do not fully understand.

The problem is complicated by the centrality of love in human life. Feelings of love mesmerize us when we experience them and occupy our fantasies when we do not. The euphoria and anguish of love dominates poetry, music, literature, soap operas, and romance novels more than any other theme. Contrary to common belief in the social sciences, love is not a recent invention of the Western leisure classes. People in all cultures experience love and have coined specific words for it.[1] Its pervasiveness convinces us that love, with its key components of commitment, idealized perceptions of loved ones, deep empathy, and overwhelming passion, is an inevitable part of the human experience, within the grasp of everyone.[2]

Our failure to understand the real and paradoxical nature of human mating is costly, both scientifically and socially. Scientifically, lack of knowledge leaves unanswered some of life's most puzzling questions, such as why people sacrifice years of their lives to the quest for love and the struggle for fulfilling relationships. Socially, our ignorance leaves us frustrated, helpless, and often hurt when mating goes wrong, whether in the jungle of online dating sites, in hookups on college campuses, in the workplace, or in our home.

We need to reconcile the profound love that humans seek with the conflict that permeates our most cherished relationships. We need to square our dreams with reality. To understand these baffling contradictions, we must gaze back into our evolutionary past—a past that has grooved and scored our minds as much as our bodies, a past in which our strategies for mating have been as critical as our strategies for survival.

Evolutionary Roots

More than a century ago, Charles Darwin offered a revolutionary explanation, sexual selection theory, for the mysteries of mating.[3] He had become intrigued by the puzzling fact that some animals have characteristics that hinder their survival. The elaborate plumage, large antlers, and other conspicuous features displayed by many species seem costly in the currency of survival. Peacocks look like a predator's dream. Not only are peacocks packages of nutritious meat, but they come attached to a long train of brilliant feathers. This train can only encumber a peacock fleeing from predators, and it also serves as a neon sign pointing those predators straight to an easy meal. Darwin's answer was that the peacocks' displays evolved because they led to their bearer's reproductive success by providing an advantage in the competition for desirable peahens. The evolution of characteristics because of their mating benefits, rather than survival benefits, is known as sexual selection.

Sexual selection, according to Darwin, takes two forms. In one form, same-sex competition, members of the same sex compete with each other, and the outcome of their contest gives the winner greater sexual access to members of the opposite sex. Two stags locking horns in combat is the prototypical image of this intrasexual competition. The characteristics that lead to success in these contests, such as greater strength, intelligence, or attractiveness to allies, evolve because the victors are able to mate more often and hence pass on genes for the qualities that have led to their success.

In the other type of sexual selection, members of one sex choose a mate based on their preferences for particular qualities in that mate. The desired characteristics evolve—that is, increase in frequency over time—because animals possessing them are chosen more often as mates and genes that cause them to be desirable get passed on with greater frequency. Animals lacking the desired characteristics are excluded from mating, and genes for undesirable qualities perish. Since peahens prefer peacocks with plumage that flashes and glitters, dull-feathered males get left in the evolutionary dust. Peacocks today possess brilliant plumage because over evolutionary history peahens have preferred to mate with dazzling and colorful males.

Darwin's theory of sexual selection began to explain mating behavior by identifying two key processes by which evolutionary change can occur: preferences for a mate and competition for a mate. But the theory was vigorously resisted by male scientists for over a century, in part because the active choosing of mates seemed to grant too much power to females, who were thought to remain passive in the mating process. The theory of sexual selection was also resisted by mainstream social scientists because its account of human nature seemed to depend on instinctive behavior and thus to minimize humans' uniqueness and flexibility. Culture, consciousness, and free will were presumed to have liberated us from evolutionary forces. The breakthrough in applying sexual selection to humans came in the late 1970s and 1980s, in the form of theoretical advances initiated by my colleagues and myself in the fields of psychology and anthropology.[4] We tried to identify underlying psychological mechanisms that were the products of evolution—adaptations that would help to explain both the extraordinary flexibility of human behavior and the active mating strategies women and men pursue. This new discipline is called evolutionary psychology.

When I began work in the field, however, little was known about actual human mating behavior. There was a frustrating lack of scientific evidence on mating in the broad array of human populations and practically no documented support for grand evolutionary theorizing. No one knew whether some mating desires are universal, whether certain gender differences are characteristic of all people in all cultures, or whether culture exerts a powerful enough influence to override the evolved preferences that might exist. So I departed from the traditional path of mainstream psychology to explore which characteristics of human mating might follow from evolutionary principles. In the beginning, I simply wanted to verify a few of the most obvious evolutionary predictions about gender differences in mating preferences—for example, whether men desire youth and physical attractiveness in a mate and whether women desire status and economic security. Toward that end, I interviewed and administered questionnaires to 186 married adults and 100 unmarried college students within the United States.

The next step was to verify whether the psychological phenomena uncovered by this study are characteristic of our species. If mating desires and other features of human psychology are products of our evolutionary history, they should be found universally, not just in the United States. So I initiated an international study to explore how mates are selected in other cultures, starting with a few European countries, including Germany and the Netherlands. I soon realized, however, that since European cultures share many features, they do not provide the most rigorous test for the principles of evolutionary psychology. Over a period of five years, I expanded the study to include fifty collaborators from thirty-seven cultures located on six continents and five islands, from Australia to Zambia. Local residents administered the instruments assaying mating desires in their native language. We sampled large cities, such as Rio de Janeiro and São Paulo in Brazil, Shanghai in China, Bangalore and Ahmedabad in India, Jerusalem and Tel Aviv in Israel, and Tehran in Iran. We also studied rural peoples, including Indians in the state of Gujarat and Zulus in South Africa. We covered the well-educated and the poorly educated. We included respondents of every age from fourteen through seventy, as well as places in the entire range of economic systems from capitalist to communist and socialist. All major racial groups, religious groups, and ethnic groups were represented. In all, our study included 10,047 people worldwide.

This study, the largest ever undertaken on human mating desires, was merely the beginning. The findings had implications that reached into every sphere of human mating life, from dating to marriage, extramarital affairs, and divorce. They were also relevant to major social issues such as sexual harassment, intimate partner violence, pornography, and patriarchy. To explore as many mating domains as possible, my lab subsequently launched over 100 new scientific studies, involving thousands of individuals. Included in these studies were men and women searching for a mate in singles bars and on college campuses, dating couples at various stages of commitment, newlywed couples in the first five years of marriage, and couples who ended up divorced. The studies explored phenomena ranging from acts of love to acts of sexual treachery.

The findings from all of these studies caused controversy and confusion among my colleagues because in many respects they contradicted conventional thinking. They forced a radical shift from the standard view of men's and women's sexual psychology. One of my aims in this book is to formulate from these diverse findings a unified theory of human mating, based not on romantic notions or outdated scientific theories but on current scientific evidence. Some of what I discovered about human mating is not nice. In the ruthless pursuit of sexual goals, for example, men and women derogate their rivals, deceive members of the opposite sex, and even subvert their own mates. These discoveries are disturbing to me; I would prefer that the competitive, conflictual, and manipulative aspects of human mating did not exist. But a scientist cannot wish away unpleasant findings. Ultimately, the disturbing side of human mating must be confronted if its harsh consequences are ever to be ameliorated.

Sexual Strategies

Strategies are methods for accomplishing goals, the means for solving problems. It may seem odd to view human mating, romance, sex, and love as inherently strategic. But humans, like other sexually reproducing species, do not choose mates randomly. We do not attract mates indiscriminately. We do not derogate our competitors out of boredom. Our mating is strategic, and our strategies are designed to solve particular problems in ways that lead to successful mating. Understanding how people solve those problems requires an analysis of sexual strategies.

Adaptations are evolved solutions to the problems posed by survival and reproduction. Over millions of years of evolution, natural selection has produced in us hunger mechanisms to solve the problem of providing nutrients; taste buds that are sensitive to fat and sugar to solve the problem of what to put into our mouths (fruit, meat, nuts, and berries, but not dirt or gravel); sweat glands and shivering mechanisms to solve the problems of extreme hot and cold; emotions such as fear and rage that motivate either flight or combat with predators or aggressive competitors; and a complex immune system to combat diseases and parasites. These adaptations are human solutions to the problems of existence posed by the hostile forces of nature—they are our survival strategies.

Correspondingly, sexual strategies are adaptive solutions to mating problems. Those in our evolutionary past who failed to mate successfully failed to become our ancestors. All of us descend from a long and unbroken line of ancestors who competed successfully for desirable mates, attracted mates who were reproductively valuable, retained mates long enough to reproduce, fended off interested rivals, and solved the problems that could have impeded reproductive success. We carry in us the sexual legacy of those success stories.

Each sexual strategy is tailored to a specific adaptive problem, such as identifying a desirable mate or besting competitors in attracting a mate. Underlying each sexual strategy are psychological adaptations, such as preferences for a particular mate, feelings of love, desire for sex, or turbulent emotions such as sexual jealousy. Each psychological mechanism is sensitive to information or cues from the external world, such as physical features, signs of sexual interest, or hints of potential infidelity. Our psychological adaptations are also sensitive to information about ourselves, such as our own mate value or ability to attract mates with certain levels of desirability. The goal of this book is to peel back the layers of adaptive problems that men and women have faced in the course of mating and uncover the complex sexual strategies they have evolved for solving them.

Although the term *sexual strategies* is a useful metaphor for thinking about solutions to mating problems, it is misleading in the sense that it connotes conscious intent. Sexual strategies do not require conscious planning or awareness. Our sweat glands are "strategies" for accomplishing the goal of thermal regulation, but we do not consciously sweat, nor are we aware of our bodies' target thermal state. Indeed, just as a pianist's sudden awareness of her hands may impede performance, most human sexual strategies are most successfully carried out without the awareness of the actor.

Selecting a Mate

Nowhere do people have an equal desire for all possible mates. Everywhere some potential mates are preferred, and others shunned. Our sexual desires have evolved in the same way as many other desires. Consider the survival problem of what food to eat. Humans are faced with a bewildering array of potential objects to ingest—berries, fruit, nuts, and fish, but also dirt, gravel, poisonous plants, twigs, and feces. If we had no taste preferences and ate objects from our environment randomly, some people would consume ripe fruit, fresh nuts, and other objects that provide caloric and nutritive sustenance. Others would eat rancid meat, rotten fruit, and toxins. Earlier humans whose preferences ever so slightly tilted them toward nutritious objects survived more often than their counterparts and hence passed on their eating proclivities to offspring.

Our actual food preferences bear out this evolutionary process. We show great fondness for substances rich in fat, sugar, protein, and salt and an aversion to substances that are bitter, sour, pathogenic, or toxic.[5] These food preferences solve a basic problem of survival. We carry them with us today precisely because they solved critical adaptive problems for our ancestors.

Our desires in a mate serve analogous adaptive purposes, but their functions do not center simply on survival. Imagine living as our ancestors did long ago—struggling to keep warm by the fire; hunting meat for our kin; gathering nuts, berries, and herbs; and avoiding parasites, dangerous animals, and hostile humans. If we were to select a mate who failed to deliver the resources promised, who had affairs, who was lazy, who lacked hunting skills, or who heaped physical abuse on us, our survival would be tenuous, and our reproduction at risk. In contrast, a mate who provided abundant resources, who protected us and our children, and who devoted time, energy, and effort to our family would be a great asset. As a result of the powerful survival and reproductive advantages reaped by those who chose a mate wisely, clear desires in a mate evolved. As descendants of those successful maters, we carry their desires with us today.

Many other species have evolved mate preferences. The African village weaverbird provides a vivid illustration.[6] When the male weaverbird spots a female in the vicinity, he displays his recently built nest by suspending himself upside down from the bottom and vigorously flapping his wings. The female watches. If the male passes her first visual inspection, the female approaches the nest, enters it, and examines the nest materials, poking and pulling them for as long as ten minutes. As she makes her inspection, the male sings to her from nearby. At any point in this sequence she may decide that the nest does not meet her standards and depart to inspect another male's nest. A male whose nest is rejected by several females will often break it down and rebuild it from scratch. By exerting a preference for males who can build a superior nest, the female weaverbird solves the problems of protecting and provisioning her future chicks. Her preferences have evolved because they bestowed a reproductive advantage over other weaverbirds who had no preferences and who mated with any males who happened along, regardless of the quality of their nests.

Women, like female weaverbirds, prefer men with desirable "nests." Consider one of the problems that women in evolutionary history had to face: selecting a man who would be willing to commit to a long-term relationship. A woman in our evolutionary past who chose to commit to mate with a man who was flighty, impulsive, philandering, or unable to sustain relationships found herself raising her children alone, without benefit of the resources, aid, and protection that another man might have offered. A woman who preferred to mate with a reliable man, one willing to commit to her over the long run, was more likely to have children who survived and thrived. Over thousands of generations, a preference for men who showed signs of being willing and able to commit to them evolved in women, just as preferences for mates with adequate nests evolved in weaverbirds. This preference solved key reproductive problems, just as food preferences solved key survival problems.

People do not always desire the commitment required of long-term mating. Men and women sometimes deliberately pursue a short-term sexual strategy—a brief fling, a one-night hookup, a weekend liaison, or a casual affair. And when they do, their preferences shift, sometimes dramatically. One of the crucial decisions for humans in selecting a mate is whether they are seeking a short-term mate or a long-term partner, a partner in whom they invest little or a partner to whom they commit a lot. The sexual strategies pursued hinge on this decision. This book documents the universal preferences that men and women display for particular characteristics in a mate, reveals the evolutionary logic behind the different desires of each gender, and explores the changes that occur when people shift their goal from casual sex to a committed relationship.

Attracting a Mate

People high in mate value, those who possess desirable characteristics, are in great demand. Appreciating their traits is not enough for successful mating, however, just as spying a ripe berry bush down a steep and treacherous ravine is not enough for successful eating. The next step in mating is to compete successfully for a desirable mate.

Among the elephant seals on the coast of California, males during the mating season use their sharp tusks to fight rival males in head-to-head physical combat.[7] Often their contests and bellowing continue day and night. The losers lie scarred and injured on the beach, exhausted victims of this brutal competition. But the winner's job is not yet over. He must roam the perimeter of his harem, which contains a dozen or more females. This dominant male must hold his place in life's reproductive cycle by herding stray females back into the harem and repelling "mate poachers" who attempt sneak copulations.

Over many generations, male elephant seals who were stronger, larger, more ferocious, and more cunning succeeded in securing mates. The larger, more aggressive males controlled sexual access to females and so passed on to their sons the genes conferring these qualities. Indeed, males now weigh roughly 4,000 pounds, or four times the weight of females, who appear to human observers to risk getting crushed during copulation.

Female elephant seals prefer to mate with the victors, and they pass on the genes conferring this preference to their daughters. But by choosing the larger, stronger winners, they also determine the genes for size and fighting abilities that will live on in their sons. The smaller, weaker, and more timid males fail to mate entirely. They become evolutionary dead ends. Because only 5 percent of the males monopolize 85 percent of the females, sexual selection pressures remain intense even today.

Male elephant seals must fight not just to beat other males but also to be chosen by females. A female emits loud bellowing sounds when a smaller male tries to mate with her. The alerted dominant male comes bounding toward them, rears his head in threat, and exposes a massive chest. This gesture is usually enough to send the smaller male scurrying for cover. Female preferences are one key to establishing competition among the males. If females did not mind mating with smaller, weaker males, then they would not alert the dominant male, and there would be less intense selection pressure for size and strength. Female preferences, in short, determine many of the ground rules of the male contests.

People are not like elephant seals in most of these mating behaviors. For example, whereas only 5 percent of the male elephant seals do 85 percent of the mating, more than 90 percent of men are able to find a mate at some point in their lives.[8] Male elephant seals strive to monopolize harems of females, and the winners remain victorious for only a season or two, whereas many humans form enduring unions that last for years and decades. But men and male elephant seals share a key characteristic: both must compete to attract females. Males who fail to attract females risk being shut out of mating.

Throughout the animal world, males typically compete more fiercely than females for mates, and in many species males are certainly more ostentatious and obvious in their competition. But competition among females is also intense in many species. Among patas monkeys and gelada baboons, for instance, females harass copulating pairs in order to interfere with the mating success of rival females. Among wild rhesus monkeys, females use aggression to interrupt sexual contact between other females and males, occasionally winning the male consort for themselves. And among savanna baboons, female competition over mates serves not merely to secure sexual access but also to develop long-term social relationships that provide physical protection.[9]

Competition among women, though typically less noisy and violent than competition among men, pervades human mating systems. The writer H. L. Mencken noted: "When women kiss, it always reminds one of prize fighters shaking hands." This book shows how members of each gender compete with each other for access to desirable mates. The tactics they use to compete are often dictated by the preferences of those they are trying to attract. Those who do not have what mate seekers desire risk remaining on the sidelines in the complicated dance of mating.

Keeping a Mate

Keeping a mate is another important adaptive problem; mates may continue to be desirable to rivals, who may poach, thereby undoing all the effort devoted to attracting, courting, and committing to the mate. Furthermore, one mate may break up a relationship because of the failure of the other to fulfill key needs and wants, or simply because someone fresher, more compelling, or more beautiful arrives. Mates, once gained, must be retained.

Consider the *Plecia nearctica*, an insect known as the lovebug. Male lovebugs swarm during the early morning and hover a foot or two off the ground, waiting for the chance to mate with a female.[10] Female lovebugs do not swarm or hover. Instead, they emerge in the morning from the vegetation and enter the swarm of males. Sometimes a male captures a female before she can take flight. Males often wrestle with other males. As many as ten males may cluster around a single female.

The successful male departs from the swarm with his mate. Then the couple glides to the ground to copulate. Perhaps because other males continue to attempt to mate with her, the male retains his copulatory embrace for as long as three full days—hence the nickname "lovebug." The prolonged copulation itself functions as a way of guarding the mate. By remaining attached to the female until she is ready to deposit her eggs, the male lovebug prevents other males from fertilizing her eggs. In reproductive currency, his ability to compete with other males and attract a female would be for naught if he failed to solve the problem of retaining his mate.

Different species solve this problem by different means. Humans do not engage in continuous copulatory embraces for days, but everyone who seeks a long-term relationship confronts the problem of holding on to a mate. In our evolutionary past, men who were indifferent to the sexual infidelities of their mates risked compromising their paternity. They risked investing time, energy, and effort in children who were not their own. Ancestral women, in contrast, did not risk the loss of parenthood if their mates had affairs, because maternity has always been 100 percent certain. But a woman with a philandering husband risked losing his resources, his commitment, and his investment in her and her children. One psychological strategy that evolved to combat infidelity was jealousy. Ancestral people who became enraged at signs of their mate's potential defection and who acted to prevent it had a selective advantage over their nonjealous peers. People who failed to prevent a mate's infidelity had less reproductive success.[11]

The emotion of jealousy motivates multiple actions in response to a threat to the relationship. Sexual jealousy, for example, may produce either of two radically different tactics, vigilance or violence. Using vigilance, a jealous man might follow his lover when she goes out, call her unexpectedly to see whether she is where she said she would be, keep an eye on her at a party, or read her text messages or email. Using violence, a man might threaten a rival discovered flirting with his lover, attack the rival with his fists, get his friends to beat up the rival, or throw a brick through the rival's window. Both mate retention tactics, vigilance and violence, are different manifestations of the same psychological adaptation of jealousy. They represent alternative ways of solving the problem of a partner's infidelity or defection.

Jealousy is not a rigid, invariant instinct that drives robotlike, mechanical action. It is highly sensitive to context and environment, including the formidability of the rival, differences in mate value between the two partners, and the alternative mating options available to the guarder. The many other behavioral options available to serve the strategy of jealousy give humans a flexibility in tailoring their responses to the nuances of a situation. This book documents the range of actions that are triggered by jealousy and the contexts in which they occur.

Replacing a Mate

Not all mates gained can be retained. Nor should they be. Sometimes there are compelling reasons to get rid of a mate, such as when a mate stops providing support, withdraws sex, or becomes physically or psychologically abusive. Those who remain with a mate through economic hardship, sexual infidelity, and cruelty may win our admiration for their loyalty today. But staying with a bad mate generally would not have helped ancestral humans to survive and reproduce successfully. We are the descendants of those who knew when to cut their losses.

Getting rid of a mate has precedent in the animal world. Ring doves, for example, are generally monogamous from one breeding season to the next, but they break up under certain circumstances. The doves experience a divorce rate of about 25 percent every season. The major reason for breaking their bond is infertility.[12] When ring doves fail to produce chicks with one partner during a breeding season, they leave the mate and search for another. Breaking up with an infertile mate aids the reproduction of ring doves, while remaining in a barren union does not.

Just as we have evolved sexual strategies to select, attract, and keep a good mate, we have also evolved strategies for jettisoning a bad mate. Divorce occurs in all known human cultures.[13] Our separation or "mate ejection" strategies involve a variety of psychological mechanisms. We assess whether the costs inflicted by a mate outweigh the benefits provided. We size up other potential partners and evaluate whether they might offer more than our current mate. We gauge the likelihood of successfully attracting more desirable partners. We calculate the potential damage that might be caused to ourselves, our children, and our kin by the breakup. And we combine all this information into a decision to stay or leave.

Once a mate decides to leave, another set of psychological adaptations is activated. Because these decisions have complex consequences for two sets of extended kin who often have keen interests in the union, breaking up is neither simple nor effortless. Complex social relationships must be negotiated and the breakup justified. The range of tactical options within the human repertoire is enormous, from simply packing one's bags and walking away to provoking a rift by revealing an infidelity. There are indeed at least fifty ways to leave a lover.

Breaking up is a solution to the problem of a bad mate, but it opens up the new problem of replacing that mate. Like most mammals, humans typically do not mate with a single person for an entire lifetime. Humans often reenter the mating market and repeat the cycle of selection, attraction, and retention. But starting over after a breakup poses its own unique problems. People reenter the mating market at a different age and with different assets and liabilities. Increased status and resources may help a person to attract a mate who was previously out of range. Alternatively, older age, the presence of children, or psychological baggage from a previous mateship may detract from a person's ability to attract a new mate.

Men and women undergo predictably different changes as they divorce and reenter the mating market. If there are children, women often take primary responsibility for child rearing, although this may be changing as some men step up to the plate. Because children from previous unions are usually seen as burdens rather than benefits when it comes to mating, a woman's ability to attract a desirable mate often suffers more than a man's. Consequently, fewer divorced women than men remarry, and this disparity gets larger with increasing age. This book documents the changing patterns of human mating over a lifetime and identifies circumstances that affect the likelihood of remating for men and women.

Conflict Between the Sexes

The sexual strategies that one sex pursues to select, attract, keep, or replace a mate often have the unfortunate consequence of creating a conflict with some members of the other sex. Among the scorpionfly, a female refuses to copulate with a courting male unless he brings her a substantial nuptial gift, typically a dead insect to be eaten.[14] While the female eats the nuptial gift, the male copulates with her. During copulation, the male maintains a loose grasp on the food, as if to prevent the female from absconding with it before copulation is complete (sometimes a female sexual exploitation strategy). It takes the male twenty minutes of continuous copulation to deposit all his sperm into the female. Male scorpionflies have evolved the ability to select a nuptial gift that takes the female approximately twenty minutes to consume. If the gift is smaller and is consumed before copulation is completed, the female casts off the male before he has deposited all his sperm. If the gift is larger and takes the female more than twenty minutes to consume, the male completes copulation, and the two then fight over the leftovers. Conflict between male and female scorpionflies thus occurs over whether he gets to complete copulation when the gift is too small and over who gets to consume the residual food when the gift is larger than needed.

Men and women also clash over resources and sexual access. In the evolutionary psychology of human mating, the sexual strategy adopted by one sex can trip up and conflict with the strategy adopted by the other sex. I call these phenomena *strategic interference*. Consider the differences in men's and women's proclivities to seek casual short-term sex. Men and women typically differ in how long and how well they need to know someone before they consent to have sex. Although there are many exceptions and individual differences, men generally have lower thresholds for engaging in sex.[15] For example, men often express the desire and willingness to have sex with an attractive stranger, whereas most women refuse anonymous encounters and prefer to know something about the potential mate prior to sex.

There is a fundamental conflict between these different sexual strategies: men cannot fulfill their short-term wishes without simultaneously interfering with women's long-term goals. An insistence on immediate sex interferes with the goal of a longer courtship phase. The interference is reciprocal, since any delay also obstructs the goal of those seeking short-term sex. Whenever the strategy adopted by one sex interferes with the strategy adopted by the other sex, strategic interference and conflict ensue.

Conflicts do not stop with a couple's commitment. Married women sometimes complain that their husbands are condescending, emotionally constricted, and unreliable. Married men sometimes complain that their wives are moody, overly dependent, and sexually withholding. Both sexes complain about infidelities, ranging from mild flirtations to serious affairs. All of these conflicts become understandable in the context of our evolved mating strategies.

Although conflict between the sexes is pervasive, it is not inevitable. There are conditions that minimize conflict and produce harmony between the sexes. Knowledge of our evolved sexual strategies gives us tremendous power to better our own lives by choosing actions and circumstances that activate some strategies and deactivate others. Indeed, understanding sexual strategies, including the cues that trigger them, is one step toward reducing conflict between men and women. This book explores the nature of sexual conflict and offers some solutions for fostering harmony between the sexes.

Sexual Orientation

"Heterosexual orientation is a paradigmatic psychological adaptation," writes Michael Bailey, one of the world's most prominent experts on sexual orientation.[16] His reasoning is compelling. Among sexually reproducing species, males and females must mate with each other for successful reproduction. Any orientation that lowers the likelihood of successful reproduction will be ruthlessly weeded out. Although controversy surrounds estimates, most scientists converge on the finding that roughly 96 to 97 percent of all men and 98 to 99 percent of all women have a *primary* orientation toward heterosexuality.

The persistence of a small percentage of primarily or exclusively homosexual men and women, however, poses a genuine evolutionary puzzle. In the several hundred public lectures I've given on human sexual strategies, the question "What about homosexuality?" is by far the most frequently asked. It's a mystery of human mating and an empirical enigma for evolutionary theory.[17] The riddle is made more intriguing by two known facts. First, a number of twin studies show that sexual orientation is moderately heritable, suggesting a partial genetic basis.[18] Second, a handful of other studies show beyond a reasonable doubt that homosexual men have a decisively lower rate of reproduction than heterosexual men.[19] How can a sexual orientation that is partly inherited continue to persist in the face of continual evolutionary selection against it?

We will explore some of these issues later in the book and discuss scientific findings about the links between sexual orientation and mate preferences and sexuality, but several key conceptual issues are worth noting here. First, there are at least three different senses of the phrase "sexual orientation." One can be called *primary sexual orientation* and refers to whom one is sexually attracted to—men, women, both (bisexual), or neither (asexual). Another is *gender identity*—whether one subjectively feels like a man or woman, feels like both, or neither. Still another is *sexual behavior,* referring to the gender of the individuals with whom one actually has sex. These distinctions are critical, since we witness many combinations and permutations in individual people. For example, some individuals may be primarily attracted to one sex but engage in sexual behavior with the other sex out of curiosity (sexual experimentation) or social constraint (lack of available sex partners corresponding to one's primary sexual orientation).

Another critical distinction is that male and female sexual orientation have different natures and developmental trajectories. Male sexual orientation tends to appear early in development and rarely changes dramatically over time, whereas female sexuality appears to be far more flexible and fluid over the life span. For example, male sexual orientation tends to be bimodally distributed, with most men either strongly heterosexual or strongly homosexual—there are relatively few bisexual men. Women's sexual orientation, by contrast, varies more smoothly along a continuum from highly heterosexual through a series of bisexual gradations to a nearly exclusive preference for same-sex partners.

Another difference is that women appear able to switch orientations more easily, evidence of the greater flexibility of their sexuality. Anecdotally, there is the "LUG" phenomenon found in women's colleges—Lesbian Until Graduation. The actress Anne Heche lived for several years in a lesbian relationship with comedienne and actress Ellen Degeneres. After they broke up, Heche married a man and had a child with him. Similarly, some women marry when they are young, have children, and then in middle age switch to a lesbian lifestyle. Although some men "come out of the closet" after a socially prescribed marriage to someone to whom they are not sexually attracted, it is still very likely that their primary sexual orientation was set relatively early in life and had never really changed.

Once we recognize that sexual orientation is not singular and that there are important differences between sexual attraction, sexual identity, and sexual behavior, scientific understanding of variations in human sexuality is likely to accelerate. We must also recognize that there is probably no single theory that can explain the many varieties of human sexuality, including gay males, lesbians, bisexuals, transgendered individuals, and asexuals, much less one that can explain the profound individual differences among those with these different orientations. We delve into the origins and nature of sexual orientation in greater detail in Chapters 2, 3, and 4, with a special focus on mate preferences, sexual motivation, and preferred mating strategies.

Culture and Context

Although ancestral selection pressures are responsible for creating the mating strategies we use today, our current conditions differ from historical ones in critical ways. Ancestral people got their fruit and vegetables from gathering and their meat from hunting; most modern people get their food from supermarkets and restaurants. Modern urban people today deploy their mating strategies on Internet dating sites and in bars rather than on the savanna. Nevertheless, the same sexual strategies used by our ancestors operate today with unbridled force. Our evolved psychology of mating, after all, plays out in the modern world because it is the only mating psychology we mortals possess.

Consider the foods consumed in massive quantities at fast-food chains. We have not evolved adaptations specifically for burgers or pizza, but the foods we eat reveal the ancestral strategies for survival we carry with us today.[20] We consume vast quantities of fat, sugar, protein, and salt in the form of burgers, shakes, fries, and pies. Fast-food chains are popular precisely because they serve these nutritional elements in concentrated quantities. They reveal the food preferences that evolved in a past environment of scarcity. Today, however, we overconsume these elements because of their unprecedented abundance, and the old survival strategies now hurt our health. Because evolution works on a time scale too slow to keep up with the radical changes of the past several hundred years, we are stuck with taste preferences that evolved under different conditions. Although we cannot go back in time and observe directly what those ancestral conditions were, our current taste preferences, like our fear of snakes and our fondness for children, provide a window for viewing what those conditions must have been. We carry with us equipment that was designed for an ancient world.

Our evolved mating strategies, just like our survival strategies, may now be maladaptive in some ways with respect to survival and reproduction. The increase in sexually transmitted infections, for example, renders casual sex more dangerous than it was under ancestral conditions. The dramatic opportunities to evaluate thousands of potential mates online sometimes paralyze our ability to decide on "the one." Only with a deep understanding of our evolved sexual strategies, their origins, and the conditions they were designed to deal with can we hope to solve the problems of mating posed by these novel environments.

One impressive advantage humans have over many other species is a repertoire of mating strategies that is large and highly sensitive to context. Consider the problem of being in an unhappy marriage and contemplating whether to get divorced. This decision depends on many complex factors, including the amount of conflict within the marriage, whether one's mate is unfaithful, the pressure applied by relatives on both sides of the family, the presence of children, the ages and needs of the children, and the prospects for attracting another mate. Humans have evolved psychological adaptations that consider and weigh the costs and benefits of these crucial features of context.

Cultural circumstances also vary in ways that are critical for activating particular sexual strategies from our complex menu of mating. Some cultures have mating systems that are polygynous, allowing men to have multiple wives. Other cultures are polyandrous, allowing women to take two or more husbands. Still others are monogamous—on the surface at least—and restrict both women and men to one marriage partner at a time. Others are promiscuous, with high rates of mate switching, or polyamorous, openly allowing love and sex with multiple partners. Our evolved strategies of mating are highly sensitive to these social, legal, and cultural patterns. In polygynous mating systems, for example, parents place tremendous pressure on their sons to compete for the status and resources needed to attract women so as to avoid the matelessness that plagues some men when others monopolize multiple women.[21] In monogamous mating cultures, in contrast, parents put less pressure on their sons.

Another key circumstance is the ratio of the sexes, or the number of available men relative to the number of available women in the mating pool. When there is a surplus of women, such as among the Ache Indians of Paraguay or in some urban centers such as Manhattan, men become more reluctant to commit to one woman, preferring instead to pursue many casual relationships. When there is a surplus of men, such as in contemporary cities of China and among the Hiwi tribe of Venezuela, monogamous marriage is the rule and divorce rates plummet.[22] As men's sexual strategies shift, so must women's. As women's sexual strategies shift, so must men's. The two coexist in a complex reciprocal relation, based in part on the crucial sex ratio.

From one perspective, context is everything. Contexts that recurred over evolutionary time created the strategies we carry with us now. Current contexts and cultural conditions determine which strategies get activated and which lie dormant. To understand human sexual strategies, this book identifies the recurrent selection pressures or adaptive challenges of the past, the psychological adaptations or strategic solutions they created, and the current contexts that activate some solutions rather than others.

Barriers to
Understanding Human Sexuality

Evolutionary theory has appalled and upset people since Darwin first proposed it in 1859 to explain the creation of new species and the adaptations that characterize their component parts. The wife of the Bishop of Worcester, his contemporary, is reported to have remarked upon hearing about his theory of our descent from nonhuman primates: "Let's hope that it's not true; but if it is, let's pray that it does not become generally known."[23] Strenuous resistance to evolutionary theory continues to this day. These barriers to understanding must be removed if we are to gain real insight into our sexuality.

One barrier is perceptual. Our cognitive and perceptual mechanisms have been designed by natural selection to perceive and think about events that occur in a relatively limited time span— over seconds, minutes, hours, days, sometimes months, and occasionally years. Ancestral humans spent most of their time solving immediate problems, such as finding food, maintaining a shelter, keeping warm, selecting and competing for partners, protecting children, forming alliances, striving for status, and defending against marauding males, so there was intense pressure to think in the short term. Evolution, in contrast, occurs gradually over thousands of generations in tiny increments that we cannot observe directly. To understand events that occur on time scales this large requires a leap of the imagination, much like the cognitive feats of physicists who theorize and infer from evidence black holes, dark matter, and eleven-dimensional universes they cannot see.

Another barrier to understanding the evolutionary psychology of human mating is ideological. From Spencer's theory of social Darwinism onward, biological theories have sometimes been used for terrible political ends—to justify oppression or to argue for racial or sexual superiority. We must be vigilant about not repeating this history of misusing biological explanations of human behavior. At the same time, we cannot be misled by this history into ignoring the most powerful theory of organic life we have—evolution by selection. As the Harvard evolutionary psychologist Steven Pinker has noted, evolutionary psychology provides powerful theories to explain aggression and cooperation as well as human sexuality and mating. Understanding human mating requires that we face our evolutionary heritage boldly and understand ourselves as products of those prior forces of natural and sexual selection.

Another basis of resistance to evolutionary psychology is the naturalistic fallacy, which maintains that whatever exists should exist. The naturalistic fallacy confuses a *scientific description* of human behavior with a *moral prescription* for that behavior. In nature, however, there are diseases, plagues, parasites, infant mortality, and a host of other natural events that we try to eliminate or reduce. The fact that they *do* exist in nature does not imply that they *should* exist.

Similarly, male sexual jealousy, which evolved in part as an adaptation to protect men's certainty of their paternity, is known to damage women worldwide in the form of intimate partner violence, stalking, and occasionally murder.[24] As a society, we may eventually develop methods for reducing male sexual jealousy and its dangerous manifestations. Because there is an evolutionary origin for male sexual jealousy does not mean that we must passively accept it or its dangerous expressions.

The naturalistic fallacy applied in the reverse direction takes the form of the romantic fallacy. Some people have exalted visions of what it means to be human. According to one of these views, "natural" humans are at one with nature, peacefully coexisting with plants, animals, and each other. War, aggression, and competition are seen as corruptions of this essentially peaceful human nature by current conditions, such as patriarchy, culture, or capitalism. Despite the evidence, some people cling to these illusions. When the anthropologist Napoleon Chagnon documented that 25 to 30 percent of all Yanomamö men die violent deaths at the hands of other Yanomamö men, his work was bitterly denounced by those who had presumed that the group lived in harmony.[25] The romantic fallacy occurs when we see ourselves through the lens of utopian visions of what we want people to be.

Opposition also arises to the presumed implications of evolutionary psychology for change. If a mating strategy is rooted in evolutionary biology, some people mistakenly think it is immutable, intractable, and unchangeable. We are therefore doomed, according to this view, to follow the dictates of our biological mandate, like blind, unthinking robots. This belief mistakenly divides human behavior into two separate categories, one biologically determined and the other environmentally determined. In fact, human action is inexorably a product of both. Every strand of DNA unfolds within a particular environmental and cultural context. Within each person's life, social and physical environments provide input to both the development and activation of evolved psychological adaptations. Every behavior is without exception a joint product of those mechanisms and their environmental influences. In identifying the historical, developmental, cultural, and situational features that formed human psychology and guide that psychology today, evolutionary psychology represents a true interactionist view.

All behavior patterns can in principle be altered by environmental intervention. The fact that currently we can alter some patterns and not others is a problem only of knowledge and technology. Advances in knowledge bring about new possibilities for change, if change is desired. Humans are extraordinarily sensitive to changes in their environment, because natural selection did not create in humans invariant instincts that manifest themselves in behavior regardless of context. It produced psychological adaptations precisely to solve the problems posed by varying contexts. Identifying the roots of mating in evolutionary biology does not doom us to an unalterable fate.

Another form of resistance to evolutionary psychology comes from the worry that evolutionary explanations might imply an inequality between the genders, support restrictions on the roles that men and women can adopt, encourage stereotypes about the genders, perpetuate the exclusion of women from power and resources, and foster pessimism about the possibilities for changing the status quo. On closer examination, however, evolutionary psychology does not carry these feared implications for human mating. In evolutionary terms, men and women are similar in many or most domains. They differ only in the circumscribed domains in which they have faced recurrently different adaptive problems over the course of human evolutionary history. For example, they diverge primarily in their preference for a particular sexual strategy, not in their innate ability to exercise the full range of human sexual strategies. Evolutionary psychology strives to illuminate the evolved mating strategies of men and women, not to prescribe what the genders could be or should be. Nor does it offer prescriptions for appropriate gender roles. It has no political agenda.

A final source of resistance to evolutionary psychology comes from the idealistic views of romance, sexual harmony, and lifelong love to which we all cling. I cleave tightly to these views myself, believing that love has a central place in human sexual psychology. I penned an essay titled "True Love" that prompted some of my graduate students to think I'd gone off the rails. But mating relationships provide some of life's deepest satisfactions. Without them, life would seem empty. After all, some people do manage to live and mate happily and harmoniously. But we have ignored the truth about human mating for too long. Conflict, competition, and manipulation also pervade human mating, and we must lift our collective heads from the sand to see them if we are to understand life's most engrossing relationships.

2

What Women Want

> To an extraordinary degree, the predilections of the
> investing sex—females—potentially determine the direc-
> tion in which species evolve. For it is the female who is
> the ultimate arbiter of when she mates and how often
> and with whom.
>
> —SARAH HRDY, *The Woman That Never Evolved*

WHAT WOMEN ACTUALLY want in a mate has puzzled both scientists and most men for centuries, for good reason. It is not andro-
centric to propose that women's preferences in a partner are more
complex and enigmatic than the mate preferences of either sex of
any other species. Discovering the evolutionary roots of women's
desires requires going far back in time, before humans evolved as
a species, before primates emerged from their mammalian ancestors, back to the origins of sexual reproduction itself.

One reason women are often more choosy about mates stems
from the most basic fact of reproductive biology—the definition
of sex. Remarkably, what defines biological sex is simply the size

of the sex cells. Males are defined as the ones with the small sex cells, females as the ones with the large sex cells. The large female gametes remain reasonably stationary and come loaded with nutrients. The small male gametes are endowed with mobility and swimming speed.[1] Along with differences in the size and mobility of sex cells comes a difference between the sexes in quantity. Men produce millions of sperm, which are replenished at a rate of roughly 12 million per hour. Women produce a fixed and unreplenishable lifetime supply of approximately 1 to 2 million ova. Of these follicles, most die. Only 400 ova mature to the point where they are capable of being fertilized.

Women's greater initial investment does not end with the large egg. Fertilization and gestation, key components of human parental investment, occur internally within women. One act of sexual intercourse, which requires minimal male investment, can produce an obligatory and energy-consuming nine-month investment by the woman that forecloses other mating opportunities. Women then bear the exclusive burden of lactation, or breast-feeding, a calorically intensive investment that may last as long as three or four years.

No biological law of the animal world dictates that females invest more than males. Indeed, among some species, such as the Mormon cricket, pipefish seahorse, and Panamanian poison arrow frog, males invest more.[2] The male Mormon cricket produces through great effort a large "spermatophore" that comes loaded with nutrients. Females compete with each other for access to the males that hold the largest spermatophores. Among these so-called sex-role reversed species, it is the males who are more discriminating about mating and females tend to be larger and more aggressive than the males. Among the more than 5,000 species of mammals, however, including the more than 250 species of primates, females bear the burden of internal fertilization, gestation, and lactation.

The great initial parental investment of women makes them an extraordinarily valuable, but limited, resource.[3] Gestating, bearing, nursing, nurturing, and protecting a child are exceptional reproductive resources that women do not allocate indiscriminately. Nor can one woman dispense these resources to many men. There is only so much time and energy in the world, and those who require a lot of each to reproduce once can only reproduce so many times in a human life. This alone means female reproductive opportunities are limited: *at most* a given female can expect to reproduce a handful of times in her life. A given male, by contrast, can expect *at most* to reproduce as many times as there are available fertile females willing to have sex. Women's reproductive resources are relatively precious. Those who have only a few shots at evolutionary success need to take those shots carefully.

Those who hold valuable resources do not give them away cheaply or unselectively. Because women in our evolutionary past risked enormous investment as a consequence of having sex, evolution favored women who were highly selective about their mates. Ancestral women suffered severe costs if they were indiscriminate—they experienced lower reproductive success, and fewer of their children survived to reproductive age. Women who were not careful to select healthy mates, for example, could bear unhealthy offspring and expose themselves and all their children to dangerous pathogens. Their offspring would die more often and reproduce less. A man in human evolutionary history could walk away from a casual coupling having lost only a few hours of time. His reproductive success was not seriously compromised. A woman in evolutionary history could also walk away from a casual encounter, but if she got pregnant as a result, she bore the costs of that decision for months, years, and even decades afterward. On the flip side, choosing a mate wisely produced a bounty of benefits ranging from good genes to a reliable provider.

Modern birth control technology has altered these costs and benefits. In places where women have access to reliable birth control, women can have short-term sexual encounters with less fear of pregnancy. And some modern women secure resources through their own professional successes, which can match and sometimes even far exceed those of the average man. But human sexual psychology evolved over millions of years to cope with ancestral adaptive problems, just as our food preferences evolved to meet ancestral food conditions. We still possess this underlying sexual psychology, even though our environment has changed.

The Many Facets of Desire

Consider an ancestral woman trying to decide between two men. One shows great generosity with his resources; the other is stingy. All else being equal, the generous man is more valuable to her than the stingy man. The generous man may share his meat from the hunt, aiding her survival. He may sacrifice his time, energy, and resources for the benefit of the children, furthering her reproductive success. In these respects, the generous man has higher value as a mate than the stingy man. If, over evolutionary time, generosity in men provided these benefits repeatedly and cues to a man's generosity were observable and reliable, then selection would favor the evolution of a preference for generosity in a mate.

Now consider a more complicated and more realistic case in which men vary not just in their generosity but also in a bewildering variety of other ways that are also significant to the choice of a mate. Men vary in their physical prowess, athletic skill, ambition, industriousness, kindness, empathy, emotional stability, intelligence, social skills, sense of humor, kin network, and position in the status hierarchy. Men also differ in the costs they impose on a mating relationship: some come with children, bad debts, a quick temper, a selfish disposition, or a tendency to be promiscuous. In addition, men differ in hundreds of ways that may be irrelevant to women. Some men have navels turned in, others have navels turned out. A strong preference for a particular navel shape would be unlikely to evolve unless male navel differences were somehow adaptively relevant to ancestral women. From among the thousands of ways in which men differ, selection over hundreds of thousands of years focused women's preferences laser-like on the most adaptively valuable characteristics.

The qualities people prefer, however, are not static. Because characteristics change, mate seekers must gauge the future potential of a prospective partner. A young medical student who lacks resources now might have excellent future promise. A very ambitious man may have already peaked and have little prospect of greater future success. Another man has children from a previous marriage, but because they are about to leave the nest, they may not drain his resources. Gauging a man's mate value requires looking beyond his current position and evaluating his potential and his future trajectories.

Evolution has favored women who prefer men who possess attributes that confer benefits and who dislike men who possess attributes that impose costs. Each separate attribute constitutes one component of a man's value to a woman as a mate. Each of her preferences tracks one component.

Preferences that favor particular components, however, do not completely solve the problem of choosing a mate. Women face further adaptive hurdles. First, a woman must evaluate her unique circumstances and personal needs. The same man might differ in value for different women. A man's willingness to do a lot of direct child care, for example, might be more valuable to a woman who does not have kin around to help her than to a woman whose mother, sisters, aunts, and uncles eagerly participate. The dangers of choosing a man with a volatile temper may be greater for a woman who is an only child than for a woman with strong brothers and sisters around to protect her. The value of potential mates, in short, depends on the individualized, personalized, and contextualized perspective of the woman doing the choosing.

In selecting a mate, women must identify and correctly evaluate the cues that signal whether a man indeed possesses a particular resource. The assessment problem becomes especially difficult in domains where men are apt to deceive women. Yes, men sometimes lie. Some pretend to have higher status than they actually possess. Some feign greater commitment than they are actually willing to give.

Finally, women face the problem of integrating their knowledge about a prospective mate. Suppose that one man is generous but emotionally unstable. Another man is emotionally stable but stingy. Which man should a woman choose? Choosing a mate calls upon psychological mechanisms that make it possible to evaluate the relevant attributes and give each its appropriate weight in the whole. There are trade-offs. A masculine man might possess good genes but may be more likely to cheat. Some attributes are granted more weight than others in the final decision about whether to choose or reject a particular man. One of these heavily weighted components is the man's resources.

Resource Potential

The evolution of the female preference for males who offer resources may be the most ancient and pervasive basis for female choice in the animal kingdom. Consider the gray shrike, a bird that lives in the Negev Desert of Israel.[4] Just before the start of the breeding season, male shrikes begin amassing caches of 90 to 120 items of edible prey, such as snails, and other useful objects, such as feathers and pieces of cloth. They impale these items on thorns and other pointed projections within their territory. Females look over the available males and prefer to mate with those with the largest caches. When the biologist Reuven Yosef arbitrarily removed portions of some males' caches and added edible objects to others, females shifted to the males with the larger bounties. Females avoided entirely males without resources, consigning them to bachelorhood. Wherever females show a mate preference, the male's resources are often, although not always, the key criterion.

Among humans, the evolution of women's preference for a committed mate with resources would have required three preconditions. First, resources would have had to be accruable, defensible, and controllable by men during human evolutionary history. Second, men would have had to differ from each other in their holdings or skill at resource acquisition, as well as in their willingness to invest those holdings in a woman and her children. If all men had possessed equal potential to acquire resources and shown an equal willingness to commit them, selection could not have favored a female preference for these qualities. Constants do not count in mating decisions. And third, the advantages of committing to one man would have had to outweigh the advantages of being with several men.

Among humans, these conditions are easily met. Territory and tools, to name just two resources, are acquired, defended, monopolized, and controlled by men worldwide. Men vary tremendously in the quantity of resources they command—from the poverty of the street bum to the riches of Bill Gates, Mark Zuckerberg, and Warren Buffett. Ancestral men similarly differed in their resource acquisition abilities, such as their hunting skills, a key ancestral analog of resource potential. Men today also differ widely in how willing they are to invest their time and resources in long-term mateships. Some men are cads, preferring to mate with many women while investing little in each. Other men are dads who prefer to channel all of their resources to one woman and her children.[5]

Women over human evolutionary history could often garner far more resources for their children through a single spouse than through several temporary sex partners. Men provide their wives and children with resources to an extent that is unprecedented among primates. Among most other primate species, for example, females must rely solely on their own efforts to acquire food, because males usually do not share food with their mates.[6] Men, in contrast, provide food, find shelter, and defend territory. Men protect children. They tutor them in the art of hunting, the craft of war, the strategies of social influence, and even the game of mating. They transfer status, aiding offspring in forming reciprocal alliances later in life. These many benefits are unlikely to be secured by a woman from a casual sex partner. Not all potential husbands can confer all of these benefits, but over thousands of generations, when some men were able to provide some of these benefits, women gained a powerful advantage by preferring them as mates.

So the stage was set for women to evolve a preference for men with resources. But women needed cues that signified a man's possession of those resources. These cues might have been indirect, such as personality characteristics that signaled a man's upward mobility. They might have been physical, such as a man's athletic ability or health. They might have included reputational information, such as the esteem in which a man was held by his peers. Economic resources, however, provided the most direct cue.

Women's current mate preferences provide a window for viewing our mating past, just as our fears of snakes and heights provide a window for viewing ancestral hazards. Evidence from dozens of studies documents that modern American women do indeed value economic resources in mates substantially more than men do in mates. In a study conducted in 1939, for example, American men and women rated eighteen characteristics for their desirability in a mate or marriage partner, ranging from irrelevant to indispensable. Women did not view good financial prospects as absolutely indispensable, but they rated them as important. Men rated them as merely desirable but not very important. Women in 1939 valued good financial prospects in a mate about twice as highly as men, and this finding was replicated in 1956 and again in 1967.[7]

The sexual revolution of the late 1960s and early 1970s failed to change this gender difference. In an attempt to replicate the studies from earlier decades, I surveyed 1,491 Americans in the mid-1980s using the same questionnaire. Women and men from Massachusetts, Michigan, Texas, and California rated eighteen personal characteristics for their value in a marriage partner. As in the previous decades, women still valued good financial prospects in a mate roughly twice as much as men did.[8] Nor did these gender differences diminish in the 1990s or the 2000s, or in published studies through the year 2015.[9]

The premium that women place on economic resources has been revealed in many contexts. The psychologist Douglas Kenrick and his colleagues devised a clever method for revealing how much people value different attributes in a marriage partner. They asked men and women to indicate the "minimum percentiles" of each characteristic that they would find acceptable.[10] American college women indicated that their minimum acceptable percentile for a husband on earning capacity was the seventieth percentile—that is, they preferred a man who earned more than 70 percent of all other men—whereas men's minimum acceptable percentile for a wife's earning capacity was only the fortieth percentile. In research conducted over the past decade, Norman Li has consistently found that women see resources in a mate as a "necessity" rather than a "luxury."

Personal ads in newspapers, in magazines, and on online dating sites confirm that women who are actually in the marriage market desire financial resources. A study of 1,111 personal ads found that female advertisers seek financial resources roughly eleven times as often as male advertisers do.[11] In short, sex differences in a preference for resources are not limited to college students and are not bound by the method of inquiry.

Nor are these female preferences restricted to the United States, or to Western societies, or to capitalist countries. The international study on choosing a mate that I conducted with my colleagues documented the universality of women's preferences. We investigated populations in thirty-seven cultures on six continents and five islands that varied on many demographic and cultural characteristics. The participants came from nations that practice polygyny, such as Nigeria and Zambia, as well as from nations that are more monogamous, such as Spain and Canada. The countries included those in which living together is as common as marriage, such as Sweden and Finland, as well as countries in which living together without marriage is frowned upon, such as Bulgaria and Greece. In all, the study sampled 10,047 individuals.[12]

Male and female participants in the study rated the importance of eighteen characteristics in a potential mate or marriage partner, on a scale from "unimportant" to "indispensable." Women across all continents, all economic systems (including socialism and communism), all ethnic groups, all religious groups, and all systems of mating (from intense polygyny to presumptive monogamy) placed more value than men did on good financial prospects. Overall, women valued financial resources about 100 percent more than men did, or roughly twice as much. There were some cultural variations. Women from Nigeria, Zambia, India, Indonesia, Iran, Japan, Taiwan, Colombia, and Venezuela valued good financial prospects a bit more than women from South Africa's Zulu communities, the Netherlands, and Finland. In Japan, for example, women valued good financial prospects roughly 150 percent more than men did, whereas women from the Netherlands deemed financial prospects only 36 percent more important than their male counterparts did—less than women from any other country. Nonetheless, the sex difference remained invariant—women worldwide desired financial resources in a marriage partner more than men. These findings provided the first extensive cross-cultural evidence supporting the evolutionary basis for the psychology of human mating. They have become established as among the most robustly documented gender differences in the entire field of psychology.[13]

Because ancestral women faced the tremendous burdens of internal fertilization, a nine-month gestation, and lactation, they would have benefited tremendously by selecting mates who possessed resources. These preferences helped our ancestral mothers solve the adaptive problems of survival and reproduction for themselves and their children.

Social Status

An examination of traditional hunter-gatherer societies, which are our closest guide to what ancestral conditions were probably like, suggests that ancestral men had clearly defined status hierarchies. In traditional societies today, resources flow freely to those at the top and trickle down slowly to those at the bottom.[14] Traditional tribes such as the Tiwi (an aboriginal group residing on two small islands off the coast of northern Australia), the Yanomamö of Venezuela, the Ache of Paraguay, and the !Kung tribe of Botswana are replete with people described as "head men" and "big men" who wield great power and enjoy the resource privileges of prestige. An ancestral man's social status provided a powerful cue to his possession of resources.

Henry Kissinger once remarked that power is a potent aphrodisiac. Women desire men who command a high position in society because social status is a universal cue to the control of resources. Along with status come better food, more abundant territory, and superior health care. Greater social status bestows on children social opportunities missed by the children of lower-ranked males. Male children in families of higher social status worldwide typically have access to more mates and better-quality mates. In one study of 186 societies ranging from the Mbuti Pygmies of Africa to the Aleut of Alaska, high-status men invariably had greater wealth and more wives than lower-status men, and their children were better nourished.[15]

Women in the United States express clear preferences for potential mates who have high social status or a high-status profession, qualities that are viewed as only slightly less important than good financial prospects.[16] In the 1990s, using a rating scale from "irrelevant" or "unimportant" to "indispensable," my colleagues and I asked participants from Massachusetts, Michigan, Texas, and California to rate the importance of a potential mate's social status; women rated it as between important and indispensable, whereas men rated it as merely desirable but not very important.[17] In a study of 5,000 college students, women listed status, prestige, rank, position, power, standing, station, and high place as important considerably more frequently than men did.[18]

David Schmitt and I conducted a study of casual and committed mating to discover which characteristics people especially value in potential spouses, as contrasted with potential sex partners.[19] Several hundred individuals rated sixty-seven characteristics for their desirability or undesirability in the short or long term. Women judged the likelihood of success in a profession and the possession of a promising career to be highly desirable in a spouse. Significantly, they saw these cues to future status as more desirable in potential spouses than in casual sex partners.

American women also place great value on education and professional degrees in mates—characteristics that are strongly linked with social status. Women rate lack of education as highly undesirable in a potential husband. The cliché that women prefer to marry doctors, lawyers, professors, successful entrepreneurs, and other professionals seems to correspond with reality. Women shun men who are easily dominated by other men or who fail to command the respect of the group.

Women's desire for status shows up in everyday life. A colleague overheard a conversation among four women at a restaurant. They were all complaining that there were no eligible men around. Yet these women were surrounded by male waiters, none of whom was wearing a wedding ring. Waiters, who do not have a high-status occupation, were apparently not even considered by these women. What the women really meant was not that there were no eligible men, but that there were no eligible men of acceptable social status.

Women on the mating market look for "eligible" men. The word *eligible* is a euphemism for "not having his resources already committed elsewhere." The frequency with which the word appears in the combination "eligible bachelor" reveals the mating desires of women. When women append an adverb to this phrase, it becomes "most eligible bachelor," referring not to the man's eligibility but rather to his social status and the magnitude of his resources. It is code for the highest-status, most resource-laden unattached man around. Most homeless and jobless men are eligible, in the sense that they are available as mates, but most women are not interested in them.

The importance that women grant to social status in mates is not limited to the United States or even to capitalist countries. In the vast majority of the thirty-seven cultures included in the international study on choosing a mate, women valued social status more than men in a prospective mate—in both communist and socialist countries, among both Croatians and Chinese, among both Christians and Muslims, in both the tropics and the northern climes.[20] For example, women valued status 63 percent more than men in Taiwan, 30 percent more in Zambia, 38 percent more in Germany, and 40 percent more in Brazil. Women see social status more as a "necessity" than as a "luxury" when it comes to long-term mating.[21]

Because hierarchies are universal features among human groups and resources flow to those who rise in the hierarchy, women solve the adaptive problem of acquiring resources in part by preferring men who are high in status. Social status gives a woman a strong indicator of the ability of a man to invest in her and her children. The scientific evidence across many cultures supports the evolutionary prediction that women are attuned to this cue to the acquisition of resources. Women worldwide prefer to marry up. Those women in our evolutionary past who failed to marry up tended to be less able to provide for themselves and their children.

Age

The age of a man also provides an important cue to his access to resources. Just as young male baboons must mature before they can enter the upper ranks in the baboon social hierarchy, human male adolescents and young men rarely command the respect, status, or position of more mature, older men. This pattern reaches an extreme among the Tiwi tribe, a gerontocracy in which the very old men wield most of the power, have most of the prestige, and control the mating system through complex networks of alliances. Even in American culture, status and wealth tend to accumulate with increasing age.

In all thirty-seven cultures in the international study on choosing a mate, women preferred men who were older than they were.[22] Averaged over all cultures, women preferred men who were roughly three and a half years older. The smallest preferred age difference was seen in French Canadian women, who sought husbands who were not quite two years older, and the largest was found among Iranian women, who sought husbands who were more than five years older. The worldwide average age difference between actual brides and grooms is three years, suggesting that women's marriage decisions often match their mating preferences.

To understand why women value older mates, we must examine what changes with age. One of the most consistent changes is access to resources. In contemporary Western societies, income generally increases with age.[23] Thirty-year-old American men, for example, make more money than men who are twenty, and men who are forty make more than thirty-year-olds. These trends are not limited to the Western world. Among traditional nonmodernized societies, older men have more social status. Among the Tiwi tribe, men are typically at least thirty years of age before they acquire enough social status to acquire a first wife.[24] Rarely does a Tiwi man under the age of forty attain enough status to acquire more than one wife. Older age, resources, and status are coupled across cultures.

In traditional societies, part of this linkage may be related to physical strength and hunting prowess. Physical strength increases in men as they get older, peaking in their late twenties and early thirties. Anthropologists find that hunting ability peaks when a man is in his thirties, at which point his slight decline in physical prowess is more than compensated for by his increased knowledge, patience, skill, and wisdom.[25] Women's preference for older men may stem from our hunter-gatherer ancestors, for whom the resources derived from hunting were critical to survival and reproduction.

Women may prefer older men for reasons other than tangible resources. Older men are likely to be more mature, more stable, and more reliable in their provisioning. Within the United States, for example, men become somewhat more emotionally stable, more conscientious, and more dependable as they grow older, at least up through the age of thirty.[26] In a study of women's mate preferences, one woman noted that "older men [are] better looking because you [can] talk to them about serious concerns; younger men [are] silly and not very serious about life."[27] The status potential of men becomes clearer with increasing age. Women who prefer older men are in a better position to gauge how high they are likely to rise.

Twenty-year-old women in all thirty-seven cultures in the international study typically preferred to marry men only a few years older, not substantially older, in spite of the fact that men's financial resources generally do not peak until their forties or fifties. One reason young women are not drawn to substantially older men may be that older men have a higher risk of dying and hence are less likely to be around to continue contributing to the provisioning and protection of children. The potential incompatibility created by a large age discrepancy may lead to strife, thus increasing the odds of divorce. Moreover, men's sperm quality tends to degrade somewhat with advanced age, which can lead to more birth defects. For these reasons, young women may be drawn more to men a few years older who have considerable promise than to substantially older men who already have attained a higher position but have a less certain future and possibly poorer sperm quality.

Not all women, of course, select older men. Some choose younger men. A study of a small Chinese village found that women who were seventeen or eighteen sometimes married "men" who were only fourteen or fifteen. The conditions in which this occurred, however, were highly circumscribed in that all the "men" were already wealthy, came from a high-status family, and had secure expectations through inheritance.[28] Apparently the preference for slightly older men can be overridden when the man possesses other powerful cues to status and resources and when his resource expectations are guaranteed.

Other exceptions occur when women mate with substantially younger men. Many of these cases occur not because of strong preferences by women for younger men but rather because both older women and younger men lack bargaining power on the mating market. Older women often cannot secure the attentions of high-status men and so must settle for younger men, who themselves have not acquired much status or value as mates. Among the Tiwi, for example, a young man's first wife is typically an older woman—sometimes older by decades—because older women are all he is able to secure with his relatively low status.

Still other exceptions occur among women who already have high status and plentiful resources of their own and then take up with much younger men. Mariah Carey, Madonna, and Cher are striking celebrity examples. They became involved with men who were years or even decades younger. But these cases are relatively rare because most women with resources prefer to mate with men at least as rich in resources as they are, and preferably more so.[29] Women may have casual sex with the proverbial "pool boy" or hook up through an online dating app with a younger man, but typically they seek an older man when they decide to settle down for a committed long-term mateship.

All these cues—economic resources, social status, and older age—add up to one thing: the ability of a man to acquire and control resources that women can use for themselves and for their children. A long history of evolution by selection has fashioned the way in which women look at men as success objects. But the possession of resources is not enough. Women also need men who possess traits that are likely to lead to the sustained acquisition of resources over time.

In cultures where people marry young, often the economic capacity of a man cannot be evaluated directly but must be inferred from observable cues. Indeed, in hunter-gatherer groups that lack a cash economy, the target of selection cannot be financial resources per se. Among the Tiwi tribe, for example, young men are scrutinized carefully by both women and older men to evaluate which ones are rising stars, destined to acquire status and resources, and which are likely to remain in the slow lane, based in part on their personality. The young men are evaluated for their promise, the key signs being good hunting skills, good fighting skills, and especially a strong proclivity to ascend the hierarchy of tribal power and influence. Women in all cultures, past and present, can select men for their apparent ability to accrue future resources, based on certain personality characteristics. And women who value the personality characteristics likely to lead to status and sustained resource acquisition are far better off than women who ignore these vital characterological cues.

Ambition and Industriousness

Which tactics do people use to elevate their position in status hierarchies? My lab discovered twenty-six distinct tactics, including deception, social networking, sexual favors, education, and industriousness. The industriousness tactic included actions such as putting in extra time and effort at work, managing time efficiently, prioritizing goals, and working hard to impress others. Among all the tactics, industriousness proved to be the best predictor of past and anticipated income and promotions. Those who worked hard achieved higher levels of education and higher annual salaries, and they anticipated greater salaries and promotions than those who failed to work hard—findings as solid in Norway as in the United States.[30] Industrious and ambitious men secure a higher occupational status than lazy, unmotivated men do.[31]

American women far more often than men desire mates who enjoy their work, show career orientation, demonstrate industriousness, and display ambition.[32] The 852 single American women and 100 married American women in the thirty-seven-culture study unanimously rated ambition and industriousness as important or indispensable. Women regard men who lack ambition as extremely undesirable, whereas men view the lack of ambition in a wife as neither desirable nor undesirable. Women are likely to discontinue a long-term relationship with a man if he loses his job, lacks career goals, or shows a lazy streak.[33]

Women in the overwhelming majority of cultures similarly value ambition and industry more than men do, typically rating it as between important and indispensable. In our study, for example, Taiwanese women rated ambition and industriousness as 26 percent more important than men did, women from Bulgaria rated it as 29 percent more important, and women from Brazil rated it as 30 percent more important.

The cross-cultural and cross-generational evidence supports the key evolutionary expectation that women have evolved a preference for men who show signs of the ability to acquire resources and a disdain for men who lack ambition. Hard work and ambition, however, are not the only available cues to potential resources. Two others, dependability and stability, provide critical information about how steady or erratic these resources will be.

Dependability and Stability

Among the eighteen characteristics rated in the thirty-seven-culture study, the second and third most highly valued characteristics were a dependable character and emotional stability or maturity. In twenty-one out of thirty-seven cultures, men and women had the same preference for dependability in a partner. Of the sixteen cultures where there was a gender difference, women in fifteen of the cultures valued dependability more than men did. Averaged across all thirty-seven cultures, women rated dependable character 2.69 (where a 3.00 signifies indispensable); men rated it nearly as important, with an average of 2.50. In the case of emotional stability or maturity, the sexes differed more. Women in twenty-three cultures valued this quality significantly more than men did; in the remaining fourteen cultures, men and women valued emotional stability equally. Averaging across all cultures, women gave this quality a 2.68, whereas men gave it a 2.47.

These characteristics may possess such a great value world-wide because they are reliable signals that resources will be provided consistently over time. Undependable people, in contrast, provide erratically and inflict heavy costs on their mates. In a study of newlywed couples, my lab found that emotionally unstable men were especially costly to women. They tended to be self-centered, to monopolize shared resources, and to be possessive, monopolizing much of the time of their wives. These men showed higher-than-average sexual jealousy, becoming enraged when their wives even talked with someone else, as well as dependency: they would insist that their mates provide for all of their needs. With a tendency to being abusive, both verbally and physically, they also displayed inconsiderateness, such as by failing to show up on time. Emotionally unstable men were also moodier than their more stable counterparts, sometimes crying after minor setbacks. Suggesting a further diversion of their time and resources was their tendency to have more affairs than average.[34] All of these costs indicate that emotionally unstable mates will absorb their partner's time and resources, divert their own time and resources elsewhere, and fail to channel resources consistently over time. Dependability and stability are personal qualities that signal increased likelihood that a woman's resources will not be drained by the man.

The unpredictable aspects of emotionally unstable men inflict additional costs by impeding solutions to critical adaptive problems. The erratic supply of resources can wreak havoc with accomplishing the goals required for survival and reproduction. Meat that is suddenly not available because an undependable mate decided at the last minute to take a nap rather than go on the hunt is a resource that was counted on but not delivered. Its absence creates problems for nourishment and sustenance. Resources prove most beneficial when they are predictable. Erratically provided resources may even go to waste when the needs they were intended to meet are met through other, more costly means. Resources that are supplied predictably can be more efficiently allocated to the many adaptive hurdles that must be overcome in everyday life.

Women place a premium on dependability and emotional stability to avoid incurring these costs and to reap the benefits that a mate can provide to them consistently over time. In ancestral times, women who chose stable, dependable men had a greater likelihood of ensuring the man's ability to acquire and maintain resources for use by them and their children. Women who made these wise choices avoided many of the costs inflicted by undependable and unstable men.

Intelligence

Dependability, emotional stability, industriousness, and ambition are not the only personal qualities that signal the acquisition and steadiness of resources. The ephemeral quality of intelligence provides another important cue. No one knows for sure what intelligence tests measure, but there is clear evidence of what high scorers can do. Intelligence is a good predictor of the possession of economic resources within the United States.[35] People who test high go to better schools, get more years of education, and ultimately get higher-paying jobs. Even within particular professions, such as construction and carpentry, intelligence predicts who will advance more rapidly to positions of power and command higher incomes. In tribal societies, the head men or leaders are almost invariably among the more intelligent members of the group.[36]

If intelligence has been a reliable predictor of economic resources over human evolutionary history, then women could have evolved a preference for this quality in a potential marriage partner. The international study on choosing a mate found that women rated education and intelligence fifth out of eighteen desirable characteristics. Ranked in a smaller list of thirteen desirable characteristics, intelligence emerged in second place worldwide. Women valued intelligence more than men in ten out of the thirty-seven cultures. Estonian women, for example, ranked intelligence third out of thirteen desired characteristics, whereas Estonian men ranked it fifth. Norwegian women valued it second, whereas Norwegian men ranked it fourth. In the remaining twenty-seven cultures, however, both sexes placed the same high premium on intelligence.

The quality of intelligence signals many potential benefits. These are likely to include good parenting skills, capacity for cultural knowledge, and adeptness at parenting.[37] In addition, intelligence is linked with oral fluency, ability to influence other members of a group, prescience in forecasting danger, and judgment in applying health remedies. Beyond these specific qualities, intelligence conveys the ability to solve problems. Some have speculated that intelligence is a marker of "good genes" that can be passed on to sons and daughters.[38] Women who select more intelligent mates are more likely to become the recipients of all of these critical benefits.

To identify some of the actions that intelligent people perform, my lab asked 140 men and women to think of the most intelligent people they knew and to describe five actions that reflected their intelligence. Their descriptions of these five types of actions imply the benefits that may flow to someone fortunate enough to choose an intelligent person as a mate: (1) intelligent people tend to have a wide perspective and to see an issue from multiple points of view, suggesting better judgment and decision making; (2) they communicate messages well to other people and are sensitive to signs of how others are feeling, suggesting good social skills; (3) they know where to go to solve problems, implying good judgment; (4) intelligent people manage money well, suggesting that resources will not be lost or squandered; and (5) they make few mistakes in accomplishing tasks they have never before attempted, suggesting an efficiency in problem solving and allocating time. By selecting an intelligent mate, women increase their chances of receiving all these benefits.

Contrast these benefits with the costs imposed by less intelligent people. Their behavior includes failing to pick up subtle hints from others, missing a joke that everyone else gets, and saying the wrong thing at the wrong time, all of which suggest a lack of social adeptness. Less intelligent people repeat mistakes, suggesting that they have less ability to learn from experience. They fail to follow simple verbal instructions, fail to grasp explanations, and persist in arguing when they are obviously wrong. This behavior implies that unintelligent mates are poor problem solvers, unreliable workers, and social liabilities.

Ancestral women who preferred intelligent mates would have raised their odds of securing social, material, and economic resources for themselves and for their children. Since intelligence is moderately heritable, these favorable qualities would have been passed on genetically to their sons and daughters, providing an added genetic benefit. Modern women and most men across all cultures hold these preferences.

Compatibility

Successful long-term mating requires a sustained cooperative alliance with another person for mutually beneficial goals. Relationships riddled with conflict impede the attainment of these goals. Compatibility between mates entails a complex mesh between two different kinds of characteristics. One kind involves complementary traits, or a mate's possession of resources and skills that differ from one's own, in a kind of division of labor between the sexes. Both partners can benefit from specialization and division.

The other kinds of traits crucial to compatibility with a mate, however, are those that are most likely to mesh cooperatively with one's own particular personal characteristics and thus are most similar to one's own. Discrepancies between partners in their political orientations, religious views, moral values, hobbies and interests, and even personalities can produce strife and conflict. The psychologist Zick Rubin and his colleagues studied 202 dating couples over several years to see which ones stayed together and which broke up.[39] They found that mismatched couples tended to break up more readily than their matched counterparts. The 103 couples who broke up had more dissimilar values on sex roles, sexual attitudes, romanticism, and religious beliefs than did the 99 couples who stayed together.

One solution to the problem of compatibility is to search for similarity in a mate. Both in the United States and worldwide, men and women who are similar to each other on a wide variety of characteristics tend to get married. The tendency for like people to mate shows up most obviously in the areas of values, intelligence, and group membership.[40] People seek mates with similar political and social values, such as their views on abortion and capital punishment. People also desire mates who are similar in race, ethnicity, and religion. Couples desire and marry mates of similar intelligence. In addition, similarity matters in personality characteristics such as extraversion, agreeableness, and conscientiousness. People like mates who share their inclination toward parties if they are extraverted and toward quiet evenings at home if they are introverted. People who are characteristically open to experience prefer mates who share their interest in wines, art, literature, and the culinary delights of fine foods. Conscientious people prefer mates who share their interest in paying bills on time and saving for the future. Less conscientious people prefer mates who share their interest in living for the moment.

The similarity within compatible couples is in part a by-product of the fact that people tend to marry others who are in close proximity, and those who are nearby tend to be similar to oneself. Similarity of intelligence in modern marriages, for example, may be an incidental outcome of the fact that people of similar intelligence tend to go to the same educational institutions. The incidental outcome explanation, however, cannot account for the widespread preference that people express for mates who are similar.[41] In a study conducted on dating couples in Cambridge, Massachusetts, my lab measured the personalities and intelligence levels of 108 individuals who were involved in a dating relationship. Separately, the couples completed a questionnaire that asked for their preferences in an ideal mate on the same qualities. The study found that women preferred mates who were similar to themselves in many respects, including boldness, dominance, and activeness; warmth, agreeableness, and kindness; responsibility, conscientiousness, and industriousness; and especially intelligence, perceptiveness, and creativity.

The search for a similar mate provides an elegant solution to the adaptive problem of creating compatibility within the couple so that their interests are maximally aligned in the pursuit of mutual goals. Consider a woman who is an extravert and loves wild parties and who is married to an introvert who prefers quiet evenings at home. Although they may decide to go their separate ways evening after evening, the mismatch causes strife. Couples in which both members are introverted or both are extraverts do not butt heads about mutually pursued activities. The marriage of a Democrat and a Republican or a gun control advocate and a gun rights proponent can make for interesting discussions, but the ensuing conflict wastes valuable energy.

Perhaps more important, matched couples maximize the smooth coordination of their efforts when pursuing mutual goals such as child rearing, maintaining kin alliances, and social networking. A couple at odds over how to rear their child waste valuable energy and also confuse the child, who receives contradictory messages. The search for similarity prevents couples from incurring these costs.

People also seek similarity in overall mate value. Because personality characteristics such as agreeableness, conscientiousness, and intelligence are all highly desirable on the mating market, those who possess more of them can command more of them in a mate.[42] Those who lack these valuable personal assets can command less and so often limit their search to those with assets that are similar to their own. By seeking similarity, individuals avoid wasting time and energy trying to attract people who are out of their reach. Consider this example. A female colleague complained that all the men she was attracted to were not interested in her, yet she was being pursued constantly by men she was not really interested in. Her friend told her: "You are an 8, going after 10s, but being sought by 6s."[43] This single observation proved more valuable to her on the mating market than three years of therapy. She adjusted her mating strategy accordingly.

Those who compete for a mate who exceeds their own mate value risk abandonment by the partner whose mating options are more expansive. Partners discrepant in mate value tend to break up because the more desirable partner can strike a better bargain elsewhere.[44]

The search for similarity thus solves several adaptive problems simultaneously: it maximizes the value one can command on the mating market; leads to the coordination of efforts; reduces conflict within the couple; avoids the costs of mutually incompatible goals; and reduces the risk of later abandonment or breakup.

Size, Strength, and V-Shaped Torso

When the great basketball player Magic Johnson revealed that he had slept with thousands of women, he inadvertently revealed women's preference for mates who display physical and athletic prowess. The numbers may be shocking, but the preference is not. Physical characteristics, such as athleticism, size, and strength, convey important information that women use in making a mating decision.

The importance of physical characteristics in the female choice of a mate is prevalent throughout the animal world. In the species called the gladiator frog, males are responsible for creating nests and defending the eggs.[45] In the majority of courtships, a stationary male is deliberately bumped by a female who is considering him. She strikes him with great force, sometimes enough to rock him back or even scare him away. If the male moves too much or bolts from the nest, the female hastily leaves to examine alternative mates. Most females mate with males who move minimally when bumped. Only rarely does a female reject a male who remains firmly planted after being bumped. Bumping helps a female frog to decide how successful the male will be at defending her clutch. The bump test reveals the male's physical ability to perform the function of protection.

Women sometimes face physical domination by men who are larger and stronger than they are, which can lead to injury and sexual aggression and prevent them from exercising choice. Such domination undoubtedly occurred regularly during ancestral times. Indeed, studies of many nonhuman primate groups reveal that male physical and sexual domination of females has been a recurrent part of our primate heritage. The primatologist Barbara Smuts lived among baboons in the savannah plains of Africa while studying their mating patterns. She found that females form enduring "special friendships" with males who offer physical protection to them and their infants. In return, these females grant their "friends" preferential sexual access during times of estrus.

Analogously, one benefit to women of committed mating is the physical protection a man can offer. A man's size, strength, and physical prowess are cues to solutions to the problem of protection. My lab and others found that women judge short men to be undesirable as long-term mates.[46] In contrast, they find it very desirable for a potential mate to be tall, physically strong, and athletic. Tall men are consistently seen as more desirable dates and mates than men who are short or of average height.[47] Two studies of personal ads revealed that, among women who mention height, 80 percent want a man who is six feet or taller. Ads placed by taller men receive more responses from women than those placed by shorter men, which may explain why men tend to "round up" by a couple of inches when describing their height to women on online dating sites. Tall men date more often than short men and have a larger pool of potential mates. Women solve the problem of protection from aggressive men at least in part by preferring a mate who has the size, strength, and physical prowess to protect them.

In addition to height, women are especially attracted to athletic men with a V-shaped torso, that is broader shoulders relative to hips.[48] Interestingly, these female preferences may have exerted sexual selection pressure on men, since modern men currently show upper body strength that is roughly twice that of women. It is one of the most sexually dimorphic attributes of the human body.

Tall men tend to have a higher status in nearly all cultures. "Big men" in hunter-gatherer societies—men high in status—are physically big men as well.[49] In Western cultures, tall men make more money, advance in their professions more rapidly, and receive more and earlier promotions. Few American presidents have been less than six feet tall. Politicians are keenly aware of voters' preference. During the televised presidential debate in 1988, George H. W. Bush made a point of standing very close to his shorter competitor, Michael Dukakis, in a strategy of highlighting their disparity in size. As the evolutionary psychologist Bruce Ellis notes:

> Height constitutes a reliable cue to dominance in social interactions . . . shorter policemen are likely to be assaulted more than taller policemen . . . suggesting that the latter command more fear and respect from adversaries . . . taller men are more sought after in women's personal advertisements, receive more responses to their own personal advertisements, and tend to have prettier girlfriends than do shorter men.[50]

This preference for taller men is not limited to Western cultures. For men of the Mehinaku tribe of the Brazilian Amazon, the anthropologist Thomas Gregor notes, size differences have acutely important effects in the wrestling arena:

> A heavily muscled, imposingly built man is likely to accumulate many girlfriends, while a small man, deprecatingly referred to as a *peritsi*, fares badly. The mere fact of height creates a measurable advantage. . . . A powerful wrestler, say the villagers, is frightening . . . he commands fear and respect. To the women, he is "beautiful" (*awitsiri*), in demand as a paramour and husband. Triumphant in politics as well as in love, the champion wrestler embodies the highest qualities of manliness. Not so fortunate the vanquished! A chronic loser, no matter what his virtues, is regarded as a fool. As he wrestles, the men shout mock advice. . . . The women are less audible as they watch the matches from their doorways, but they too have their sarcastic jokes. None of them is proud of having a loser as a husband or lover.[51]

The presence of aggressive men who tried to dominate women physically and to circumvent their sexual choices may have been an important influence on women's mate selection in ancestral times. Barbara Smuts argues that, consequently, during human evolutionary history physical protection from other men was one of the most important things a man could offer a woman. Given the alarming incidence of sexual coercion and rape in many cultures, a mate's protection value may well remain relevant to mate selection in modern environments. Many women simply do not feel safe on the streets, and a strong, tall, athletic mate acts as a deterrent to other sexually aggressive men.

Good Health, Symmetry, and Masculinity

It may come as no surprise that women and men worldwide prefer mates who are healthy.[52] In the thirty-seven-culture study, women judged good health to be anywhere from important to indispensable in a marriage partner. In another study on American women, poor physical conditions, ranging from bad grooming habits to having a sexually transmitted infection (STI), were regarded as extremely undesirable characteristics in a mate. The biologists Clelland Ford and Frank Beach found that signs of ill health, such as open sores, lesions, and unusual pallor, are universally regarded as unattractive.[53]

In humans, good health may be signaled by behavior as well as by physical appearance. A lively mood, high energy level, and sprightly gait, for example, may be attractive precisely because they are calorically costly and can be displayed only by people brimming with good health.

The tremendous importance we place on good health is not unique to our species. Some animals display large, loud, and gaudy traits that are costly and yet signal great health and vitality. Consider the bright, flamboyant, ostentatious plumage of the peacock.

It is as if the peacock is saying: "Look at me; I'm so fit that I can carry these large, cumbersome feathers, and yet still I'm thriving." The mystery of the peacock's tail, which seems so contrary to utilitarian survival, is finally on the verge of being solved. The biologists William D. Hamilton and Marlena Zuk proposed that the brilliant plumage serves as a signal that the peacock carries a light load of parasites, since peacocks who carry more than the average number of parasites have duller plumage.[54] The burdensome plumage provides a cue to health and robustness. Peahens prefer the brilliant plumage because it provides clues to the male's health.

Women are especially attracted to men who show two observable markers of good health—symmetrical features and masculinity. Bodies are supposed to be bilaterally symmetric, so deviations in symmetry represent errors a body made in constructing itself. These superficial errors may signal other errors made in constructing important systems, such as the immune system. Errors have two sources—genetic mutations and environmental stresses such as injuries or disease during development. More symmetrical men tend to be healthier and to experience fewer illnesses such as respiratory diseases, and women find them more attractive than their more lopsided peers.[55]

Masculine features in men provide another set of health cues. These features include longer and broader lower jaws, stronger brow ridges, deeper voices, and the classic male V-shaped torso. Masculine qualities are primarily the product of testosterone production during adolescence when a male's facial, body, and vocal qualities are forming. The problem is that too much testosterone can be bad for men, compromising their immune system and leading to shorter lives. So why do some men develop such masculine features? The theory is that only very healthy men, those with strong immune systems, can afford to produce a lot of testosterone during adolescence. Men with weaker immune systems cut back on testosterone production (not consciously, of course) to prevent compromising their already tenuous health. According to this theory, masculine features are honest signals of good health. And indeed, women find masculine features to be somewhat attractive in long-term mating, although they find these features even more attractive when choosing a casual sex partner.

In ancestral times, four bad consequences were likely to follow if a woman selected a mate who was unhealthy or disease-prone. First, she put herself and her family at risk of contracting the disease. Second, her mate was less able to perform essential functions and provide crucial benefits to her and her children, such as food, protection, health care, and child rearing. Third, her mate was at increased risk of dying, prematurely cutting off the flow of resources and forcing her to incur the costs of searching for a new mate and courting all over again. And fourth, if health is partly heritable, she would risk passing on genes for poor health to her children. A preference for healthy mates solves the problem of mate survival and ensures that resources are likely to be delivered over the long run.

Love, Kindness, and Commitment

A man's possession of assets such as health, status, resources, intelligence, and emotional stability, however, does not guarantee his willingness to commit them to a particular woman. Some men show a tremendous reluctance to marry or commit. Some prefer playing the field of singledom and seek a series of casual sex partners. Some popular online dating apps, such as Tinder, facilitate this short-term strategy. Women sometimes derogate men for this hesitancy, calling them "commitment dodgers," "commitment phobics," "paranoid about commitment," and "fearful of the M word."[56] And women's negative reaction to these proclivities makes sense given the large asymmetries in the costs of sex. Because women historically incurred large costs and heavy investment as a result of sex, pregnancy, and childbirth, it often has been reproductively advantageous for them to seek some level of commitment from men with whom they have sex.

The weight that women attach to commitment is revealed in the following true story (the names are changed). Mark and Susan had been going out with each other for two years and had been living together for six months. He was a well-off forty-two-year-old professional, she a medical student of twenty-eight. Susan pressed for a decision about marriage—they were in love, and she wanted to have children within a few years. But Mark balked. He had been married before, and divorced. If he ever married again, he wanted to be absolutely sure it would be permanent. As Susan continued to press for a decision, Mark raised the possibility of a prenuptial agreement. She resisted, feeling that this violated the spirit of marriage. Finally, they agreed that by a date four months in the future he would have decided one way or the other. The date came and went, and still Mark could not make a decision. Susan told him that she was leaving him, moved out, and started dating another man. Mark panicked. He called her up and begged her to come back, saying that he had changed his mind and would marry her. He promised a new car. He promised that there would be no prenuptial agreement. But it was too late. Mark's failure to commit was too strong a negative signal to Susan. It dealt the final blow to their relationship. She was gone forever.

Women past and present face the adaptive problem of choosing men who not only have the necessary resources but also show a willingness to commit those resources specifically to them. This problem may be more difficult than it seems at first. Although resources can often be directly observed, commitment cannot. Instead, gauging commitment requires looking for probabilistic cues. Love is one of the most important cues to commitment.

Feelings and acts of love are not recent products of particular Western views, contrary to some conventional beliefs in the social sciences. Love is universal. Thoughts, emotions, and actions of love are experienced by people in all cultures worldwide—from the Zulu in the southern tip of Africa to the Inuit in the north of Alaska. In a survey of 168 diverse cultures from around the world, the anthropologist William Jankowiak found strong evidence for the presence of romantic love in nearly 90 percent of them. For the remaining 10 percent, the anthropological records were too sketchy to definitely verify the presence of love. When the sociologist Sue Sprecher and her colleagues interviewed 1,667 men and women in Russia, Japan, and the United States, they found that 61 percent of the Russian men and 73 percent of the Russian women were currently in love. Comparable figures for the Japanese were 41 percent of the men and 63 percent of the women. Among Americans, 53 percent of the men and 63 percent of the women acknowledged being in love. Clearly, love is not a phenomenon limited to Western cultures.[57]

To identify precisely what love is and how it is linked to commitment, my lab initiated a study of acts of love.[58] First, we asked fifty women and fifty men from the University of California, Berkeley, and the University of Michigan to think of people they knew who were currently in love and to describe actions performed by those people that reflected or exemplified their love. A different group of college men and women evaluated each of the nominated 115 acts for how typical it was of love. Acts of commitment topped the women's and men's lists, being viewed as most central to love. Such acts included giving up romantic relations with others, talking of marriage, and expressing a desire to have children with the person. When performed by a man, these acts of love signaled the intention to commit resources to one woman.

Commitment has many facets. One major component of commitment is fidelity, exemplified by the act of remaining faithful to a partner when apart. Fidelity signals the exclusive commitment of sexual resources to a single partner. Another aspect of commitment is the channeling of resources to the loved one, such as buying an expensive gift or ring. These acts signal a serious intention to commit economic resources to a long-term relationship. Emotional support is yet another facet of commitment, revealed by behavior such as being available in times of trouble and listening to the partner's problems. Commitment entails a channeling of time, energy, and effort to the partner's needs at the expense of fulfilling one's own personal goals. Acts of reproduction, such as planning to have children, also represent a direct commitment to one's partner's genes. All these acts of love signal the commitment of sexual, economic, emotional, and genetic resources to one person.

Since love is a worldwide phenomenon, and since a primary function of acts of love is to signal commitment of reproductively relevant resources, women should place a premium on love in the process of choosing a mate. To find out if they do, Sue Sprecher and her colleagues asked American, Russian, and Japanese students whether they would marry someone who had all the qualities they desired in a mate if they were not in love with that person.[59] Fully 89 percent of American women and 82 percent of Japanese women said that they would still require love for marriage, even if all other important qualities were present. Among Russians, only 59 percent of women would not marry someone with whom they were not in love, no matter how many desirable qualities that person had. Although a clear majority of Russian women required love, the lower threshold may reflect the tremendous difficulty Russian women have in finding a mate because of the severe shortage of men in their country, especially men capable of investing resources. These variations reveal the effects of cultural context on mating. Nonetheless, the majority of women in all three cultures saw love as an indispensable ingredient in marriage.

Direct studies of preferences in a mate confirm the centrality of love. In a study of 162 Texas women college students, out of 100 characteristics examined, the quality of being loving was the most strongly desired in a potential husband.[60] The thirty-seven-culture study confirmed the universal importance of love. Among eighteen possible characteristics, mutual attraction or love proved to be the most highly valued in a potential mate by both sexes, being rated a 2.87 by women and 2.81 by men (out of 3.00). Nearly all women and men, from the enclaves of South Africa to the bustling streets of Brazilian cities, gave love the top rating, indicating its indispensability for a committed mateship. Women place a premium on love in order to secure the commitment of men's economic, emotional, and sexual resources.

Two additional personal characteristics, kindness and sincerity, are critical to securing long-term commitment. In one study of 800 personal advertisements, sincerity was the single most frequently listed characteristic sought by women.[61] Another analysis of 1,111 personal advertisements again showed that sincerity was the quality most frequently sought by women—indeed, women advertisers sought sincerity nearly four times as often as men advertisers.[62] Sincerity in personal advertisements is a code word for commitment, and women use it to screen out men seeking casual sex without any commitment.

People worldwide depend on kindness not from strangers, but rather from their mates. As shown by the thirty-seven-culture study, women have a strong preference for mates who are kind and understanding. In thirty-two out of the thirty-seven cultures, in fact, the sexes were identical in valuing kindness as one of the three most important qualities out of a possible thirteen in a mate. Only in Japan and Taiwan did men give greater emphasis than women to kindness. And only in Nigeria, Israel, and France did women give greater emphasis than men to kindness. In no culture, however, was kindness in a mate ranked lower than third out of thirteen for either sex. Women desired kindness in a mate especially when it was directed toward them, and less so when it was directed toward other people or other women, supporting the notion that women prize dispositions in men to commit their resources selectively rather than indiscriminately.[63]

Kindness is an enduring personality characteristic that has many components, but at the core of all of them is the commitment of resources. The trait signals an empathy toward children, a willingness to put a mate's needs before one's own, and a willingness to channel energy and effort toward a mate's goals rather than exclusively and selfishly to one's own goals.[64] Kindness, in other words, signals the ability and willingness of a potential mate to commit energy and resources selflessly to a partner.

A lack of kindness signals selfishness, an inability or unwillingness to commit, and a high likelihood that costly burdens will be inflicted on a spouse. The study of newlyweds, for example, found that women married to unkind men complained that their spouses abused them both verbally and physically by hitting, slapping, or spitting at them. Unkind men tend to be condescending, putting down their wife's opinions as stupid or inferior. They are selfish, monopolizing shared resources. They are inconsiderate, failing to do any housework. They are neglectful, failing to show up as promised. Finally, they have more extramarital affairs, suggesting that these men are unable or unwilling to commit to a monogamous relationship.[65] Unkind men look out for themselves and have trouble committing to anything much beyond that.

Because sex is one of the most valuable reproductive resources women can offer, they have evolved psychological mechanisms that cause them to resist giving it away indiscriminately. Requiring love, sincerity, and kindness is a way of securing a commitment of resources commensurate with the value of the resource that women give to men. Requiring love and kindness helps women to solve the critical adaptive mating problem of securing the commitment of resources from a man that can aid in the survival and reproduction of her offspring.

Deal Breakers

The flip side of what women want is what women do not want—the proverbial deal breakers. Incest avoidance is one of the most important. Reproducing with a genetic relative creates "inbreeding depression," which results in children with genetic abnormalities such as Down's syndrome and lower levels of intelligence. Although most people experience the emotion of disgust when contemplating sex with close kin, women are especially repulsed. This gender difference follows from the facts of parental investment—the costs of making a poor sexual decision are typically higher for women than for men. Even the thought of tongue-kissing a sibling or parent typically evokes strong disgust in women.[66] Alongside "beats me up," "will have sex with other people when he is with me," and "is addicted to drugs," "is my sibling" is one of the most powerful deal breakers for women.[67]

Most deal breakers, however, are simply the inverses of the qualities that women desire—lacking resources, drive, ambition, or status; lacking intelligence; being undependable or emotionally unstable; being small, weak, or feminine in appearance; being unhealthy or asymmetrical; being mean or cruel; and lacking love specifically for the woman doing the mate selecting.

Do Women's Desires Change When They Have Power and Resources?

Many years ago, I offered a different possible explanation for women's preferences for men with resources, based on the so-called structural powerlessness and sex-role socialization of women.[68] According to this view, because women are typically excluded from power and access to resources, which are largely controlled by men, women seek mates who have power, status, and earning capacity. Women try to marry upward in socioeconomic status to gain access to resources. Men do not value economic resources in a mate as much as women do because men already have control over these resources and because women have fewer resources anyway.

The society of Bakweri, from Cameroon in West Africa, casts doubt on this theory by illustrating what happens when women have real power. Bakweri women hold greater personal and economic power because they have more resources and are in scarcer supply than men.[69] Women secure resources through their own labors on plantations, but also from casual sex, which is a lucrative source of income. There are roughly 236 men for every 100 women, an imbalance that results from the continual influx of men from other areas of the country to work on the plantations. Because of the extreme imbalance in numbers of the sexes, women have more money than men and more potential mates to choose from. Yet despite this greater latitude, Bakweri women persist in preferring to have a mate with resources. Wives often complain about receiving insufficient support from their husbands. Indeed, lack of sufficient economic provisioning is the most frequently cited divorce complaint of women. Bakweri women change husbands if they find a man who can offer them more money and pay a larger bride price. When women are in a position to fulfill their evolved preference for a man with resources, they do so. Having the dominant control of economic resources does not diminish this key mate preference.

Professionally and economically successful women in the United States also value resources in men. My lab's newlywed study identified women who were financially successful, measured by their salary and income, and contrasted their preferences in a mate with those of women with lower salaries and income. Many of the financially successful women earned more than $100,000 per year in today's dollars. These women were well educated, tended to have professional degrees, and had high self-esteem. Perhaps surprisingly, the study showed that successful women place an even greater value than less successful women on mates who have professional degrees, high social status, and greater intelligence, as well as desiring mates who are tall, independent, and self-confident. These women also express an even stronger preference for high-earning men than do women who are less financially successful. In a separate study the psychologists Michael Wiederman and Elizabeth Allgeier found that college women who expected to earn the most after college placed more importance on the financial prospects of a potential husband than did women who expected to earn less. Professionally successful women, such as medical students and law students, also assigned great importance to a mate's earning capacity.[70] Furthermore, men who were low in financial resources and status did not value economic resources in a mate any more than financially successful men did.[71]

Cross-cultural studies also find that women with their own economic resources value resources in a potential mate more, not less, than women lacking these resources. A study of 1,670 Spanish women found that high-resource women wanted mates with more status and more resources.[72] A study of 288 Jordanians found the same thing, as did a study of 127 Serbians and an Internet study of 1,851 English women.[73] Taken together, these results not only fail to support the structural powerlessness or sex-role hypothesis but directly contradict it.

Structural powerlessness has an element of truth in that men in many cultures do control resources and sometimes do exclude women from power. But the theory cannot explain several facts: men strive to exclude other men from power at least as much as they do women; the origins of the male motivation to control resources remain unexplained; women have not evolved bigger, stronger bodies to acquire resources directly; and men's preferences in a mate remain entirely mysterious. Evolutionary psychology accounts for this constellation of findings. Men strive to control resources and to exclude other men from resources to fulfill women's mating preferences. In human evolutionary history, men who failed to accumulate resources failed to attract mates. Men's more powerful status and resource acquisition drives are due, at least in part, to the preferences that women have expressed over the past few million years. To paraphrase the evolutionary anthropologist Sarah Hrdy, "Men are one long breeding experiment run by women."

Sexual Orientation and Mate Preferences

As mentioned in Chapter 1, the origins of same-sex sexual orientation remain largely a mystery. The mate preferences of women who self-identify as lesbian, however, are better known. In 2007, Richard Lippa published the largest study on this topic, reporting the mate preferences of 2,548 lesbian women and comparing them to those of 82,819 heterosexual women.[74] He found two clusters of findings. First, many of the mate preferences of the two groups were quite similar. Both valued health, kindness, industriousness, sense of humor, and similar values in a mate. Lesbian women differed from heterosexual women, however, in placing less importance on fondness for children, parenting abilities, and religion. Interestingly, although both groups placed tremendous importance on honesty and intelligence, lesbian women valued these traits even more strongly.

Another study examined individual differences among lesbian women, focusing on differences between those who self-identified as "butch" and as "femme."[75] Butch women tended to be more masculine, dominant, and assertive; femme women tended to be more sensitive, cheerful, and feminine. The femme tended to express a stronger desire to have children and placed more importance on the financial resources of a potential romantic partner. Butch lesbians tended to place less emphasis on the financial resources of a potential partner but experienced greater jealousy over rival competitors who were more financially successful.

Thus, in many ways lesbian women are somewhat similar to heterosexual women in their mate preferences, but differ in a few of the qualities desired. More importantly, there are large individual differences among self-identified lesbians, and these variations caution against sweeping generalizations.

Context-Dependent Shifts in Women's Desires

In addition to a woman's personal economic power, several other circumstances cause predictable changes in which men she desires. These include whether other women find a man attractive, whether she is seeking a committed partner or casual sex, and her own mate value.

One of the most successful beer commercials of all time depicts a well-dressed man with a bottle of Dos Equis in his hand. Depending on the version, there are either two or three very attractive women surrounding him. This commercial might appeal to men because it implies that they will enhance their attractiveness to women if they drink this brand of beer. But being surrounded by beautiful women also makes the man more attractive to women. Animal biologists have given this phenomenon the clunky name *mate copying*. From fish to birds, females use the apparent preferences of other females as critical information about a potential mate's mate value. Mate copying has also been found in humans in my lab (in a study led by Sarah Hill) and in four other labs. Women find men surrounded by other women especially attractive if those women are themselves physically attractive and if they seem attentive to, and interested in, the man.

Temporal context—whether a woman is seeking a sexual hookup or a committed partner—also influences desire. In long-term mating, women prioritize character traits such as kindness, dependability, and emotional stability, as well as qualities that signal excellent future status and resource potential, such as ambition, industriousness, and education. For casual sex partners, however, these qualities become considerably less important. Instead, women emphasize physical attractiveness, desirability to other women, and higher levels of masculinity—qualities that might be linked with "good genes," a topic we cover in greater depth in Chapter 4.

Finally, women's own level of desirability influences their desires. It may not come as a shock that women who are 8's are generally choosier than women who are 6's or 5's. More desirable women have more bargaining power on the mating market, and they can elevate their standards. Women with high mate value in Canada, America, Croatia, Poland, Brazil, and Japan have been found to list a longer set of sought-after traits in their personal ads. They want higher levels of resources, education, and intelligence; higher social status; good parenting skills; good partner skills; and a raft of other traits. What may be less intuitively obvious is that women with high mate value are especially drawn to masculine men compared with their lower-mate-value counterparts. This disparity has been found for vocal masculinity as well as facial masculinity. One speculation for this preference shift pivots on the finding that masculine men tend on average to be less faithful than less masculine men. Perhaps only a woman who is high in mate value herself feels that she can control the wandering eye of an attractive, masculine man by reminding him that he risks losing her.

Effects of Women's Desires
on Actual Mating Behavior

Mate preferences cannot evolve unless they affect actual mating behavior at least some of the time. Of course, people cannot always get what they want. Most must settle for someone less than their ideal mate. A raft of scientific studies demonstrate, however, that women's desires do influence their actual mating decisions.

One source of evidence comes from personal ads. Which ads placed by men get more "hits," clicks, or "right swipes" from women? Age is a key predictor. More mature men get more hits than younger men, although women generally set the limit at ten years older than themselves. Men who indicate higher levels of income and education get more hits, a trend that has been replicated in Poland as well as the United States.[76]

A study of 21,973 men found that those higher in socioeconomic status were more likely to attract wives.[77] Poor men are more likely to remain bachelors. Among the Kipsigis of Kenya, men with land resources are more likely to attract wives, and men with a lot of land attract multiple wives.[78] American men with resources are more likely to marry physically attractive women. And women worldwide in all cultures across the globe tend, on average, to marry men who are somewhat older than they are.[79]

Women's desires in a mate also influence men's behavior, precisely as predicted from the logic of sexual selection theory. Studies of mate attraction find that men display resources such as cars, houses, gifts, and expensive dinners to attract women. And men derogate their rivals verbally by impugning their status, ambition, physical prowess, and resources. Even in online dating ads, men are more likely than women to exaggerate their income, education level, and height, rounding up by about 10 to 20 percent. In all these ways, women's mate preferences influence actual mating behavior, both their own and that of the men seeking to attract them.

Women's Many Preferences

We now have the outlines of an answer to the enigma of what women want. Women are judicious, prudent, and discerning about the men they consent to mate with because they have so many valuable reproductive resources to offer. Those with valuable resources rarely give them away indiscriminately. The costs in reproductive currency of failing to exercise choice were too great for ancestral women, who would have risked beatings, food deprivation, disease, abuse of children, and abandonment. By contrast, the benefits of exercising choice—in nourishment, protection, gene quality, and paternal investment in children—were abundant.

Committed mates may bring with them a treasure trove of resources. Selecting a long-term mate who has the relevant resources is clearly an extraordinarily complex endeavor. For women, it involves at least a dozen distinctive preferences, each corresponding to a resource that helps them solve critical adaptive problems.

That women seek resources in a long-term mate may seem obvious to the casual observer, but until the thirty-seven-culture study, that preference had not been scientifically documented worldwide. Moreover, because men's resources and resource acquisition skills often cannot be directly discerned, women's preferences are keyed to other qualities that signal the likely possession, or future acquisition, of resources. Indeed, women may be less influenced by money per se than by qualities that lead to resources, such as ambition, drive, status, intelligence, emotional stability, and mature age. Women scrutinize these personal qualities carefully because they reveal a man's potential.

Potential, however, is not enough. Because many men with a high resource potential are themselves discriminating and are at times content with casual sex, women are faced with the problem of commitment. Seeking love and sincerity are two solutions to the commitment problem. Sincerity signals that the man is capable of commitment. Acts of love signal that he has in fact committed to a particular woman.

To have the love and commitment of a man who could be easily defeated by other men in the physical arena, however, would have been a problematic asset for ancestral women. Women mated to small, weak men lacking in physical prowess would have risked damage from other men and loss of the couple's joint resources. Tall, strong, athletic men with V-shaped torsos offered ancestral women protection. In this way, their resources and commitment could be secured against incursion. Women who selected men in part for their strength and prowess were more likely to be successful at surviving and reproducing.

Resources, commitment, and protection do a woman little good if her husband sickens or dies, or if the couple is so mismatched that they fail to function as an effective team. The premium that women place on a man's health ensures that husbands will be capable of providing these benefits over the long haul. And the premium that women place on similarity of interests and traits with their mate helps to ensure the convergence of mutually pursued goals. These multiple facets of current women's mating preferences correspond precisely with the multiple facets of the adaptive problems faced by our women ancestors thousands of years ago.

Women, of course, do not evaluate potential mates one trait at a time. Men come as whole packages of qualities that must be accepted or rejected altogether.[80] This inevitably requires trade-offs. A kind man may be willing to devote his entire life to one woman and have great potential as a father but may have fewer resources to provide. A strong, healthy, attractive man may be a sterling provider of resources and good genes but may be more tempted to be unfaithful. Moreover, many circumstances create shifts in women's mate preferences—her personal resource acquisition ability, whether she is seeking a long-term mate or a casual sex partner, close kin in proximity, the sex ratio in the mating pool, and the presence of other women who are attracted to a particular man. The reason men have been baffled for so long about what women want is that women's mate preferences are inherently complex, multifaceted, and context-dependent, reflecting the large number of intricate adaptive challenges our ancestral mothers confronted repeatedly over the long course of human evolutionary history.

Ancestral men were confronted with a different set of adaptive problems. So we must now shift perspective to gaze at ancestral women as potential mates through the eyes of our male forebears.

3

What Men Want

Beauty is in the adaptations of the beholder.
—DONALD SYMONS, "What Do Men Want?"

WHY MEN WOULD ever commit to just one woman poses a puzzle. Since all an ancestral man needed to do to reproduce was to impregnate a woman, casual sex without commitment would have achieved this goal. For evolution to produce men who desire commitment or marriage and who are willing to devote years of investment to one woman, powerful adaptive advantages to that strategy over one of seeking casual sex, at least under some circumstances, must have been present.

One solution to this puzzle comes from the ground rules set by women. Since it is clear that many ancestral women required reliable signs of male commitment before consenting to sex, men who failed to commit would have suffered on the mating market. They might have failed to attract any women at all. Or perhaps they failed to attract the more desirable women and had to settle

for those lower in mate value. Women's requirements for consenting to sex made it costly for most men to pursue a short-term
mating strategy exclusively. In the economics of reproductive effort, the costs of not pursuing a long-term mate would have been
prohibitively high for most men, and men would have benefited
as their odds of attracting a mate, as well as attracting a more desirable mate, increased with their willingness to commit.

Another way in which men benefited from sustained commitment to one woman was by increasing the odds that he would
be the father of any children she bore—upping his probability of
genetic paternity. By committing for the long term, men typically
gained repeated and exclusive sexual access, and their close proximity put them in a position to fend off potential mate poachers.
Without commitment, repeated sex became questionable and paternity more uncertain.

A further benefit of committing to one woman was the increased survival and reproductive success of the man's children.
In human ancestral environments, infants and young children
were more likely to die without sustained investment from two
parents or related kin.[1] Among the Ache of Paraguay, for example,
when a man dies in a club fight, the other villagers often make a
collective decision to kill his children, even when the children
have a living mother. In one case reported by the anthropologist
Kim Hill, a boy of thirteen was killed after his father had died in a
club fight. Overall, Ache children whose fathers die suffer a death
rate more than 10 percent higher than children whose fathers remain alive.

Over human evolutionary history, even children who did
survive without the father's investment would have suffered by
missing out on the knowledge he could impart and the political
alliances he could bestow. Both of these assets help solve mating
problems later in life. Fathers in many cultures past and present
have a strong hand in arranging beneficial marriages for their sons

and daughters.[2] The absence of these benefits challenges the evolutionary fitness of children without fathers. These evolutionary pressures, operating over thousands of generations, gave an advantage to men who pursued a long-term strategy of commitment.

The economics of the mating marketplace typically produces an asymmetry between the sexes in their ability to obtain a desirable mate in a committed as opposed to a temporary relationship.[3] Most men can obtain a much more desirable mate if they are willing to commit to a long-term relationship because women typically desire a lasting commitment, and highly desirable women are in the best position to get what they want. In contrast, most women can obtain a much more desirable casual partner by offering sex without requiring commitment, since high-status men are willing to relax their standards and have sex with a variety of women if the short-term hookup carries no commitment. High-status men impose more stringent standards for a partner to whom they are willing to commit.

Men also gain in two other ways by committing. One is an increase in social status. In many cultures, males are not considered "real men" until they have married. Increased status, of course, brings a man other bounties, including better resources for his children and sometimes an increased attractiveness to additional mates. A final benefit of commitment or marriage is the formation of a more expansive coalitional network that includes his spouse's friends and kin. Men, in short, have much to gain by committing to one woman.

Much of what men want in a long-term mate coincides with what women want. Like women, men want committed partners who are intelligent, kind, dependable, emotionally stable, and healthy. For men as well as for women, these qualities are linked with mates who will make excellent partners, excellent allies, and excellent parents. These qualities could also signal good genetic material and low mutation loads, that is fewer copying errors within the partner's genome—qualities that make for healthier and more robust children.

But men face an adaptive problem not faced by women, at least not as poignantly—choosing a fertile partner. To be reproductively successful, the most obvious criterion would be a woman's ability to bear children. A woman with high reproductive capacity would be extremely valuable in evolutionary currencies. Men need some basis, however, on which to judge a woman's reproductive capacity.

The solution to this problem is diabolically difficult. Ancestral men had few obvious aids for figuring out which women possessed the highest reproductive value. A woman's fertility is not stamped on her forehead or advertised with flashing neon signs. It cannot be observed directly, and it is not imbued in her social reputation. Her family is clueless. Even women themselves lack direct knowledge of their reproductive value.

The adaptive problem of detecting which women are fertile comes into clear view when we consider chimpanzees, our closest primate relatives. When a female chimp is fertile, she goes into an estrus phase. Her genitals become engorged, creating bright red swellings that are indeed somewhat like neon signs in their visibility. She emits ovulatory scents at ovulation. These estrus signals send male chimps into a sexual frenzy. To make it even easier on these male chimps, estrus females often energetically solicit sex, "presenting" themselves to males they prefer. Men do not have it this easy. Although there are subtle changes that women undergo when ovulating, such as a slight lightening of their skin and a slight rise in voice pitch, women have nothing approaching the vivid visible ovulation signals emitted by female chimps. Over evolutionary history, vivid signs of human ovulation were largely driven underground, irrevocably changing the ground rules of mating.

A preference nevertheless evolved for fertility. Ancestral men evolved mechanisms to sense cues to a woman's underlying reproductive value, and two obvious and observable cues were youth and health.[4] Old or unhealthy women clearly could not reproduce as much as young, healthy women. Ancestral men solved the problem of finding reproductively valuable women in part by preferring those who were young and healthy. But how can youth and health be discerned?

Youth

It is a fact of fertility that women's reproductive capacity declines steadily with increasing age after the midtwenties. By the age of forty, a woman's reproductive capacity is low. By fifty, it is close to zero. Women's capacity for reproduction is compressed into a fraction of their lives.

Men's preferences capitalize on this critical cue. In the United States, men uniformly express a desire for mates who are younger than they are. Among college students surveyed from 1939 through 2005 on campuses coast to coast, the preferred age difference hovered around two and a half years.[5] Twenty-one-year-old men preferred, on average, women who were eighteen and a half.

Men's preoccupation with a woman's youth is not limited to Western cultures. When the anthropologist Napoleon Chagnon was asked which females are most sexually attractive to Yanomamö men of the Amazon, he replied without hesitation, "Females who are *moko dude*."[6] The word *moko,* when used with respect to fruit, means that the fruit is harvestable, and when used with respect to a woman, it means that the woman is fertile. Thus, fruit that is *moko dude* is perfectly ripe, and a woman who is *moko dude* is postpubescent but has not yet borne her first child, or about fifteen to eighteen years of age. Comparative information on other tribal and traditional peoples suggests that the Yanomamö men are typical in their preference.

Nigerian, Indonesian, Iranian, and Indian men are similarly inclined. Without exception, in every one of the thirty-seven societies examined in the international study, men preferred wives who were younger than themselves. Nigerian men who were twenty-three and a half years old, for example, preferred wives who were six and a half years younger, or just over seventeen years old. Croatian men who were twenty-one and a half years old expressed a desire for wives who were approximately nineteen. Chinese, Canadian, and Colombian men shared with their Nigerian and Croatian brethren a powerful desire for younger women. On average, men from the thirty-seven cultures expressed a desire for wives approximately two and a half years younger than themselves.

Although men universally preferred younger women as wives, the strength of this preference varied somewhat from culture to culture. Scandinavian men in Finland, Sweden, and Norway preferred their brides to be only one or two years younger. Men in Nigeria and Zambia preferred their brides to be six and a half and seven and a half years younger, respectively. In Nigeria and Zambia, which practice polygyny, like many cultures worldwide, men who can afford it are legally permitted to marry more than one woman. Men in polygynous mating systems are typically older than men in monogamous systems by the time they have acquired sufficient resources to attract wives. The larger age difference preferred by Nigerian and Zambian men probably reflects their greater age when they acquire wives.[7]

This interpretation is supported by a raft of scientific studies showing that, as men get older, they prefer as mates women who are increasingly younger than they are. Consider the statistics derived from online personal advertisements.[8] A man's age has a strong effect on his preferences: men in their thirties prefer women who are roughly five years younger, whereas men in their fifties prefer women ten to twenty years younger.[9]

Although these findings support the evolutionary hypothesis that men prefer younger, and hence more fertile, women, this perspective actually leads to a very counterintuitive prediction—namely, that young adolescent males should prefer women who are slightly *older* than they are. Scientific studies bear this prediction out. Adolescent males age fifteen, for example, express a desire for females who are seventeen or eighteen.[10] What is fascinating is that this attraction is almost entirely unreciprocated. Women in their late teens do not even notice these young adolescent males, much less find themselves attracted to them. They prefer men a few years older, not a few years younger.

These findings regarding adolescent males contradict two potential alternative explanations for why older men are attracted to younger women. One—an old standby in psychology—is reinforcement theory: that people repeat behaviors for which they are rewarded. Adolescent males are hardly reinforced or rewarded by the women they are most attracted to; indeed, they are ignored or actively shunned by these women. A second explanation is that men are attracted to younger women as a means of exercising power and control. But the mid-adolescent males have no power or control at all over the late-adolescent women they find so beautiful. The fertility explanation, in short, provides the most compelling explanation for the entire pattern of findings, from the attractions of adolescent males to men's attractions toward women who are increasingly younger relative to their own age as the men get increasingly older.

Actual marriage decisions confirm the preference of men for women who are increasingly younger than they are as they age. American grooms exceed their brides in age by roughly three years at first marriage, five years at second marriage, and eight years at third marriage.[11] Men's preference for younger women also translates into actual marriage decisions worldwide. In Sweden during the 1800s, for example, church documents reveal that men who remarried following a divorce selected new brides 10.6 years younger on average. In all countries around the world where information is available on the ages of brides and grooms, men on average exceed their brides in age.[12] Among European countries, the age difference ranges from about two years in Poland to roughly five years in Greece. Averaged across all countries, grooms are three years older than their brides, or roughly the difference expressly desired by men worldwide. In polygynous cultures, the age difference runs even larger. Among the Tiwi of northern Australia, for example, high-status older men often have wives who are two and three decades younger than they are.[13] In summary, contemporary men prefer young women because they have inherited from their male ancestors an evolved preference that focused intensely on this cue to a woman's reproductive value. This psychological preference translates into actual mating decisions much of the time—although as we will see later, people can't always get what they want.

Standards of Physical Beauty

A preference for youth is merely the most obvious of men's preferences linked to a woman's reproductive capacity. Evolutionary logic leads to an even more powerful set of expectations for universal standards of beauty. Just as our standards for attractive landscapes embody cues such as water, game, and refuge, mimicking environments beneficial to our ancestors, so our standards for female beauty embody cues to women's reproductive capacity.[14] Beauty may be in the eyes of the beholder, but those eyes, and the minds behind the eyes, have been shaped by millions of years of human evolution.

Our ancestors had access to two types of observable evidence of a woman's health and youth: features of physical appearance, such as full lips, clear skin, smooth skin, clear eyes, lustrous hair, and good muscle tone, and features of behavior, such as a bouncy, youthful gait, an animated facial expression, and a high energy level. These physical cues to youth and health, and hence to reproductive capacity, constitute key elements of male standards of female beauty.

Because physical and behavioral cues provide the most powerful observable evidence of a woman's reproductive value, ancestral men evolved a preference for women who displayed these cues. Men who failed to prefer qualities that signaled high reproductive value—men who preferred to marry gray-haired grandmothers lacking in smooth skin and firm muscle tone—would have left fewer offspring.

Clelland Ford and Frank Beach discovered several universal cues that correspond precisely with this evolutionary theory of beauty.[15] Signs of youth, such as clear skin and smooth skin, and signs of health, such as the absence of sores and lesions, are universally regarded as attractive. Any cues to ill health or older age are seen as less attractive. Imagining passionately kissing a lover's acne is more likely to provoke feelings of disgust than feelings of sexual desire. Poor complexion is always considered a sexual turnoff. Pimples, ringworm, facial disfigurement, and dirtiness are universally seen as unattractive. Clarity and smoothness of skin and freedom from disease are universally attractive.

For example, the anthropologist Bronislaw Malinowski reported that, among the Trobriand Islanders in northwestern Melanesia, "sores, ulcers, and skin eruptions are naturally held to be specially repulsive from the viewpoint of erotic contact." The "essential conditions" for beauty, in contrast, were "health, strong growth of hair, sound teeth, and smooth skin."[16] Specific features, such as bright eyes and full, well-shaped lips rather than thin or pinched lips, were especially important to the Islanders.

Cues to youth are also paramount in the aesthetics of women's attractiveness. When men and women rate a series of photographs of women differing in age, judgments of facial attractiveness decline with the increasing age of the woman.[17] The ratings of women's beauty decline regardless of the age or sex of the judge.

Most traditional psychological theories of attraction have assumed that standards of attractiveness are learned gradually through cultural transmission and therefore do not emerge clearly until a child is at least three or four years old. The psychologist Judith Langlois and her colleagues have overturned this conventional wisdom by studying infants' social responses to faces.[18] Adults evaluated color slides of white and black female faces for their attractiveness. Then infants of two to three months of age and six to eight months of age were shown pairs of these faces that differed in their degree of attractiveness to adults. Both younger and older infants looked longer at the more attractive faces, suggesting that standards of beauty apparently emerge quite early in life. In a second study, Langlois found that twelve-month-old infants showed more observable pleasure, more play involvement, less distress, and less withdrawal when interacting with strangers who wore attractive masks than when interacting with strangers who wore unattractive masks.[19] In a third study, Langlois found that twelve-month-old infants played significantly longer with attractive dolls than with unattractive dolls. No training seems necessary for these standards to emerge. This evidence challenges the common view that the idea of attractiveness is learned through gradual exposure to current cultural standards.

Many, but not all, constituents of beauty are neither arbitrary nor culturally capricious. When the psychologist Michael Cunningham asked people of different races to judge the facial attractiveness of photographs of women of various races, he found great consensus about who was and was not good-looking.[20] Asian and American men, for example, agree with each other on which Asian and American women are most and least attractive. Consensus has also been found among Chinese, Indian, and English samples, between South Africans and Americans, and between black and white Americans.[21]

Photographic manipulation provides evidence supporting evolutionary theories of female beauty. To find out what makes for an attractive face, Langlois and her team generated composites of the human face by means of computer graphics technology. These faces were then superimposed upon each other to create new faces. The new composite faces were made up of a differing number of individual faces—four, eight, sixteen, or thirty-two. People then rated the attractiveness of each composite face, as well as the attractiveness of each individual face that made up the composite. Results proved startling. The composite faces were uniformly judged to be more physically attractive than any of the individual ones. The sixteen-face composite was deemed more attractive than the four-face or eight-face composites, and the thirty-two-face composite was deemed the most attractive of all. Because superimposing individual faces tends to eliminate their irregularities and make them more symmetrical, the average or symmetrical composite faces were more attractive than actual individual faces.[22]

One explanation for why symmetrical faces are considered more attractive comes from research conducted by the psychologist Steve Gangestad and the biologist Randy Thornhill, who examined the relationship between facial and bodily asymmetries and judgments of attractiveness.[23] Repeated environmentally induced injuries and diseases produce asymmetries during development. These include not just injuries and other physical insults, which may provide a cue to health, but also the parasites that inhabit the human body and the mutations that inhabit the human genome. Because parasites and genetic mutations cause physical asymmetries, the degree of asymmetry can be used as a cue to the health status of the individual and as an index of the degree to which the individual's development has been perturbed by various stressors. In scorpionflies and swallows, for example, males prefer to mate with symmetrical females and tend to avoid those that show asymmetries. In humans as well, when Gangestad and Thornhill measured people's features, such as foot breadth, hand breadth, ear length, and ear breadth, and independently had these people evaluated on attractiveness, they found that less symmetrical people were seen as less attractive. Human asymmetries also increase with age. Older people's faces are far more asymmetrical than younger people's faces, so that symmetry provides another cue to youth as well. This evidence provides yet another confirmation of the theory that cues to health and cues to youth are embodied in standards of attractiveness—standards that emerge remarkably early in life.

Body Shape

Facial beauty is only part of the picture. Features of the rest of the body provide abundant cues to a woman's reproductive capacity. Standards for bodily beauty vary somewhat from culture to culture, along such dimensions as a plump versus slim body build or light versus dark skin. Emphasis on particular physical features, such as eyes, ears, buttocks, or genitals, also varies by culture. Some cultures, such as the Nama, a branch of Hottentots residing in southwest Africa, consider an elongated labia majora to be sexually attractive, and they work at pulling and manipulating the vulvar lips to enhance attractiveness. Men in many cultures prefer large, firm breasts, but in a few, such as the Azande of eastern Sudan and the Ganda of Uganda, men are reported to view long, pendulous breasts as the more attractive.[24]

The most culturally variable standard of beauty seems to be in the preference for a slim versus plump body build. This variation is linked partly with the social status that body build conveys. In cultures where food is scarce, such as among the Bushmen of Australia, plumpness signals wealth, health, and adequate nutrition during development.[25] In cultures where food is relatively abundant, such as the United States and many western European countries, the relationship between plumpness and status is reversed and the rich signal their status through relative thinness.[26] Men apparently do not have an evolved preference for a particular amount of body fat per se. Rather, they have an evolved preference for whatever features are linked with status, which vary in predictable ways from culture to culture. Clearly such a preference does not require conscious calculation or awareness.

Studies by the psychologist Paul Rozin and his colleagues have revealed a disturbing aspect of women's and men's perceptions of the desirability of plump versus thin body types.[27] American men and women viewed nine female figures that varied from very thin to very plump. The women were asked to indicate their ideal for themselves, as well as their perception of men's ideal for the female figure. In both cases, women selected a figure slimmer than average. When men were asked to select which female figure they preferred, however, they selected the figure of average body size. American women erroneously believe that men desire thinner women than they actually do prefer. These findings refute the belief that men desire women who are runway-model thin; most men do not.

While men's preferences for a particular body size vary, one preference for body shape that is fairly invariant, the psychologist Devendra Singh discovered, is the preference for a small waist size relative to hip size.[28] Before puberty, boys and girls show a similar fat distribution. At puberty, however, a dramatic change occurs. Boys lose fat from their buttocks and thighs, while the release of estrogens in pubertal girls causes them to deposit fat in their lower trunk, primarily on their hips and upper thighs. Indeed, the volume of body fat in this region is 40 percent greater for women than for men.

In other words, the waist-to-hip ratio is similar for the sexes before puberty, but after puberty women's hip fat deposits cause their waist-to-hip ratio to become significantly lower than men's. Healthy, reproductively capable women have a waist-to-hip ratio between 0.67 and 0.80, while healthy men have a ratio in the range of 0.85 to 0.95. Abundant evidence now shows that the waist-to-hip ratio is an accurate indicator of women's reproductive status. Women with a lower ratio show earlier pubertal endocrine activity. Women with a higher ratio have more difficulty becoming pregnant, and those who do become pregnant do so at a later age than women with a lower ratio. The waist-to-hip ratio is also an accurate indication of long-term health status. Diseases such as diabetes, hypertension, heart problems, previous stroke, and gallbladder disorders are linked with the distribution of fat, as reflected by the ratio. The link between the waist-to-hip ratio and both health and reproductive status made it a reliable cue for ancestral men's preferences in a mate.

Singh discovered that waist-to-hip ratio is indeed a powerful cue to women's attractiveness. In a dozen studies conducted by Singh, men rated the attractiveness of female figures, which varied in both their waist-to-hip ratio and their total amount of fat. Men find the average figure to be more attractive than a thin or fat figure. Regardless of the total amount of fat, however, men find women with a low waist-to-hip ratio to be the most attractive. Women with a ratio 0.70 are more attractive than women with a ratio of 0.80, who in turn are more attractive than women with a ratio of 0.90. Finally, Singh's analysis of *Playboy* centerfolds and winners of beauty contests in the United States over thirty consecutive years confirmed the invariance of this cue. Although both centerfolds and beauty contest winners got thinner, their waist-to-hip ratio remained roughly the same at around 0.70.

There is one more possible reason for the importance of waist-to-hip ratio. Pregnancy alters this ratio dramatically. A higher ratio mimics pregnancy and therefore may render women less attractive as mates or sexual partners. A lower ratio, in turn, signals health, reproductive capacity, and lack of current pregnancy. Men's standards of female attractiveness have evolved over thousands of generations to detect and find attractive this reliable cue.

The Importance of Physical Appearance

Because of the bounty of fertility cues conveyed by a woman's physical appearance, and because male standards of beauty have evolved to correspond to these cues, men have evolved to prioritize appearance and attractiveness in their mate preferences. In the United States mate preferences for physical attractiveness, physical appearance, good looks, or beauty have been lavishly documented. When 5,000 college students were asked in the 1950s to identify the characteristics they wanted in a future husband or wife, men listed physical attractiveness far more often than women did.[29] The sheer number of terms that men listed betrayed their values. They wanted a wife who was pretty, attractive, beautiful, gorgeous, comely, lovely, ravishing, and glamorous. American college women, at that time at least, rarely listed physical appearance as paramount in their ideal husband.

Multi-decade mating studies in the United States from 1939 to 1996 found that men rate physical attractiveness and good looks as more important and desirable in a potential mate than do women.[30] Men tend to see attractiveness as important, whereas women tend to see it as desirable but not very important. The gender difference in the importance of attractiveness remains constant from one generation to the next. Its size does not vary throughout the decades. Men's greater preference for physically attractive mates is among the most consistently documented psychological sex differences.[31]

This does not mean that the importance people place on attractiveness is forever fixed. On the contrary, the importance of attractiveness increased dramatically in the United States in the twentieth century.[32] For nearly every decade since 1930, physical appearance grew in importance for men and women about equally, corresponding with the rise in television, fashion magazines, advertising, and other media depictions of attractive models. For example, the importance attached to good looks in a marriage partner on a scale of 0.00 to 3.00 increased between 1939 and 1989 from 1.50 to 2.11 for men and from 0.94 to 1.67 for women. Similar shifts have been observed in China, India, and Brazil well into the twenty-first century.[33] These shifts show that mate preferences can change. But the sex difference so far remains invariant. The gap between men and women has been constant since the late 1930s in all countries studied thus far.

These sex differences are not limited to the United States or to Western cultures. Regardless of the location, habitat, marriage system, or cultural living arrangement, men in all thirty-seven cultures included in the international study on choosing a mate valued physical appearance in a potential mate more than women did. China typified the average difference in importance attached to beauty: Chinese men gave it a 2.06 and women gave it a 1.59. This internationally consistent sex difference persists despite variations in ranking, in wording, and in race, ethnicity, religion, hemisphere, political system, and mating system. Among the Hadza, more than five times as many men as women placed great importance on fertility in a spouse.[34] When asked how they could tell that a woman could have many children, most Hadza men responded by saying, "You can tell just by looking," suggesting their awareness that appearance conveys vital information about fertility. Men's preference for physically attractive mates is a species-wide psychological mechanism that transcends culture. Women too value appearance in a mate, as they should because appearance conveys health for both sexes, but they do not prioritize it as much as men.

Men's Status and Women's Beauty

Men value a woman's attractiveness for reasons other than her reproductive value. The consequences of women's attractiveness for a man's social status are critical. Everyday folklore tells us that our mate is a reflection of ourselves. Men are particularly concerned about status, reputation, and hierarchies because elevated rank has always been an important means of acquiring the resources that make men attractive to women. It is reasonable, therefore, to expect that a man will be concerned about the effect that his mate has on his social status—an effect that has consequences for gaining additional resources and mating opportunities.

A person's status and resource holdings, however, often cannot be observed directly. They must instead be inferred from tangible characteristics. Among humans, one set of cues is people's ornamentation. Gold chains, expensive artwork, or fancy cars may signal to both sexes an abundance of resources that could be directed toward parental investment.[35] Men seek attractive women as mates not simply for their reproductive value but also as signals of status to same-sex competitors and to other potential mates.[36]

Experiments have documented the influence of attractive mates on men's social status. When shown photographs of unattractive men paired with attractive spouses, people attribute status and professional prestige to those men more than in other pairings, such as attractive men with unattractive women, unattractive women with unattractive men, and even attractive men with attractive women. People suspect that an unattractive man must have high status if he can interest a stunning woman, presumably because people know that attractive women have high mate value and usually can get what they want.

In my study of human prestige criteria, dating someone who is physically attractive greatly increases a man's status, whereas it increases a woman's status only somewhat.[37] In contrast, a man who dates an unattractive woman experiences a moderate decrease in status, whereas a woman who dates an unattractive man experiences only a trivial decrease in status.

These trends occur across cultures. When my research collaborators and I surveyed native residents of China, Poland, Guam, Romania, Russia, and Germany in parallel studies of human prestige criteria, we found that in each of these countries, acquiring a physically attractive mate enhances a man's status more than a woman's. In each country, having an unattractive mate hurts a man's status more than it does a woman's. Men across cultures today value attractive women not only because attractiveness signals a woman's reproductive capacity but also because it signals status, and status, in turn, creates more mating opportunities.

Sexual Orientation and Mate Preferences

The premium that men place on a mate's appearance is not limited to heterosexuals. Some scientists contend that same-sex relationships provide an acid test for the evolutionary basis of sex differences in the desires for a mate.[38] Do gay men show preferences more or less like those of other men, differing only in the sex of the person they desire? Do they show preferences similar to those of women? Or do they have unique preferences unlike the typical preferences of either sex?

No one knows the exact percentage of homosexuals in any culture, past or present. Part of the difficulty lies with definitions. The sexologist Alfred Kinsey estimated that more than one-third of all men engage at some point in life in some form of homosexual activity, typically as part of adolescent experimentation. Far fewer people, however, express a strong preference for the same sex as a mate. Most estimates put the figure at about 3 to 4 percent for men and 1 to 2 percent for women.[39] The discrepancy between the percentages of people who have engaged in some kinds of homosexual acts and people who express a core preference for partners of the same sex suggests an important distinction between the underlying psychology of preference and the outward manifestation of behavior. Some men who prefer women as mates may nonetheless substitute a man as a sex partner, because of either circumstance or opportunity.

No one knows why some people have a strong preference for members of their own sex as mates, although this lack of knowledge has not held back speculation. One suggestion is the so-called kin selection theory of homosexuality, which holds that homosexuality evolved when some people served better as aides to their close genetic relatives than as reproducers.[40] No current evidence exists to support this theory. Gay men do not invest more in their nephews and nieces than do heterosexual men. Other theories point to the mother's intrauterine environment, birth order, and other nongenetic causes. If there exists one single large cause of sexual orientation, it is likely that scientists would know it by now. That the origins of homosexuality remain somewhat of a mystery suggests that the causes of sexual orientation are likely to be multiple and complex.

Homosexual preferences in a mate, in contrast, are far less mysterious. Studies document the great importance that homosexual men place on the youth and physical appearance of their partners. William Jankowiak and his colleagues asked homosexual and heterosexual individuals, both men and women, to rank sets of photographs of men and women differing in age on physical attractiveness.[41] Gay and heterosexual men alike ranked the

younger individuals as consistently more attractive. Neither lesbian nor heterosexual women, in contrast, placed any importance
on youth in their ranking of attractiveness. These results suggest
that lesbian women are very much like heterosexual women in
their mate preferences, except with respect to the sex of the person they desire, and that homosexual men are similar to heterosexual men in their mate preferences.

The psychologists Kay Deaux and Randel Hanna conducted a
systematic study of homosexual mate preferences.[42] They collected
800 ads from several East Coast and West Coast newspapers,
equally sampling male heterosexuals, female heterosexuals, gay
men, and lesbians. Using a coding scheme, they calculated the
frequency with which members of each of these groups offered
and sought particular characteristics, such as physical attractiveness, financial security, and personality traits.

Lesbians tended to be similar to heterosexual women in placing little emphasis on physical appearance, with only 19.5 percent
of the heterosexual women and 18 percent of the lesbians mentioning this quality. In contrast, 48 percent of heterosexual men
and 29 percent of gay men stated that they were seeking attractive partners. Among all groups, lesbians listed their own physical attractiveness less often than any other group; such mentions
appeared in only 30 percent of their ads. Heterosexual women,
in contrast, offered attractiveness in 69.5 percent of the ads, gay
men in 53.5 percent, and heterosexual men in 42.5 percent. Only
16 percent of the lesbians requested a photograph of respondents
to their ads, whereas 35 percent of heterosexual women, 34.5 percent of gay men, and 37 percent of heterosexual men made this
request.

Lesbian women are distinct from the other three groups in
specifying fewer physical characteristics, such as weight, height,
eye color, or body build. Whereas only 7 percent of lesbians men-

tioned their desire for specific physical attributes, 20 percent of heterosexual women, 38 percent of gay men, and 33.5 percent of heterosexual men requested particular physical traits. And as with overall attractiveness, lesbians stood out in that only 41.5 percent listed physical attributes among the assets they offered, whereas 64 percent of heterosexual women, 74 percent of gay men, and 71.5 percent of heterosexual men offered particular physical assets. It is clear that gay men are similar to heterosexual men in the premium they place on appearance. Lesbian women are more like heterosexual women in their desires, but differ in placing less value on physical qualities, both in their offerings and in the qualities they seek.

Less formal studies confirm the centrality of youth and physical appearance for male homosexuals. Surveys of the gay mating market consistently find that physical attractiveness is the key determinant of the desirability of a potential partner. Male homosexuals place great emphasis on dress, grooming, and physical condition. And youth is a key ingredient in judging attractiveness: "Age is the monster figure of the gay world."[43]

The sociologists Philip Blumstein and Pepper Schwartz found that the physical beauty of a partner was critical to the desires of homosexual and heterosexual men more than to lesbian or heterosexual women, even among already coupled individuals.[44] They found that 57 percent of gay men and 59 percent of heterosexual men felt that it was important that their partner be sexy-looking. In contrast, only 31 percent of the heterosexual women and 35 percent of the lesbian women stated that sexy looks were important in a partner. Male homosexuals and male heterosexuals seem to have similar mate preferences, except with respect to the sex of their preferred partner. Both place a premium on appearance, and youth and youthful features are central ingredients in their definition of beauty.

Men Who Achieve Their Desires

Although most men place a premium on youth and beauty, it is clear that not all men succeed in satisfying their desires. Men who lack the status and resources that women want, for example, generally have the most difficult time attracting good-looking young women and must settle for less than their ideal. Evidence comes from men who have historically been in a position to get exactly what they prefer, such as kings, emperors, despots, and other men of unusually high status. In the 1700s and 1800s, for example, wealthier men from the Krummerhörn population of Germany married younger brides than did men lacking wealth. Similarly, high-status men, from the Norwegian farmers of 1700 to 1900 to the Kipsigis in contemporary Kenya, have consistently secured younger brides than their lower-status counterparts.[45]

Kings and despots routinely stocked their harems with young, attractive, nubile women and had sex with them frequently. The Moroccan emperor Moulay Ismail the Bloodthirsty, for example, acknowledged having sired 888 children. His harem had 500 women. When each woman reached the age of thirty, she was banished from the emperor's harem, sent to a lower-level leader's harem, and replaced by a younger woman. Roman, Babylonian, Egyptian, Incan, Indian, and Chinese emperors all shared the tastes of Emperor Ismail and instructed their trustees to scour the land for as many young pretty women as they could find.[46]

Marriage patterns in modern America confirm the fact that the men with the most resources are the best equipped to actualize their preferences. High-status men, such as the aging rock stars Rod Stewart and Mick Jagger and the movie stars George Clooney and Johnny Depp, frequently select women decades younger. One study examined the impact of a man's occupational status on the woman he marries. Men who are high in occupational status are able to marry women who are considerably more physically attractive than are men who are low in occupational status.[47] Indeed, a man's occupational status seems to be the best predictor of the attractiveness of the woman he marries. Men in a position to attract younger women often do.

Men who enjoy high status and income are apparently aware of their ability to attract women of higher value. In a study of a computer dating service involving 1,048 German men and 1,590 German women, the ethologist Karl Grammer found that as men's income goes up, they seek younger partners.[48] Each increment in income is accompanied by a decrease in the age of the woman sought.

Not all men, however, have the status, position, or resources to attract young women, and some men end up mating with older women. Many factors determine the age of the woman at marriage, including the woman's preferences, the man's own age, the man's mating assets, the strength of the man's other mate preferences, and the woman's appearance. Mate preferences are not invariably translated into actual mating decisions for all people all of the time, just as food preferences are not invariably translated into actual eating decisions for all people all of the time. But men who are in a position to get what they want often partner up with young, attractive women. Ancestral men who actualized these preferences experienced greater reproductive success than those who did not.

Media Effects on Standards

Advertisers exploit the universal appeal of beautiful, youthful women. Some argue that the media and Madison Avenue construct a single, arbitrary standard of beauty that everyone must live up to.[49] Advertisements are thought to convey unnatural, photoshopped images of beauty and to tell people to strive to embody those images. This interpretation may be partially true, particularly when it comes to depicting unnaturally thin female models, but it is also at least partially false. Standards of beauty are not arbitrary but rather embody reliable cues to reproductive value. Advertisers have no special interest in inculcating a particular set of beauty standards; they do want to use whatever sells products. Advertisers perch a clear-skinned, regular-featured young woman on the hood of the latest-model car, or gather several attractive young women to stare fondly at a man drinking a brand-name beer, because these images exploit men's evolved psychological mechanisms and therefore sell cars and beer, not because advertisers want to promulgate a single standard of beauty.

The media images with which we are bombarded daily, however, have a potentially damaging consequence. In one study, after groups of men looked at photographs of either highly attractive women or women of average attractiveness, they evaluated their commitment to their current romantic partner.[50] The men who had viewed pictures of attractive women thereafter judged their actual partner to be less attractive than did the men who had viewed analogous pictures of women who were average in attractiveness. Perhaps more important, the men who had viewed attractive women thereafter rated themselves as less committed to, less satisfied with, less serious about, and less close to their actual partners. Parallel results were obtained in another study in which men viewed physically attractive nude centerfolds—they rated themselves as less attracted to their partners.[51]

The reason for these changes is found in the unrealistic nature of the images. The few attractive women selected for advertisements are chosen from thousands of applicants. In many cases, literally thousands of pictures are taken of a chosen woman. *Playboy*, for example, was reputed to shoot roughly 6,000 pictures for its centerfold each month. From thousands of pictures, a few are selected for advertisements and centerfolds. And then those images are photoshopped. So what men see are the most attractive women in their most attractive poses with the most attractive background in the most attractive photoshopped images. Contrast these photographs with what ancestral man would have witnessed, living in a band of no more than 150 individuals. It is doubtful that he would see hundreds or even dozens of attractive women in that environment. If there were plenty of attractive fertile women, however, he might reasonably consider switching mates and decreasing his commitment to his existing mate.

We carry with us the same evaluative mechanisms that evolved in ancient times. Now, however, these psychological adaptations are artificially stimulated by the dozens of attractive women whose images men witness daily in our visually saturated culture on the Internet, in magazines, on billboards, on television, and in movies. These images do not represent real women in our actual social environment. Rather, they hijack adaptations designed for a different mating environment. They sometimes create unhappiness by interfering with existing real-life relationships. The ability to scroll through thousands of potential mates on Internet dating sites and apps such as Tinder, Match.com, and OKCupid may trick our psychology of mating into thinking that there is always someone better out there if only we can swipe or click through enough options.

As a consequence of viewing these images, men become dissatisfied and less committed to their mates. The potential damage inflicted by these images affects women as well, because they create a spiraling and unhealthy competition among women to embody the images they see daily—images of women who presumably are desired by men, but in actuality are much thinner than most men really find attractive. The unprecedented rates of eating disorders, such as anorexia nervosa, and cosmetic surgery, such as tummy tucks and breast enlargement, may stem in part from these media images; some women go to extreme lengths to fulfill what they perceive to be men's desires. But the images do not cause this unfortunate result by creating standards of beauty that were previously absent. Rather, they work by exploiting men's existing evolved standards of beauty and women's competitive mating mechanisms on an unprecedented and unhealthy scale.

Facial and bodily beauty, as important as they are in men's mating preferences, solve for men only one set of adaptive problems—identifying and becoming sexually aroused by women who show signs of fertility. Selecting a reproductively valuable woman, however, provides no guarantee that her value will be monopolized exclusively by one man. The next critical adaptive problem is to ensure paternity.

Chastity and Fidelity

Mammalian females typically enter estrus only at intervals. Vivid visual cues and strong scents often accompany estrus and powerfully attract males. Sexual intercourse occurs primarily in this narrow envelope of time. Women, however, do not send any sort of genital signal when they ovulate. Nor is there much evidence that women secrete detectable olfactory cues. Indeed, women are rare among primates in possessing the unusual adaptation of comparatively concealed or cryptic ovulation.[52] Yes, there are some subtle changes—a slight lightening of the skin, a slightly more attractive voice pitch, and even a higher sexual drive. But relatively cryptic ovulation obscures a woman's reproductive status.

Concealed ovulation dramatically changed the ground rules of human mating. Women became attractive to men not just when ovulating but throughout their menstrual cycles. Cryptic ovulation created a special adaptive problem for men by decreasing the certainty of their paternity. Consider a primate male who monopolizes a female for the brief period that she is in estrus. In contrast to human males, he can be fairly "certain" of his paternity, although obviously not consciously. The period during which he must guard the female and have sex with her is sharply constrained. Before and after her estrus, he can go about his other business without running the risk of cuckoldry.

Ancestral men did not have this luxury. Our human ancestors never knew when a woman was ovulating. Because mating is not the sole activity that humans require to survive and reproduce, women could not be guarded around the clock. And the more time a man spent guarding, the less time he had available for grappling with other critical adaptive challenges. Ancestral men therefore were faced with a unique paternity problem not faced by other primate males—how to be certain of their paternity when ovulation was concealed.

Marriage or long-term committed mating provided one solution.[53] Men who married would benefit reproductively relative to other men by substantially increasing their probability of paternity. Repeated sexual intercourse with one woman throughout her ovulation cycle raised a man's odds that she would bear his child. The social traditions of marriage function as public ties that bind a couple, with fidelity enforced by family members as well as by each partner. Marriage also provides men with opportunities to learn intimately about their mate's personality and subtle patterns of behavior, making it difficult for her to hide signs of infidelity. These benefits of marriage would have outweighed the costs of forgoing the sexual opportunities sometimes available to ancestral bachelors, at least under some conditions.

For an ancestral man to reap the reproductive benefits of marriage, he had to seek reasonable assurances that his mate would indeed remain sexually faithful to him. Men who failed to be aware of these cues would have lost out in the currency of relative reproductive success. Failure to be sensitive to these cues so as to ensure their partner's fidelity would have diverted years of her parental investment to another man's children. Men who were indifferent to the potential sexual contact between their wives and other men would not have been successful in the game of differential reproductive success.

Our male forebears solved this uniquely male adaptive problem by seeking qualities in a potential mate that might increase the odds of securing their paternity. At least two preferences in a mate could solve the problem for males: the desire for premarital chastity and the quest for postmarital sexual loyalty. Before the use of modern contraceptives, chastity provided a cue to the future certainty of paternity. On the assumption that a woman's proclivities toward chaste behavior would be stable over time, her premarital chastity signaled her likely future fidelity.

In the modern United States, men value virgin brides modestly more than women value virgin grooms. But the value they place on it has declined over the past seventy years, coinciding with the increasing availability of reliable birth control methods.[54] In the 1930s, men viewed chastity as close to indispensable, but in the past few decades men have rated it as desirable but not crucial. Among the eighteen characteristics rated, chastity declined from the tenth most valued in 1939 to the seventeenth most valued in the late 1980s and 1990s and into the 2000s and 2010s. Furthermore, American men differ regionally in how they value chastity. College students in Texas, for example, desire a chaste mate more than college students in California, rating it a 1.13 as opposed to 0.73 on a 3.00 scale. Despite the decline in the value of virginity in the twentieth century and despite regional variations, the sex difference remains—men more than women emphasize chastity in a potential committed mateship.

The trend for men to value chastity more than women holds up worldwide, but cultures vary tremendously in the value placed on chastity. At one extreme, people in China, India, Indonesia, Iran, Taiwan, and the Palestinian areas of Israel attach a high value to chastity in a potential mate. At the opposite extreme, people in Sweden, Norway, Finland, the Netherlands, Germany,

and France believe that virginity is largely irrelevant or unimportant in a potential mate.

In contrast to the worldwide consistency in the different preferences by gender for youth and physical attractiveness, only 62
percent of the cultures in the international study placed a significantly different value on chastity in a committed mateship by
sex. Where sex differences in the value of virginity were found,
however, men invariably placed a greater value on it than women
did. In no culture did women desire chastity more than men did.

The cultural variability in the preference of each sex for chastity is explained by several factors, including the prevailing incidence of premarital sex, the degree to which chastity can be
demanded in a mate, the economic independence of women,
and the reliability with which chastity can be evaluated. Chastity
differs from other attributes, such as a woman's physical attractiveness, in that it is less directly observable. Even physical tests
of female virginity are unreliable, whether from variations in the
structure of the hymen, rupture due to nonsexual causes, or de-
liberate alteration.[55]

Variation in the value that people place on chastity may be
traceable in part to variability in the economic independence of
women and in women's control of their own sexuality. In some
cultures, such as Sweden, premarital sex is not discouraged and
practically no one is a virgin at marriage. One reason may be that
women in Sweden are far less economically reliant on men than
women in most other cultures. The legal scholar Richard Posner notes that marriage provides few benefits for Swedish women
relative to women in most other cultures.[56] The Swedish social
welfare system includes day care for children, long paid maternity
leaves, and many other material benefits. The Swedish taxpayers
effectively provide women with what partners otherwise would or
might. Women's economic independence from men lowers the
cost to them of a free and active sex life before marriage, or as an

alternative to marriage. Thus, practically no Swedish women are virgins at marriage, and hence the value that Swedish men place on chastity has declined to a worldwide low of 0.25.[57]

Differences in the economic independence of women, in the benefits provided by husbands, and in the intensity of competition for husbands all drive the critical cultural variation.[58] Where women benefit from marriage and where competition for husbands is fierce, women compete to signal chastity, causing the average amount of premarital sex to go down. Where women control their economic fate, do not require so much of men's investment, and need to compete less for reliable providers, they are freer to disregard men's preferences, which causes the average amount of premarital sex to go up. Men everywhere might value chastity in a long-term mate if they could get it, but in many cultures they simply cannot demand it of their brides.

From a man's reproductive perspective, a more important cue to the certainty of paternity than virginity per se is the assurance of future fidelity. If men cannot reasonably require virginity, they can choose mates for sexual loyalty or fidelity. In fact, the study of short-term and long-term mating found that American men viewed having little sexual experience as desirable in a spouse. Furthermore, men saw promiscuity as especially undesirable in a permanent mate, rating it −2.07 on a scale of −3.00 to +3.00. The actual amount of prior sexual activity in a potential mate, rather than virginity per se, would have provided an excellent guide for ancestral men who sought to solve the problem of uncertainty of paternity. Indeed, the single best predictor of extramarital sex is premarital sexual permissiveness—people who have many sex partners before marriage tend to be more unfaithful than those who have few sex partners before marriage.[59]

Modern men place a premium on fidelity. When American men in the study of short-term and long-term partners evaluated sixty-seven possible characteristics for their desirability in a committed mateship, faithfulness and sexual loyalty emerged as the most highly valued traits.[60] All men give these traits the highest rating possible, an average of +2.85 on a scale of −3.00 to +3.00. Men regard unfaithfulness as the least desirable characteristic in a wife, rating it a −2.93, reflecting the high value that men place on fidelity. Men abhor promiscuity and infidelity in their wives. Unfaithfulness proves to be more upsetting to men than any other pain a spouse can inflict on her mate. Women also become extremely upset over an unfaithful mate, but several other factors, such as sexual aggressiveness, exceed infidelity in the grief they cause women.[61]

The sexual revolution of the 1960s and 1970s, with its promises of sexual freedom and lack of possessiveness, apparently has had a limited impact on men's preferences for sexual fidelity. Nor has the overhyped hookup culture on college campuses today significantly changed these preferences. Cues to fidelity still signal that the woman is willing to channel all of her reproductive value exclusively to her husband. A woman's future sexual conduct looms large in men's commitment decisions. The fact that nonpaternity rates—that is, the prevalence of children in a marriage mistakenly believed to have been fathered by the husband—tend to be quite low in most cultures, many as low as 1 to 3 percent, suggests that most men who commit to marriage have largely succeeded in solving this key adaptive problem.[62]

Evolutionary Bases of Men's Desires

The great emphasis that men place on a woman's physical appearance is not some immutable biological law of the animal world. Indeed, in many other species, such as the peacock, it is the females who place the greater value on physical appearance. Nor is men's preference for youth a biological universal in the animal world. Some primate males, such as orangutans, chimpanzees, and Japanese macaques, prefer older females, who have already demonstrated their reproductive abilities by giving birth; they show low sexual interest in adolescent females because they have low fertility.[63] But human males have faced a unique set of adaptive problems and so have evolved a unique sexual psychology. They prefer youth because of the centrality of marriage in human mating. Their desires are designed to gauge a woman's future reproductive potential, not just the chance of immediate impregnation. They place a premium on physical appearance because of the wealth of reliable cues it provides to the reproductive potential of a potential mate.

Men worldwide want physically attractive, young, and sexually loyal wives who will remain faithful to them over the long run. These preferences cannot be attributed to Western culture, to capitalism, to white Anglo-Saxon bigotry, to the media, or to incessant brainwashing by advertisers. They are universal across cultures and are absent in none. They are deeply ingrained psychological adaptations that drive our mating decisions, just as our evolved taste preferences drive our decisions on food consumption.

Homosexual mate preferences, ironically, provide a testament to the depth of these evolved psychological mechanisms. The fact that physical appearance figures centrally in gay men's mate preferences, and that youth is a key ingredient in their standards of beauty, suggests that not even variations in sexual orientation alter these fundamental male adaptations.

These preferences upset some people because they are unfair. We can modify our physical attractiveness only in limited ways, and some people are born, or develop into, better-looking individuals than others. Beauty is not distributed democratically. A woman cannot alter her age, and a woman's reproductive value declines more sharply with age than a man's; evolution has dealt women a cruel hand, at least in this regard. (Later we will see how evolution has dealt men a cruel hand in causing their earlier death.) Women fight the decline through cosmetics, through plastic surgery, through fitness classes. An $8 billion cosmetics industry has emerged in America to exploit these trends.

After a lecture on the subject of sex differences in mate preferences, one woman suggested that I suppress the findings because of the distress they would cause women. Women already have it hard enough in this male-dominated world, she felt, without having scientists tell them that their mating problems may be based in men's evolved psychology. Yet suppression of this truth is unlikely to help, just as concealing the fact that people have evolved preferences for succulent, ripe fruit is unlikely to change their preferences. Railing against men for the importance they place on beauty, youth, and fidelity is like railing against meat eaters because they prefer animal protein. Telling men not to become aroused by signs of youth and health is like telling them not to experience sugar on their tongues as sweet.

Many people hold an idealistic view that standards of beauty are arbitrary, that beauty is only skin-deep, that cultures differ dramatically in the importance they place on appearance, and that Western standards stem from the media, parents, the culture, or other agents of socialization. But standards of attractiveness are not arbitrary—they reflect cues to youth and health, and hence to reproductive value. Beauty is not merely skin-deep. It reflects internal reproductive capabilities. Although modern fertility technology grants women greater latitude for reproducing across a wider age span, men's preferences for women who show apparent signs of reproductive capacity continue to operate today in spite of the fact that they were designed in an ancestral world that may no longer exist.

Cultural conditions, economic circumstances, and technological inventions, however, play a critical role in men's evaluation of the importance of chastity. Where women are less economically dependent on men, as in Sweden, sexuality is highly permissive, and men do not desire or demand chastity from potential wives. These shifts highlight the sensitivity of some mate preferences to features of culture and context.

Despite cultural variations, sexual fidelity tops the list of men's long-term mate preferences. Although many men in Western culture cannot require virginity, they usually insist on sexual loyalty. Birth control technology may have rendered this mate preference unnecessary for its original function of ensuring paternity, but the mate preference nevertheless persists. A man does not relax his desire for fidelity in his wife just because she takes birth control pills. This constant demonstrates the importance of our evolved sexual psychology—a psychology that was designed to deal with critical cues from an ancestral world but that continues to operate with tremendous force in today's modern world of mating.

That world of mating, however, involves more than marriage. If ancestral couples had always remained faithful, there would have been no selection pressure for the intense concern with fidelity. The existence of this concern means that both sexes must also have engaged in casual sex and sometimes infidelity. So we must turn now to this mysterious region of human sexuality.

4

Casual Sex

The biological irony of the double standard is that males could not have been selected for promiscuity if historically females had always denied them opportunity for expression of the trait.

—ROBERT SMITH, *Sperm Competition and the Evolution of Mating Systems*

IMAGINE THAT AN attractive person of the opposite sex walks up to you on a college campus and says: "Hi, I've been noticing you around town lately, and I find you very attractive. Would you go to bed with me?" How would you respond? If you are like 100 percent of the women in one study in Florida, you would give an emphatic no. You might be offended, insulted, or plain puzzled by the request out of the blue. But if you are a man, the odds are 75 percent that you would say yes.[1] You would most likely feel flattered by the request.

Perhaps there is something odd about the culture in Florida, so other researchers sought to replicate these findings. Particularly informative are studies based in sexually liberal cultures such as France and Denmark. In France, for example, women are increasingly consuming pornography, having sex with men they meet on the Internet, and having a larger number of casual sex partners. When French women were approached with a request for sex, however, only 3 percent agreed to have sex with the approaching stranger if he was highly attractive, and 0 percent if he was only average.[2] In contrast, a full 83 percent of French men consented to sex with an attractive woman, and 60 percent agreed if she was average in attractiveness. Studies carried out in Denmark produced similar results, although men in committed romantic relationships were considerably less likely to consent to sex than were single men.[3] Men and women react differently when it comes to casual sex, and willingness to consent to sex with strangers differs strongly by gender across cultures.

Casual sex typically requires mutual consent, however. Ancestral men could not have had temporary hookups unaided. At least some ancestral women must have been sexually willing or eager some of the time, barring coerced sex (a topic explored in depth in Chapter 7). If all women had mated for life with a single man—and in most traditional cultures most postpubertal females are married—opportunities for casual sex would seem to have vanished.[4] So short-term sex would have meant that women were engaging in extramarital affairs. One of the keys to ancestral women's extramarital sexual opportunities was a lapse in mate guarding. Hunting opened windows of opportunity, because men went off for hours, days, or weeks to procure meat.

In spite of the prevalence and evolutionary significance of casual sex, until recently most scientific research on human mating has centered on long-term mating. The typically transient and secretive nature of casual sex makes it difficult to study. In Alfred Kinsey's classic research on sexual behavior, for example, questions about extramarital sex prompted many people to refuse to be interviewed altogether. Among those who did consent to an interview, many declined to answer questions about extramarital sex.

Our relative ignorance about casual sexual encounters also reflects deeply held values. Many of us shun the promiscuous and scorn the unfaithful because such people often interfere with our own sexual strategies. From the perspective of a married woman or man, for example, the presence of promiscuous people endangers marital fidelity. From the perspective of a single woman or man seeking marriage, the presence of promiscuous people lowers the likelihood of finding someone willing to commit. We derogate male short-term strategists as cads, womanizers, or "man whores" because we want to discourage casual sex, at least among some people. People also derogate women by "slut-shaming." Casual sex is in many ways still a taboo topic. But it fascinates us. We must look closer and ask why it looms so large in our mating repertoire.

Although women and men alike have the whole repertoire of mating strategies—long-term mating, short-term mating, mate poaching, infidelity, and so on—there do exist somewhat stable individual differences, sometimes called *sociosexual orientation*. Some people are strongly inclined to long-term, high-investment mating. They want sex in the context of a loving committed relationship. Others are more inclined to short-term mating; casual sex without love or encumbering commitment feels fine to them. Whereas long-term maters search for "the one and only," short-term maters thrive on sexual variety and tend to experience a larger number of sex partners. So we turn now to the clues present in a deep-time evolutionary history of short-term mating.

Physiological Clues to Sexual Strategies and the Mystery of Female Orgasm

Existing adaptations in our psychology, anatomy, physiology, and behavior reflect prior evolutionary selection pressures. Just as our current fear of snakes betrays an ancestral hazard, so our sexual anatomy and physiology reveal an ancient story of short-term sexual strategies. Important clues to that story have come to light through careful studies of men's testes size, ejaculate volume, variations in sperm production, and a possible function of female orgasm.

Large testes typically evolve as a consequence of intense sperm competition when the sperm from two or more males occupy the reproductive tract of the female at the same time.[5] Sperm competition exerts a selection pressure on males to produce large ejaculates containing numerous sperm. In the race to the valuable egg, the more voluminous sperm-laden ejaculate has an advantage in displacing the ejaculate of other men inside the woman's body.

The testes size of men, relative to their body weight, is far larger than that of gorillas and orangutans. Male testes account for 0.018 percent of body weight in gorillas and 0.048 percent in orangutans. In contrast, men's testes account for 0.079 percent of body weight—60 percent more than that of orangutans and more than four times that of gorillas. Men's relatively large testes provide one solid piece of evidence that women in human evolutionary history sometimes had sex with more than one man within a time span of a few days. The comment made in many cultures that a man has "big balls" may be a metaphorical expression with a literal referent. But humans do not possess the largest testes of all the primates. Human testicular volume is substantially smaller than that of the highly promiscuous chimpanzee, whose testes account for 0.269 percent of body weight, which is more than three times the percentage of men. These findings suggest that our human ancestors rarely reached the chimpanzee's extreme of promiscuity.[6]

Another clue to the evolutionary existence of casual mating comes from variations in sperm production and insemination.[7]

In a study to determine the effect of separating mates from each other on sperm production, thirty-five couples agreed to provide ejaculates resulting from sexual intercourse, either from condoms or from the flowback (the gelatinous mass of seminal fluid spontaneously ejected by a woman at various points after intercourse).[8] All the couples had been separated from each other for varying intervals of time.

Men's sperm count increased dramatically with the increasing amount of time the couple had been apart. The more time spent apart, the more sperm the husbands inseminated in their wives when they finally had sex. When the couples spent 100 percent of their time together, men inseminated only 389 million sperm per ejaculate. But when the couples spent only 5 percent of their time together, men inseminated 712 million sperm per ejaculate, or almost double the amount. Sperm insemination increases when other men's sperm might be inside the wife's reproductive tract at the same time, as a consequence of the opportunity provided for extramarital sex by the couple's separation. This increase in sperm is precisely what would be expected if humans had an ancestral history of some casual sex and marital infidelity.

The increase in sperm insemination by the husband upon prolonged separation gives his sperm a greater chance in the race to the egg by crowding out or displacing any interlopers' sperm. A man appears to inseminate just enough sperm to replace the sperm that have died inside the woman since his last sexual episode with her, thereby "topping off" his mate to a particular level to keep the population of his sperm inside her relatively constant. Men appear to carry a physiological mechanism that elevates sperm count when their wives may have had opportunities to be unfaithful.

The physiology of women's orgasm provides another clue to an evolutionary history of short-term mating. Once it was thought that a woman's orgasm functions to make her sleepy and keep her reclined, thereby decreasing the likelihood that sperm will flow out and increasing the likelihood of conceiving. But if the function of orgasm were to keep the woman reclined so as to delay flowback, then more sperm would be retained when flowback is delayed. That does not happen. Rather, there is no link between the timing of the flowback and the number of sperm retained.[9]

Women on average eject roughly 35 percent of the sperm within thirty minutes of the time of insemination. If the woman has an orgasm, however, she retains 70 percent of the sperm and ejects only 30 percent. Lack of an orgasm leads to the ejection of more sperm. This evidence is consistent with the theory that women's orgasm functions to suck up the sperm from the vagina into the cervical canal and uterus, increasing the probability of conception.

A key to the mystery of female orgasm appears to be the link between female orgasm and sperm retention, combined with a hidden side of female sexuality—women's sexual infidelities. Kinsey found that women were almost twice as likely to achieve orgasms with their affair partners as with their husbands. A British study found that women have more frequent high-sperm-retention orgasms—those that occur within two minutes after the male orgasm—with their affair partners than with their husbands. The clincher, however, may be the timing of lunchtime romance at the No-Tell Motel: women who have affairs appear to time their sexual liaisons to coincide with the most fertile phase of their cycle—prior to or at ovulation. Indeed, the rate of sexual intercourse with an affair partner during peak fertility is three times as high as the rate during the low-fertile post-ovulatory phase.[10]

Female orgasm may function as a selection device to choose which man will end up fertilizing her eggs, a man who is not necessarily her husband. Women are more orgasmic with regular mates who have good genetic quality, as indexed by anatomical measures of symmetry and judgments of physical attractiveness.

But if they are having affairs, women preferentially choose affair partners of high genetic quality and then experience more frequent sexual orgasms in the context of their liaisons. For women having affairs, orgasm may facilitate a mating strategy of getting the best of both worlds—investment from one man who provides parenting and resources for her children and good genes from another man who provides little investment but who increases the genetic quality of her children.

Although my reading of scientific evidence leads me to conclude that the female orgasm shows at least some design hallmarks of adaptation, skeptics of this conclusion—advocates of the hypothesis that female orgasm is a non-adaptive by-product analogous to male nipples—still have plenty of ammunition to work with. No current adaptationist hypothesis, for example, can explain why there appear to be huge individual differences and cultural differences in the occurrence of female orgasm. Furthermore, it is entirely possible that the female orgasm is neither 100 percent adaptation nor 100 percent by-product, but rather contains certain features that are by-products combined with some adaptive modification.

This may not be good news for the husbands of women seeking sex outside marriage, but it suggests that women have evolved strategies that function for their own reproductive benefit in the context of extramarital affairs, perhaps by securing good genes from one man and investment from their regular mate.

In addition to this anatomical and physiological evidence, psychological and behavioral evidence also suggest a long evolutionary history of casual, short-term mating.

Lust

Psychological adaptations point to a human evolutionary past of casual sex. Because the adaptive benefits of temporary liaisons differ for each gender, however, evolution has forged different psychological mechanisms for men and women. For ancestral men, the primary benefit of casual sex was a direct increase in the number of offspring. Men consequently faced a key adaptive problem—how to gain sexual access to a variety of women.

One psychological solution to the problem of securing sexual access to a variety of partners is old-fashioned lust. Men have evolved a powerful desire for sexual access to a variety of women. When President Jimmy Carter told a reporter that he "had lust in his heart," he expressed honestly a universal male desire for sexual variety. Men do not always act on this desire, but it is a motivating force: "Even if only one impulse in a thousand is consummated, the function of lust nonetheless is to motivate sexual intercourse."[11]

To find how many sexual partners people desire, the study of short-term and long-term mating asked unmarried college students to identify how many sex partners they would ideally like to have within various time periods, ranging from the next month to their entire lifetime.[12] Men desired more sex partners than women at each of the different time intervals. Within the next year, for example, men stated on average that ideally they would like to have more than six sex partners, whereas women said that they would like to have only one. Within the next three years, men desired ten sex partners, whereas women wanted only two. In their lifetime, men on average wanted to have eighteen sex partners and women only four or five.

David Schmitt's massive study of fifty-two different cultures located on six continents and thirteen islands uncovered the same pattern.[13] Norwegian culture provides an especially interesting test case for these sex differences, since it is a culture with a high degree of gender equality.[14] Over the next thirty years, Norwegian women desired roughly five sex partners; Norwegian men desired roughly twenty-five. Some psychologists argue that increased gender equality will reduce or eliminate these and other sex differences.[15] This clearly has not happened in Norway or in any other culture studied so far. Men's inclination to count their "conquests" and to "put notches on their belt," long incorrectly attributed in Western culture to male immaturity or masculine insecurity, in fact reflects an adaptation to motivate brief sexual encounters.

Studies of sex drive reveal similar gender differences. The most massive study, involving more than 200,000 individuals from 53 countries, measured sex drive by asking participants to respond to statements such as "I have a strong sex drive" and "It doesn't take much to get me sexually excited."[16] In every nation, from Thailand to Croatia to Trinidad, men reported having a higher sex drive than did women. Similarly, large gender differences emerge from studies of masturbation rates and pornography consumption. The sex differences in sex drive prove just as large in nations with high levels of gender equality, such as Sweden and Denmark, as they do in nations with lower levels of gender equality, such as Bangladesh, Egypt, and Nigeria—findings that contradict the notion that these sex differences are caused by economic gender inequality.

Another psychological solution to the problem of gaining sexual access to a variety of partners is to let little time elapse before seeking sexual intercourse. The less time he permits to elapse before obtaining sexual intercourse, the larger the number of women a man can successfully bed. Large time investments absorb more of a man's mating effort and interfere with solving the problem of number and variety. In the business world, time is money. In the mating world, time is sexual opportunity.

Men and women in the study of short-term and long-term mating rated how likely they would be to consent to sex with someone they viewed as desirable if they had known the person for only an hour, a day, a week, a month, six months, a year, two years, or five years. Both men and women said that they would probably have sex upon knowing an attractive person for five years. At every shorter interval, however, men exceeded women in their reported likelihood of having sex. Five years or six months—it was all the same for men. They expressed equal eagerness for sex with women they had known for either length of time. In contrast, women dropped from probable consent to sex after five years' acquaintance to neutral feelings about sex after knowing a person for six months.

Having known a potential mate for only one week, men are still on average positive about the possibility of consenting to sex. Women, in sharp contrast, report being unlikely to have sex after knowing someone for just a week. Upon knowing a potential mate for merely one hour, men are slightly disinclined to consider having sex, but the disinclination is not strong. For most women, sex after just one hour is a virtual impossibility. These fundamental sex differences have been extensively documented across the globe, including in Norway, Denmark, and Sweden.[17] As with men's desires, men's inclination to let little time elapse before seeking sexual intercourse offers a partial solution to the adaptive problem of gaining sexual access to a variety of partners.

Studies of Internet dating point to the same conclusion. Barry Kuhle conducted a study of users of Tinder, a dating site geared heavily toward short-term mating.[18] Even though it is widely seen as a site for sexual hookups, men more than women expressed significantly greater interest in immediate short-term sex. Men reported "swiping right" on dozens or even hundreds of female profiles in the hope that a few would reciprocate. Women were considerably more selective, picking just one or a few for potential matches. Male lust, seemingly insatiable, drives men's search for sexual variety in the modern world of Internet mating.

Standards for Short-Term Mates

Another psychological solution to securing a variety of casual sex partners is men's relaxation of their standards for acceptable partners. High standards for attributes such as age, intelligence, personality, and marital status function to exclude the majority of potential mates from consideration. Relaxed standards ensure the presence of more eligible players.

College students provided information about the minimum and maximum acceptable ages of a partner for a short-term or long-term sexual relationship. For a brief hookup, college men accepted an age range that was roughly four years wider than women did. Men were willing to have sex in the short run with members of the opposite sex who were as young as sixteen and as old as twenty-eight, whereas women required men to be at least eighteen but no older than twenty-six. This relaxation of age restrictions by men did not apply to committed mating, for which the minimum age was seventeen and the maximum twenty-two. For women the minimum age for committed mating was nineteen and the maximum twenty-five.

Men also relaxed their standards for a wide variety of other characteristics. Out of the sixty-seven characteristics nominated as potentially desirable in a casual mate, men required lower levels of such assets as charm, athleticism, education, generosity, honesty, independence, kindness, intellectuality, loyalty, sense of humor, sociability, wealth, responsibility, spontaneity, cooperativeness, and emotional stability. Men's relaxation of standards helps to solve the problem of gaining access to a variety of sex partners.

When the college students rated sixty-one undesirable characteristics, women rated roughly one-third of them as more undesirable than men did in the context of casual sex. In this context, men had less objection to drawbacks such as mental abuse, violence, bisexuality, dislike by others, excessive drinking, ignorance, lack of education, possessiveness, promiscuity, selfishness, lack of humor, and lack of sensuality. In contrast, men rated only four negative characteristics as significantly more undesirable than women did: a low sex drive, physical unattractiveness, a need for commitment, and hairiness. Men clearly relaxed their standards more than women did for brief sexual encounters.

Lowered standards, however, are still standards. Indeed, men's standards for sexual affairs reveal a precise strategy to gain sexual variety. Compared with their long-term preferences, men seeking casual sex disliked women who were prudish or conservative or had a low sex drive. In contrast to their long-term preferences, men valued sexual experience in a potential temporary sex partner, which reflects a belief that sexually experienced women are more sexually accessible to them than women who are sexually inexperienced. Men disliked promiscuity or indiscriminate sexuality in a potential wife or committed mate but believed that promiscuity was either neutral or even mildly desirable in a potential sex partner. Promiscuity, high sex drive, and sexual experience in a woman probably signal an increased likelihood that a man can gain sexual access for the short run. Prudishness and low sex drive, in contrast, signal a difficulty in gaining sexual access and thus interfere with men's short-term sexual strategy.

One distinguishing feature of men's relaxation of standards for short-term sex partners involves the need for commitment. In contrast to the tremendous positive value of +2.17 out of 3.00 that men placed on commitment when seeking a marriage partner, men seeking a casual hookup disliked a quest for commitment in a woman, judging it −1.40, or undesirable, in a short-term partner.[19] Furthermore, men were not particularly bothered by a woman's marital status when they evaluated casual sex partners; a woman's commitment to another man reduced the odds that she would try to extract a commitment from them. These findings confirm that men shift their desires to minimize their investment in a casual mating, providing an additional clue to an evolutionary history in which men sometimes sought casual, uncommitted sex.

The Coolidge Effect

The story is told that President Calvin Coolidge and his wife, Grace, were being given separate tours of newly formed government farms. Upon passing the chicken coops and noticing a rooster vigorously copulating with a hen, Mrs. Coolidge inquired about how often the rooster performed this duty. "Dozens of times each day," replied the guide. Mrs. Coolidge asked the guide to "please mention this fact to the president." When the president passed by later and was informed of the sexual vigor of the rooster, he asked, "Always with the same hen?" "Oh, no," the guide replied, "a different one each time." "Please tell *that* to Mrs. Coolidge," said the president. And so the "Coolidge effect" was named—the male tendency to be sexually re-aroused upon the presentation of novel females, giving males an impulse to mate with multiple females.

The Coolidge effect is a widespread mammalian trait that has been documented many times.[20] Male rats, rams, cattle, and sheep all show the effect. In a typical study, a cow is placed in a bull pen, and after copulation the cow is replaced with another cow. The bull's sexual response continues unabated with each new cow but diminishes quickly when the same cow is left in the pen. Males continue to become aroused to the point of ejaculation in response to novel females. The response to the eighth, the tenth, or the twelfth female is nearly as strong as the response to the first.

Sexual arousal to novelty occurs despite a variety of attempts to diminish it. For example, when researchers disguised ewes postcopulation with a canvas covering, the rams were never fooled.[21] Their response to a female with whom they had already copulated was always lower than with a novel female. The diminished drive was not a result of the female's having had sex per se; the renewed drive occurred just as often if the novel female had already copulated with another male. And the male remained relatively uninterested if the original female was merely removed and reintroduced.

Men across cultures also show the Coolidge effect. In Western culture, the frequency of intercourse with a long-term partner declines as the relationship lengthens. Compared to the first month of marriage, intercourse is roughly half as frequent after one year of marriage, and it declines more gradually thereafter. As Donald Symons notes, "The waning of lust for one's wife is adaptive . . . because it promotes a roving eye."[22] Human wanderlust takes many forms. Men in most cultures pursue extramarital sex more often than do their wives. The Kinsey study, for example, found that 50 percent of men but only 26 percent of women had extramarital affairs.[23] Some studies show that the gap may be narrowing. One study of 8,000 married men and women found that 40 percent of the men and 36 percent of the women reported at least one affair. The Hite reports on sexuality suggest figures as high as 75 percent for men and 70 percent for women, although these samples are acknowledged not to be representative.[24] More representative samples, such as Morton Hunt's survey of 982 men and 1,044 women, yielded an incidence of 41 percent for men and 18 percent for women.[25] Despite these varying estimates, and a possible narrowing of the gap between the sexes, all studies show sex differences in the incidence and frequency of affairs: more men have affairs more often, and with more partners, than women do.[26]

Spouse swapping, "swinging," and polyamory are nearly always initiated by husbands, not by wives.[27] A Muria man from India summarized the male desire for variety succinctly: "You don't want to eat the same vegetable every day."[28] A Kgatla man from South Africa described his sexual desires about his two wives: "I find them both equally desirable, but when I have slept with one for three days, by the fourth day she has wearied me, and when I go to the other I find that I have greater passion, she seems more attractive than the first, but it is not really so, for when I return to the latter again there is the same renewed passion."[29]

The anthropologist Thomas Gregor describes the sexual feelings of Amazonian Mehinaku men in this way: "Women's sexual attractiveness varies from 'flavorless' (*mana*) to the 'delicious' (*awirintya*) . . . sad to say, sex with spouses is said to be mana, in contrast with sex with lovers, which is nearly always *awirintyapa*."[30] Gustav Flaubert writes of Madame Bovary that she is "like any other mistress; and the charm of novelty, gradually slipping away like a garment, laid bare the eternal monotony of passion, whose forms and phrases are forever the same."[31]

Studies of men's sexual arousal to pornography support the existence of the Coolidge effect in humans.[32] Using physiological measures of penile tumescence and self-reports of sexual arousal, researchers have shown that men viewing the same erotic images repeatedly experience progressively diminished arousal with each viewing. Over the same time period, men exposed to erotic images of different women became consistently re-aroused. The modern explosion of Internet pornography, now a multibillion-dollar business, owes its success largely to hijacking men's evolved sexual psychology.

Kinsey sums it up best: "There seems to be no question but that the human male would be promiscuous in his choice of sexual partners throughout the whole of his life if there were no social restrictions. . . . The human female is much less interested in a variety of partners."[33]

Sexual Fantasies

Sexual fantasies provide another psychological clue to men's desire for low-commitment sex. One of several music videos targeted to adolescent men shows a male rock star cavorting across a beach strewn with dozens of beautiful bikini-clad women. Another shows a male rock star caressing the shapely legs of one woman after another as he sings. Yet another shows a rapper gazing at dozens of women who are wearing only underwear. Since these videos are designed to appeal to male audiences, the implication is clear. A prominent male sexual fantasy is to have sexual access to dozens of different young, beautiful women who respond eagerly and willingly.

Men's and women's sexual fantasies differ greatly. Studies from Japan, the United Kingdom, and the United States show that men have roughly twice as many sexual fantasies as women.[34] In their sleep men are more likely than women to dream about sexual events. Men's sexual fantasies more often include strangers, multiple partners, and anonymous partners. Most men report that during a single fantasy episode they sometimes change sexual partners; most women rarely change sex partners within one fantasy. In Hunt's survey, 32 percent of men but only 8 percent of women reported having imagined sexual encounters with over 1,000 different partners in their lifetime. Fantasies about group sex occurred among 33 percent of the men but only 18 percent of the women.[35] A typical male fantasy, as one man told another researcher, is having "six or more naked women licking, kissing, and fellating me."[36] Another man reported the fantasy of "being the mayor of a small town filled with nude girls from 20 to 24. I like to take walks, and pick out the best-looking one that day, and she engages in intercourse with me. All the women have sex with me any time I want."[37] Numbers and novelty are key ingredients of men's fantasy lives.

Male fantasies are heavily visual, focusing on smooth skin and body parts, notably breasts, genitals, buttocks, legs, and mouths. During their sexual fantasies, 81 percent of men but only 43 percent of women focus on visual images rather than feelings. Attractive women with lots of exposed skin who show signs of easy access and no commitment are key components of men's fantasies. As Bruce Ellis and Donald Symons observe, "The most striking feature of [male fantasy] is that sex is sheer lust and physical gratification, devoid of encumbering relationships, emotional elaboration, complicated plot lines, flirtation, courtship, and extended foreplay."[38] These fantasies reveal a psychology attuned to seeking sexual access to multiple partners.

Women's sexual fantasies, in contrast, often contain familiar partners. Fifty-nine percent of American women but only 28 percent of American men reported that their sexual fantasies typically focused on someone with whom they were already romantically and sexually involved. Emotions and personality are crucial for women. Forty-one percent of the women but only 16 percent of the men reported that they focused most heavily on the personal and emotional characteristics of the fantasized partner. And 57 percent of women but only 19 percent of men reported that they focused on feelings as opposed to visual images. As one woman observed: "I usually think about the guy I am with. Sometimes I realize that the feelings will overwhelm me, envelop me, sweep me away."[39] Women emphasize tenderness, romance, and personal involvement in their sexual fantasies. They also pay more attention to how their partner responds to them than to visual images of the partner.[40]

Hooking Up and Sexual Regret

The differing nature of sexual regret in men and women offers further evidence of men's evolved psychology of short-term mating. Regret is a powerful emotion. We rue the mistakes we have made, a feeling that probably functions to help us make better decisions in the future. Sexual regret occurs in two domains—missed sexual opportunities (sexual omission) and committed sexual actions (sexual commission). In studies of more than 23,000 individuals, men more than women reported regretting missed sexual opportunities.[41] These included not having more sex when younger, not having more sex when single, and failing to act on a sexual opportunity with a particularly attractive person. Women were more likely to regret sexual acts of commission, such as losing virginity to the wrong person, hooking up with a person with low mate value when drunk, and having sex with someone who was not interested in a relationship.

Women are more likely than men to experience negative emotions after a hookup. Men are more likely to regret when the woman they hooked up with wants a more serious relationship. Men report that their ideal outcome of a hookup would be more hookups in the future. Women are more likely to report that their ideal outcome would be a romantic relationship. Following hookups, women are more likely than men to report feeling "used" and experiencing depressed mood.[42] There are important individual differences within each gender, of course; some women just want casual sex, and some men yearn for deeper connection. The overall gender differences in sexual regret and post-hookup feelings, however, provide additional clues that reveal a fundamental difference in men's and women's sexual psychology.

The Closing Time Effect and the Post-Orgasm Shift

Another psychological clue to men's strategy of casual sex comes from studies that examine shifts in men's judgments of attractiveness over the course of an evening at a singles bar. In one study, 137 men and 80 women were approached at 9:00 p.m., 10:30, and 12:00 midnight and asked to rate the attractiveness of members of the opposite sex in the bar using a 10-point scale.[43] As closing time approached, men viewed women as increasingly attractive. The judgments at 9:00 were 5.5, but by midnight they had increased to over 6.5. Women's judgments of men's attractiveness also increased over time. But women's ratings overall of the male bar patrons were lower than men's ratings of women. At 9:00, women rated the men at the bar as just below the average of 5.0, which increased near midnight to only 5.5.

Men's shift in perceptions of women's attractiveness near closing time occurs regardless of how much alcohol they have consumed. Whether a man has consumed a single drink or six drinks has no effect on the shift in his view of women as more attractive near closing time. The often noted "beer goggles" phenomenon, whereby women presumably are viewed as more attractive with men's increasing intoxication, may instead be attributable to a psychological mechanism sensitive to decreasing opportunities for sexual success. As the evening progresses and a man has not yet been successful in picking up a woman, he views the remaining women in the bar as increasingly attractive, a shift that should increase his motivation to seek sex from the remaining women in the bar.

Another perceptual shift may take place after men have an orgasm with a casual sex partner with whom they wish no further involvement. Some men report viewing a sex partner as highly attractive before orgasm, but then after orgasm, a mere ten seconds later, viewing her as less attractive or even unappealing. Martie Haselton and I found that these shifts occur primarily among men who are dispositionally inclined to pursue a short-term mating strategy.[44] They do not occur for long-term-oriented men, and they do not occur for women regardless of mating strategy. The negative shift in attraction following orgasm may function to prompt a hasty postcopulatory departure to reduce risks to the man such as getting involved in an unwanted commitment.

Sexual Orientation and Casual Sex

A further clue to the significant role of casual mating in men's sexual repertoire comes from examining the sexual behavior of homosexual men and women. Donald Symons notes that male homosexual sexuality is unconstrained by women's dictates of romance, involvement, and commitment. Similarly, lesbian sexuality is unconstrained by men's dictates and demands. The actual behavior of those with a same-sex sexual orientation therefore provides a window for viewing the nature of all men's and women's sexual desires, unclouded by the compromises imposed by the sexual strategies of the other sex.

Gay men are much more interested in casual sex with strangers than are lesbian women.[45] Whereas male homosexuals often pursue brief encounters, lesbians rarely do. Whereas male homosexuals frequently search for new and varied sex partners, lesbians are more likely to settle into intimate, lasting, committed relationships. One study found that 94 percent of male homosexuals had more than fifteen sex partners, whereas only 15 percent of lesbians had that many.[46] The more extensive Kinsey study conducted in San Francisco in the 1980s found that almost one-half of the male homosexuals who participated had over 500 different sex partners, mostly strangers met in baths or bars.[47] Some modern dating apps such as Grindr are specifically designed to facilitate these sexual opportunities. When men are unconstrained by the courtship and commitment requirements women often want, they freely satisfy their desires for casual sex with a variety of partners.

In their proclivities for casual sex, as in their long-term mate preferences, homosexual males are similar to heterosexual males and lesbian women are similar to heterosexual women. Homosexual proclivities reveal fundamental differences between men and women in the centrality of casual sex. Symons notes that "heterosexual men would be as likely as homosexual men to have sex most often with strangers, to participate in anonymous orgies in public baths, and to stop off in public rest rooms for five minutes of fellatio on the way home from work if women were interested in these activities. But women are not interested."[48]

Prostitution

Men's desire for casual sex creates a demand for prostitution; many men, including married men, are willing to pay for casual sex.[49] Prostitution occurs in nearly every society. In the United States, there are an estimated 1 million active prostitutes, although prostitution is legal only in some counties of the state of Nevada. In Germany, where prostitution is legal, there are roughly 400,000 part-time or full-time prostitutes. Estimates suggest 500,000 prostitutes in Mexico, 800,000 in the Philippines, 3 million in India, and 5 million in China. In all cultures, men are overwhelmingly the consumers. Kinsey found that 69 percent of American men had been to a prostitute, and for 15 percent of them prostitution was a regular sexual outlet. The corresponding numbers for women were so low that they were not even reported.[50]

The prevalence of prostitution does not imply that it is an adaptation, something targeted by selection. Rather, it can be understood as a consequence of two factors operating simultaneously—men's desire for low-cost casual sex and women either choosing or being compelled by economic necessity or other factors to offer sexual services for material gain.

The psychological clues that reveal men's strategies for casual sex are numerous: sexual fantasies, the Coolidge effect, lust, sex drive, inclination to seek intercourse rapidly, relaxation of standards, attitudes toward hookups, emotions of sexual regret, the closing time effect, post-orgasm shifts in judgments of women's attractiveness, homosexual proclivities, and willingness to use prostitution as a sexual outlet. These psychological clues reveal an evolutionary past that favored men who had short-term mating in their sexual repertoire alongside the pursuit of a long-term mate. But heterosexual men need consenting women for casual sex.

The Hidden Side of
Women's Short-Term Sexuality

The reproductive benefits to men of casual sex are large and direct, but the benefits that women reap from short-term mating were largely neglected until evolutionary psychologists began to investigate them. Although women cannot increase the number of children they bear by having sex with multiple partners, they can gain other important advantages from casual sex as one strategy within a flexible sexual repertoire.[51] Ancestral women must have sought casual sex for its benefits in some contexts at some times, because if there had been no willing women, men could not possibly have pursued their own interest in short-term sex.

For ancestral women, unlike men, seeking sex as an end in itself is unlikely to have been a powerful goal of casual mating, for the simple reason that sperm have never been scarce. Access to more sperm would not have increased a woman's reproductive success. Minimal sexual access is all a woman needs, and there is rarely a shortage of men willing to provide the minimum. Additional sperm are unnecessary for fertilization.

One key benefit of casual sex to women is immediate access to resources. Imagine a food shortage hitting an ancestral tribe thousands of years ago. Game is scarce. The first frost has settled ominously. Bushes no longer yield berries. A lucky hunter takes down a deer. A woman watches him return from the hunt, hunger pangs gnawing. She flirts with him. Although they do not discuss any explicit exchange, her sexual enticements make him more than willing to provide her with a portion of the deer meat. Sex for resources, or resources for sex—the two have been exchanged in millions of transactions over the millennia of human existence.

In many traditional societies, such as the Mehinaku of Amazonia and the natives of the Trobriand Islands, men bring gifts such as food, jewelry, tobacco, betel nuts, turtle shell rings, or armlets to their mistresses. Women deny sex if the gifts stop flowing. A woman might say, "You have no payment to give me—I refuse."[52] A Trobriand man's reputation among women suffers if he fails to bring gifts, and this interferes with his future ability to attract mistresses. Trobriand women benefit materially through their affairs.

Modern women's preferences in a lover provide psychological clues to the evolutionary history of the material and economic benefits women gained from brief sexual encounters. Women especially value four characteristics in temporary lovers more than in committed mates—spending a lot of money on them from the beginning, giving them gifts from the beginning, having an extravagant lifestyle, and being generous with their resources.[53] Women judge these attributes to be mildly desirable in husbands but quite desirable in casual sex partners. Women dislike frugality and signs of stinginess in a lover; these qualities signal that the man is reluctant to devote an immediate supply of resources. These psychological preferences reveal that securing immediate resources is a key adaptive benefit that women secure through affairs.

The benefit of economic resources from casual sex is most starkly revealed in extreme cases such as prostitution. In cross-cultural perspective, many women who become prostitutes do so out of economic necessity because they lack suitable opportunities for marriage. Women who have been divorced by a man because of adultery, for example, have often become unmarriageable in cultures such as Taiwan Hokkien or the Somalis.[54] Chinese

and Burmese women may be unmarriageable if they are not virgins. Women among the Aztec and Ifugao are unmarriageable if
they have a disease. In all these societies, unmarriageable women
sometimes resort to prostitution to gain the economic benefits
needed for survival.

Some women, however, say that they turn to prostitution to
avoid the drudgery of marriage. Maylay women in Singapore, for
example, become prostitutes to avoid the hard work expected of
wives, which includes the gathering of firewood and the launder-
ing of clothes. And among the Amhara and Bemba, prostitutes
earn enough through casual sex to hire men to do the work that
is normally expected of wives. Immediate economic resources, in
short, remain a powerful benefit to women who engage in temporary sexual liaisons.

Sexual affairs also provide an opportunity to evaluate potential husbands by supplying additional information that is unavailable through mere dating without sexual intercourse. Given the
tremendous reproductive importance of selecting the right husband, women devote great effort to evaluation and assessment.
Affairs prior to marriage allow a woman to assess the intentions
of the prospective mate—whether he is seeking a brief sexual encounter or a marriage partner, and hence the likelihood that he
will abandon her. An affair allows her to evaluate his personality
characteristics—how he holds up under stress and how reliable
he is. It allows her to see through any deception that might be
present—whether he is truly free or already involved in a serious
relationship. And it allows her to assess his value as a mate or to
learn how attractive he is to other women.

Sexual intercourse before marriage provides important information about the long-term viability of a couple's relationship
by giving them the opportunity to evaluate their sexual compatibility. Through sex women can gauge such qualities as a man's

sensitivity, his concern with her happiness, and his flexibility. Sexually incompatible couples divorce more often and are more likely to experience adultery.[55] Twenty-nine percent of men and women questioned by the sex researchers Samuel Janus and Cynthia Janus stated that sexual problems were the primary reason for their divorce—the reason most often mentioned. The potential costs inflicted by an unfaithful mate and by divorce potentially can be avoided by assessing sexual compatibility before making a commitment.

Women's preferences for short-term mates reveal hints that they use casual sex to evaluate possible marriage partners. If women sought short-term mates simply for opportunistic sex, as many men do, certain characteristics would not be particularly bothersome, such as a man's preexisting committed relationship or his promiscuity. Women, like men, would find promiscuity in a prospective lover to be neutral or mildly desirable.[56] In truth, however, women regard a preexisting relationship or promiscuous tendencies in a prospective lover as highly undesirable, since they signal unavailability as a potentially committed partner or the repeated pursuit of a short-term sexual strategy. These characteristics decrease the woman's odds of entering a long-term relationship with the man. They convey powerfully that the man cannot remain faithful and is a poor long-term mating prospect. And they interfere with the function of extracting immediate resources, since men who are promiscuous or whose resources are tied up in a serious relationship have fewer unencumbered assets to allocate.

Women's desires in a short-term sex partner strongly resemble their desires in a husband.[57] In both cases, women want someone who is kind, romantic, understanding, exciting, stable, healthy, humorous, and generous with his resources. In both contexts, women desire men who are tall, athletic, and attractive. Men's preferences, in marked contrast, shift abruptly with the mating context.

The relative constancy of women's preferences in both scenarios supports the hypothesis that some women see casual mates as potential husbands and thus impose high standards for both.

Mate Switching and Backup Mates

Through casual sex, women may also secure added protection against conflicts that arise with other men or with competitors. Having a second mate who will defend and protect her may be especially advantageous for women in societies where they are at considerable risk of attack or rape. In some societies, such as the Yanomamö of Venezuela, women are vulnerable to male violence, including physical abuse, rape, and even the killing of their children, when they lack the protection of a mate.[58] This vulnerability is illustrated by the account of a Brazilian woman who was kidnapped by Yanomamö men.[59] When men from another village tried to rape her, not a single Yanomamö man came to her defense because she was not married to any of them and had no special male friends to protect her.

The use of such special friendships for protection has a primate precedent among savanna baboons.[60] Female baboons form special friendships with one or more males other than their primary mates, and these friends protect them against sexual harassment from other males. Females show a marked preference for mating with their friends when they enter estrus, suggesting a strategy of exchanging sex for protection. As Robert Smith points out:

> A primary mate cannot always be available to defend his wife and children and, in his absence, it may be advantageous for a female to consort with another male for the protection he may offer. . . . Absence of the primary mate [for example, when he is off hunting] may create the opportunity and need for extrabond mating. . . . A male may be inclined to protect the

children of a married lover on the chance that his genes are represented among them.[61]

A lover may also serve as a potential replacement for a woman's regular mate if he should desert, become ill or injured, prove to be infertile, or die, which were not unusual events in ancestral environments. Her regular mate might fail to return from the hunt, for example, or be killed in a tribal war. Men's status might change over time—for instance, a woman married to a head man who is deposed, whose position is usurped, and whose resources are co-opted might benefit by positioning herself to replace him quickly, without having to start over again. A woman who must delay replacing her mate by starting over is forced to incur the costs of a new search for a mate while her own desirability declines. Women benefit from having other men as potential backup mates.

The mate-switching function has been observed in the spotted sandpiper (*Actitis macularia*), a polyandrous shorebird studied on Little Pelican Island in Leech Lake, Minnesota. The biologists Mark Colwell and Lewis Oring, through 4,000 hours of field observation, discovered that a female spotted sandpiper who engages in extra-pair copulations with another male has an increased likelihood of becoming an enduring mate with that male in the future.[62] The females use the copulation as a way to test the receptivity and availability of the male. Male spotted sandpipers, however, sometimes foil these attempts at mate switching. Some males move several territories away from their home base when seeking extra-pair copulations, apparently so that the female will not detect that they are already mated. Despite this conflict between the sexes, the fact that the adulterers often end up as committed mates suggests that the extra-pair matings function as a means to switch mates.

Evidence for the mate-switching function of casual sex in humans comes from several sources. Women tend to have affairs when they are unhappy with their primary relationship, whereas men who have affairs are no less happy with their marriages than men who refrain.[63] Heidi Greiling and I conducted the second study, which revealed that women sometimes have affairs when they are trying to replace their current mate or in order to make it easier to break off with a current mate.[64]

Casual sex partners sometimes bestow elevated status on their temporary mates. Women sometimes elevate their status by mating with a prestigious man, even if it is just an affair. In the economics of the mating marketplace, people assume that the woman must be special, since prestigious men generally have their pick of the most desirable women. Women may gain access to a higher social stratum, from which they might secure a permanent mate. Women also can elevate their status within their own social circles and potentially secure a more desirable husband.

Possible Genetic Benefits of Short-Term Sex

It is also possible for women to gain superior genes through casual sex that are passed on to their children. Given men's proclivities for opportunistic sex, the economics of the mating marketplace render it far easier for a woman to get a man from a higher stratum or with better genes to have sex with her than it is for her to get him to marry her. A woman might try to secure the investment of a lower-ranking man by marrying him, for example, while simultaneously securing the genes of a higher-ranking man by mating with him casually. This dual strategy apparently exists in Great Britain, where the biologists Robin Baker and Mark Bellis have discovered that women typically have affairs with men who are higher in status than their husbands.[65]

One version of the better genes theory has been called the "sexy son hypothesis."[66] According to this view, women prefer to have casual sex with men who are attractive to other women because they will have sons who possess the same charming characteristics. Women in the next generation will therefore find these sons attractive, and the sons will enjoy greater mating success than the sons of women who mate with men who are not regarded as attractive by most women.

Evidence for this theory comes from a study that identified key exceptions to women's more stringent selection criteria for long-term partners. Women are more exacting with regard to physical attractiveness in a casual encounter than they are in a permanent mate.[67] The preference for physically attractive casual sex partners may be a psychological clue to a human evolutionary history in which women benefited through the success of their sexy sons.

The strongest evidence of the good genes hypothesis comes from studies of women's preference shifts when ovulating. Large-scale statistical reviews of the three dozen or so studies of cycle shifts find that ovulating women not on hormonal contraceptives do indeed show stronger preferences for masculine men, especially for masculine bodies and voices, as well as symmetrical men.[68] Only women with mates low in genetic quality, however, stand to reap genetic benefits from an affair with a man who has the hypothesized good-genes indicators. And some researchers argue that other hypotheses better explain ovulation preference shifts. Ovulating women, for example, experience a higher sex drive, may feel sexier and more desirable, and so feel that they can successfully attract men of higher mate value.[69] The next decade of research will undoubtedly delve more deeply into the hidden genetic benefits to women of pursuing a short-term sexual strategy.

One type of mating system puts sharp constraints on women's short-term mating and any benefits that might accrue from them—arranged marriages. Although we can never know for sure, anthropologists believe that many women during human evolutionary history did not contract their own marriages; the evidence for this belief is the prevalence of marriages arranged by fathers and other kin in today's tribal cultures, which are assumed to resemble the conditions under which humans evolved.[70] The practice of arranged marriage is still common in many other parts of the world as well, such as India, Kenya, and the Middle East. Arranged marriages restrict the opportunities for women to reap the benefits of short-term mating. Even where matings are arranged by parents and kin, however, women often exert some influence over their sexual and marital decisions by manipulating their parents, carrying on clandestine affairs, defying their parents' wishes, and sometimes eloping. These forms of personal choice open the window to the benefits for women of short-term mating, including genetic benefits, even when their marriage is arranged by others.

Costs of Casual Sex

All sexual strategies carry costs, and casual sex is no exception. Men risk contracting sexually transmitted diseases, acquiring a reputation as a womanizer or "man-whore," or suffering injury from a jealous husband. A significant proportion of murders across cultures occur because jealous men suspect their mates of infidelity.[71] Unfaithful married men risk retaliatory affairs by their wives and costly divorces. Short-term sexual strategies also take time, energy, and economic resources.

Women sometimes incur more severe costs than men do. Women risk impairing their desirability if they develop a reputation for promiscuity, since men prize fidelity in a potential long-term mate. Women known as promiscuous suffer reputational damage even in relatively promiscuous cultures, such as among the Swedes and the Ache Indians.[72] A woman who adopts an exclusively short-term sexual strategy is at greater risk of physical and sexual abuse. Although women in marriages are also subjected to battering and even rape by husbands, the alarming statistics on the incidence of date rape, which some estimate to be 15 or 20 percent of all college women, reveal that women who are not in long-term relationships are at considerable risk.[73] Mate preferences, if judiciously applied to avoid potentially dangerous men, can minimize these risks.

Unmarried women who pursue casual sex risk getting pregnant and bearing a child without the benefits of an investing partner. In ancestral times, these children would have been at much greater risk of disease, injury, and death.[74] Some women commit infanticide in the absence of an investing man. In Canada, for example, single women delivered only 12 percent of the babies born between 1977 and 1983, but they committed just over 50 percent of the sixty-four maternal infanticides reported to the police.[75] This trend occurs across cultures as well, such as among the Baganda of Africa. But even this solution does not cancel the substantial other costs that women incur: nine months of gestation, reputational damage, and lost mating opportunities.

An unfaithful married woman risks the withdrawal of resources by her husband. From a reproductive perspective, she may be wasting valuable time in an extramarital liaison, obtaining sperm that are unnecessary for reproduction.[76] Furthermore, she risks increasing the sibling competition among her children, who may have weaker ties because they were fathered by different men.[77]

Short-term mating, in short, poses hazards for both sexes. But because there are powerful benefits as well, women and men have evolved psychological mechanisms to select circumstances in which the costs of short-term mating are minimized and the benefits increased.

Circumstances Favorable for Casual Sex

Everyone knows some men who are womanizers and others who are exclusively monogamous. Everyone knows some women who enjoy casual sex and others who would not dream of sex without commitment. Individuals differ in their proclivities for casual mating. Individuals also shift their proclivities at different times and in different contexts. These variations in sexual strategy depend on a range of personal, social, cultural, and ecological conditions.

The absence of an investing father during childhood has been reliably linked to the pursuit of a short-term sexual strategy. Among the Mayan of Belize and the Ache of Paraguay, for example, father absence has been correlated with men stating that they are unwilling to commit the time, energy, and resources needed to sustain a long-term mateship.[78] Women and men who grow up in father-absent homes are likely to reach puberty sooner, to start having intercourse earlier, and to pursue a short-term strategy after their sexual debut.[79] Their father's absence may lead women to infer that men are not reliable investors and thus to pursue a short-term sexual strategy of obtaining some benefits from multiple men rather than trying to secure the sustained investment of one man.

There is some scientific controversy over the direction of effects and precisely what causes individual differences in sexual strategy. Is the shift to a short-term strategy when one's father is absent due to the harsher or more unpredictable environment resulting from the father's lack of investment? Or is it due to genes that father-absent dads pass on to their children? Yet another possibility is that stepfather presence, rather than father absence, prompts kids to spring into sexual action sooner. Moreover, biological fathers engage in heavier "daughter guarding," which prevents girls from acting on their sexual impulses and encourages a long-term mating strategy. Future research is required to sort out these causal alternatives, but it is clear that individuals differ markedly in their inclination for short-term sex.

Casual sex is also related to people's developmental stage in life. Adolescents in many cultures are more likely to use temporary mating as a means of assessing their value on the mating market, experimenting with different strategies, honing their attraction skills, and clarifying their own preferences. After they have done so, they are often ready for commitment or marriage. The fact that premarital adolescent sexual experimentation is tolerated and even encouraged in some cultures, such as the Mehinaku of Amazonia, provides a clue that short-term mating is related to one's stage in life.[80]

The transitions between committed matings offer additional opportunities for casual sex. Upon divorce, for example, it is crucial to reassess one's value on the current mating market. The presence of children from the marriage generally lowers the desirability of divorced people. The elevated status that comes with being more advanced in their career, conversely, may raise their desirability. Precisely how all these changed circumstances affect a particular person may be evaluated by brief encounters, which allow a person to gauge more precisely his or her desirability on the mating market.

The abundance or shortage of eligible men relative to eligible women is another critical context for temporary mating. Many factors affect this sex ratio, including wars, which kill larger numbers of men than women; risky activities such as fights, which more frequently affect men; intentional homicides, in which roughly seven times more men than women die; and differential remarriage rates by age, whereby women remarry less and less often than men with increasing age. The modern phenomenon of more women than men enrolling in many colleges and universities in North America and western Europe creates a sex ratio imbalance among the college-educated mating pool. At the University of Texas at Austin, for example, the student body in 2016 was 54 percent women and 46 percent men. This may not sound like a huge disparity, but in fact it translates into a surplus of 17 percent more women than men. China's historical one-child policy, in contrast, created a surplus of men because parents selectively aborted female fetuses.

Men shift to short-term sexual strategies when many women are sexually available because the sex ratio is in their favor and they are better able to implement their desire for variety. Among the Ache, for example, men are highly promiscuous because there are 50 percent more women than men. Women shift to casual sex when there is a shortage of investing men available for marriage or when there are few benefits to marriage.[81] In some subcultures, notably in areas of concentrated poverty, men often lack the resources that women desire in a permanent mate. Where men do not have resources, women have less reason to mate with only one man. Similarly, when women receive more resources from their kin than from their husbands, they are more likely to engage in extramarital sex.[82] Women in these contexts sometimes mate opportunistically with different men, securing greater benefits for themselves and their children. The rise of the hookup culture on many modern college campuses has been partly created by the increasing sex ratio imbalance as higher percentages of women compared to men seek higher education.

In cultures where food is shared communally, women have less incentive to marry and often shift to temporary sex partners. The Ache of Paraguay, for example, communally share food secured from large game hunting. Good hunters do not get a larger share of meat than poor hunters. Women receive the same allotment of food, regardless of whether they have a husband and regardless of the hunting skill of their husband. Hence, there is less incentive for Ache women to remain mated with one man, and about 75 percent of them favor short-term relationships.[83] The socialist welfare system of Sweden provides another example. Since food and other material resources are provided to everyone, women have less incentive to marry. As a result, only half of all

Swedish couples who live together get married, and members of both sexes often pursue more casual relationships.[84]

Another factor that is likely to foster brief sexual encounters—although differently for men and women—is one's future desirability as a mate. A man at the apprenticeship stage of a promising career may pursue only brief affairs, figuring that he will be able to attract a more desirable long-term mate later on, when his career is closer to its peak. A woman whose current desirability is low may reason that she cannot attract a husband of the quality she desires and so may pursue carefree short-term relationships as an alternative to settling for someone who does not meet her standards.

Certain legal, social, and cultural sanctions encourage short-term mating. Roman kings, for example, were permitted to take hundreds of concubines, and like Moroccan emperor Moulay Ismail the Bloodthirsty (see Chapter 3), they cycled the young women out of the harem by the time they reached the age of thirty.[85] In Spain and France, it is an accepted cultural tradition that men who can afford it keep mistresses in apartments, a short-term arrangement outside the bounds and bonds of marriage. The ideologies of some isolated groups and communes—a living arrangement that was especially popular during the late 1960s and early 1970s and is present today among those practicing polyamory—encourage sexual experimentation with short-term relationships.

The sexual strategies pursued by other people affect the likelihood of casual sex. When many men pursue short-term relationships, as in Russia in many large-population cities, women are effectively forced into casual mating because fewer men are willing to commit, although some women choose to opt out of the mating game entirely. Or when one spouse has an extramarital affair, then the other may be motivated to even the score. Casual sex is never pursued in a vacuum. It is influenced by stage of life, mate value, sex ratios, cultural traditions, legal sanctions, and the strategies pursued by others. All of these circumstances affect the likelihood that a person will choose casual sex from the menu of human mating strategies.

Casual Sex as a Source of Power

Historically, the scientific study of mating has focused nearly exclusively on marriage. Human anatomy, physiology, psychology, and behavior, however, betray an ancestral past filled with opportunistic sex and affairs. The obvious reproductive advantages of such affairs to men may have blinded scientists to the benefits they had for women as well. Affairs involve willing women. Willing women seek or require benefits.

This picture of human nature may be disturbing to some. Women may not be comforted by the ease with which men are sometimes willing to jump into bed with near-strangers. Men may not be comforted by the knowledge that their partners continue to scan the mating terrain, encourage other men by flirting, offer hints of sexual accessibility, cultivate backup mates, and sometimes cheat with impunity. Human nature can be alarming.

But viewed from another perspective, our possession of a complex repertoire of mating strategies gives us far more power, far more flexibility, and far more control of our own destiny. We choose from a large mating menu and are not doomed to a single, invariant strategy. We tailor our mating strategies to our circumstances, be they an environment characterized by a sex ratio imbalance or a return entry into the mating market after a breakup. Moreover, the rapid rise of Internet dating sites and mobile apps greatly expands the pool of potential mates, providing access to thousands of potential partners we would never otherwise encounter in our day-to-day lives.

Modern technology and contemporary living conditions also allow people to escape many of the costs of casual sex that our ancestors experienced. Effective birth control, for example, allows us to avoid the costs of an unwanted or ill-timed pregnancy. The relative anonymity of urban living diminishes the reputational damage incurred by casual sex. Geographic mobility lowers the often restrictive influence of parents on the mating decisions of their children. And government safety nets lower the risks to survival for children produced by short-term liaisons. These reduced costs foster a fuller expression of the range of human mating within our complex repertoire.

Acknowledging the full diversity of our mating strategies may violate our socialized conceptions of one-and-only bliss. But simultaneously, this knowledge gives us greater power to design our own mating destiny than any humans in our evolutionary past ever possessed.

5

Attracting a Partner

Hearts have as many changing moods as the face has expressions. To capture a thousand hearts demands a thousand devices.

—OVID, *The Erotic Poems: The Art of Love*

KNOWING WHAT WE desire in a mate provides no guarantee that we will succeed in getting what we want. Success hinges on providing signals that we will deliver what the partner we desire is seeking. Because ancestral women valued high status in men, for example, men have evolved motivation for acquiring and displaying status. Because ancestral men desired youth and health in potential mates, women have evolved motivations to appear young and healthful. Competition to attract a mate therefore involves besting one's rivals in developing and displaying the characteristics most keenly sought by one's desired partners.

In this coevolutionary cycle, psychological mechanisms evolve in one sex to solve the adaptive problems imposed by the other sex. Just as the successful angler uses the lure that most closely resembles food that fits the fish's evolved preferences, so the successful competitor employs psychological tactics that most closely fit the evolved desires of the other sex. The characteristics that men and women value are keys to understanding the means of attracting a mate.

Attracting a mate does not occur, however, in a social vacuum. Desirable partners elicit strong social competition for their attention. Successful attraction therefore depends not merely on providing signals that one will fulfill a potential mate's desires but also on counteracting the seductive signals of rivals. Humans have evolved a method for running interference that is unique in the animal kingdom—the verbal derogation of competitors. Damaging a rival's reputation with a put-down, a slur, or an insinuation is part of the process of successfully attracting a mate.

Derogatory tactics, like tactics of attraction, work because they exploit the psychological adaptations that predispose people to be sensitive to certain valuable qualities in possible mates, such as their resources or appearance. A man's communication to a woman that his rival lacks ambition can be effective only if the woman is predisposed to reject men who have a low future resource potential. Similarly, a woman who tactically "slut-shames" her rival works only if men are predisposed to reject women who might have difficulty remaining faithful.

The success of both attractive and derogatory tactics hinges on whether the target of desire is seeking a casual sex partner or a long-term committed mate. Consider the case of a woman who denigrates a rival by casually mentioning that the rival has slept with many men. If the man is seeking a spouse, this tactic is highly effective, because men dislike promiscuity in a potential wife. If the man is seeking casual sex, however, the woman's tactic is likely to backfire, because most men pursuing easy sex are not bothered by a woman's past promiscuity. Similarly, overt displays of sexuality are effective short-term tactics for women but are ineffective in the long run: such displays get men's sexual attention but do not motivate them to invest or commit. The effectiveness of attraction, in short, depends critically on the temporal context of the mating. Men and women tailor their attraction techniques to the length of the relationship they seek.

The rules of play on the sexual field differ substantially from those of the marriage market. In long-term mating, both men and women prefer a long courtship—a process that permits evaluation of the nature and magnitude of the assets each person possesses and the costs they carry. Initial exaggerations of status or resources are revealed. Prior commitments to other mates surface. Children by former mates emerge. Prolonged assessment also allows both individuals to evaluate their mutual compatibility, which is essential for long-term mating.

Casual affairs truncate this assessment, dramatically increasing the opportunities for deception. Exaggeration of prestige, status, and income may go undetected. Prior commitments remain concealed. Information that damages a reputation comes too late. Casual mating, in short, is a rocky terrain where manipulation and deception can trip the unwary with every step. To compound this problem, deception usually occurs in the domains that are most important—status, resources, and commitment for women, appearance and sexual fidelity for men, and personality qualities for both.

The battle for casual sex is joined by both sexes, but not equally. The fact that more men than women seek casual sex partners creates a hurdle for men because there are fewer willing women. Women therefore tend to be more in control in short affairs than in the marital arena. For every attractive and sexually willing woman there are usually dozens of men who would consent to have sex with her. Women can be very choosy because they have so many options to choose from. In committed relationships, in contrast, this level of choosiness is a luxury that only very desirable women can afford.

Attracting a committed or casual mate requires display. Just as weaverbirds display their nests and scorpionflies display their nuptial gifts, men and women must advertise their assets on the mating market. Because men's and women's desires differ, the qualities they display must differ.

Generosity and Resource Display

The evolution of male strategies for accruing and displaying resources pervades the animal kingdom. The male roadrunner, for example, catches a mouse or baby rat, pounds it into a state of shock or death, and offers it to a female as her next meal, but without actually handing it over.[1] Rather, the male holds it away from her while croaking and waving his tail. Only after the birds have copulated does he release his gift to the female, who uses it to nourish the eggs that the male has just fertilized. Males who fail to offer this food resource fail in the effort to attract females.

Men, too, go to great lengths to display their resources to attract mates. The mate attraction studies conducted by my lab identified dozens of tactics that men and women use to attract a mate. We asked several hundred students from the University of California at Berkeley, Harvard University, and the University of Michigan to describe all the tactics they had observed in others or had used themselves. Their examples included bragging about accomplishments, talking about their importance at work, showing sympathy for the problems of others, initiating visual contact, and wearing sexy clothes. A team of four researchers reduced the larger set of more than 100 actions into 28 relatively distinct categories. The category "display athletic prowess," for example, included actions such as working out with weights, impressing someone by twisting open difficult jars, and talking about athletic successes. Subsequently, 100 adult married couples and 200 unmarried university students evaluated each tactic for how effective it is in attracting a mate, whether it is more effective when employed in casual or long-term relationships, and how frequently they, their close friends, and their spouses employ it.[2]

One of the techniques employed by men is to display their tangible resources: showing a high earning potential, flashing a lot of money, driving an expensive car, telling women how important they are at work, and subtly revealing their accomplishments. Another technique men use is to deceive women about their resources by misleading them, for example, about their career expectations, or exaggerating their prestige at work. Like the male roadrunner offering up his kill, men offer women resources as a primary method of attraction.

Men also derogate their rivals' resources. Typical behavior includes spreading false rumors about a rival, making fun of a rival's appearance, scoffing at a rival's achievements, and telling others that a rival has a sexually transmitted disease. All of these actions would fall into one of the 28 categories classified by our research team. For example, the category of "derogating a competitor's intelligence" includes making the rival seem dumb, telling others that the rival is stupid, and mentioning that the rival is an "airhead."

Men also counteract the attraction tactics of other men by derogating a rival's resource potential. Typically, men tell women that their rivals are poor, have no money, lack ambition, or drive cheap cars. Women are far less likely to derogate a rival's resources; when they do, the tactic is less effective than when men do it.[3]

Timing plays a key role in determining the effectiveness of different types of resource display. Immediate displays of wealth—such as flashing money, buying a woman gifts, or taking her out to an expensive restaurant on the first date—prove more effective for attracting casual sex partners than long-term mates. In bars, where opportunities for imparting resources are limited, men frequently initiate contact with prospective sex partners by offering to buy them drinks.[4]

Generosity with resources is critical in both casual and committed mate attraction. Giving a waitress a large tip, for example, indicates not just the possession of wealth but also the critical willingness to share it. One study found that men contributed more to charity when they were being observed by women, but not when being observed by men.[5] Women's charity contributions, in contrast, did not vary across different observer conditions. Men benefit by showing generosity with resources because women are turned off by signs of stinginess in all mating contexts.[6]

Showing the potential for having resources by exhibiting studiousness at college or describing ambitious goals to a woman is more effective for attracting long-term mates than casual sex partners. Derogation tactics also reveal the importance of timing. Putting down the financial potential of a rival is most effective in long-term mating. Telling a woman that the rival will do poorly in his profession or lacks ambition is highly effective in the committed mating market but relatively ineffective when it comes to competition for casual sex. These findings mesh perfectly with the preferences that women express in the same two contexts—desiring immediate resources from brief affairs and reliable future resources from enduring mates.

Wearing costly clothing works equally well in both contexts. Women shown slides of different men are more attracted to men who wear expensive clothing, such as three-piece suits, sports jackets, and designer jeans, than to men who wear cheap clothing, such as tank tops and T-shirts.[7] Clothing has this effect on women whether they are evaluating a man as a marital or sex partner, perhaps because expensive clothing signals both immediate resources and future resource potential. The anthropologists John Marshall Townsend and Gary Levy have verified that the effect of the expense and status of clothing in attracting women is robust across any sort of involvement, from merely having coffee with a man to marriage.[8] The same men were photographed wearing either a Burger King uniform with a blue baseball cap and a polo-type shirt or a white dress shirt with a designer tie, a navy blazer, and a Rolex watch. Based on these photographs, women stated that they were not at all open to dating, sex, or marriage with the men in the low-status clothing but were willing to consider all these relationships with men wearing the high-status attire.

The importance of resources to attraction is not limited to Western cultures. Among the Sirionó of eastern Bolivia, one man was a particularly unsuccessful hunter. He suffered a loss of status and had lost several wives to men who were better hunters. The anthropologist A. R. Holmberg began hunting with this man, gave him game that others were told he had killed, and taught him how to kill game with a shotgun. Eventually, as a result of the man's increased hunting prowess, he "was enjoying the highest status, had acquired several new sex partners, and was insulting others, instead of being insulted by them."[9]

The power of imparting resources is no recent development. Ovid observed precisely the same phenomenon 2,000 years ago, testifying to the long-standing nature of this tactic over human written history: "Girls praise a poem, but go for expensive presents. Any illiterate oaf can catch their eye provided he's rich. Today is truly the Golden Age: gold buys honor, gold procures love."[10] We still live in that golden age.

Demonstrating Commitment

Displays of love, commitment, and devotion are powerful attractions to a woman. They signal that a man is willing to channel his time, energy, and effort to her over the long run. Commitment is difficult and costly to fake, because commitment is gauged from repeated signals over time. Men who are interested only in casual sex are unlikely to invest this much effort. The reliability of commitment display as a signal renders it an especially effective technique for attracting women.

The mate attraction studies confirm the power of displaying commitment in the long-term mating market. Discussing cohabitation or marriage signals that a man would like to integrate the woman into his social and family life, commit his resources to her, and perhaps have children with her. Offering to convert to her religion shows a willingness to accommodate to her needs. Showing a deep concern for her problems communicates emotional support and a commitment to be there in times of need. The 100 newlywed women we surveyed all reported that their husbands displayed these signals during their courtship, confirming that they were highly effective when used.

One strong signal of commitment is a man's persistence in courtship. It can take the form of spending a lot of time with a woman, seeing her often, dating her for an extended period of time, calling her frequently on the phone, and texting or emailing her frequently. These tactics are highly effective at attracting long-term mates, with average effectiveness ratings of 5.48 on a 7-point scale, but only moderately effective (4.54) at attracting sex partners. Furthermore, persistence in courtship proves to be more effective for a man than for a woman because it signals that he is interested in more than casual sex.

The effectiveness of sheer persistence in courtship is illustrated by a story told by one newlywed: "Initially, I was not interested in John at all. I thought he was kind of nerdy, so I kept turning him down and turning him down. But he kept calling me up, showing up at my work, arranging to run into me. I finally agreed to go out with him just to get him off my back. One thing led to another, and six months later, we got married."

Persistence also worked for a German university professor. While returning to Germany by train from a professional conference in Poland, he started talking to an attractive physician, twelve years his junior. The conversation became animated as their attraction for one another grew. The physician was on her way to Amsterdam, not Germany, and before long the station where she had to change trains was upon them. The physician said good-bye to the professor, but he insisted on helping her with her luggage and carried it to a station locker for her. As his train pulled away from the station the professor berated himself for failing to seize the moment. He decided to take action. At the next station he got off and boarded another train back to where he had left the physician. He searched the station in vain—there were no signs of her. On foot, he searched all the stores and shops surrounding the station. No luck. Finally, he went back to the station and planted himself in front of the locker into which he had loaded her luggage. When she eventually returned, she was surprised to see him and impressed by his persistence in tracking her down. A year later she left her native Poland to marry him in Germany. Without tenacity, the professor would have lost her irretrievably. Persistence pays.

Displays of kindness, which also signal commitment, figure prominently in successful attraction techniques. Men who demonstrate an understanding of a woman's problems, show sensitivity to her needs, act compassionately toward her, and perform helpful deeds succeed in attracting women as long-term mates. Kindness works because it signals that the man cares for the woman, will be there for her in good times and bad, and will channel resources to her. It signals long-term romantic interest rather than purely sexual interest.

Another tactic for revealing kindness is to display nurturance toward children. In one study, women saw photos of the same man in three different conditions—standing alone, interacting positively with a baby, and ignoring a baby in distress.[11] Women were most attracted to the man when he acted warmly toward the baby and were least attracted to him when he ignored the baby in distress. When men, however, were shown analogous photos of a woman standing alone, showing positive feelings toward a baby, and ignoring a baby in distress, their attraction to her was identical in all these contexts. Showing nurturance toward the young is apparently an attraction tactic that is effective mainly for men and works by signaling a proclivity to commit to and care for children. Showing warmth toward a cute puppy or kitten might have similar effects.

Men also signal their commitment by showing loyalty and fidelity. Signs of promiscuity, in contrast, indicate that the man is pursuing a purely sexual mating strategy. Short-term strategists typically distribute their attentions and resources over several women. Out of 130 possible ways for men to attract a mate, women regard showing fidelity as the second most effective action, just a shade behind displaying an empathic understanding of the woman's problems.

Because fidelity signals commitment, an effective tactic for denigrating a rival is to question the rival's sexual intentions. When a man tells a woman that his rival just wants casual sex, for example, women are turned off to that rival for committed mating. Similarly, saying that a rival cheats on women and cannot stay loyal to just one woman is highly effective at decreasing a rival's long-term attractiveness to women.[12]

Displays of love provide another sign of commitment. A man can attract a woman by doing special things for her, showing a loving devotion to her, and saying "I love you." Men and women rate these actions as among the top 10 percent of all tactics for attracting a woman for commitment. Demonstrations of love convey cues to long-term intentions.

Whereas signals of commitment prove highly effective in attracting long-term mates, creating an illusion of commitment can be effective in attracting and seducing a woman. Men looking for casual liaisons compete by mimicking what women desire in enduring mateships. This tactic is especially potent when women use casual sex to evaluate prospective husbands. Women are more receptive, even in the short term, to men who appear to embody their ideals in a long-term mate.

Some men exploit this tactic to attract women as casual sex partners. The psychologists William Tooke and Lori Camire studied exploitative and deceptive attraction tactics in a university population.[13] From a nomination procedure parallel to the one used in the attraction studies, they assembled a list of eighty-eight ways in which men and women deceive one another in the service of attracting a mate. Participants reported misleading the other sex about career expectations, sucking in their stomachs when walking near members of the opposite sex, appearing to be more trusting and considerate than they really were, and acting uninterested in having sex when sex actually loomed large in their thoughts.

A singles bar study produced similar results. Four researchers spent approximately 100 person-hours sitting in singles bars in Washtenaw County in Michigan, writing down each attraction tactic they witnessed. Through this procedure, they observed 109 attraction tactics, such as sucking seductively on a straw, offering to buy someone a drink, sticking out one's chest, and staring at someone's body. Then a different sample of 100 university students evaluated these tactics for their probable effectiveness at attracting them when employed by a person of the other sex. Women stated that the most effective tactics for attracting them would be displaying good manners, offering help, and acting sympathetic and caring.[14] Mimicking what women want in a husband by showing kindness and sincere interest, in short, is also an effective technique for luring women into brief sexual liaisons.

The deception study found that men use several tactics to deceive women about their intentions. Men pretend to be interested in starting a relationship when they are not really interested and act as if they care about a woman even though they really do not. Most men are fully aware that feigning commitment is an effective tactic for short-term sexual attraction, and they admit to deceiving women by this means. Men using Tinder, Hinge, and other dating apps admit that they pretend to be open to being in a relationship even though their real interest lies in racking up large numbers of short-term sexual conquests. One man who estimated that he had hooked up with thirty or forty women over the past year through dating apps admitted, "I sort of play that I could be a boyfriend kind of guy," in order to win them over, "but then they start wanting me to *care* more . . . and I just don't."[15]

As the biologist Lynn Margulis notes: "Any animal that can perceive can be deceived." "Deception consists of mimicking the truth," comments the biologist Robert Trivers in describing how the technique works. "[It is] a parasitism of the preexisting system for communicating correct information." Whenever females look for investing males, some males deceive about their willingness to invest. Certain male insects offer females food, only to take it back after the copulation is complete.[16] They then use the same resources to court another female. For females, this strategy poses the problem of detecting deception, discovering insincerity, and penetrating disguise. One of the human solutions to this problem is to place a premium on honesty.

Displaying honesty is in fact a powerful tactic a man can use to obtain a long-term mate. This tactic conveys that the man is not simply seeking a transient sex partner. Of the 130 identified tactics to attract a female mate, three of the top ones suggest openness and honesty—acting truthful with the woman, communicating feelings to her directly and openly, and simply being oneself. All of these tactics are among the most effective 10 percent of all attraction tactics that men can use.

Because of the adaptive problem historically imposed on women by men's dual sexual strategy of short-term and long-term relationships, tactics that allow women a clear window for evaluating a man's actual characteristics and intentions prove to be highly attractive. Signals of dishonesty conceal those characteristics and intentions, rendering that assessment window cloudy or opaque.

If signs of commitment are highly effective, cues that resources are already committed elsewhere undermine attraction. Roughly 30 percent of the men on the Tinder app, which is widely regarded as a short-term mating app, are married. Among the men who patronize singles bars, many are married or have steady relationships. Some have children who command large shares of their resources. These men report removing their wedding rings before entering the bars. After intensive grilling of men at one singles bar, researchers found that "12 people admitted that they were married. . . . We suspected that others were married, by somewhat rather undefinable qualities, sometimes connected with a rather mysterious withholding of various kinds of information about everyday life styles."[17] Because being married clearly interferes with attracting women, it becomes a liability for men who fail to conceal it.

University students confirm that knowledge of prior commitments hinders a man's efforts to attract a woman. Indeed, out of eighty-three tactics that men can perform to render a rival less attractive to women, mentioning that he has a serious girlfriend is seen as the most effective one.

Signals of commitment help men to attract women because they signal that they are pursuing a long-term sexual strategy. These displays communicate that his resources will be channeled exclusively to her.

Revealing Physical Prowess

Men display physical and athletic prowess in modern times as part of their tactical arsenal for attracting women. Newlywed and undergraduate couples alike report that men display their strength roughly twice as often as women and display athletic prowess roughly 50 percent more often than women as part of their courtship tactics. Furthermore, displays of strength and athleticism are judged to be significantly more effective for attracting mates when used by men. Flexing muscles, playing sports, mentioning feats of athletic prowess, and lifting weights all figure more prominently in men's attraction tactics. College students' evaluations of derogation tactics reveal that displays of physical and athletic prowess are significantly more effective for attracting casual sex partners than for attracting spouses. Perhaps this is why men are more likely to show photos of themselves revealing upper torso shots with bulging biceps and six-pack abs on hookup sites like Tinder than on more serious dating sites like eHarmony or OKCupid. The derogation tactics that stand out as more effective in casual contexts than permanent ones include putting down a rival's strength and athletic ability. Mentioning that a rival is physically weak, outshining a competitor in sports, and physically dominating a rival are more effective short-term than long-term tactics. These studies support the common observation that male athletes, especially star players, enjoy success at attracting women for casual sex.

Among the Yanomamö, a man's status is heavily determined by his physical feats, which include chest-pounding duels, ax fights, combat against neighboring villages, and physically vanquishing rivals. The status gained through physical prowess translates into greater sexual access, which historically was a key route to greater reproductive success. Indeed, men who have demonstrated their prowess through killing other men (*unokai*) have more wives and more children than same-aged non-*unokai* men.[18] Physical and athletic displays, in short, have always been powerful attractors in traditional and modern societies alike.

Showing Bravado and Self-Confidence

Displays of masculine self-confidence prove effective for men seeking to attract mates but are significantly more effective in attracting casual than committed mates. Acting conceited or macho, bragging about one's accomplishments, and showing off are all judged by college students to be more effective for men in attracting sex partners than wives. The effectiveness of bravado and confidence is reflected in a story told by a woman in a singles bar:

> I was sitting at a corner table talking to my girlfriend and sipping on a gin and tonic. Then Bob walked in. He acted like he owned the place, smiling broadly and very confident. He caught my eye, and I smiled. He sat down and started talking about how horses were his hobby. He casually mentioned that he owned a horse farm. When the last call for alcohol came, he was still talking about how expensive his horses were, and said that we should go riding together. He said, "In fact, we could go riding right now." It was 2:00 a.m., and I left the bar and had sex with him. I never did find out whether he owned horses.

Self-confidence signals status and resources.[19] Among newlyweds, for example, men scoring high on self-confidence earn significantly more money than men with lower self-confidence. Self-confidence translates into success in finding sex partners. A woman at a singles bar put it this way: "Some guys just seem to know what they are doing. They know how to approach you and just make you feel good. Then you get those nerds . . . who can't get anything right. They come on strong at first, but can't keep it together. . . . They just hang around until you dump them by going to the rest room or over to a friend to talk."[20] Women distinguish false bravado from real self-confidence, and they find the genuine article more attractive. Men high in self-esteem tend to approach physically attractive women and ask them for dates, regardless of their own physical attractiveness. Men low in self-esteem, in contrast, avoid approaching attractive women, believing that their chances are too slim.[21]

Self-confidence is responsive to feedback. In singles bars, men rebuffed by women in their first few attempts produce successively less confident approaches. Rejection produces a downward cycle of resentment, hostility, and sometimes a cessation of all tactics. One man in a singles bar commented after a third woman had rebuffed him, "You need steel balls to make it in this place." Apparently the psychological pain and lowered confidence experienced by rejected men cause them to reevaluate their sexual techniques, lower their sights to women who have lower appeal, and wait until circumstances are more favorable for further attempts.[22]

Another tactic is to feign confidence. According to the deception study, men boast and brag to make themselves appear better, act more masculine than they really feel, and behave more assertively around women than they really are. Men strut for a reason— to increase their odds of succeeding in sex.

Not all displays of bravado and confidence are directed toward attracting the opposite sex. They are also directed toward other men in an attempt to elevate status and prestige within the group. College men exaggerate the number of their sex partners, mislead others about how many women express a desire for them, exaggerate their own sexual skills, and act braver than they really feel. These are tactics of status competition. Men compete for position, resources, and signs of elevated prestige. If a man can obtain the deference of other men by elevating his position in the sexual domain, his status typically translates into greater access to desirable women.

The fact that men select this tactic primarily in casual mating contexts provides circumstantial support for the sexy son hypothesis. Men who display their bravado and sexual conquests signal to women that they are sexually attractive to women in general. Like the peacock displaying his plumage, these strutting men may be more likely to have sons who are attractive to women in the next generation, assuming some heritability to these proclivities.

This display of bravado is sometimes exploited by other males. To attract females, for example, male bullfrogs sit at the edge of a pond and emit loud, resonant croaks. Females listen carefully to the chorus of male sounds and select one to move toward. The louder and more resonant the croak, the more attractive it is to females. The larger, healthier, and more dominant the male, the more resonant his croaks. The dominant male strategy, therefore, is to emit the loudest and most resonant croaks possible. Sitting silently near a dominant male is a smaller, weaker male. He emits no croaks and attracts no attention. But as a female approaches the dominant sounds, the silent male darts from his hiding place, intercepts her, and quickly copulates. This strategy, called a satellite or sneak strategy, illustrates the exploitation of dominant males by less dominant males who cannot compete directly.[23]

Humans also use this strategy, which is humorously depicted in the Woody Allen film *Everything You Always Wanted to Know About Sex* (**But Were Afraid to Ask*). The scene opens with men dressed up as sperm who are fighting with each other over access to an egg. The macho male sperm battle furiously. When they have defeated each other and all lie down exhausted, a small sperm played by Woody Allen steps out cautiously from behind a curtain where he has been cowering and proceeds to hop onto the egg.

Men also sometimes use this sneak strategy, as we found in studies of mate poaching. We asked fifty men and fifty women which strategies they would use to attract someone who was already mated with someone else.[24] One of the most frequently used tactics is pretending to be friends with the couple and then switching into mating mode when the opportunity arises. Once in close proximity, mate poachers encourage rifts in the couple's relationship: "I don't think your partner appreciates you"; "You are too good for him"; "I think you deserve someone better, someone who treats you like the princess you are . . . someone like me!"

A less common male poaching tactic is to feign femaleness. Among the sunfish in the lakes of Ontario, for example, a small male mimics a female and enters the nesting site of the dominant male. This mimicry reduces the odds of being attacked. Once inside the territory, however, the small male quickly fertilizes the eggs that have already been deposited by the females, cuckolding the dominant, territory-holding male. A rare tactic among humans is to feign homosexuality so as not to incur the suspicion of the dominant man and then attempt to have sex with the woman when he is not around. Nonetheless, it is interesting that a few college men report having observed it. In general, pretending to be nonthreatening as a potential mate poacher—for instance, by pretending to be a friend of the man or pretending to be already committed to another woman—is more common. Like bullfrogs and sunfish, humans occasionally use sneaky strategies.

Enhancing Appearance

Just as men's successful tactics for attracting women depend on women's desires in a mate, women's attraction tactics depend on men's preferences. Women who succeed appear reproductively valuable by embodying physical and behavioral cues that signal their youth and physical attractiveness. Women who fail to fulfill these qualities lose a competitive edge.

Because men place a premium on appearance, competition among women to attract men centers heavily on enhancing their physical attractiveness along youthful and healthful lines. Bolstering this practice is the cosmetics industry, which is supported mainly by women; although men are spending increasing amounts on cosmetic products, women still outspend men roughly nine to one. Women's magazines include an avalanche of advertisements for beauty products. Men's magazines, in contrast, advertise cars, electronics, and alcoholic beverages. Advertisements in men's magazines that promise appearance enhancement are typically for muscle-building products or for deodorants and shower gels with scents advertised as being attractive to women.

Women do not compete to signal accurate information. Rather, they compete to activate men's evolved psychological standards of beauty, which are keyed to youth and health. Because flushed cheeks and high color are cues that men use to gauge a woman's health, women rouge their cheeks artificially to trigger men's attraction. Because smooth, clear skin is one of men's evolved desires, women cover up blemishes, use moisture cream, apply astringents, and get facelifts. Because lustrous hair is one of men's evolved desires, women highlight, bleach, tint, or dye their hair, and they give it extra body with conditioners, egg yolks, beer, or weaves. Because full red lips trigger men's evolved desires, women apply lipstick skillfully and even get injections to enlarge their lips for the "bee-stung" look. And because firm, youthful breasts stimulate men's desires, women obtain breast implants and wear push-up bras.

Women report using makeup to accentuate their looks twenty times as often as men. Women go on diets to improve their figures, get new and interesting haircuts, and spend over an hour a day on their appearance—twice as much time as men spend on theirs. They lie out in the sun or go to tanning salons to achieve a healthy-looking glow. Appearance enhancement for attracting a mate is twice as effective for women as for men.[25] In contrast, men who devote excessive attention to enhancing their appearance can hurt their competitive chances; people sometimes infer that they are narcissistic or self-absorbed.[26]

Women do more to improve their appearance than meets the eye. They use deceptive tactics to manipulate their appearance. They wear false fingernails to make their hands appear longer and their fingers more elegant; wear heels to accentuate leg length, bum protrusion, and calf shape; wear dark clothing and vertical stripes to appear thinner; apply spray tan to appear sun-kissed; pull in their stomachs or cinch their waists to enhance their waist-to-hip ratio; wear body-shaping undergarments like Spanx to appear leaner and firmer; wear padded bras to appear bustier; and highlight their hair to appear more youthful.

Women are well aware of the importance of appearance on the mating market. After interviews with women in singles bars, researchers reported that many of them "said that they went home from work before going out to the bars to do a whole revamping." Often, before going out for the evening, they would take a bath, wash their hair, put on fresh makeup, and go through three changes of outfits before selecting one. "Primping for us counts more than for guys—they don't need to worry about their looks as much."[27] The ability to make men's heads turn signals a highly desirable mate and evokes advances from more men. This effect enlarges the pool of men and, in turn, gives women a greater ability to choose high-mate-value men.

Women do not merely strive to improve their own looks; they also disparage the looks of other women. Women in the derogation study mentioned that their rivals were fat, ugly, and unattractive, had "thunder thighs," and had shapeless bodies. Making fun of a rival's appearance is more effective for women in the sexual marketplace than in the marriage marketplace. And it is more effective for women than for men in both short-term and long-term mating contexts.

Women derogate other women's appearance both to the desired men, to other women in their social circles, and directly to the rivals themselves. One woman in an upscale hotel bar described her tactic of looking at a rival's hair and, without saying anything, taking out a hairbrush and handing it to her. Her rivals sometimes got up and left the bar. Often the practice succeeded in driving away her competition. Damaging the self-image of a rival is one way to clear the field.

Making public one's disdain for another woman's appearance enhances the effectiveness of this derogation tactic. One man from a fraternity reported being ridiculed mercilessly by his brothers after it became known that he had sex with a particularly unattractive woman. Men discovered having sex with unattractive women suffer social humiliation and lose status in the eyes of their peers.[28]

Since physical attractiveness is an attribute that is easy for men to observe directly, these findings raise an interesting puzzle: Why would derogatory verbal comments about other women work when men can gauge attractiveness with their own eyes? Derogation works in part by guiding men's perceptions of women. Women can draw attention to flaws that are otherwise not noticed or salient, such as heavy thighs, a long nose, short fingers, close-set eyes, or an asymmetrical face, and make them salient. No human is without imperfections. Drawing attention to them magnifies their importance, especially if attention is drawn to efforts to conceal or disguise a weak spot. Women also exploit the fact that our judgments of attractiveness are influenced by other people's judgments.[29] Knowing that others find a woman unattractive causes a downward shift in our view of her appearance. Moreover, knowing that other people in our social environment do not believe that a woman is attractive actually renders her a less valuable asset as a mate. Even in a context with easily observed qualities, such as physical appearance and stature, there is plenty of room for the effective use of belittling tactics.

Modern cosmetology exploits women's evolved psychology of competing for mates, and women who do not make effective use of methods to enhance their appearance hurt their chances at attracting valuable mates. This situation has created a runaway beauty competition in which the time, effort, and money expended on appearance have reached levels unprecedented in human history. Women in all cultures alter their appearance, but perhaps none as much as those in the West, which has the technology to exploit women's desire to appear attractive through visual media unavailable to more traditional societies. The cosmetics industry does not create desires so much as it exploits the desires that are already there.

The journalist Naomi Wolf has described advertisements as creating a false ideal, which she calls "the beauty myth," in order to subjugate women sexually, economically, and politically. The beauty myth is presumed to have taken on causal properties, undoing all the accomplishments of feminism in improving conditions for women. Some argue that the surgical technologies of breast implants and facelifts are designed to medically control women.[30] They contend that the diet, cosmetics, and cosmetic surgery industries combined, totaling more than $53 billion a year, are motivated by the desire to subjugate women. Standards of beauty, the argument goes, are arbitrary—capriciously linked with age, highly variable across cultures, not universal in nature, and hence not a function of evolution.

These naive arguments fly in the face of the scientific evidence. Myths cannot have causal force; only the individuals who embrace myths can. Power structures cannot have causal force; only the individuals who wield power can. Wolf's account of the beauty myth is terribly unflattering to women. It implies that women are passive pawns with no preferences of their own and no individuality, buffeted and brainwashed by forces like power structures, myths, and men conspiring to subjugate them.

In contrast, an evolutionary psychological perspective reveals that women have far more autonomy and choice in their deployment of attraction tactics than proponents of the beauty myth would have us believe. Women who seek a lasting mate, for example, have at their disposal a wide range of tactics, including displays of loyalty, signals of common interests, and acts of intelligence. Women purchase beauty products not because they have been brainwashed by the media, but because they have determined that using beauty products will increase their power to get what they want. Women are not unsuspecting dupes manipulated by the forces of Madison Avenue, but determine through their preferences which products they will consume—products that they perceive will enhance their value as a mate, friend, or group member.

Advertisements, however, do damage women. Women are bombarded with exploitative, photoshopped images that depict ideals unattainable by most women. These magnify a woman's focus on appearance and at the same time fail to highlight the deeper personal qualities that are also critical to men's desires, such as intelligence, personality, social skills, and compassion. The cosmetics industry exploits women's evolved concern over appearance and then increases their insecurity by elevating the standards of attractiveness to which women aspire with images of a deluge of seemingly flawless, world-class models that are in fact deceptively photoshopped. This duplicity increases the apparent beauty of other women—their competition—and may lower women's self-esteem. It may also distort women's and men's understanding of the actual mating pool and mating market.

All women today are unique, distinctive winners of a 5 million year beauty contest of sexual selection. Every female ancestor of the readers of these words was attractive enough to obtain enough investment to raise at least one child to reproductive age. Every male ancestor was attractive enough to attract a woman to have his child. It is worth keeping in mind, when confronted with a sea of troubles in the mating game, that every one of us is an evolutionary success story.

Displaying Fidelity

In light of men's emphasis on fidelity in a committed relationship, displays of fidelity should be paramount in women's tactics of attraction. Faithfulness displays, such as honesty and trustworthiness, signal that the woman is pursuing a long-term mating strategy and that she is doing so without deception and exclusively with one man.

Out of 130 acts of attraction, remaining faithful, avoiding sex with other men, and showing devotion proved to be the three most effective tactics for attracting a committed mate. Participants rated all three over 6.5, with 7.0 indicating the highest possible effectiveness. Signals of fidelity offer a man a solution to one of the most important mating challenges he faces—the problem of ensuring his paternity in his children.

The centrality of fidelity shows up indirectly in the tactics employed by women to derogate mating competitors. Saying that a rival cannot stay loyal to one man was judged to be the single most effective derogation tactic for a woman to use in the marriage market. Calling a rival a slut, saying she was loose, or telling others that she slept around were in the top 10 percent of effective derogation tactics.[31]

This tactic can backfire if a man is seeking casual sex. Mae West once noted that "men like women with a past because they hope history will repeat itself." Men seeking short-term partners typically are not bothered by promiscuity in a woman and in fact find it mildly desirable, since it increases their chances of success. Calling another woman promiscuous therefore does not have the intended effect of dissuading men who are pursuing a brief sexual encounter. Women who mistakenly gauge a man's mating goals can fail in their quest to render their rivals undesirable.

The fact that women exploit men's desire for faithful mates to undermine their rivals is reinforced by the prevalence of derogatory sexual terms in human language. Although there are terms for men who are promiscuous, such as player, lady's man, Lothario, and Don Juan, they are fewer in number and carry less negative valence than comparable words for women. And sometimes such terms are applied to men with admiration or envy rather than as put-downs. In contrast, John Barth's *The Sot Weed Factor* illustrates the range of insults hurled by women at other women.[32] An English woman competes against a French woman by using these labels to cast aspersions on her character: harlot, whore, sow, bawd, strawgirl, tumbler, mattressback, windowgirl, galleywench, fastfanny, nellie, nightbird, shortheels, bum-bessie, furrowbutt, coxswain, conycatcher, tart, arsebender, canvasback, hipflipper, hardtonguer, bedbug, breechdropper, giftbox, craterbutt, pisspallet, narycherry, poxbox, flapgap, codhopper, bellylass, trollop, joy-girl, bumpbacon, strumpet, slattern, chippie, pipecleaner, hotpot, back-bender, leasepiece, spreadeagle, sausage-grinder, cornergirl, codwinker, nutcracker, hedgewhore, fleshpot, cotwarmer, hussy, and stumpthumper. The French woman uses a comparably long list of counter-derogations in her native language, including *bas-cul, consoeur, poupinette, briballeuse, gaure, gourgandine, saffrete, redresseuse, drue, fille de joie, champisse,* and *marane*. In literature as in life, denigrating a competitor's promiscuity decreases her attractiveness in the mating market.

The importance of context is also shown by the attraction tactic of acting coy or unavailable. Appearing indifferent to a person one likes and playing hard to get are judged to be more effective for women than for men. Furthermore, these forms of coyness are more effective for women in the context of long-term as opposed to casual mates.[33]

This outcome meshes perfectly with the sexual strategies of both women and men. The coyness tactic works for women seeking committed mates because it signals both desirability and fidelity. Men think that if a woman is easy for them to get sexually, then she may be easy for other men too. College men, for example, point out that women who are easy to get are probably desperate for a mate and might also have an STI—signals of low desirability and high promiscuity.[34]

Another study found that playing hard to get is most successful as a mate-attracting tactic when it is used selectively, that is, when a woman is hard to get in general but is selectively accessible to a particular man.[35] For example, a woman might publicly spurn the advances of all men except the specific man she wants. This signals that he is getting an excellent bargain on the mating market and, importantly, that she is likely to be faithful in the long run. Successful women convey being discriminating without turning off the particular man they desire. The effectiveness of playing hard to get as a long-term attraction technique stems from providing men with two key reproductive assets: desirability on the mating market and a signal that he alone will have sexual access.

When a woman has a long history of casual sex, it may be difficult to appear faithful, loyal, and devoted. Mate-attracting tactics

are not deployed in a social vacuum, and people are keenly interested in transmitting information about the sexual reputation of
others. Gossip columnists, talk show hosts, and their audiences
dwell on who is sleeping with whom, savoring salacious details.
Reputations sullied are difficult to repair.

In the small social groups in which humans evolved, damage to
reputation was likely to have been lasting. Concealing sexual information from others in a small group is virtually impossible. Among
the Ache of Paraguay, for example, everyone knows who has slept
with whom, so there is little room for deception. When a male anthropologist queried Ache men about who had slept with whom,
and a female anthropologist did likewise with Ache women, there
was perfect correspondence between their accounts.[36] In modern
Western culture, with its great mobility and anonymous urban living, there is considerably more room for rehabilitating one's reputation and starting fresh in a new social environment where one's
past is unknown. Having a history of promiscuity in the modern
world no longer precludes the subsequent use of signs of fidelity
to attract a mate.

Sexual Signaling

Most men want one benefit from casual mating: low-cost sex with
attractive women. For women, therefore, explicit overtures that
signal sexual availability or receptivity are exceptionally effective
tactics. These include talking seductively, making a man think of
having sex with her, and simply asking a man if he wants to have
sex. These attraction tactics are maximally effective for women in
casual mating contexts.

Men in singles bars corroborated these findings. When they
evaluated 103 mate-attracting tactics for their effectiveness, they
singled out the actions of a woman making direct eye contact,
looking at him seductively, brushing up against him, running her

hands through his hair, puckering her lips and blowing kisses, sucking on a straw or finger, leaning forward to expose her chest, and bending over to accentuate her curves. In sharp contrast, women judged these same actions when performed by men to be a great turnoff. The more overt the sexual advances by men, the less attractive women find them. On a 7-point scale, men placed a woman's action of rubbing her chest or pelvis up against a man at 6.07—the second most effective act of all 103 acts, exceeded only by simply agreeing to have sex with the man. Women, however, placed a man's use of such an action at only 1.82, suggesting that it is highly ineffective. So-called dick-pics, sent by some men in the erroneous belief that they will turn a woman on, in fact repulse most women.

Women also sometimes sexualize their appearance. Men in the single bars studied stated that a woman's wearing sexy, revealing, tight clothes; wearing a shirt with a low-cut back or a low-cut front; letting the strap or shirt slip off her shoulders; wearing a short skirt; walking with a hip swivel; and dancing provocatively all placed in the top 25 percent of the tactics most likely to attract them. A study by T. Joel Wade and Jennifer Slemp similarly found that the most effective flirtation tactics for women include touching, dressing in revealing clothing, moving closer, kissing on the cheek, and rubbing against the man.[37] Effective nonverbal seduction tactics for women in Lisbon, Portugal, included wearing tight skirts, wearing low-neck blouses, and exposing legs through short skirts or wearing attention-getting black or red nylons.[38] Women who sexualize their appearance and behavior succeed in evoking approaches from men.

The power for women in sexualizing their appearance is further shown by a study of clothing style and skin exposure. Men and women watched photos of the opposite sex in which models differed in the amount of skin exposed and the tightness of their clothing. After each image, people judged the model's attractiveness as a dating partner, marital partner, and sex partner. Men found women in tight-fitting and revealing clothing more attractive than fully clothed women as dating partners and sex partners, but not as marriage partners. Women, in contrast, judged men in tight-fitting and revealing clothes to be less attractive than fully clothed men in all conditions, probably because these men were signaling that they were primarily interested in casual sex.[39]

Women's sexualization of their appearance becomes quite overt in singles bars. Researchers Natalie Allon and Diane Fishel report that women "often walked around the room, standing tall, protruding their chests, holding in their stomachs, stroking their own arms or hair—they seemed to exhibit themselves on public display." Sometimes a woman's sexy looks are so effective that they crowd out all other male thoughts. Allon and Fishel describe one woman who was very thin, attractive, and large-breasted:

> She often tended to say things that were scatterbrained and she had a nervous giggle. Her talk and her erratic laughter seemed quite secondary in the singles bar, as most men who talked to her were preoccupied with her chest and the way she displayed her chest by twisting and turning. Some men commented to us that they hardly heard what this woman said—or for that matter, even cared what she said. Such men seemed to prefer to look at this woman's chest than to listen to her.[40]

Initiating visual contact also proves to be a highly effective tactic for women who seek to attract a sex partner. Looking intensely into a man's eyes and allowing him to see her staring are judged to be among the top 15 percent of effective tactics women can use to attract short-term sex partners. In contrast, this tactic proves only moderately effective in attracting committed mates, scoring near the midpoint of the 7-point scale.

A woman who initiates visual contact signals good odds of sexual success. In one study, a man and a woman were videotaped interacting.[41] After a brief period of time, the woman looked into the man's eyes and smiled at him. Men and women witnessed the videotape and then made judgments about the woman's intentions. Men interpreted eye contact and smiling as signs of sexual interest and seductive intent. Women who observed the same actions by other women interpreted them as signs of friendliness rather than seductiveness. Clearly, eye contact and smiles are often ambiguous—sometimes they signal sexual interest, and sometimes they do not—but men are more likely to err in the direction of inferring sexual interest, exhibiting a male sexual overperception bias. That is, when confronted with ambiguous cues, men over-infer sexual interest when it is often not actually there (see Chapter 7 on error management theory).

While women convey sexual availability as a tactic, they also question the sexual availability of other women as a means of derogating them. When a college woman derogates a rival in a short-term context, she mentions that her rival is merely a tease, indicates that her rival leads men on, and tells the man that her rival is frigid. All of these acts of derogation imply that the other woman will not be sexually available to the man and that he is likely to waste his time and energy if he pursues her as a casual partner.

Women also call their sexual competitors prudish, priggish, or puritanical. Questioning the sexual accessibility of rivals is an effective female strategy, because unavailable women are costly for men who seek casual sex—they risk channeling time and resources toward dubious prospects.

Some ways in which women question a rival's sexual accessibility, such as calling a competitor a tease and saying that she leads men on, seem extraordinarily clever, because at the same time such remarks do not imply that the woman is loyal, faithful, or a good long-term prospect. Rather, they imply that she uses an exploitative strategy of feigning sexual approachability, perhaps to obtain resources and attention, but then fails to deliver. Furthermore, saying that a rival is frigid or prudish implies that she is a problematic casual sex partner without implying that she is also a desirable long-term mate, because men also dislike sexual coldness in both mating contexts. Tactics that simultaneously derogate a rival's short-term and long-term value on the mating market are especially effective.

Mae West once commented, "Brains are an asset, if you hide them." That may indeed be true for casual sex. Women sometimes act submissive, helpless, and less intelligent than they really are to attract short-term mates. Women report pretending to be helpless, letting the man control the conversation, acting dumb, acting "ditzy," and pretending to be meek and submissive. A woman's submissiveness conveys to a man that he need not expect hostile reactions to his advances.[42] Subservient signals implicitly give men permission to approach. Since men are more likely to initiate approaches, signs of submissiveness and helplessness lower barriers to approach. Acting submissive elicits approaches from a larger number of men, expands the pool of potential mates, creates greater opportunities for choice, and ultimately increases the quality of the mate obtained.

Acting submissive, helpless, or dumb may also signal that the man will be able to control or manipulate the woman easily for his own ends. A woman's apparent helplessness may signal ease of sexual exploitation—sex without the cost of commitment.[43] The stereotype of the "bubble-headed blonde" may be misleading; this public presentation is intended as a strategic signal of approachability or even sexual accessibility rather than of actual intellectual ineptness. Women sometimes present the allure of vulnerability for their own strategic purposes.[44]

Signals of sexual accessibility are sometimes part of a larger strategy to lure a man into a long-term relationship. Sometimes the only way a woman can gain the attention and interest of a man is by offering herself as sexually available with no apparent strings attached. If the costs in resources and commitment are made low enough, many men succumb to sexual opportunity. Once a woman gains sexual access to a man of her choice, her proximity offers opportunities for insinuating herself, for making the man depend on her for various functions, and for gradually escalating both the benefits he will receive by staying in the relationship and the costs he will incur if he leaves her. What seems initially like costless sex without strings attached ends up being transformed into commitment.

Women sometimes bait men with sex. Because men's psychological adaptations orient them so vigilantly to short-term sexual opportunities, women can exploit them as a first step toward luring them into a committed relationship.

The Fitness Signaling Hypothesis: Humor, Creativity, Art, Music, and Morality

Because women prefer mates who have a good sense of humor, men should display humor in their tactics of attraction.[45] Humor has many facets, two of which are humor production (making witty remarks, telling jokes) and humor appreciation (laughing when someone else produces humor). In long-term mating, women prefer men who produce humor, whereas men prefer women who are receptive to their humor.[46] Precisely why do women value humor in a mate? One theory is that displaying humor signals interest in initiating and maintaining a mating relationship.[47] This theory predicts that humor signals long-term intentions and commitment cues toward a specific person. Making someone laugh and appreciating their humor convey excellent mind-reading abilities, perspective taking, playfulness, verbal adeptness, mutual compatibility, and good long-term mate potential. Not everyone is convinced, however, that humor is really important in mate attraction. The comedian Jimi McFarland noted: "One of the things women claim is most important in a man is a sense of humor. In my years as a comedian, I've learned that they're usually referring to the humor of guys like Brad Pitt, Tom Cruise, and Russell Crowe. Apparently, those guys are hilarious."

Another theory proposes that humor is a cue that its user possesses good genes, a fitness indicator signaling excellent functioning of complex cognitive skills unimpaired by a high mutation load.[48] According to Geoffrey Miller's fitness signaling hypothesis, humor is one among an array of uniquely human abilities that convey genetic quality to a potential mate. Others include high verbal dexterity (a large and fluent vocabulary and facility with language and its nuances), intelligence, artistic ability, musicality, and creativity. Even displaying moral virtues such as honesty, cooperativeness, fairness, and conscientiousness can be signals. The fitness signaling hypothesis draws an analogy with the peacock's tail—the tail is flashy, cumbersome, and costly, but only peacocks in the best condition, those with the highest fitness, can afford to produce these mesmerizing displays. High mutation and parasite loads, for example, dull the plumages' luminescence. Peacocks do no investing in peahens, nor do they aid offspring, so the only benefits these males can provide are good-quality genes. Females who sexually select males with the best genes bear offspring who are healthier in the next generation, have sons who inherit qualities that will make them attractive to females, and have daughters who inherit the female sexual preference. That is, the daughters will, in turn, choose mates with genes that confer high fitness on their own offspring.

The fitness signaling theory builds on the work of prior evolutionists, such as the geneticist R. A. Fisher and the biologist Amotz Zahavi. For fitness signals to be reliable and honest, Zahavi argues, they must be costly to produce.[49] If they were easy and metabolically cheap to generate, then every individual would do so. It is precisely their costliness that makes them honest signals of genetic quality. Miller argues that the same logic applies to creative, artistic, musical, and intellectual displays in the context of courtship. These abilities confer no direct survival benefit, but do convey cues to genetic quality. They evolved, Miller contends, through a process of mutual mate choice in which men and women both exhibited high levels of choosiness in selecting mates. And indeed, men and women are quite similar in their intelligence, musical abilities, creativity, and many other qualities.

Although humans have unquestionably evolved through mutual mate choice, as I have argued throughout this book, and the genetic quality of mates is undoubtedly part of that picture (for example, the sexy son hypothesis), critics of the fitness signaling hypothesis have identified some problems with this explanation for the evolution of music, art, humor, and so on. The evolutionary psychologist Steven Pinker, for example, argues that there are no specific adaptations for art, music, literature, and the like. Rather, they are nonfunctional by-products of adaptations that evolved for other purposes and allow humans to take pleasure in "shapes and colors and sounds and jokes and stories and myths."[50] Creating paintings that mimic the color patterns present in fruit, for example, can pleasurably activate an adaptation of color vision designed for locating ripe fruit. Pinker argues that music is "auditory cheesecake, an exquisite confection crafted to tickle the sensitive spots of at least six of our mental faculties."[51] So rather than being costly fitness signals that are displayed for mate attraction, human artistic and musical abilities may simply be by-products of adaptations that evolved for other functions.

Another criticism of the fitness signaling hypothesis is that some of the qualities it is designed to explain, such as intelligence and morality, do have compelling adaptive functions beyond merely serving as cues to genetic quality. Consider intelligence, which is linked with good resource acquisition skills, good parenting skills, prescience in forecasting danger, good health practices, and capacity to acquire and skillfully use cultural knowledge. Selecting an intelligent mate confers this bounty of adaptive benefits on oneself and one's children. The genetic benefits that intelligence provides to offspring may be important as well, but it seems rash to discount how intelligence helps to solve a host of adaptive problems linked with enabling the mate selector and children to survive and thrive. Displays of morality, undoubtedly important in attracting a mate, also signal that one will be a good and generous partner, a good and fair cooperator, a self-sacrificing parent, and a high-quality long-term ally—all qualities that directly solve practical adaptive problems.

A third set of problems with the fitness signaling hypothesis centers on its testability and its ability to lead to new discoveries previously unknown. The hypothesis runs into trouble in explaining sex-differentiated qualities. If both men and women are choosing the same fitness indicators, why do women value humor production in potential mates, for example, while men value humor appreciation in potential mates? Some critics argue that the fitness signaling hypothesis is an after-the-fact explanation for phenomena that are widely known—that people tell jokes and find things funny, display moral qualities in public, devote seemingly wasteful time producing music and art, and so on. They contend that it has not led to novel empirical discoveries, one of the key criteria for evaluating scientific hypotheses. Nonetheless, the fitness signaling hypothesis does focus greater attention on genetic quality in mate selection, which historically has been relatively neglected. And it might turn out to be an important addition to the theoretical tools that evolutionary psychologists possess to explain the complexities of human mate attraction.

The Sexes at Cross-Purposes

Success at attracting a mate depends on more than grasping the context and the intentions of a potential partner. It also hinges on surpassing the competition. For this reason, men and women do not merely enhance their own attractiveness; they also derogate their rivals. While making themselves appear attractive by exhibiting the qualities sought by the other sex, people also denigrate their rivals by making them appear to lack these desired qualities.

Perhaps more than in any other part of the mating arena, in casual sex men and women suffer from the strategies of the opposite sex. Men deceive women by feigning an interest in commitment to achieve a quick sexual score. They also feign confidence, status, kindness, and resources that they lack. Women who succumb to this deception give up a valuable sexual benefit at bargain-basement prices. But women battle back by insisting on stronger cues to commitment and by feigning interest in casual sex as a means of concealing their long-term intentions. Just as men deploy tactics to sexually exploit women, women turn the tables and exploit men's sexual desires. Some men take the bait and risk becoming ensnared in a web of hidden costs.

But offering sexual enticement poses risks for women. To suggest sexual availability is, without question, the most effective way for a woman to lure a man into a casual relationship. But because men dislike signs of promiscuity in a long-term mate, the sexual strategy that works so well for the woman in the short run often backfires if she is seeking a committed mate. Because men use similar strategies in both contexts, they can determine at a later stage, with more information in hand, whether they want the woman as a short-term or long-term partner. Women often have more to lose if they make errors in sexual strategies.

Men and women both are alert to deception at the hands of the opposite sex. Women sometimes hold out sexually, seek demonstrations of intentions and investment, and penetrate possible deceptions. Men conceal their emotions, disguise their external commitments, and remain uncommunicative and noncommittal. They try to abscond with the sexual benefit without paying the cost of commitment.

The ratio of available women to men affects the prevailing tactics used to attract a partner. The typical ratio in online dating sites like Tinder and Hinge, for example, favors women, because many more men than women are seeking short-term sex partners. Women looking for a brief encounter can exercise a great deal of choice. The sex ratio imbalance pressures men to best other men with better lines, better deceptions, and better simulations of the criteria that women impose. The losers typically outnumber the winners, and many men strike out.

Where the sex ratio is reversed and there are many more available women than men, the balance of power shifts to men because they can more easily attract women for casual sex. This imbalance is especially great today on college campuses and among college-educated individuals. More women than men attend college, and women are less likely than men to select a mate who is less educated than they are. This combination creates a surplus of educated women in the mating market. The rise of Tinder and other hookup apps and dating sites reflects the advantage that educated men have on the short-term mating market today.[52] For women seeking long-term mates, these unfavorable conditions tax their attraction tactics and make sexual competition among them fiercer.

This trend is exacerbated by women's high standards for a mate: their choosiness dramatically shrinks the effective pool of eligible men. Many men are eliminated from contention for failing to pass even preliminary screening. This leaves just a few survivors—men of reasonable social status, with adequate self-confidence and good resource potential, who are willing to commit—over whom women then compete. Those who succeed in attracting a lasting mate then face the next adaptive problem—staying together.

6

Staying Together

> When two people are first together, their hearts are on
> fire and their passion is very great. After a while . . . they
> continue to love each other, but in a different way—
> warm and dependable.
>
> —MARJORIE SHOSTAK,
> *Nisa: The Life and Words of a !Kung Woman*

TREMENDOUS BENEFITS FLOW to couples who remain committed.
From this unique alliance come efficiencies that include complementary skills, a division of labor, and a sharing of resources,
as well as mutual benefits such as a unified front against mutual
enemies, a stable home environment for rearing children, and a
more extended kin network. To reap these benefits, people must
be able to retain the mates they have succeeded in attracting.

People who fail to stay together incur severe costs. Bonds be-
tween extended kin are ripped apart. Essential resources are lost.
Children may be exposed to potentially dangerous stepparents.
Failure to keep a committed mate can mean wasting all the effort

189

expended in the selection, attraction, courting, and commitment process. Men who fail to prevent the defection of their mate risk losing access to valuable childbearing capabilities and maternal investment. Women who fail to retain their mate risk losing the mate's resources, protection, and paternal investment. Both sexes incur opportunity costs, the lost opportunities for exploring other mating prospects.

Given the high rate of divorce in Western cultures, and the existence of divorce in all cultures, it is obvious that staying together is neither automatic nor inevitable. Rivals loom on the periphery, waiting for an opportunity to mate-poach. Existing mates sometimes fail to provide the promised benefits. Some start imposing costs that become too burdensome to bear. Couples are surrounded by people who have agendas at odds with their own and who attempt to loosen or fracture their bond. Staying together can be difficult unless the couple undertakes strategies designed to ensure a successful, committed union.

Mate-keeping tactics occupy an important place in nonhuman animal mating. Although they are phylogenetically far removed from humans, insects offer instructive contrasts with humans because of the great diversity of their tactics and because human ways of solving the adaptive problem of keeping a mate are strikingly analogous to those of insects.[1] One of the most frequent strategies insects use is to conceal their mate from competitors. Concealment tactics include physically removing a mate from an area dense with competitors, covering up the attractive cues of a mate, and reducing the conspicuousness of the courtship display. Male wasps who successfully follow the scents of a female to her perch immediately whisk her away to prevent the mating attempts of other males who may also be tracking her scent.[2] If the male wasp fails to remove the female, he risks a physical battle with other males who converge on the perch. Male beetles release a scent that reduces their mate's attractiveness, preventing other males from noticing the female or making it more likely that other males will search for unmated females. A male cricket starts out with loud calls, but he softens them as he gets close to the female in order to avoid alerting competitors to their union and the interference that might follow.[3] All of these concealment tactics reduce a mate's contact with potential interlopers.

Another strategy is to physically prevent a takeover by other males. Many insects maintain close contact with the mate and repel interfering competitors. The male veliid water strider, for example, grasps his mate and sometimes rides on her back for hours or days, even while not copulating, to prevent encroachment. Faced with rival males, insects may use their antennae to lash out at them, turn and wrestle with them, or simply chase them off.[4] Perhaps the most unusual form of physical interference is the insertion of copulatory plugs. One species of worm, for example, adds a special substance to the seminal fluid that coagulates once deposited in the female, preventing other males from inseminating her and literally cementing his own reproductive bond with her. And in one species of fly, the *Johannseniella nitida,* males leave their genitalia broken off from their own bodies after copulation to seal the reproductive opening of the female. These adaptations to hinder sperm competition illustrate the extraordinary lengths to which males go to prevent reproductive takeovers by rivals.[5]

Although humans and insects are only distantly related, the basic adaptive logic behind holding on to a mate shows striking parallels. Males in both cases strive to inseminate females and to prevent cuckoldry. Females in both cases strive to secure investments in return for mating access. But human mate retention tactics take on uniquely intricate forms of psychological manipulation that set them apart from the rest of the animal kingdom.

Humans differ from most nonhuman animals in forming long-term and highly committed mateships. Remaining bonded is crucial for women and men alike. Although mate-keeping tactics among insects are performed primarily by males, among humans both men and women use them. Indeed, women are equal to men in the effort they channel toward the adaptive problem of staying together. This equality follows from the evolutionary logic of the value of the reproductive resources that would be lost by a breakup compared with the potential gains an individual could accrue by a breakup. Because men and women who embark on a committed relationship tend to couple with individuals of equivalent desirability, the 8's with other 8's and the 6's with other 6's, both sexes lose equally, on average, as a result of a breakup.[6]

The Menace of Mate Poachers

One reason mate-keeping tactics are crucial is because mate poaching is an ever-present threat. Desirable mates are always in short supply. Glamorous, interesting, attractive, socially skilled people are heavily courted and rapidly removed from the mating pool. Those who succeed in attracting the 9's and 10's tend to hold on to them, escalating the effort they allocate to mate guarding.[7] Transitions between relationships are brief for the beautiful. In modern monogamous societies, for those left on the sidelines of the mating dance, mate shortages get more severe with each passing year. In traditional polygynous societies, where most desirable women marry shortly after puberty, single men suffer the most. How can a person find a desirable mate when all these factors conspire to take attractive mates out of the mating market?

One unpretty solution to this recurrent quandary is mate poaching. Although many regard efforts to lure someone out of an existing mateship as morally reprehensible, it has a long recorded history.[8] One of the earliest written records of mate poaching is the biblical account of King David and Bathsheba. One day King David happened to spy the beautiful Bathsheba, wife of Uriah, bathing on the roof of a neighboring house. David's passion for her consumed him. He succeeded in seducing her, and consequently Bathsheba became pregnant. King David set out to destroy Uriah by sending him to the battle front and commanding his troops to retreat, exposing him to mortal danger. After Uriah was killed, King David married Bathsheba. Although their first child died, their union proved fruitful, and they went on to produce four children.

Mate poaching is a common mating strategy. David Schmitt and I discovered that 60 percent of men and 53 percent of women admitted to having attempted to lure someone else's mate into a committed relationship. Although more than half of these attempts failed, nearly half succeeded. This similarity between the genders in long-term poaching attempts contrasted with poaching efforts targeting brief sexual encounters—60 percent of the men but only 38 percent of the women reported attempting to lure someone else's mate into a casual sexual encounter. Far higher percentages of both genders said that others had attempted to entice them to leave their own existing relationship—93 percent of the men and 82 percent of the women for long-term love, and 87 percent of the men and 94 percent of the women for a brief sexual encounter.

Somewhat smaller percentages reported that someone had attempted to poach their own mate, suggesting that poaching ploys are often initiated away from the prying eyes of the unsuspecting "victim." Roughly one-third of our sample—35 percent of the men and 30 percent of the women—reported that a partner had been *successfully* taken away from them by a mate poacher. Although many attempts at mate poaching fail, nearly one-third appear to succeed. Schmitt has replicated these basic findings in a massive cross-cultural study involving more than thirty nations.[9] Mate poaching has probably been successful often enough to have evolved as a distinct sexual strategy.

People poach for many of the same reasons they mate to begin with—to find emotional intimacy, experience passionate sex, secure protection, gain resources, enhance social status, fall in love, or have children. But mate poachers perceive additional benefits unique to the context of mate poaching. One is *gaining revenge against a rival* by stealing the rival's mate. Vengeance could only have evolved as a motive, of course, if it served an adaptive function, such as inflicting a cost on a rival that lowered the rival's relative reproductive success or deterring other potential rivals from inflicting costs. Another benefit is *securing access to a pre-approved mate,* one who has already established credibility by passing another's screening criteria. Although enticing a mate who is already "taken" can provide these benefits, it sometimes comes at a price. Mate poachers risk violence—injury or even death—at the hands of the jealous partner. A poacher also incurs damage to his or her social reputation if branded as a deceiver. Poachers may be shunned when word of their deceit gets around, impairing their ability to attract other potential mates. Furthermore, if the mate poacher is successful, it might be costly to have a mate who is revealed to be potentially poachable and thus requires more expensive mate guarding.

Schmitt and I found that many of the tactics used to attract mates in other contexts—enhancing appearance, displaying resources, showing kindness, presenting a sense of humor, revealing empathy, and so on—are also effective for the purpose of poaching. Two tactics, however, are specially tailored to enticing mates away from others. The first is *temporal invasion,* which includes acts such as changing one's schedule in order to be around the target more often than the target's current partner, or dropping by when the current partner is off at work or out of town. The second is *driving a wedge*—infiltrating the existing mateship and actively promoting a breakup. One way to drive a wedge is to boost the target's self-esteem, conveying messages that enhance their self-perceptions of their own desirability. At the same time, the poacher might communicate that the target is not appreciated by the regular partner: "He doesn't treat you well," or "You deserve better," or "You're too good for him." The boost in self-esteem combined with the feeling of being underappreciated is sometimes enough to widen a small crack in a relationship. Through this double-pronged strategy, the mate poacher frees up an already taken mate and sits waiting in the wings when it happens.

Although not terribly admirable, there is good evidence that mate poaching can be an effective mating strategy. Indeed, those who pursue a mate poaching strategy have a larger number of lifetime sex partners and dating partners.[10]

Humans have evolved their own special strategies for defending against mate poachers and retaining a mate. Women in relationships are especially vigilant about rival women, whereas men tend to be more vigilant about monitoring their own partner.[11] One of the most important mate retention strategies involves continuing to fulfill the desires of one's mate—the desires that led to the mate selection to begin with. But merely fulfilling these desires may not be enough if rivals are attempting the same thing. Ancestral humans needed a psychological mechanism specifically designed to alert them to potential threats from the outside, an adaptation that would regulate when to deploy mate-guarding strategies. That mechanism was sexual jealousy.

Gender-Linked Adaptive Functions of Sexual Jealousy

Whenever males contribute to their offspring, they confront the problem of uncertain paternity. This problem occurs whenever fertilization and gestation occur inside the female's body. It intensifies whenever males invest in offspring after they are born. Compared with many other male mammals, men invest tremendously in their offspring. Cuckoldry is therefore a serious adaptive problem that men have had to solve throughout human evolutionary history. The prevalence of the problem in the animal kingdom is reflected in the fact that so few mammalian males invest at all in their young.[12] Among chimpanzees, our closest primate relatives, males defend their troop against chimp aggressors, but they invest little or nothing in their own offspring. Males would incur a double penalty if they invested in their children without some certainty of paternity: their parental effort would not only be wasted but might also get channeled to a rival's offspring. The general failure of male mammals to invest in their young is telling—most have not solved the problem of ensuring paternity. The fact that men do invest heavily in their young provides powerful evidence that our ancestors evolved effective paternity assurance adaptations. Studies of sexual jealousy, in all its diverse manifestations, provide direct evidence that jealousy is one of the primary adaptations.

Imagine getting off work early and returning home. As you enter the house you hear sounds coming from the back room. You call your partner's name, but no one answers. As you approach the back room, sounds of heavy breathing and moaning become louder. You open the bedroom door. On the bed is a stranger, naked and having passionate sexual intercourse with your partner. What emotions would you experience? If you are human, you would most likely experience some combination of humiliation, rage, betrayal, despondency, and grief.[13]

Sexual jealousy consists of emotions that are evoked by a perceived threat to a sexual relationship. The perception of a threat leads to actions designed to reduce or eliminate that threat.[14] These can range from vigilance, which functions to monitor the mate for signs of extra-pair involvement, to violence, which inflicts a heavy cost on the mate or rival. Sexual jealousy is activated by cues that someone else has an interest in one's mate or by indications of a mate's defection, such as flirting with someone else. The rage, sadness, and humiliation following these cues motivate action intended either to cut off a rival, prevent the mate's defection, or, sometimes, cut one's losses.

Men who fail to solve this adaptive problem risk not only suffering direct reproductive costs but also losing status and reputation, which can seriously impair their ability to attract other mates. Consider the reaction in Greek culture to cuckoldry: "The wife's infidelity . . . brings disgrace to the husband who is then a Keratas—the worst insult for a Greek man—a shameful epithet with connotations of weakness and inadequacy. . . . While for the wife it is socially acceptable to tolerate her unfaithful husband, it is not socially acceptable for a man to tolerate his unfaithful wife and if he does so, he is ridiculed as behaving in an unmanly manner."[15] Cuckolded men are universal objects of derision. The penalties for failure to keep a mate, including the loss of social status, are compounded by diminished future success in the game of mating.

Most research on jealousy has focused on male sexual jealousy, probably because of the asymmetry between men's and women's confidence about their parenthood. Nonetheless, women experience jealousy just as intensely; a mate's contact with other women can lead him to redirect his resources and commitment away from her and her children and toward another woman and her children. Men and women do not differ in either the frequency or the magnitude of their jealousy experience. In one study, 300 individuals who were partners in 150 romantic relationships were asked to rate how jealous they were in general, how jealous they were of their partner's relationships with members of the other sex, and the degree to which jealousy was a problem in their relationship. Men and women admitted to equal amounts of jealousy, confirming that both experience jealousy and overall do not differ in the intensity of their jealous feelings.[16]

These reactions are not limited to the United States. Over 2,000 individuals from Hungary, Ireland, Mexico, the Netherlands, the United States, and the former Soviet Union and Yugoslavia were asked their reactions to a variety of different sexual scenarios. Men and women in all of these places expressed identically negative emotional reactions to thoughts of their partner's flirting with someone else or having sexual relations with someone else. The genders are also the same in their jealous reactions to a sexual partner's hugging someone else or dancing with someone else, although their responses to these events are less negative than to flirting and sexual relations. For both men and women worldwide, as in the United States, jealousy is an adaptation that becomes activated in response to a threat to a valued relationship.[17]

Despite these similarities, there are intriguing gender differences in the content and focus of jealousy and in the specific events that trigger jealousy. In one study, twenty men and twenty women were asked to play a role in a scenario in which they became jealous.[18] But first the participants had to choose their scenario from among a group of possible scenarios, which typically involved either jealousy over a partner's sexual involvement with someone else or jealousy over a partner's devotion of time and resources to someone else. Seventeen women chose infidelity in the allocation of either resources or time as the jealousy-inducing event, and only three women chose sexual infidelity. In marked contrast, sixteen of the twenty men chose sexual infidelity as the jealousy-inducing event, and only four men chose the diversion of time or resources. This study provides the first clue that, although both men and women have the jealousy adaptation, it is triggered by different events, and that those events correspond to the adaptive problems of ensuring paternity for men and ensuring resources and commitment for women.

In another study, fifteen couples listed situations that would make them jealous. Men identified sexual involvement between their partner and another man as the primary cause of jealousy, and secondarily comparison between themselves and a rival. Women, in contrast, indicated that they would become jealous primarily in response to their partner's spending time with other women, talking with a rival, and kissing a female rival.[19] Women's jealousy, in short, is triggered by cues to the possible diversion of their mate's investment to another woman, whereas men's jealousy is triggered primarily by cues to their mate's having sex with another man.

These gender differences reveal themselves both psychologically and physiologically. In a study of sex differences in jealousy, my colleagues and I asked 511 college men and women to compare two distressing events—if their partner had sexual intercourse with someone else and if their partner formed a deep emotional attachment to someone else.[20] Fully 83 percent of the women found their partner's emotional infidelity more upsetting, whereas only 40 percent of the men did. In contrast, 60 percent of the men experienced their partner's sexual infidelity as more upsetting, whereas only 17 percent of the women did.

To evaluate a different group—this one comprising sixty men and women—on their physiological distress in response to sexual and emotional infidelity, we placed electrodes on the corrugator muscle in the brow, which contracts when people frown; on the first and third fingers of the right hand to measure skin conductance, or sweating; and on the thumb to measure heart rate. Then we asked people to imagine two types of infidelity, sexual and emotional. Men became more physiologically distressed by the sexual infidelity. Their heart rates accelerated by nearly five beats per minute, equivalent to drinking three cups of coffee in one sitting. Their skin conductance increased 1.5 micro-siemens with the thought of sexual infidelity, but showed little change from baseline in response to the thought of emotional infidelity. And their frowning increased, showing 7.75 microvolt units of contraction in response to sexual infidelity, as compared with only 1.16 units in response to emotional infidelity. Women tended to show the opposite pattern, exhibiting greater physiological distress at the thought of emotional infidelity. Women's frowning, for example, increased to 8.12 microvolt units of contraction in response to emotional infidelity, from only 3.03 units of contraction in response to sexual infidelity. Other researchers have replicated the physiological gender differences using multiple measures.[21] The coordination of psychological distress with physiological distress illustrates the precision with which humans have adapted over time to the specific threats they have faced to keeping a mate.

Sex differences in the causes of jealousy are not limited to Americans. In one study of jealous men and women in central Europe, 80 percent of the men expressed fears of a sexual nature, such as worrying about their mate's having intercourse with another man or worrying about their own sexual adequacy.[22] Only 22 percent of the jealous women expressed sexual concerns, the majority focusing instead on the emotional relationship, such as the degree of closeness between their mate and another woman. Men in Hungary, Ireland, Mexico, the Netherlands, the Soviet Union, the United States, and Croatia all showed more intense jealousy than women in response to their partner's having sexual fantasies about another person.[23] These gender differences in the triggers of jealousy appear to characterize the entire human species.

Competing Explanations for Gender Differences in Jealousy

The evolutionary interpretation of sex differences in jealousy has been challenged.[24] Some have proposed that sexual infidelity and emotional infidelity are often correlated, and indeed they are. People tend to get emotionally involved with those with whom they have sex and, conversely, tend to become sexually involved with those with whom they are emotionally close. But men and women might differ in their beliefs about the correlation. According to this hypothesis, perhaps women get more upset about a partner's emotional involvement with someone else because they think it implies that their partner will also become sexually involved. Women might believe that men can have sex, in contrast, without getting emotionally involved, and so imagining a partner's sexual involvement with another person is less upsetting. Men's beliefs might differ. Perhaps men get more upset about a partner's sexual involvement with another man because they think that she is likely to have sex with him only if she is also emotionally involved, whereas they think that a woman can easily become emotionally involved without having sex with a man.

My team and I conducted four empirical studies in three cultures to test predictions from the competing evolutionary and belief hypotheses.[25] The first study involved 1,122 undergraduates at a liberal arts college in the southeastern United States. The original infidelity scenarios were altered to render the two types of infidelity mutually exclusive. Participants reported their relative distress in response to a partner's sexual infidelity with no emotional involvement and their response to the partner's emotional involvement with no sexual infidelity. A large gender difference emerged, as predicted by the evolutionary model. If the belief hypothesis were correct, then the gender difference should have disappeared. It did not.

Our second study provided four additional tests of the predictions from the two models, using three research strategies. One strategy employed three versions of rendering the two types of infidelity mutually exclusive. A second strategy posited that both types of infidelity had occurred and asked participants to indicate which aspect they found more upsetting. A third strategy used a statistical procedure to test the independent predictive value of sex and beliefs in accounting for which form of infidelity would be more distressing. The results were conclusive: large gender differences were discovered, precisely as predicted by the evolutionary model. No matter how the questions were worded, no matter which methodological strategy was employed, and no matter how stringently the conditional probabilities were controlled, the gender differences remained robust.

Our third study replicated the infidelity dilemmas in a non-Western sample of native Koreans. The original sex differences were replicated. With two strategies to control for the co-occurrence of sexual and emotional infidelity, the gender differences again remained robust. The evolutionary hypothesis survived this empirical hurdle. In our fourth study, we tested the predictions about jealousy and about the nature of beliefs in a non-Western Japanese sample. The results again provided support for the evolutionary hypothesis. In yet another study, Brooke Scelza surveyed a small-scale population, the Himba of Namibia, and also found that men more than women were more distressed by the sexual aspect of the infidelity when both forms of infidelity occurred.[26] And finally, the evolutionary psychologist Barry Kuhle analyzed spontaneous jealous interrogations following the discovery of an actual infidelity. He found that men more than women wanted to know, "Did you have sex with him?" whereas women more than men wanted to know, "Do you love her?"[27]

Perhaps more important than the details of any one study is evaluation by the key scientific criterion—the weight of the evidence.[28] The sex differences in jealousy have now been discovered using an astonishingly wide array of diverse methods. The sex differences in jealousy using the forced-choice method are robust across cultures such as Brazil, England, Romania, Korea, Japan, the Netherlands, Norway, and Sweden, suggesting universality.[29] The sex differences remain robust when participants are asked "which aspect" of the infidelity would be most distressing when both sexual infidelity and emotional infidelity have occurred. Most, although not all, researchers examining physiological responses to jealousy have replicated the sex differences in physiological distress. The sex differences become even more pronounced among those who have experienced an actual infidelity in their lives and when participants undergo a procedure that requires them to vividly imagine the experience of infidelity. Men have more difficulty than women in forgiving a sexual than an emotional infidelity and indicate a greater likelihood of ending a relationship following a sexual infidelity than an emotional one.

Cognitively, men, compared to women, show greater memorial recall of cues to sexual than to emotional infidelity; preferentially search for cues to sexual rather than to emotional infidelity; involuntarily focus attention on cues to sexual rather than to emotional infidelity; and show faster decision times in response to cues to sexual than to emotional infidelity.

A study of brain activation, using fMRI brain scans of participants as they viewed imagery of sexual and emotional infidelity, found striking sex differences.[30] Men showed far greater activation than women in the amygdala and hypothalamus—brain regions involved in sexuality and aggression. Women, in contrast, showed greater activation than men in the posterior superior sulcus—a brain region involved in the process of mind-reading, such as inferring a partner's future intentions. These findings are precisely what we would expect if male and female jealousy adaptations were designed to solve somewhat different adaptive problems.[31] In sum, the sex differences in jealousy remain robust across cultures and across a wide range of methods, including psychological dilemmas, physiological recordings, cognitive experiments, and fMRI recordings of brain activation.

Several other gender-differentiated design features of the jealousy adaptation have been documented. Men's jealousy is especially attuned to rivals who have status and resources; women's jealousy is especially attuned to rivals who are physically attractive.[32] One man said, "The thought of my ex having sex with another was excruciating. . . . I would stay awake with this thought going through my head, could feel my temperature rise to boiling point."[33] One woman said that, "with girls, if they are pretty, or if he says they are pretty, I don't like it at all."[34] Interestingly, these sex differences in distress over the attributes of rivals—women's anger at a rival's attractiveness and men's anger at a rival's status and resources—show up even in women and men diagnosed as having "pathological" jealousy.[35]

Men more than women display an "infidelity overperception bias" in overestimating their partner's likelihood of sexual infidelity.[36] Finally, among women and men who are prone to chronic jealousy and worry a lot about relationship threats, the gender differences in response to sexual versus emotional infidelity are especially large.[37]

Mate Retention Through Fulfilling a Partner's Desires

Once jealousy has become activated by threats to the security of one's mateship, it can motivate tactics directed at the mate, at the rival, or at oneself. Men and women use an astonishing variety of tactics to keep a mate. A partner's original mate preferences form the basis for one major strategy: fulfilling the partner's preferences—that is, providing the sorts of resources he or she initially sought—should be a highly effective method of preserving the relationship.

To investigate this possibility, I initiated mate retention studies.[38] First, I asked dating men and women to describe specific

behaviors they had observed in people trying to hold on to partners to prevent them from becoming involved with someone else.
They came up with 104 identifiable acts, which a team of four
investigators classified into nineteen discrete clusters. The cluster
called "vigilance," for example, included calling a partner at unexpected times to see who he or she was with, having one's friends
check up on the partner, snooping through personal belongings,
and dropping by unexpectedly to see what the partner was doing. Finally, I asked 102 college students who were involved in
dating relationships and 210 newlyweds to rate how frequently
they performed each of these acts of vigilance. In their fifth year
of marriage, the newlywed couples again reported on their use of
mate retention tactics. A separate panel of judges evaluated the
tactics for their effectiveness in keeping a mate when performed
by a man and when performed by a woman.

Fulfilling the initial mating desires of the partner did indeed
prove to be an effective mate-keeping tactic. Because women desire love and kindness in their initial selection of a mate, continuing to provide love and kindness is a highly effective tactic for
men who want to keep their mates. Men who tell their mates that
they love them, are helpful when their mates need assistance,
and regularly display kindness and affection succeed in retaining their mates. These were judged to be the most effective acts
that men could perform, with an effectiveness rating of 6.23 on a
7-point scale, and were significantly more effective for men than
the same acts performed by women, which received an effectiveness rating of 5.39. Furthermore, the performance of these
acts was directly linked with the length of the relationship among
dating couples and with the duration of marriage after five years.
Husbands who failed to perform acts of love and commitment
were more likely to have a wife who was contemplating or seeking
divorce than husbands who were kind and loving. Acts of love and
kindness succeed because they signal an emotional commitment

to the relationship, they bestow a benefit rather than inflicting a cost, and they fulfill women's psychological preferences for a desirable partner.

Because women also value economic and material resources, continuing to provide them is another highly effective tactic for men to keep their mates. In the service of this goal, men reported spending a lot of money on their mates and buying them expensive gifts. Among committed dating couples, men provided these external resources more often than women did. Providing resources was the second most effective tactic for men in retaining a mate, with an average effectiveness rating of 4.50, in contrast to a rating of 3.76 when used by women. Men more than women provided resources in the service of keeping their mates during the newlywed phase of marriage, and they continued to use this tactic more often than their wives after five years of marriage.[39] Like successful tactics for attracting a mate, successful tactics for keeping a mate fulfill the mate's desires—in this case, providing the economic and material resources on which women place a premium.

Analogously, men value physical attractiveness, and I found that women were most likely to cite enhancing their appearance as one of their primary mate retention tactics—a finding that is replicable across cultures, including Brazil, Croatia, and the United States.[40] Out of the nineteen clusters evaluated, enhancing their appearance was the second most effective tactic used by women, after love and kindness. Women go out of their way to make themselves attractive to their partners, making up their faces to look nice, dressing to maintain a partner's interest, and acting sexy to distract a partner's attention from other women. Not only newlywed women but also women married for five years enhance their physical appearance in the service of keeping a mate, which shows that, for women, continuing to fulfill men's initial mating desires is a key to staying together.

The importance of appearance was dramatically illustrated by a study in which men and women watched a videotape of a couple sitting on a couch talking.[41] After forty-five seconds, during which the couple cuddle, kiss, and touch one another, one of the partners gets up and leaves the room to refill their wineglasses. Seconds later, an interloper enters and is introduced as the previous girlfriend or boyfriend of the partner who has remained on the couch. (The men watched the version with a previous boyfriend as the interloper, and the women watched the version with an old girlfriend as the interloper.) The partner stands up and briefly hugs the interloper, then the two sit down on the couch. Over the next minute they perform intimate actions, such as kissing and touching. The absent partner then returns, stops, and looks down at the two people who are showing affection to each other on the couch. The tape ends there. Women who saw the tape were nearly twice as likely as men to report that, in response to this threat to keeping a mate, they would try to make themselves more attractive to their partner. Men, in contrast, were more likely to say that they would become angry, suggesting a more aggressive strategy for keeping a mate. Women enhance their appearance because it activates men's evolved desires.

Emotional Manipulation

When tactics such as providing resources, love, and kindness fail, people sometimes resort to desperate emotional tactics to retain their mates, particularly if they are lower in mate value. Examples are crying when the partner indicates interest in others, making the partner feel guilty about such interest, and telling the partner that they are hopelessly dependent on him or her.

Submission or self-abasement is another tactic of emotional manipulation. For example, people may go along with everything their mate says, let that person have his or her way, and promise to change—a desperation tactic if there ever was one. In spite of the common stereotype that women are more submissive than men, the mate retention studies show the opposite in mate retention tactics. Men submit to, and abase themselves before, their mates roughly 25 percent more than women do. This gender difference shows up among college dating couples, among newlywed couples, and even among couples after several years of marriage. The gender difference in self-abasement cannot be attributed to a male reporting bias, because their spouses corroborate those reports.

Precisely why men submit and self-abase more than women remains a puzzle. Perhaps a man who perceives himself to be lower in mate value than his partner uses submission to try to prevent her from ditching him. Perhaps the tactic represents an attempt to placate a woman who is on the verge of leaving. But these speculations are not satisfactory because they do not answer the question of why men need to resort to this tactic more than women. Only future research can unravel the answer to this mystery.

Another emotional manipulation is intentionally trying to provoke sexual jealousy with the goal of keeping a mate. This tactic includes actions such as dating others to make a mate jealous, talking with people of the opposite sex at parties to incite jealousy, and showing an interest in people of the opposite sex to make a mate angry. People perceive these tactics to be nearly twice as effective for women as for men. A woman who flirts with other men in order to elicit jealousy and thereby hold on to a mate, however, is walking a fine line: eliciting jealousy injudiciously might provoke either violence or abandonment if her mate perceives her as promiscuous.

Although women admit to inducing jealousy more than men do, not all women resort to this tactic. One study has identified a key context in which women do intentionally elicit jealousy.[42] It examined discrepancies between partners in their emotional commitment to the relationship. Such discrepancies can signal differences in the desirability of the partners, since the less involved person is generally higher in mate value. Whereas 50 percent of the women who viewed themselves as more involved than their partner intentionally provoked jealousy, only 26 percent of the women who were equally or less involved used this tactic. These women acknowledged that they were motivated to elicit jealousy in order to increase the closeness of the relationship, to test the strength of the relationship, to see if the partner still cared, and to inspire possessiveness. Discrepancies between partners in desirability, as indicated by differences in involvement in the relationship, apparently cause women to provoke jealousy as a tactic to gain information about, and to increase, men's commitment.

Repelling Mate Poachers

Like many species, humans show proprietary attitudes toward their possessions and toward their mates. One method for signaling ownership is a public marking that tells rivals to stay away. Public signals of possession can be verbal, as in introducing a person as a spouse or lover and bragging about a mate to friends. Public signals can be physical, such as holding hands with or putting one's arm around a mate in front of other people. Public signals can also be ornamental, such as asking a mate to wear one's jacket, giving jewelry that signifies that the person is taken, and displaying a Facebook relationship status to signify that the person is taken.

Although men and women do not differ in how often they use these public measures to repel mate poachers, our expert panel judged the signals to be significantly more effective when used by men than by women.[43] The reason may be that public signals provide a strong cue to the woman of a man's intent to commit. An engagement ring, for example, sends a strong signal to potential mate poachers. Verbal, physical, and ornamental displays attain their effectiveness by dissuading potential competitors, just as the male insect who mingles his scent with that of the female causes rivals to seek other mates who are uncontested. These displays also communicate a commitment that fulfills women's long-term desires.

Maintaining vigilance is an additional means that both sexes use to keep their mates away from others. An animal analogue occurs among the male elephant seals on the California coast. They maintain a vigil against rivals and female defections by patrolling the perimeter of their harem. Calling a mate at unexpected times, reading his or her email, or monitoring Facebook posts are human exercises of vigilance. Vigilance represents an effort to detect whether there are any signs of defection in the mate. Vigilance also conveys a message to a mate that evidence of consorting with rivals will be detected and acted upon. People in our evolutionary past who were not vigilant experienced more defections than those who kept a watchful eye.

The tactic of concealing mates is closely related to vigilance. The male wasp whisks his mate away from the path that might be tracked by other males. Men and women conceal their mates by refusing to take them to parties where competitors will be present, refusing to introduce them to friends who might mate-poach, and taking them away from gatherings filled with potential competitors. Concealment attains its effectiveness by reducing the contact of mates with rivals and reducing the opportunities for mates to assess alternative mating prospects.

A close cousin of concealment is monopolizing a mate's time—insisting that all free time be spent together and monopolizing the mate at social gatherings. Monopolizing a mate prevents that person from having contact with potential rivals who could poach him or her or be appealing as an attractive alternative.

These forms of mate retention have historical and cross-cultural precedents. Claustration, or the concealment of women to prevent their contact with potential sexual partners, provides a vivid example of mate monopolization. Historically, Indian men have secluded women in the interior of dwellings. Arab men have concealed the faces and bodies of women with veils or burkas. Japanese men have bound the feet of women to restrict their mobility. In societies that practice veiling, weddings are the venue for the most extreme forms of this variety of concealment—that is, those in which the greatest surface area of the skin is covered—because a woman getting married is close to peak fertility. Young prepubescent girls and older postmenopausal women are less severely concealed because they are viewed as less enticing to other men.[44]

Another common practice throughout human history has been for men to gather women into guarded harems. The term *harem* means "forbidden." Indeed, it was often as difficult for women to leave harems as it was for outside men to get in. Kings and other rulers used eunuchs to guard their harems. In India during the sixteenth century, merchants supplied rich men with a steady supply of Bengali slave eunuchs, who not only were castrated but had their entire genitalia cut off.[45]

The number of women collected into harems is staggering by any standard. The Indian emperor Bhuponder Singh had 332 women in his harem when he died, "all of [whom] were at the beck and call of the Maharaja. He could satisfy his sexual lust with any of them at any time of day or night."[46] In India, the harems of sixteenth-century kings were estimated to have between 4,000 and 12,000 occupants.[47] In Imperial China, emperors around 771 BC kept one queen, three consorts or wives of the first rank, nine wives of the second rank, twenty-seven wives of the third rank, and eighty-one concubines.[48] In Peru, an Inca lord kept a minimum of 700 women "for the service of his house and on whom to take his pleasure . . . [having] many children by these women."[49]

All of these public signals of mate retention served the sole goal of preventing contact between the mates and potential rivals.

Because high-status men historically have been in a position of power, their ability to apply extreme tactics has reduced women's freedom of choice. In modern industrial societies, with greater gender equality, both sexes deploy public signals—albeit typically less drastic ones than those used by medieval lords—to retain their mates.

Cost-Inflicting Mate Retention Tactics

Another mate retention tactic is to inflict costs on competitors or on mates through derogation, threats, and violence. These contrast sharply with benefit-conferring tactics such as providing resources or bestowing love and kindness. Destructive tactics acquire their effectiveness by deterring interlopers from poaching and deterring mates from straying.

One set of these cost-inflicting tactics is aimed at rivals. Verbal denigration of competitors is perhaps the mildest form of this tactic, although in Ecclesiasticus (28:17) it is noted that "the blow of a whip raises a welt, but a blow of the tongue crushes the bones." To dissuade their mates from becoming attracted to a rival, both men and women may belittle the rival's appearance or intelligence or start damaging rumors about him or her. Derogation of competitors continues even after vows of undying commitment are taken, because mate switching is always a possibility. When used judiciously, it is an effective method for rendering rivals less attractive and lowers the odds of a mate's defection.

A costlier tactic is subjecting a rival to verbal threats and violence. Just as chimpanzees bare their teeth in a threat that sends rivals scurrying from a female, newlywed men yell at rivals who look at their bride, threaten to strike those who make passes at her, and stare coldly at men who look too long at her. These threatening retention tactics are performed almost exclusively by men. Although they are not performed often, we discovered that

46 percent of married men had threatened an intrasexual competitor within the past year, whereas only 11 percent of the married women had done so. These tactics convey strong signals that mate poaching attempts come with large risks.

Men sometimes inflict even more extreme costs on their rivals. Married men may hit men who make passes at their wives, get their friends to beat up a rival, slap men who show too much interest in their wives, or vandalize their property. These acts impose heavy costs in the form of bodily injury or, in rare cases, death. The reputation that these acts earn for their perpetrator deters other men. Most men would think twice before flirting with the girlfriend of a large, rough-looking, burly man with a reputation for hair-trigger violence.

Another set of cost-inflicting tactics are sometimes directed at mates to deter them from straying. Male baboons and other primates wound females through bites or beatings when they consort with other males.[50] Married men and women become angry when their partner flirts with others, yell if the partner flirts, and threaten to break up if their partner ever cheats. Men perceived by their partner as lower in mate value are especially likely to verbally insult her, possibly because these men, with fewer benefits to bestow, are trying to reduce her perception that she is the more desirable partner.[51] Moreover, both genders sometimes threaten never to speak with their partner again if they catch the partner with someone else. Occasionally they hit their partner when he or she flirts with others. Men in committed dating relationships and men who are married inflict these costs nearly twice as often as men who do not expect to be with their current mate in the future.

Punishing a mate who shows signs of interest in others acquires its effectiveness from the deterrent value of the threatened costs. Some of these costs are physical, such as bodily injury. Other costs are psychological, such as the lowered self-esteem that comes from being yelled at or otherwise verbally abused.[52]

Since a person's self-esteem is, in part, an internal tracking device reflecting self-perceived mate value, these forms of abuse may be functional in mate retention, however morally abhorrent they are.

Clues to the functionality of partner abuse come from the specific contexts in which it is deployed.[53] One circumstance is the perception or discovery of sexual infidelity. A second is when there exists a mate value discrepancy: the less desirable partner may abuse the other to reduce that partner's perceptions of the discrepancy. A third is when a woman is pregnant and the man suspects that the child might not be his. Blows in this circumstance are often directed to the woman's abdomen, suggesting the disturbing possibility that the function of this form of violence is to abort a rival's child.

These vicious sorts of spousal abuse are seen across cultures. Studies of the Baiga, for example, reveal cases in which husbands have attacked their wives with blazing logs as punishment for flirting with another man, a form of violence against women in which jealousy is the key motive.[54] In studies of abused women in Canada, 55 percent of the women reported that jealousy was one of the reasons for their husband's assault on them; half of the women who reported jealousy as a motive acknowledged that their sexual infidelity had provoked the violence.[55]

Brutal beatings occur not just after an infidelity is suspected but to prevent its occurrence. Moreover, several culturally created means have been developed to prevent extramarital sexual activity through genital mutilation in various cultures across northern and central Africa, Arabia, Indonesia, and Malaysia. Clitoridectomy, the surgical removal of the clitoris to prevent a woman from experiencing sexual pleasure, is practiced on millions of African women. Another practice common in Africa is infibulation, the sewing shut of the labia majora. According to one estimate, 200 million women living today in twenty-three countries in northern and central Africa have been genitally mutilated through infibulation.[56]

Infibulation effectively prevents sexual intercourse. It is sometimes performed by the woman's kin as a guarantee to a potential husband that the bride is virginal. After marriage, infibulated women must be cut open to allow for sexual intercourse. If the husband goes away for a while, his wife may be reinfibulated. In the Sudan, the woman is reinfibulated after she bears a child and then must be reopened to allow for intercourse. Although the decision to reinfibulate a woman usually rests with her husband, some women demand reinfibulation after delivery, in the belief that it increases the husband's pleasure. A Sudanese woman who fails to please her husband risks being divorced, thus losing her children, losing economic support, and bringing disgrace on her entire family.[57]

There are no cultures in which men are not sexually jealous. In every supposedly nonjealous culture previously thought to contain no barriers to sexual conduct beyond the incest taboo, evidence for sexual jealousy has now been found. The Marquesa Islanders, for example, were once thought to impose no formal or informal prohibitions on adultery. This notion is contradicted by the ethnographic report: "When a woman undertook to live with a man, she placed herself under his authority. If she cohabited with another man without his permission, she was beaten or, if her husband's jealousy was sufficiently aroused, killed."[58]

Another presumed example of the absence of sexual jealousy is the Inuit, a culture that practices wife sharing. Contrary to popular myth, however, male sexual jealousy is a leading cause of spousal homicide among the Inuit, and these homicides occur at an alarmingly high rate.[59] Inuit men share their wives only under highly circumscribed conditions, such as when there is a reciprocal expectation that the favor will be returned in kind. Wife swapping apparently can mitigate the onset of men's jealousy. All of these findings demonstrate that there are no paradises populated with sexually liberated people who share mates freely and do not get jealous.

Some societies require the mate poacher to pay reparation to the husband when he is caught having intercourse with the wife. Even in the United States, monetary payments to the husband have been imposed on mate poachers for "alienation of affection." In North Carolina, for example, an ophthalmologist was required to pay a woman's ex-husband $200,000 for having enticed her away from him. These legal strictures reflect an intuitive understanding of human evolutionary psychology: in men's eyes, cuckoldry represents the unlawful stealing of another's resources. When it comes to sex, men everywhere seem to regard wives as "theirs" to be owned and controlled. Men react to cuckoldry as they would to theft and sometimes leave a trail of destruction in their wake.[60]

A Dangerous and Deadly Passion

Men's sexual jealousy is neither a trivial nor a peripheral emotion in human life. It sometimes becomes so powerful that it causes the person who experiences it to kill a mate or an interloper. In one case a wife killing was apparently fueled by an awareness of the reproductive damage of cuckoldry, as the husband explained:

> You see, we were always arguing about her extramarital affairs. That day was something more than that. I came home from work and as soon as I entered the house I picked up my little daughter and held her in my arms. Then my wife turned around and said to me: "You are so damned stupid that you don't even know she is someone else's child and not yours." I was shocked! I became so mad. I took the rifle and shot her.[61]

A wife's infidelity is sometimes viewed as so extreme a provocation that a "reasonable man" may legally respond with lethal violence. In Texas until 1974, for example, it was legal for a husband to kill his wife and her lover if he did so while the adulterers were engaging in the act of intercourse; their murder was considered a reasonable response to a powerful provocation. Laws exonerating men from killing adulterous wives are found worldwide and throughout human history. Among the Yaps, for example, rules permit husbands to kill wives and their lovers and to burn them up in the house if caught in the act of adultery. Similar provisions are made for offended husbands among the Toba-Batak of Sumatra. Old Roman law granted the husband the right to kill only if the adultery occurred in his own house, and similar laws remain in effect in some European countries today.[62]

Male sexual jealousy is the single most frequent cause of all types of violence directed at wives, including physical abuse and actual murder. In one study of forty-four physically abused wives seeking refuge, 55 percent stated that jealousy was their husband's key motive for assaulting them.[63] Sexual jealousy is a major motive for murder. In a study of homicides among the Tiv, Soga, Gisu, Nyoro, Luyhia, and Luo in British colonial Africa, of seventy murders of wives by their husbands, 46 percent were explicitly over sexual matters, including adultery, the woman's abandonment of the husband, and the woman's refusal of sex with the husband.[64]

Many of the homicides perpetrated by women also appear to have male sexual jealousy at their root. Women who kill men frequently do so to defend themselves against an enraged, threatening, and abusive husband from whom they fear bodily harm. In a sample of forty-seven homicide cases precipitated by a jealous man, sixteen women were killed by men for real or suspected infidelity, seventeen male rivals were killed by enraged men, and nine men were killed in self-defense by women whom the men had accused of infidelity.[65]

Homicidal jealousy is by no means limited to American or even to Western cultures. Sexual jealousy is a leading motive behind homicide in Sudan, Uganda, and India.[66] One study in the Sudan, for example, found that the leading motive for 74 of 300 male-perpetrated murders was sexual jealousy.[67] Most cases of spousal homicide in every society studied are apparently precipitated by male accusations of adultery or by the woman's leaving or threatening to leave the husband. Furthermore, about 20 percent of the homicides of men by men have as their motive rivalry over a woman or offense taken at advances made to a spouse, daughter, or female relative.[68]

The adaptive functions of jealousy to prevent infidelity and ensure paternity are hard to reconcile with the seemingly maladaptive act of killing one's wife, which interferes with reproductive success by destroying a key reproductive resource. There are several possible explanations. Because the overwhelming majority of unfaithful wives are not killed, the actual killing of a wife might represent an accidental slip of the adaptation, in which violent jealousy becomes pathological, is carried too far, and intentionally or accidentally results in death.[69] Although this explanation fits some cases of wife killing, it does not square with the seeming intentionality of the many men who acknowledge that they intended to kill their partner and even hunted the woman down to do so.

An alternative explanation is that the killings that stem from jealousy represent extreme but nonetheless evolved manifestations of the adaptation. Killing one's wife would not necessarily have been reproductively damaging under all conditions during human evolutionary history. In the first place, if a wife is going to abandon her husband, not only will he lose her reproductive resources anyway, but he also may suffer the additional cost of finding that those resources are channeled to a competitor, which is a double blow to relative reproductive success.

Men who allow themselves to be cuckolded are subject to ridicule and damage to their reputation, especially if they take no retaliatory action. In a polygynous marriage, for example, killing an unfaithful wife might salvage a man's honor and also serve as a powerful deterrent to infidelity by his other wives. Polygynous men who took no action may have risked being cuckolded with impunity in the future. In some circumstances in our evolutionary past, killing a wife may have represented an effort at damage containment designed to stop the hemorrhaging of reproductive resources.

In the face of the conflicting costs and benefits of homicide, it is reasonable to speculate that, in some circumstances, killing a spouse who was unfaithful or was determined to leave would have been reproductively more beneficial than allowing oneself to be cuckolded or abandoned with impunity. Thoughts of killing and occasional actual killings may have been adaptive over human evolutionary history and hence may be part of men's evolved psychological machinery. This is a horrifying possibility and obviously does not justify or excuse murder, but if society is ever going to grapple successfully with the serious problem of spousal homicide, it must confront the psychological mechanisms that give rise to it, especially the circumstances that activate violent adaptations and make them especially dangerous.

The Fragile Union

It is a remarkable human achievement that a man and a woman who have no genes in common can stay together in a union of solidarity over years, decades, or a lifetime. Because of the many forces that pull couples apart, however, staying together is a fragile proposition that poses a unique set of adaptive problems. Successful solutions typically incorporate several ingredients. First, the mate is supplied with the adaptively relevant resources needed to prevent defection. Second, competitors are kept at bay, for example, by public signals of possession or through concealing the mate from others. Third, mate guarders use emotional manipulation, for example, by provoking jealousy to increase perceptions of desirability, submitting or abasing oneself to the mate, or convincing the mate that alternatives are undesirable. Fourth, cost-inflicting measures come into play, such as punishing a mate for signals of defection or physically assaulting a rival.

These diverse tactics for retaining mates succeed by exploiting the psychological adaptations of mates and rivals. The beneficial tactics, such as giving love and resources, work for a man because they fulfill the psychological desires that led the woman to choose him to begin with. For a woman, enhancing her physical appearance and providing sexual resources succeeds because they match men's psychology of desire. Indeed, our study of married couples found that men intensify their mate retention efforts when they perceive their partner to be attractive, just as women ramp up their mate retention efforts with partners who are higher in status and income.[70]

Unfortunately, the tactics of threats and violence, which inflict costs on mates and rivals, also work by exploiting the psychological adaptations of others. Just as physical pain leads people to avoid the environmental hazards that can harm them, psychological fear causes people to avoid the wrath of an angry mate. Aggression sometimes pays.

Male sexual jealousy, a key adaptation underlying many tactics of mate retention, is also the dangerous emotion responsible for a majority of men's acts of violence against their mates. It may seem paradoxical that this adaptation, which is designed to keep a mate, causes so much destruction. It does so because the reproductive stakes are so high and the reproductive interests of the players can diverge so dramatically. The goals of a married man conflict with those of his rival, who seeks to lure his desirable wife away. A man's goals can conflict with those of his wife or girlfriend, who may become the victim of violent sexual jealousy. And when one partner wants to stay together while the other wants to break up, both parties are in for suffering—which brings us to the broader topic of conflict between the sexes.

7

Sexual Conflict

As we learn more about the patterns and structures that have shaped us today, it sometimes seems men are the enemy, the oppressors, or at the very least an alien and incomprehensible species.

—CAROL CASSELL, *Swept Away*

NOVELS, SONGS, SOAP operas, and tabloids tell us about battles between men and women and the pain they inflict on each other. Wives bemoan their husbands' neglect; husbands are bewildered by their wives' moodiness. "Men are emotionally constricted," say women. "Women are emotional powder kegs," say men. Men want sex too soon, too fast; women impose frustrating delays. Are these just stereotypes?

When I first started exploring the topic of conflict between the sexes, I wanted to survey this potentially expansive terrain. Toward this end, I asked several hundred women and men simply to list all the things that members of the opposite sex did that upset, angered, annoyed, or irritated them.[1] People were talkative on the topic. They listed 147 distinct things that someone could do to upset or anger someone of the opposite sex, ranging from condescension, insults, and physical abuse to sexual aggression, sexual withholding, sexism, and sexual infidelity. With this basic list of conflicts in hand, my colleagues and I conducted studies of singles, dating couples, and married couples to identify which sources of conflict occur most often and which produce the greatest distress.

Conflict between the sexes is best understood in the broader context of social conflict. Social conflict occurs whenever one person interferes with the achievement of the goal of another person. Interference can take various forms. Among men, for example, conflict occurs when they compete for precisely the same resources, such as position in a status hierarchy or access to a desirable sex partner. Because young, attractive women are in scarcer supply than men who seek them, some men get shut out. One man's gain becomes other men's loss. Similarly, two women who desire the same responsible, kind, or high-achieving man come into conflict; if one woman gets what she wants, the other woman does without.

Conflict also erupts between men and women whenever one sex interferes with the goals and desires of the other sex. In the sexual arena, for example, a man who seeks sex without investing in his partner short-circuits a mating goal of many women, who want greater emotional commitment and higher investment. The interference runs both ways. A woman who requires a long courtship and heavy investment interferes with a man's short-term sexual strategy.

Conflict per se serves no evolutionary purpose, and it is generally not adaptive at all for individuals to get into struggles with the other sex. On the contrary, conflict is typically costly. Sexual conflict is an undesirable outcome of the fact that people's sexual strategies interfere with each other. We have inherited from our ancestors, however, psychological solutions to problems of conflict management.

The emotions of anger, distress, and upset are key psychological solutions that have evolved in part to alert people to interference with their mating goals. These emotions serve several related functions. They draw our attention to the problematic events, focusing attention on them and momentarily screening out less relevant events. They mark those events for storage in memory and easy retrieval from memory. Emotions also lead to action, causing people to strive to eliminate the source of the problem or to head off future battles.

Because men and women have different sexual strategies, they differ in which events activate negative emotions. Men who seek casual sex without commitment or involvement, for example, often upset women, whereas women who lead men to invest for a period of time and then withhold sex that was enticingly implied will cause men to get angry.

Sexual Accessibility and Conflict over Perceived Mate Value

Disagreements about sexual access or availability may be the most common sources of conflict between men and women. When 121 college students kept daily diaries of their dating activities for four weeks, 47 percent reported having one or more disagreements about the desired level of sexual intimacy.[2] Men sometimes seek sex with a minimum of investment. Men guard their resources and are extraordinarily choosy about whom they invest in. They are "resource coy" in order to preserve their investments for a long-term mate or for multiple casual sex partners, sometimes serially and sometimes in rotation. Because women's long-term sexual strategies loom large in their repertoire, they often seek signals of investment before agreeing to sex. The investment that women covet is precisely the investment that men most selectively allocate. The sexual access that men seek is precisely the resource that women are so selective about apportioning.

Conflict over perceived desirability, where one person feels resentment because the other ignores him or her as a potential mate, is often where the first battle line is drawn in the mating market. People with higher desirability have more resources to offer and so can attract a mate with a higher value. Those with a low value must settle for less. Sometimes, however, a person may feel worthy of consideration and yet the other person disagrees.

This point is illustrated by a female colleague who frequents country-and-western bars. She reports that she is sometimes approached by a beer-drinking, T-shirted, baseball-capped, stubble-faced blue-collar worker who asks her to dance. When she declines, men like this sometimes get verbally abusive, saying, for example, "What's the matter, bitch, I'm not good enough for you?" Although she simply turns her back, that is precisely what she thinks: they are not good enough for her. Her unspoken message is that she can obtain someone better, and this message angers rebuffed men. The rock star Jim Morrison of The Doors once noted that women seem wicked when one is unwanted. Differences between people's perceptions of mate value cause conflict.

Cognitive Biases in Sexual Mind Reading

Humans live in an uncertain mating world. We must make inferences about others' intentions and emotional states. How attracted is he to her? How committed is she to him? Does that smile signal sexual interest or mere friendliness? Some psychological states, such as smoldering passion for another person, are intentionally concealed, rendering uncertainty greater and speculation more tortuous. We are forced to make inferences about hidden intentions and concealed deeds using a collage of cues that are only probabilistically related to their actual existence. An unexplained scent on one's romantic partner, for example, could signal sexual betrayal, or it could be an innocuous aroma acquired during a casual conversation or a walk through a shopping mall.

In reading the minds of others, there are two ways to go wrong. You can infer a psychological state that is not there, as when one assumes sexual interest when it is absent. Or you can fail to infer a psychological state that is there, as when one remains oblivious to another's burning yearnings, sexual or romantic. According to error management theory (EMT), it would be exceedingly unlikely that the cost-benefit consequences of the two types of errors would be identical across their many occurrences.[3] We intuitively understand this in the context of smoke alarms, which are typically set to be hypersensitive to any hint of smoke. The costs of occasional false alarms are minor compared to the catastrophic costs of failing to detect a real house fire. EMT extends this logic to cost-benefit consequences in the metric of evolutionary fitness.

According to EMT, asymmetries in the cost-benefit consequences of mind-reading inferences, if they recur over evolutionary time, create selection pressures that produce predictable cognitive biases. Just as smoke alarms are biased to produce more false positives than false negatives, EMT predicts that evolved mind-reading mechanisms will be biased to produce more of one type of inferential error than another. The *sexual overperception bias,* whereby men possess mind-reading biases designed to minimize the costs of missed sexual opportunities, is a perfect example. EMT provides a cogent explanation for the finding that men appear to falsely infer that women are sexually interested in them when they merely smile, incidentally touch their arm, or are simply friendly.

In one study, 98 men and 102 women watched a ten-minute videotape of a conversation between a male professor and a female student.[4] The student visits the professor's office to ask for a deadline extension for a term paper. The actors in the film are a female drama student and a male drama professor. Neither actor acts flirtatious or provocative, although both have been instructed to behave in a friendly manner. Participants witnessed the tape and then rated the likely intentions of the woman using 7-point scales. Women watching the interaction were more likely to say that the student was trying to be friendly (6.45), not sexy (2.00) or seductive (1.89). Men, while also perceiving friendliness (6.09), were more likely than women to infer seductive (3.38) and sexual (3.84) intentions. Similar results were obtained from a study using photos of a man and women studying together.[5] Men rated the photographed women as showing moderate intent to be sexy (4.87) and seductive (4.08), whereas women rating the identical photographs saw considerably less sexual intent (3.11) and less seductive intent (2.61).

Interestingly, men who view themselves as especially high in mate value are especially prone to experience the sexual overperception bias.[6] Men who are dispositionally inclined to pursue a short-term mating strategy also exhibit a more pronounced sexual overperception bias—a bias that would facilitate the success of a short-term mating strategy by minimizing lost opportunities.[7] A speed-dating study conducted in my lab, led by Carin Perilloux, found that men were especially susceptible to the sexual overperception bias when interacting with physically attractive women—an ironic finding since attractive women are generally very choosy.[8] The men were inferring interest in the minds of the women least likely to actually be interested. Nevertheless, as men act on their inferences they do occasionally open up sexual opportunities. If over evolutionary history even a tiny fraction of these sexual misperceptions led to sex, then men would have evolved lower thresholds for inferring women's sexual or romantic interest. Men's sexual overperception bias evolved to motivate approach.

Once this male mechanism was in place, it became susceptible to manipulation. Women sometimes use their sexuality as a tactic in such manipulation. In one study of 200 university students, women significantly more than men reported smiling and flirting as a means of eliciting special treatment from members of the opposite sex, even though they had no interest in having sex with those men.[9] Women, in short, sometimes exploit men's sexual overperception bias for their own ends.[10] Men's perception of sexual interest in women combines with women's intentional exploitation of this psychological adaptation to create a potentially volatile mix. These sexual strategies lead to conflict over the desired level of sexual intimacy, over men's feeling that women lead them on, and over women's feeling that men are too pushy in the sexual sphere.

Sexual pushiness sometimes slips over the line into sexual aggressiveness—the vigorous pursuit of sexual access despite a woman's reluctance or resistance. Sexual aggressiveness is one strategy men use to minimize the costs they incur for sexual access, although this strategy carries its own costs in the possibility of retaliation and damage to their reputation. Acts of sexual aggression include demanding or forcing sexual intimacy, failing to get mutual agreement for sex, and touching a woman's body without her permission. In one study, my lab asked women to evaluate 147 potentially upsetting actions that a man could perform. Women rated sexual aggression on average to be 6.50, or close to the 7.00 maximum of distress. No other kinds of acts that men could perform, including verbal abuse and nonsexual physical abuse, were judged by women to be as upsetting as sexual aggression. Contrary to a view held by some men, women do not want forced sex. Women sometimes have fantasies that involve forced sex with a man who turns out to be rich and handsome, and sometimes the theme of forced sex occurs in romance novels, but neither of these circumstances means that women actually desire forced or nonconsensual sex.[11]

Men, in sharp contrast, seem considerably less bothered if a woman is sexually aggressive; they see it as relatively innocuous compared with other sources of discomfort. On the same 7-point scale, for example, men judged the group of sexually aggressive acts to be only 3.02, or only lightly upsetting, when performed by a woman. A few men spontaneously commented that they would find such acts sexually arousing if a woman performed them. Other sources of distress, such as a mate's infidelity and verbal or physical abuse, were seen by men as far more upsetting—6.04 and 5.55, respectively—than sexual aggression by a woman.

A disturbing difference between the genders is that men consistently underestimate how unacceptable sexual aggression is to women. When asked to judge its negative impact on women, men rated it only 5.80 on the 7-point scale, which is significantly lower than women's own rating of 6.50. The implication of this alarming source of conflict between the sexes is that some men may be inclined to use aggressive sexual acts because they fail to comprehend how distressing these acts really are to women. In addition to creating conflict, men's failure to correctly understand the psychological pain that women experience from sexual aggression may be one cause of men's lack of empathy for rape victims.[12] The callous remark by a Texas politician that if a woman cannot escape a rape, she should just lie back and enjoy it, could only have been uttered by someone who fails to understand the magnitude of the trauma experienced by women who are victims of sexual aggression.

Women, in contrast, overestimated how upsetting sexual aggression by a woman is to a man, judging it to be 5.13, or moderately upsetting, in contrast to men's rating of only 3.02.[13] Men and women both err in cross-sex mind-reading. These cognitive biases may result from false beliefs about the other gender, mistakenly extrapolating from their own projected reactions. Men seem to think that women are more like them than they really are, and women seem to think that men are more like them than they really are. Acquiring knowledge about gender differences in perceptions of sexual aggression might be one step toward reducing sexual conflict.

The flip side of the coin of sexual aggression is sexual withholding. Men consistently complain about women's sexual withholding, defined by such acts as sexual teasing, saying no to having sex, and leading a man on and then turning him away. On the same 7-point scale of magnitude of upset, men judged sexual withholding to be 5.03, whereas women judged it to be 4.29. Both genders are bothered by sexual withholding, but men significantly more so than women.

For women, sexual withholding fulfills several possible functions. One is to preserve their ability to choose men of high mate value—those who are willing to commit emotionally, to invest materially, or to contribute high-quality genes, or ideally all three. Women withhold sex from certain men and selectively allocate it to others of their own choosing. Moreover, by withholding sex, women increase its value and render it a scarce resource. Scarcity ratchets up the price that men are willing to pay for it. If the only way men can gain sexual access is by heavy investment, then they will make that investment. Under conditions of sexual scarcity, men who fail to invest fail to mate. This creates another conflict between a man and a woman, since her withholding interferes with his strategy of gaining sex sooner and with fewer emotional strings attached.

Another function of sexual withholding is to manipulate a man's perception of a woman's value as a mate. Because highly desirable women are less sexually accessible to the average man

by definition, a woman may influence a man's perception of her
desirability by withholding sexual access. Highly desirable women
are, in fact, hard to get, so men interpret the difficulty of gaining
sexual access to a woman as a cue to her mate value. Finally, sexual withholding, at least initially, may encourage a man to evaluate
a woman as a long-term mate rather than a sexual fling. Granting
sexual access early often causes a man to see a woman as a casual
mate.

By withholding sex, women create challenges for men. They
circumvent the component of men's mating strategy that involves
seeking low-cost sex. Certainly, women have a right to choose
when, where, and with whom they want to have sex. But the exercise of that choice interferes with one of men's deep-seated sexual
strategies and is therefore experienced by men as bothersome or
upsetting; hence, it is one of the key sources of conflict between
the sexes.

Emotional Commitment

In the most abstract sense, people solve adaptive problems by
one of two means—by their own labor or by securing the labor of
others. In principle, people who can successfully obtain the effort of others with a minimal investment can be more successful
in solving life's adaptive problems. It is often in a woman's best
interest, for example, to have a man so devoted to her that all of
his energies are channeled to her and her children. It is often in
a man's best interest, however, to allocate only a portion of his
resources to one woman, reserving the rest for additional adaptive problems, such as seeking additional mating opportunities or
achieving higher social status. Hence, individual women and men
are often at odds over each other's commitments.

A key sign of conflict over commitment centers on the irritation women express about men's tendency not to express their

feelings openly. One of the most frequent complaints women have about men is that they are emotionally constricted. Among newlyweds, for example, 45 percent of women, in contrast to only 24 percent of men, complain that their mates fail to express their true feelings. During the dating phase, roughly 25 percent of women complain that their partners ignore their feelings; this increases to 30 percent in the first year of marriage. By the fourth year of marriage, 59 percent of women complain that their husbands ignore their feelings. In contrast, only 12 percent of newlywed men and 32 percent of men in their fourth year of marriage make this complaint.[14]

From a woman's vantage point, what are the benefits she gains by getting a man to express his emotions, and what are the costs she incurs if he fails to express them? From a man's vantage point, are there benefits to withholding the expression of emotions and costs to expressing them? One source of this gender difference stems from the fact that men's reproductive resources are more easily divided than women's. Within any one-year period, for example, a woman can only get pregnant by one man, and so the bulk of her reproductive resources cannot be easily partitioned. Within that same year, a man can divide his resources by investing in two or more women.

One reason men fail to express their emotions is that investing less emotionally in a relationship frees up resources that can be channeled toward other women or other goals. As in many negotiable exchanges, it is often in a man's best interest not to reveal how strong his desires are or how intensely he is willing to commit. Turkish rug dealers wear dark glasses to conceal their interest. Gamblers strive for a poker face to disguise telltale emotions that give away their hands. Emotions often betray the degree of investment. If emotions are concealed, one's sexual strategies remain concealed as well. The lack of information causes women to agonize, to sift through the available signs trying to discern where men really stand. College women, far more than college men, report spending time recalling and dissecting with friends conversations and activities they experienced with the people they are dating. They try to analyze their partner's "real" inner states, intentions, emotions, and motivations.[15] Conflict over commitment resides at the core of complaints about men's emotional constrictedness.

Concealment of sexual strategies is not the only force driving men to remain stoic, nor are men necessarily inept at expressing emotions under different circumstances. Similarly, women sometimes conceal their emotions for strategic reasons. In the mating arena, however, discerning the long-term intentions of a potential partner is less critical for men than for women. Women in ancestral times who erred in their assessment suffered severe costs by granting sexual access to men who failed to commit to them. Getting a man to express himself emotionally represents one tactic that women use to gain access to the important information they need to discern a man's degree of commitment. Perhaps that's why singer Madonna exhorts women to put love to the test by getting men to express themselves; only then will they know if his love is real.

While women complain that men are emotionally constricted, men commonly complain that women are too moody and emotional. Roughly 30 percent of dating men, in contrast to 19 percent of dating women, complain about their partner's moodiness. These figures increase to 34 percent of men during the first year of marriage and jump to 49 percent of men by the fourth year of marriage, in contrast with married women, of whom only 25 percent make these complaints.[16]

Moody partners absorb time and psychological energy. Appeasing responses, such as efforts to get the partner out of the bad mood and putting one's own plans aside temporarily, take up energy at the expense of other goals. Women impose these costs on men as a tactic for eliciting commitment. A moody woman may be saying: "You had better increase your commitment to me, or else I will burden you with my emotional volatility." It is one tactic in women's repertoire for eliciting male commitment. Men dislike it because it requires that they expend effort that could be allocated to solving other adaptive challenges.

Moodiness also functions as an assessment device to test the strength of the bond.[17] Women use moodiness to impose small costs on their mates and then use men's reactions to the costs as a gauge of their degree of commitment. If a man is unwilling to tolerate these costs, it is a cue that his commitment is low. Men's willingness to tolerate the costs and to be responsive to the increasing demands for investment signals a greater level of commitment. Either way, the woman gains valuable information about the strength of the bond.

Neither the functions of moodiness nor the functions of emotional reserve require conscious thought to be strategically enacted. Women need not be aware that they are attempting to test the strength of the man's commitment. Men need not be aware that they are trying to minimize their commitment to preserve some for efforts outside the couple. The functions of adaptations for dealing with sexual conflict over emotional expression remain largely hidden from view.

Resource Investment

In addition to emotional commitment, couples also skirmish over the investment of time, energy, and resources. Neglect and unreliability are manifestations of commitment conflicts. More than one-third of all dating and married women complain that their partners neglect them, reject them, and subject them to unreliable treatment. Among their common complaints are that men do not spend enough time with them, fail to call when they say they will, show up late, and cancel arrangements at the last minute. Roughly twice as many women as men complain about these events. Approximately 38 percent of dating women, for example—but only 12 percent of dating men—complain that their partners sometimes fail to call them when they say they will.[18]

Upset over neglect and unreliability reflects a conflict over investment of time and effort. It takes effort to be on time. Reliability requires relinquishing time and resources that could be channeled toward other goals. Neglect signals a low investment, indicating that the man lacks the depth of commitment necessary to perform acts that require even minimal cost for the woman's benefit.

Marriage does not extinguish conflict over investments. Indeed, as the marriage progresses from the newlywed year to the fourth year, women's complaints about neglect and unreliability increase. Roughly 41 percent of newlywed women and 45 percent of women married for four years express irritation that their partners do not spend enough time with them. The analogous figures for men are only 4 percent during the newlywed year and 12 percent during the fourth year of marriage.[19]

The flip side of the coin of neglect is dependency and possessiveness. Conflict develops when one mate absorbs so much energy that the partner's freedom is restricted. A common grievance of married men, far more than of married women, is that their spouse takes up too much of their time and energy. Thirty-six percent of married men, in contrast with only 7 percent of married women, express irritation that their spouse demands too much of their time. Twenty-nine percent of married men, but only 8 percent of married women, complain that their mates demand too much attention.[20]

These gender differences in demands on time and attention reflect a continuing conflict about investment. Women try to sequester their mate's investment. Some men resist monopolization, striving to channel a portion of their effort toward other adaptive problems such as raising their status or acquiring additional mates. More than three times as many men as women voice possessiveness complaints. For men, historically, there was a large and direct reproductive payoff to preserving some investment for acquiring status and additional mates. For women, the benefits were smaller, less direct, and often more costly because they risked the loss of the existing mate's investment of time and resources. Wives may be possessive and demanding because they do not want their husband's limited investment to be diverted away from them.

Another manifestation of investment conflict centers on grievances about a partner's selfishness. Among married couples, 38 percent of men and 39 percent of women complain that their partner acts selfishly. Similarly, 37 percent of married women and 31 percent of married men lament their partner's self-centeredness. The core of selfishness centers on allocating resources to oneself at the expense of others, such as a spouse or children. Complaints about self-centeredness rise dramatically during the course of marriage. During the first year of marriage, only 13 percent of women and 15 percent of men complain that their partner is self-centered. By the fourth year of marriage, the numbers more than double.[21]

To understand these dramatic changes, consider the critical signals of investment during the courting stage. Effective courting communicates a willingness to put a mate's interests before your own, or at least on par with your own. These cues are powerful tactics for attracting a mate and are displayed most floridly while courting. After the mateship is reasonably secure, the tactics signaling selflessness subside because their initial function of attracting a mate recedes. Each gender becomes freer to indulge the self and to channel less effort toward the partner. This is what long-term couples mean when they grumble that their partner takes them for granted.

The picture is not a very pretty one, but humans were not designed by natural selection to coexist in mating bliss. They were designed for individual survival and genetic reproduction. The psychological mechanisms fashioned by these ruthless evolutionary criteria are sometimes selfish.

Conflicts over investment often center on money. A study of American couples found that money is one of the most frequent sources of conflict. Seventy-two percent of married couples fight about money at least once a year, with 15 percent fighting more than once a month.[22] Interestingly, couples fight more about how the money they have is to be allocated than about how much money they have in their joint pool of resources.[23]

American men, far more often than women, complain that their spouse spends too much money on clothes. The percentage of men who express this grievance starts at 12 percent during the newlywed year and increases to 26 percent by the fourth year of marriage. In contrast, among women, only 5 percent during the newlywed year and 7 percent during the fifth year of marriage are bothered by their husband's spending on clothes. Both, however, complain equally that their spouse spends too much money in general. Nearly one-third of men and women by the fourth year of marriage complain about their spouse's overexpenditure of mutual resources.

More women than men complain that their spouse fails to channel the money they do earn to them, especially noting their failure to buy them gifts. By the fifth year of marriage, roughly one-third of married women voice this complaint; in contrast, only 10 percent of husbands express similar complaints.[24] Conflict between the sexes corresponds remarkably well with the initial gender-linked preferences in a mate. Women select mates in part for their economic resources and, once married, complain more than men that those resources are not forthcoming or abundant enough.

Deception

Conflicts between the sexes over sexual access, emotional commitment, and investment of resources reach more dramatic proportions when we add deception to the mix. Deception flourishes in the plant and animal world. Some orchids, for example, have brilliantly colored petals and centers that mimic the colors, shapes, and scents of female wasps of the species *Scolia ciliata*.[25] Male wasps, powerfully attracted by these scents and colors, land on the orchids the way they would land on a female's back. This event is followed by a pseudo-copulation, in which the male moves rapidly over the rigid hairs of the upper surface of the flower, which mimic the hairs on a female wasp's abdomen. He probes the orchid in an apparent search for complementary female genital structures, incidentally picking up the plant's pollen. Failing to find the exact structures needed for ejaculation, however, the male moves on to another pseudo-female. Orchids deceive the male wasp for the function of cross-pollination.

Humans also engage in sexual deception. A colleague used to go to upscale hotel bars and pick up men who would take her out to dinner. During dinner, she was friendly, flirtatious, sexy, and engaging. Toward the end of dinner, she would excuse herself to go to the women's room, then slip out the back door and disappear into the night. Sometimes she did this alone, sometimes with a girlfriend. Her targets were often businessmen from out of town, whom she would be unlikely to encounter again. Although she spoke no lies, she was a sexual deceiver. She used sexual cues to elicit resources and then left sneakily without following through with sex. One can't feel too sorry for the guys, though, since many were married and pursuing their own forms of deception.

Although this tactic may be unusual, its underlying theme occurs repeatedly in ordinary behavior in various guises. Women are apparently aware of the sexual effects they have on men. When 104 college women were asked how often they flirted with a man to get something they wanted, such as a favor or special treatment, knowing that they did not want to have sex with him, they gave this action on average a frequency of 3 on a 4-point scale, where 3 signified "sometimes" and 4 signified "often." The comparable figure for men was 2. Women gave similar responses to questions about using sexual hints to gain favors and attention, yet admitted that they had no intention of having sex with the targets of these hints.[26] Some women acknowledge being sexual deceivers as one tactic in their strategic arsenal.

Although women are more likely to be sexual deceivers, men are more likely to be commitment deceivers. Consider what a thirty-three-year-old man had to say about the commitment implied by declarations of love:

> You would think saying "I love you" to a woman to thrill and entice her isn't necessary anymore. But that's not so. These three words have a toniclike effect. I blurt out a declaration of love whenever I'm in the heat of passion. I'm not always believed, but it adds to the occasion for both of us. It's not exactly a deception on my part, I have to feel *something* for her. And, what the hell, it usually seems like the right thing to say at the time.[27]

When my lab asked 112 college men whether they had ever exaggerated the depth of their feelings for a woman in order to have sex with her, 71 percent admitted to having done so, compared with only 39 percent of the women who were asked a parallel question. When the women were asked whether a man had ever deceived them by his exaggeration of the depth of his feelings in order to have sex with her, 97 percent admitted that they had experienced this tactic at the hands of men; in contrast, only

59 percent of the men had experienced this tactic at the hands of women.[28]

Among married couples, deception continues in the form of sexual infidelity. The motivations for male infidelity are clear, since ancestral men who had extramarital affairs might sire additional children and thereby gain a reproductive advantage over their more loyal rivals. Women get extremely upset by male infidelity because it signals that the man is diverting resources to other women and might even defect from their relationship. Women stand to lose the entire investment secured through the marriage, and replacing a husband is not always easy, especially if a woman has children. Consequently, evolutionists have predicted that women will be far more upset by an affair that contains emotional involvement than about one that does not, because emotional involvement typically signals outright defection rather than the less costly siphoning off of a fraction of resources. Women turn out to be more forgiving and less upset if no emotional involvement accompanies their husband's fling.[29] Men seem to know this. When caught having an affair, men often plead that the other woman "means nothing."

In the human mating dance, the costs of being deceived about a potential mate's resources and commitment are carried more heavily by women. An ancestral man who made a poor choice in sex partners risked losing only a small portion of time, energy, and resources, although he may also have evoked the rage of a jealous boyfriend or protective father. An ancestral woman who made a poor choice of a casual mate, allowing herself to be deceived about the man's long-term intentions, risked enduring pregnancy, childbirth, and child care unaided and being less able to attract an alternative mate, since existing children are seen as costs by potential mates on the mating market.

Because the deceived can suffer large losses, selection favored the evolution of psychological vigilance to detect cues to deception and to prevent its occurrence. Humans today are experiencing one more cycle in the endless spiral of an evolutionary arms race between deception by one gender and detection by the other. As the deceptive tactics get more subtle, the ability to detect deception becomes more sensitive.

Women guard against deception. When they are seeking a committed relationship, an important first-line defense is imposing courtship costs by requiring extended time, energy, and costly signals before consenting to sex. More time buys more assessment. It allows a woman greater opportunity to evaluate a man, to assess how committed he is to her, and to detect whether he is burdened by prior commitments to other women and children. Men who seek to deceive women about their ultimate intentions typically tire of extended courtship. They go elsewhere for sex partners who are more readily available.

Although women have developed strategies for penetrating men's deception, men clearly cannot ignore deception at the hands of women. This is especially true when men seek spouses. Accurate assessments of women's reproductive value, resources, alliances, and fidelity become paramount. This is vividly illustrated in a scene from Tennessee Williams's play *A Streetcar Named Desire*. Mitch is on a date with Blanche DuBois, a former high school teacher to whom he is engaged to be married but who has deceived him about her sexual past with other men, including a sexual relationship with a student that caused her expulsion from the school. A friend has just alerted Mitch to Blanche's past, so he aggressively tells her that he has always seen her only at night under a dim light, never in a well-lit room. He turns on a bright light, from which Blanche recoils, but he sees that she is older than she had led him to believe. He confronts her with what he has heard about her flamboyant sexual past. She plaintively asks Mitch whether he will still marry her. He says, "No, I don't think I'll marry you now," as he nevertheless approaches her menacingly for sex.[30]

Given the importance that men attach to looks and sexual exclusivity in a potential mate, they are especially sensitive to deception about a woman's age and sexual history. Men are keenly attuned to information about women's sexual reputations. Vigilance guards them against deception about two of the most reproductively important considerations for a man seeking a long-term mate—her reproductive value and the likelihood that her value will be channeled exclusively to him.

Unfortunately, conflict between the sexes does not end with battles about sexual access, commitment, or deception. Sometimes it takes more violent forms.

Intimate Partner Violence

Violence takes several forms. One is psychological abuse, which causes a wife to feel less valuable in the relationship, to lower her sense of desirability and make her feel lucky to have secured the husband, and to diminish her perceived prospects on the mating market if she is contemplating abandoning the mateship.[31]

Two functional tactics of psychological abuse are condescension and contempt. Condescension manifests through two methods. In one, a man places more value on his opinions simply because he is a man. In another, a man treats his mate as if she were stupid or inferior. Newlywed men condescend roughly twice as often as their wives do. These acts have the effect of lowering the wife's sense of her own desirability.[32] Condescension, one form of which is "mansplaining," may function to increase the victim's investment and commitment to the relationship and to bend the victim's energies toward the goals of the abuser.[33] Victims often feel that, because their mating alternatives are not rosy, they must strive valiantly to placate the current mate. They also appease the partner to avoid incurring his further wrath.

Psychological abuse sometimes escalates from verbal abuse to physical violence. Men's motives for battering women center heavily on coercive control. One researcher attended the trials of 100 Canadian couples engaged in litigation over the husband's violence toward the wife. The researcher concluded that at the core of nearly all the cases was the husband's frustration about his inability to control his wife, whom he frequently accused of being a whore or of having sex with other men.[34] A study of thirty-one battered American women found that jealousy was the main topic of spousal arguments. Jealousy led to physical abuse in 52 percent of the cases, with 94 percent listing jealousy as a frequent cause of the history of battering in the relationship.[35] In yet another study, for 95 percent of sixty battered wives who had sought the assistance of a clinic in North Carolina, "morbid jealousy," such as jealousy if the wife left the house for any reason or if she maintained friendships with other men or women, had evoked violent reactions from their husbands.[36] The coercive constraint of women, particularly in sexual matters, underlies most cases of physical abuse.

Spouse abuse is obviously a dangerous game to play. The abuser may be seeking increased commitment and investment, but the tactic may backfire and produce a desire to leave instead. Alternatively, this form of abuse may represent a last-ditch attempt to hold on to a mate who is on the brink of leaving. In this sense, the abuser treads on thin ice. He risks triggering the decision that the relationship is too costly to endure. Perhaps this is why abusers are often profusely apologetic after the abuse, crying, pleading, and promising that they will never do it again.[37]

Partner abuse is not a Western invention; it occurs cross-culturally. Among the Yanomamö, for example, husbands regularly strike their wives with sticks for offenses as slight as serving tea too slowly.[38] Interestingly, Yanomamö wives often regard physical abuse as a sign of the depth of their husband's love for them—an interpretation probably not shared by their modern American counterparts. Whatever the interpretation, these beatings have the effect of subordinating Yanomamö women to their husbands.

Men sometimes abuse their partner by insulting her physical appearance. Although only 5 percent of newlywed men do so, the percentage triples by the fourth year of marriage. In marked contrast, only 1 percent of newlywed women insult their husband's appearance, and only 5 percent of longer-married women do so. Given that a woman's physical appearance is typically a key component of her mate value, women find these derogations especially distressing. Men may insult their appearance to lower women's perception of their own desirability, thereby securing a more favorable power balance within the relationship.

As with other destructive tendencies, the fact that abuse has an adaptive logic behind it does not mean that people should accept it, desire it, or be lax about curtailing it. On the contrary, greater understanding of the logic behind abusive tactics and the contexts in which they occur should lead to more effective means of curtailing them. Men who have certain personality dispositions, such as being emotionally unstable, are four times as likely to abuse their wives as emotionally stable men.[39] Discrepancies in the desirability of the two partners, a long distance between the couple's residence and that of the woman's kin, and the absence of legal penalties for abuse are contexts that put women at increased risk.

Sexual Harassment

Although abuse and other forms of conflict are common within couples, sexual conflict is also common outside of mating relationships. For instance, disagreements over sexual access sometimes occur in the workplace, where people often seek casual and romantic mates. The search may cross a line and become sexual harassment, which can be defined as "unwanted and unsolicited sexual attention from other individuals in the workplace."[40] It includes mild forms such as unwanted staring at a woman's breasts and body, what one woman described as the "up-down" as a man scans her physique from head to toe. It includes sexual comments, such as "nice ass" or "beautiful body." And it includes physical violations, such as the touching of breasts, buttocks, or thighs. Sexual harassment clearly produces conflict between the sexes.

Evolutionary psychology offers insight into the psychology that motivates sexual harassment and the circumstances that trigger it. Sexual harassment is typically motivated by the desire for short-term sexual access, although it is sometimes motivated by power or by a search for a lasting romantic relationship. Evolved sexual strategies shed light on sexual harassment through the profiles of typical victims, including such features as their age, marital status, and physical attractiveness; their reactions to unwanted sexual advances; and the conditions under which they were harassed.

Victims of sexual harassment are not random. In one study of complaints filed with the Illinois Department of Human Rights over a two-year period, seventy-six complaints were filed by women and only five by men.[41] Another study of 10,644 federal government employees found that 42 percent of the women, but only 15 percent of the men, had experienced sexual harassment at some point in their career.[42] Among complaints filed in Canada under human rights legislation, ninety-three cases were filed by women and only two by men. In both cases filed by men, the harassers were men rather than women.[43] Women are generally the victims and men the perpetrators. Nonetheless, because women experience greater distress than do men in response to acts of sexual aggressiveness, women might be more likely to file official complaints than men when harassed.

The victims of sexual harassment are disproportionately young, physically attractive, single women. Women over forty-five are less likely to be victims.[44] One study found that women between the ages of twenty and thirty-five filed 72 percent of the complaints of harassment, whereas they represented only 43 percent of the workforce at the time. Women over forty-five, who represented 28 percent of the workforce, filed only 5 percent of the complaints.[45] The victims of sexual harassment are women whose relative youth evokes male sexual interest in general.

Single and divorced women are subjected to more sexual harassment than married women. In one study, single women represented only 25 percent of the workforce but filed 43 percent of complaints; married women, comprising 55 percent of the workforce, filed only 31 percent of the complaints.[46] There may be several reasons for these differences. Husbands sometimes function as "bodyguards," deterring would-be harassers. Moreover, men perceive single women to be more receptive to sexual advances or more easily sexually exploitable.

Reactions to sexual harassment also follow evolutionary psychological logic. When men and women were asked how they would feel if a coworker of the opposite sex asked them to have sex, 63 percent of the women said that they would be insulted, while only 17 percent said that they would feel flattered.[47] Men's reactions were just the opposite—only 15 percent would be insulted, and 67 percent would feel flattered. These reactions fit with the evolutionary psychology of human mating—men generally have more positive emotional reactions to the prospect of casual sex. Women react more negatively to being treated as mere sex objects.

The degree of anguish women experience from unwanted sexual advances, however, depends in part on the status of the harasser. My lab asked 109 college women how upset they would feel if a man they did not know, whose occupational status varied from low to high, persisted in asking them out on a date despite repeated refusals, a relatively modest form of harassment. On a 7-point scale, women said that they would be most upset by advances from construction workers (4.04), garbage collectors (4.32), cleaning men (4.19), and gas station attendants (4.13), and least upset by persistent advances from premedical students (2.65), graduate students (2.80), and successful rock stars (2.71).[48] Women's distress in response to the same acts of harassment varies depending on men's status.

Women's reactions to sexual harassment also depend heavily on whether the motivation of the harasser is perceived to be sexual or romantic. Sexual bribery, attaching job promotions to sex, and other cues that the person is interested only in casual sex are more likely to be labeled as harassment than are signals of potential interest that may transcend the purely sexual, such as nonsexual touching, complimentary looks, or flirting.[49] When 110 college women used a 7-point scale to rate how sexually harassing a series of acts by their coworkers would be, acts such as putting his hand on a woman's genital area (6.81) or trying to corner a woman when no one else was around (6.03) were seen as extremely harassing. In contrast, acts such as telling a woman that he sincerely liked her and would like to have coffee with her after work was judged to be only 1.50 (1.00 signifying no harassment at all).[50] Clearly, short-term sexual and coercive intentions are more harassing than sincere romantic intentions.

These findings about the profiles of sexual harassment victims, the sex differences in emotional reactions, and the importance of the status of the harasser all follow from the evolutionary psychology of human mating strategies. Men have evolved lower thresholds for seeking casual sex, and their sexual overperception bias leads them to infer sexual interest where none exists. These sexual adaptations become activated in the workplace perhaps no less than in any other social context.

Sexual Assault

Rape may be defined as the use of force, or the threat to use force, to obtain sex. Estimates of the number of women who have been raped vary, depending on how inclusive a definition the researcher uses. Some researchers use broad definitions that include instances in which a woman did not perceive that she was raped at the time but admitted later that she did not really want to have intercourse or regretted doing so. Other researchers use stricter definitions that delimit rape to clear cases of forced intercourse against the woman's will. One large-scale study of 2,016 university women, for example, found that 6 percent had been raped.[51] Another study found, however, that almost 15 percent of 380 college women had been involved in sexual intercourse against their will.[52] Given the large social stigma attached to victims and the well-known underreporting of rape, these figures probably underestimate the actual numbers of women who have been raped.

The issue of rape has a bearing on human mating strategies, in part because many rapes occur within the context of mating relationships. Dating is a common context for rape. One study found that almost 15 percent of college women had experienced unwanted sexual intercourse in a dating encounter.[53] Another study found that, for 63 percent of 347 women, all instances of sexual victimization were perpetrated by dates, lovers, husbands, or de facto partners.[54] The most extensive study of rape in marriage found that of nearly 1,000 married women, 14 percent had been raped by their husband.[55] Rape in the modern world often does not fit the stereotype of a menacing stranger jumping out of a dark alley.

Men are almost invariably the perpetrators of rape, and most victims are women, although victims also include children and men. It is a matter of controversy within the scientific community whether rape represents an evolved sexual strategy of men or is better understood as a horrifying side effect of men's general sexual strategy of seeking low-cost casual sex.[56] Among scorpionflies, however, the evidence for rape as an evolved strategy is strong. The males have a special anatomical clamp that functions solely in the context of raping a female and not in consensual mating, for which a male offers a nuptial gift.[57] Experiments that seal the clamp with wax prevent the male from achieving a forced copulation. Scorpionflies have rape adaptations, but what about humans?

Have Men Evolved Adaptations to Rape?

Controversy about the possibility that men have evolved adaptations to rape erupted in the year 2000 when the biologist Randy Thornhill and the anthropologist Craig Palmer published a book called A Natural History of Rape: Biological Bases of Sexual Coercion.[58] Although evolutionary theories of human rape had been published for two decades preceding its publication, their book proved to be a flash point. The authors outline two competing theories of rape, one endorsed by each author. Thornhill proposes the theory that men have *evolved rape adaptations*—specialized psychological mechanisms for forcing sex on unwilling women as a reproductive strategy. Palmer proposes instead that *rape is a by-product* of other evolved mechanisms, such as the male desire for sexual variety, a desire for low-cost consensual sex, a psychological sensitivity to sexual opportunities, and the general capacity of men to use physical aggression to achieve a wide variety of goals.

The rape-as-adaptation theory proposes six specialized adaptations that may have evolved in the male mind:

- Assessment of the vulnerability of potential rape victims (for example, in the context of warfare or a non-warfare

situation in which a woman lacks the protection of a
husband or kin)
- A context-sensitive switch that motivates rape by men
  who lack sexual access to consenting partners (such as
  low-status males who cannot obtain mates through regular channels of courtship)
- A preference for maximally fertile rape victims
- An increase in sperm counts of rape ejaculates compared with those occurring in consensual sex
- Male sexual arousal specifically to the use of force or to
  signs of female resistance to consensual sex
- Context-specific marital rape when sperm competition
  might exist, such as when there is evidence or suspicion
  of female infidelity

Evidence supporting these hypothesized adaptations is either
absent or ambiguous. Rape is common in war, clearly a context
where women are often vulnerable, but so is theft, looting, and
property damage. Are there specialized adaptations for all these
behaviors, or are they instead either by-products of other psychological mechanisms or merely the output of more general
cost-benefit evaluation mechanisms? Decisive studies have not
yet been conducted.

Although there is no conclusive evidence supporting the
rape-as-adaptation theory, psychological and physiological experiments have revealed some disturbing findings. Laboratory studies
that expose men to audio and visual depictions of rape versus mutually consenting sexual encounters find that men display sexual
arousal, assessed both by self-report and by penile tumescence, to
both consenting and nonconsenting situations. Men apparently
are sexually aroused when exposed to sexual scenes, whether or
not consent is involved. Nonetheless, other conditions, such as
the presence of violence, evidence that the victim experiences

pain, and a disgust reaction from the victim, inhibit the sexual arousal of most men.[59]

These findings cannot differentiate between the two explanatory alternatives: that men have only a general tendency to be sexually aroused in response to witnessing sexual encounters and hence have no distinct adaptations to forced sex, or that men have evolved a distinct rape psychology. Consider a food analogy. Humans, like dogs, salivate when they smell appetizing food, especially if they have not eaten for a while. Suppose that a scientist hypothesizes that humans have a specific adaptation to take food forcibly from others. The scientist then conducts studies in which people are deprived of food for twenty-four hours and thereafter exposed visually to one of two scenes: appetizing food that is given willingly by one person to another person, or equally appetizing food that is forcibly taken from one person by another.[60] If this hypothetical experiment finds that people salivate an equal volume to both food scenes, we cannot conclude that people have a distinct food adaptation to "take food forcibly." All we can conclude is that, when hungry, people seem to salivate when exposed to scenes of food, regardless of the circumstances surrounding the method of procurement. This hypothetical example is analogous to the findings that indicate sexual arousal in men in response to sexual scenes, regardless of whether those scenes depict mutually consenting sex or forced sex. The data do not constitute evidence that rape is a distinct evolved strategy of men.

Another possible piece of evidence for rape adaptation theory is that convicted rapists come disproportionately from lower socioeconomic groups, supporting the mate deprivation hypothesis.[61] Some interviews with rapists support this view. One serial rapist, for example, reported that "I felt that my social station would make her reject me. And I didn't feel that I would be able to make this person. I didn't know how to go about meeting her. . . . I took advantage of her fright and raped her."[62] For men who lack the status, money, or other resources to attract women, coercion may represent a desperate alternative. Men scorned by women because they lack the qualities for attracting desirable mates may develop hostility toward women, an attitude that short-circuits the normal empathic response and so promotes coercive sexual behavior.

But this finding could also be caused by lower rates of reporting when rape is committed by men from higher social groups, or from the greater ability of privileged men to evade arrest and conviction because they can afford to hire expensive lawyers. Or perhaps women raped by high-status men are less likely to press charges, given the lower odds of being believed and obtaining justice.

There is also direct evidence *against* the mate deprivation hypothesis of rape. In a study of 156 heterosexual men, average age of twenty, the evolutionary psychologist Martin Lalumiere and his colleagues measured the use of sexual coercion with items such as: "Have you ever had sexual intercourse with a woman even though she didn't really want to because you used some degree of physical force?"[63] Separately, they measured mating success. Men who scored high on mating success *also* scored high on sexual aggression. Men who had had a lot of sexual partners were *more* likely to report using force. Furthermore, men who evaluated their future earning potential as high reported using more, not less, physical coercion in their mating tactics. Although additional studies are needed, we can tentatively conclude that a simple version of the mate deprivation theory of rape is unlikely to be correct.

These results, however, do not rule out a more complex hypothesis—perhaps men have evolved two kinds of context-specific rape adaptations, one contingent on when they experience mating failure and one when the costs are so low that they can get away with it, as might occur among the upper socioeconomic stratum of society.[64] There is no current evidence for or against this modified hypothesis.

Rape victims tend to be disproportionately concentrated among young, reproductive-age women. Despite the fact that some women of all ages are raped, the victims of rape are heavily concentrated among young women. In one study of 10,315 rape victims, women between the ages of sixteen and thirty-five were far more likely to be raped than women in any other age category.[65] Eighty-five percent of all rape victims are less than thirty-six years old. By way of comparison, victims of other crimes, such as aggravated assault and murder, show a markedly different age distribution. Women between forty and forty-nine, for example, are just as likely to suffer an aggravated assault as women between twenty and twenty-nine, but the older women are far less likely to be raped. Indeed, the age distribution of rape victims corresponds quite closely to the age distribution of women's reproductive value, in marked contrast to the age distribution of victims of other violent crimes. This evidence strongly suggests that rape is not independent of men's broader evolved sexual psychology.

That rapists disproportionately victimize young fertile women, however, is not decisive evidence for or against the competing theories of rape. This finding can be attributed to men's evolved attraction to cues to fertile women in regular mating contexts rather than a rape-specific adaptation. That is, although there is abundant evidence that men are attracted to young fertile women across mating contexts, there is no evidence that this attraction is a rape-specific adaptation.

One source of evidence that many scientists believe to be relevant to theories of rape is the pregnancy rate that follows from rape. If rape evolved as a reproductive strategy, it must historically have resulted in reproduction some of the time. Modern rape-pregnancy rates, of course, are not necessarily relevant to whether rape resulted in pregnancy in the past; modern routine contraceptives may reduce current rape-pregnancy rates below those that occurred in ancestral times. Thus, it is all the more startling that one study discovered that pregnancy rates resulting from *penile-vaginal rape among reproductive-age women* are extraordinarily high—6.42 percent—compared to a consensual per-incident rate of only 3.1 percent.[66] This finding can be partially explained by selection bias in the victims whom rapists target—young fertile women. Nonetheless, even controlling for age, the study's authors find a rape-pregnancy rate that is roughly 2 percent higher than the consensual-sex pregnancy rate. This counterintuitive finding, *if it turns out to be replicable,* cries out for some kind of explanation.

Jonathan and Tiffani Gottschall offer a hypothesis anchored in the premise that men who court women using normal mating strategies are "at the mercy of discriminating females," whereas rapists are not. Rapists, although constrained by opportunity and the defense mechanisms of women, nonetheless can and do choose victims who would otherwise refuse to mate with them. Rapists might choose women who, in addition to being young, are especially physically attractive. Since attractive women are more fertile on average (see Chapter 3), this may partially explain the unusually high rape-pregnancy rate.

The rape-pregnancy findings, however, do not directly support the rape-as-adaptation hypothesis. We already know that men are attracted to features that correlate with fertility, such as cues to youth and health, in consensual mating contexts, and so no specialized rape adaptation is required to explain these results. The rape-pregnancy findings do, however, contradict the so-called argument from inconceivable conception, according to which some opponents of the rape-as-adaptation theory claim that rape cannot possibly have evolved because it so rarely leads to conception.[67]

Individual men differ in their proclivity toward rape. In one study, men were asked to imagine that they had the possibility of forcing sex on someone else against her will with no chance of getting caught, no chance that anyone would find out, no risk of disease, and no possibility of damage to their reputation. Thirty-five percent indicated that there was some likelihood they would force sex on the woman under these conditions, although in most cases the likelihood was slight.[68] In another study that used a similar method, 27 percent of the men indicated that there was some likelihood they would force sex on a woman if there was no chance of getting caught.[69] Although these percentages are alarmingly high, if taken at face value they also indicate that most men are not potential rapists.

Men who do use coercion to get sex exhibit a distinct set of characteristics. They tend to be hostile toward women, to endorse the myth that women secretly want to be raped, and to show a personality profile marked by impulsiveness, hostility, low agreeableness, low empathy, and hypermasculinity, combined with a high degree of sexual promiscuity.[70]

Marital rapes are more likely when the husband is concerned about a potential sexual infidelity, as well as during or immediately following a breakup.[71] This finding suggests the possibility of rape as a sperm competition adaptation. Nonetheless, the direction of causality is unclear—perhaps women are more likely to break up with partners who tend to force them into unwanted sex. In short, a conclusion reached by Donald Symons in 1979 appears to be apt today: "I do not believe that available data are even close to sufficient to warrant the conclusion that rape itself is a facultative adaptation in the human male."[72]

I speculate that scientific progress will advance when theorists distinguish different types of rape, rather than viewing sexual assault as a singular crime. Consider date rape, stranger rape, warfare rape, rape by husbands, homosexual rape, and rape of stepdaughters by stepfathers. The causes of one type of rape may differ substantially from the causes of others. Date rape, for example, may be partly a by-product of the modern conditions of living, where young women live in social circumstances devoid of the close protection of extended kin—a known deterrent to violence against women. Serial stranger rapists often manage to avoid detection owing to the unusual modern conditions of high geographic mobility and anonymous urban living. The limited geographical mobility and small-group living of our ancestors would have rendered certain kinds of stranger rape virtually impossible. Rape in the context of warfare, in contrast, appears to have a cross-cultural prevalence and historical depth that may have favored selection for rape. Some kinds of rape may be caused by pathology or dysfunction of evolved mechanisms; others may be by-products; still others may be caused by specific rape adaptations. Lumping all instances of forced sex under a single label "rape" may impede progress in discovering the unique underlying causal conditions that lead to each distinct type of crime.

Do Women Have Evolved
Sexual Assault Defenses?

The feminist author Susan Griffin has written: "I have never been free of the fear of rape. From a very early age, I, like most women, have thought of rape as part of my natural environment— something to be feared and prayed against like fire or lightning. I never asked why men raped; I simply thought it one of the many mysteries of human nature."[73]

Although the controversy over the scientific study of rape has focused primarily on what motivates men to force sex on women, almost lost in the furor is attention to the psychology of rape victims. There is one point about victim psychology, however, on which all sides of the debate agree: *rape is an abhorrent atrocity that typically inflicts heavy costs on victims.* We need no formal theory to arrive at this insight. Nonetheless, it is important to determine *why* rape is experienced as extraordinarily traumatic.

From an evolutionary perspective, the costs of rape begin with the fact that it circumvents female choice, a core component of women's sexual strategy. A raped woman risks untimely pregnancy with a man she has not chosen—a man who imposes himself against her will, a man who is unlikely to invest in her children, and a man who may have genes inferior to those she would otherwise have chosen. A raped woman risks being blamed, punished, or abandoned by her regular mate, who may suspect that her experience was consensual or that she somehow brought it on herself. The costs of being raped are dramatically illustrated in a case in Pakistan:

> Zafran Bibi, a 26-year-old devout Muslim residing in Pakistan, was sentenced to death by stoning. Her crime was adultery, punishable by death according to Islamic law. The evidence: A child born more than a year after her husband had abandoned her, but had not yet divorced her. This was no ordinary adultery. Zafran Bibi had been raped by her brother-in-law, she testified. That did not matter. The birth of the illegitimate child proved adultery, according to the judge. Her accusation that her brother-in-law had raped her was tantamount to a criminal confession.[74]

Raped women suffer psychologically. They experience fear, humiliation, embarrassment, anxiety, depression, rage, and fury. They feel guilty, used, violated, and polluted. Women view forced sex as more upsetting to them than any of at least 147 other things that a man can do to hurt a woman, more upsetting even than savage nonsexual beatings at the hands of a man.[75] Raped women also suffer in the aftermath. Some victims fear leaving their houses, avoid contact with men, isolate themselves socially, and live in a psychological prison with no apparent reprieve.

On top of the psychological torment, raped women suffer socially. As the case of Zafran Bibi illustrates, victims are sometimes held responsible for the crime perpetrated on them. They experience damage to their reputations. They suffer a loss in perceived desirability on the mating market. Their kin may reject or ostracize them for bringing shame on their family. They sometimes become socially shunned. Whatever the causes of rape, no one except the clueless and callused doubts the appalling damage it inflicts on the victim.

Given these often catastrophic costs, *if* rape has occurred throughout human history, it would defy evolutionary logic if selection had not fashioned defenses in women to prevent its occurrence. This is a separate issue from that of whether men have evolved adaptations to rape. Women could have evolved anti-rape adaptations, in principle, even if rape has been entirely a by-product of non-rape mechanisms. We can never determine with absolute certainty whether rape was frequent enough historically to have forged a female anti-rape psychology. But we can assemble available historical and cross-cultural evidence to make an educated guess. Written history dating back to the Bible brims with episodes of rape, and even specifications by religious leaders about the conditions under which men can sexually assault women. For example, the Sages of the Talmud, codified by Maimonides, provide this injunction:

A soldier in the invading army may, if overpowered by passion, cohabit with a captive woman . . . [but] he is forbidden to cohabit a second time before he marries her. . . . Coition with her is permitted only at the time when she is taken captive . . .

he must not force her in the open field of battle . . . that is, he
shall take her to a private place and cohabit with her.[76]

Although no systematic studies have been conducted on the
occurrence and frequency of rape among traditional societies
across cultures, an informal review of published ethnographies
reveals that rape is reported in many of them—from the Amazonian jungle of Brazil to the more peaceful !Kung San of Botswana.
The Semai of central Malaysia were frequently victimized by Ma-
lay raiders, who would ambush them, kill the men, and take the
women by force.[77] The Amazonian peoples studied by Thomas
Gregor have special words for both rape (*antapai*) and gang rape
(*aintyawakakinapai*).[78] Rapes in war occurred as far back as there
are written records, as amply documented by Susan Brownmiller
in her classic treatise *Against Our Will*.[79] Genghis Khan, more
than 800 years ago, talked with relish about the gratification received through rape: "The greatest pleasure in life is to vanquish
your enemies and chase them before you, to rob them of their
wealth and see those dear to them bathed in tears, to ride their
horses and clasp to your bosom their wives and daughters."[80]
The evolutionary anthropologist Barbara Smuts summarizes the
cross-cultural evidence in this way: "Although the prevalence of
male violence against women varies from place to place, cross cultural surveys indicate that societies in which men rarely attack or
rape women are the exception, not the norm."[81]
    A number of evolutionary scientists have been at the forefront
in articulating potential evolved defenses against rape. Hypothesized anti-rape adaptations include:

- Psychological pain upon rape that motivates avoiding
  rape in the future
- Formation of alliances with males as "special friends"
  for protection

- Formation of female-female coalitions for protection
- Specialized fears that motivate women to avoid situations in which they might be in danger of rape
- The shunning of risky activities during ovulation to decrease the odds of sexual assault when conception is most likely

The first clue to the possibility that women have evolved adaptations to prevent being raped comes from two studies that analyzed the distribution of rapes across the female menstrual cycle. In one study of 785 rape victims, proportionately fewer women were raped during midcycle, defined as days 10 to 22 (an unfortunately wide and hence imprecise interval).[82] Another study found that ovulating women were less often victims of sexual assault.[83] To explore these patterns, Tara Chavanne and Gordon Gallup studied risk-taking among 300 undergraduate women.[84] Women indicated whether they had engaged in each of eighteen activities that varied in their risk of making someone vulnerable to sexual assault. Going to church and watching television were examples of low-risk activities. Going to a bar and walking in a dimly lit area were examples of high-risk activities.

For women taking birth control pills, Chavanne and Gallup find no effect of menstrual cycle on risk-taking.[85] Among women not taking the pill, however, ovulating women showed a decrease in risk-taking activities. Contending that risk avoidance is a candidate for an anti-rape adaptation, these authors successfully rule out several alternative explanations for the reduction in risk taking. For example, this reduction in risk taking is not a reflection of diminished sexual receptivity at ovulation; in fact, women usually peak in sexual motivation and receptivity at midcycle when they are with a consensual partner. Midcycle risk avoidance also cannot be attributed to a decrease in women's general activity level, since pedometer-recorded activity level in women tends to increase during ovulation.[86] In short, ovulating women appear to avoid behaviors that put them at increased risk of rape, suggesting the possibility of *specialized risk avoidance* as an anti-rape adaptation.

Many women *routinely* engage in risk-avoidance maneuvers to avoid putting themselves in harm's way.[87] In one study of urban women, 41 percent reported "isolation tactics," such as not going out on the street at night, and 71 percent reported using "street-savvy tactics," such as wearing shoes that would enable them to run away should they be attacked. In a study in Seattle, 67 percent of women said that they avoided certain dangerous locations of the city, 42 percent reported not going out unaccompanied, and 27 percent sometimes refused to answer their door. A study of Greek women reported that 71 percent avoided venturing out alone at night and 78 percent shunned dangerous locations within the city. Women also show wariness around men who talk about sex a lot, men who are sexually aggressive, and men who have a reputation for sleeping with a lot of women. Women report choosing public places for dates with men they do not know well. They intentionally avoid giving mixed sexual signals to certain men. They sometimes carry pepper spray, mace, whistles, or weapons. And they sometimes limit their drinking around men they do not know well.[88]

These risk avoidance strategies may be learned prudence measures, much like installing a burglar alarm after reading about a rash of burglaries in the neighborhood. Alternatively, risk avoidance may be motivated, in part, by a *specialized fear of rape*—a second potential anti-rape adaptation that induces women to avoid contexts conducive to sexual assault. Evidence for this specialized fear comes from a strong positive association between women's reports of rape-fear and their reports of how many different behavioral precautions they take to avoid rape.[89] Women who are fearful of rape, more than women who are less fearful, avoid being alone with men they do not know well, decline rides from men, leave when a man comes on too strong sexually, avoid outdoor activities when alone, and exercise caution in their drinking. One New Zealand study found that young women experience more fear of sexual assault than older women; older women's fears were more likely to center on being robbed or burgled than on being raped.[90] Women residing in neighborhoods with a high incidence of rape report more fear than those living in safer neighborhoods. These studies, of course, cannot determine whether women have evolved a specialized fear of rape contingent on their age and vulnerability, or whether these fears are expressions of more general mechanisms such as a rational appraisal of danger combined with fear mechanisms possessed by all people.

The psychologists Susan Hickman and Charlene Muehlenhard found that women were more fearful of being raped by strangers than by acquaintances. This difference occurred despite the fact that stranger rape is rare, accounting for only 10 to 20 percent of all rapes, compared with acquaintance rape, which is far more common, roughly 80 to 90 percent.[91] Hickman and Muehlenhard conclude that women's fears do not match the realities of rape. An alternative interpretation is that women's apprehensions are actually effective: stranger fear motivates precautionary behaviors, lowering the real incidence of stranger rape below what it would have been without these functional fears. According to this view, women's stranger fears function to prevent rape. Alternatively, women's fear of stranger rape could have evolved in ancestral environments in warfare contexts in which rapists were, in fact, mostly strangers—very much unlike the modern environment. These hypotheses could both be partially true, and both remain to be empirically tested.

Sarah Mesnick and Margo Wilson have explored a third potential anti-rape adaptation, which they call the bodyguard hypothesis. According to this hypothesis, women form heterosexual pair-bonds with men in part to reduce their risk of sexual aggression from other men.[92] According to the bodyguard hypothesis, women should be especially attracted to physically large and socially dominant men in contexts in which they are at risk of sexual aggression. To test the bodyguard hypothesis, Wilson and Mesnick studied 12,252 women, each interviewed over the phone by trained female interviewers. Questions about sexual assault began with: "Has a male stranger ever forced you or attempted to force you into any sexual activity by threatening you, holding you down or hurting you in some way?" Subsequent questions dealt with unwanted sexual touching: "[Apart from this incident you have just told me about], has a male stranger ever touched you against your will in any sexual way, such as unwanted touching, grabbing, kissing, or fondling?"[93] The statistical analyses focused on sexual victimizations that had occurred within the twelve months prior to the interview and excluded sexual assaults by husbands or boyfriends.

A total of 410 unmarried and 258 married women reported experiencing one or more of these sexual violations. Marital status proved to have a dramatic effect on sexual victimization. Among women in the youngest age bracket of eighteen to twenty-four, eighteen out of one hundred unmarried women reported sexual victimization by a stranger, whereas only seven out of every one hundred married women reported sexual victimization. Messick and Wilson conclude that their results support the bodyguard hypothesis, although they acknowledge that they have not identified the causal mechanism by which married women are less likely to be raped than comparably aged single women. The lower rape rates among married than single women might reflect lifestyle differences—single women might spend more time in public places, such as bars and parties where alcohol is consumed, rather than at home, making them more vulnerable to predatory rapists. It might reflect individual differences in mating strategies, whereby single women might be more likely to pursue short-term matings that place them in contexts where they are exposed to greater danger of sexual coercion. Or it might reflect the deterrent effects of husbands on potential rapists, as the bodyguard hypothesis suggests. The bodyguard hypothesis requires more direct tests: Are women especially likely to choose large, physically imposing men when living in social circumstances that indicate a relatively higher risk of rape? Are women with such men for partners less likely to be raped than women with less formidable partners? Although one study found that women put in crime-prone areas of a city ramp up their preferences for physically formidable mates, this shift appears to reflect a general anticrime protective reaction rather than a rape-specific defense.[94]

A fourth hypothesized anti-rape adaptation is *specialized psychological pain,* articulated in Thornhill and Palmer's *A Natural History of Rape*.[95] According to this hypothesis, the psychological trauma that women experience from rape motivates them to avoid similar recurrences in the future. Evidence for this hypothesis comes from a study that purports to show that the women who experience the most intense pain and psychological trauma from rape are (a) young and fertile women rather than prepubescent girls or postmenopausal women, (b) married rather than single women, and (c) victims who were vaginally raped rather than orally or anally raped. Furthermore, (d) women who experience the most visible signs of physical violence during rape experience the least psychological pain, presumably because they would be less likely to be blamed for or suspected of complicity in the rape. An advocate of the psychological pain hypothesis might have added an additional prediction—(e) that women raped by men low in mate value (for example, men who are unattractive and of low socioeconomic status) will experience more psychological trauma than women raped by men higher in mate value (more attractive and higher-status men).

Regardless of these points of theoretical and empirical contention, one thing is quite clear—sound scientific evidence is lacking on the specifics of women's defenses against rape. Research is urgently needed on women's anti-rape strategies and their relative effectiveness, whether or not such strategies ultimately turn out to be specialized evolved adaptations or products of more general cognitive and emotional mechanisms.

The Evolutionary Arms Race

Conflicts between men and women pervade their interactions on the mating market, in the workplace, and within relationships. These range from conflicts over sexual access in dating couples to fights over commitment and investment among married couples, to sexual harassment in the workplace, date rape, and warfare rape. Even taking into account the many scientific questions that still remain about how best to explain rape, most sexual conflicts have their origins in men's and women's evolved mating strategies. The strategies pursued by members of one sex often interfere with those of the other sex as each tries to influence the other toward gender-linked mating goals.

Both genders have psychological adaptations, such as anger, sadness, and jealousy, that alert them to interference with their mating strategies. A woman's anger is evoked most intensely in the specific contexts in which a man interferes with her mating strategies—for example, if he acts in condescending, abusive, controlling, or sexually coercive ways toward her, constricting her personal power or freedom of choice. A man's anger is most intensely evoked when a woman interferes with his mating strategies, for example, by spurning his advances, refusing to have sex with him, or hooking up with another man.

These battles create spiraling arms races over evolutionary time. For every incremental gain in men's ability to deceive women, women evolve comparable incremental gains in their ability to detect deception. Better abilities to detect deception, in turn, create the evolutionary conditions for the other sex to develop increasingly subtle forms of deception. For each escalating test that women impose on men to gauge the depth of their commitment, men develop increasingly more elaborate strategies to mimic or minimize commitment. This development in turn favors more refined and subtle tests by women to weed out the pretenders. And for every form of abuse inflicted by one sex on the other, the other evolves methods for circumventing the manipulations. As women evolve better and more sophisticated strategies to achieve their mating goals, men evolve increasingly sophisticated strategies to achieve theirs. Because the mating goals of the sexes interfere with each other within evolutionarily delimited domains, there is no evolutionary end to the spiral.

Adaptive emotions such as anger and psychological pain, however, help women and men reduce the costs they incur when someone attempts to interfere with their mating strategies. In the context of dating or marriage, these emotions sometimes lead to the end of the relationship.

8

Breaking Up

Women marry believing that their husbands will change.
Men marry believing that their wives will not change.
They are both wrong.

—ANONYMOUS

HUMAN MATING IS rarely a once-in-a-lifetime occurrence. Divorce and remarriage are so common in the United States that nearly 50 percent of all children do not live with both of their genetic parents. Stepfamilies are rapidly becoming the norm, not the exception. Contrary to some beliefs, this is not a recent phenomenon, nor does it reflect a dramatic decline in family values. Divorce specifically and the dissolution of long-term mating relationships more generally are universal across cultures. Roughly 85 percent of Americans have experienced at least one breakup of a committed mating relationship.[1] Among the !Kung of Botswana, 134 marriages out of 331 recorded ended in divorce—about 40 percent.[2] Among the Ache of Paraguay, the average man and

269

woman are married and divorced more than eleven times each by the time they reach the age of forty.[3]

People end committed relationships for many reasons. A spouse may start imposing new or larger costs, for example, or a better opportunity for a mate may come along. Staying in a bad relationship can be costly—lost resources, missed mating opportunities, physical abuse, inadequate care for children, and emotional abuse. These costs all interfere with successful solutions to the critical adaptive problems of survival and reproduction. New mating opportunities, superior resources, better child care, and better allies are some of the benefits that may flow to people who leave bad relationships.

Adaptive Problems Leading to Breakups

Many mates in ancestral times became injured and died before old age. Men, for example, sustained wounds or were killed in combat between warring tribes. The paleontological record reveals fascinating evidence of aggression between men. Pieces of spears and knives have been found lodged in the remains of human rib cages. Injuries to skulls and ribs are found more frequently on male than on female skeletons, revealing that physical combat was primarily a male activity. Intriguingly, more injuries are located on the left sides of skulls and rib cages, suggesting a greater prevalence of right-handed attackers. The earliest known homicide victim in the paleontological record is a Neanderthal man who was stabbed in the chest by a right-hander roughly 50,000 years ago.[4] These highly patterned injuries cannot be explained as accidents. They demonstrate that injury and death at the hands of other people have been recurrent hazards in human evolutionary history.

Traditional tribes today do not escape the damage done by male aggression. Among the Ache, for example, ritual club fights occur only among men, and they often result in permanent disabilities and death.[5] A woman whose husband goes off to a club fight can never be sure that he will return unharmed. Among the Yanomamö, a boy does not achieve full status as a man until he has killed another man. Yanomamö men display their scars proudly, often painting them bright colors to draw attention to them.[6] Men have fought in wars throughout human history, exposing themselves to grave risks.

Violence at the hands of other men was not the only way an ancestral man could die. Hunting has always been a male-dominated human enterprise, and ancestral men risked injury, particularly when hunting large game, such as wild boar, bison, or buffalo. Lions, panthers, and tigers roamed the African savanna, inflicting injury or death on the unwary, the unskilled, the imprudent, or the unlucky. Some men accidentally plunged off cliffs or fell from trees. In human ancestral environments, since a woman's husband had a chance of dying first or becoming so seriously injured as to cripple his ability to hunt or to protect her, it would have been highly adaptive for her to assess and encourage alternative mates.

Ancestral women never warred and rarely hunted. Women's gathering activities, which yielded 60 to 80 percent of the family's food resources, were far less dangerous.[7] Childbirth, however, took its toll. Without modern medical technology, many women failed to survive the dangerous journey of pregnancy and childbirth. A man left mateless by his wife's death would have had to start the search and courting process from scratch, unless he had psychological adaptations that anticipated this possibility and caused him to lay the groundwork for securing a replacement. It would have paid for both men and women not to wait until their mate's death to start evaluating potential alternatives.

Injury, disease, or the death of a mate were not the only hazards to force ancestral mates to look elsewhere. A woman's husband could lose status within the group, be ostracized, become dominated by a rival male, prove to be a bad father, prove to be infertile, fail as a hunter, start abusing her, initiate affairs, direct resources to other women, or turn out to be sexually impotent. A man's wife could fail at gathering food, mishandle family resources, prove to be a bad mother, prove to be infertile, decline his sexual advances, cheat on him, or get pregnant by another man. Either sex could contract debilitating diseases or become riddled with parasites. Life events sometimes take a terrible toll on a mate full of vitality when initially chosen. Once a selected spouse decreases in value, alternatives become attractive.

A mate's decline in value and potential death represented only two of the conditions that might have diverted a person's attention to alternatives. Another critical condition is an increase in one's own desirability, which opens up an array of alternatives that were previously unobtainable. A man, for example, could sometimes dramatically elevate his status by performing an unusually brave deed, such as killing a large animal, defeating another man in combat, or saving someone's child from harm. Sudden increases in a man's status opened up new mating possibilities with younger, more attractive mates or multiple mates, who could make a current mate pale by comparison. Mating options mushroomed for men who managed to boost their status. Because a woman's value as a mate was closely tied with her reproductive value, she usually could not elevate her desirability to the same extent that men could. Nevertheless, women could improve their mate value by acquiring status or power, showing unusual adeptness at dealing with crises, displaying exceptional wisdom, or having sons, daughters, or other kin who achieved elevated positions within the group. These possibilities for changes in mating value are still with us today.

Another important impetus to break up a mateship was the presence of more desirable alternatives. A desirable mate who had previously been taken could suddenly become available. A previously uninterested person could develop a strong attraction. A member of a neighboring tribe could appear on the scene. And any of these people could be sufficiently desirable to warrant breaking an existing marital bond.

In sum, three major general circumstances could have led an ancestral person to leave a long-term mate: when a current mate became less desirable because of a decrease in abilities or resources or a failure to provide the reproductively relevant resources expected in the initial selection; when the person experienced an increase in his or her own resources or reputation that opened up previously unobtainable mating possibilities; and when compelling alternatives became available. Because these three conditions are likely to have regularly recurred among our ancestors, it is reasonable to expect that humans evolved psychological mechanisms to evaluate the costs and benefits of existing relationships in comparison with the perceived alternatives. These adaptations would have been attuned to changes in the value of a mate, continued to identify and gauge mating alternatives, and led to the pursuit of backup mates or potential replacement mates.

Adaptations for Breaking Up

Ancestral conditions that favored breakups posed recurrent adaptive challenges over human evolutionary history. People who were oblivious to a decrease in their mate's value, who were totally unprepared to find a new mate in the event of their mate's death, or who failed to trade up to a higher-quality mate when offered the opportunity would have been at a tremendous reproductive disadvantage compared with those who perceived and acted on these conditions.

It may be disconcerting to acknowledge it, but most people continue to assess outside options while in a committed relationship. Men's banter, when it does not center on sports or work, often revolves around the appearance and sexual availability of women in their social circles. Married women talk as well about which men are attractive, available, and high in status. These discussions accomplish the critical goals of exchanging information and assessing the mating terrain. It pays to monitor alternatives with an eye toward mating opportunities. Those who stick it out with an undesirable mate through thick and thin may receive our admiration, but their kind would not have reproduced as successfully in ancestral times and are not well represented among us today. Men and women evaluate alternative mating possibilities even if they have no immediate intention to act on them. It pays to plan ahead.

Mate preferences continue to operate during marriage, being directed not just at comparing the array of potential mates but at comparing those alternatives with the current mate. Men's preference for young, attractive women does not disappear once they make a long-term commitment to a mate; nor does women's attention to the status and prestige of other men. Indeed, one's mate provides a handy standard for repeated comparisons. Research from my lab, spearheaded by Dan Conroy-Beam, discovered that happiness in a mateship is partly determined by the discrepancies between one's partner's mate value and the value of alternative mates in the local environment. People assess how well their mates stack up to the competition and become unhappy if their mates suffer by these comparisons.[8] A decision to keep or get rid of one's mate depends on the outcome of these calculations, which may not be made consciously.

A man whose increased status opens up better mating alternatives does not think to himself, *Well, if I leave my current wife, I can increase my reproductive success by mating with younger, more reproductively valuable women.* He simply finds other women increasingly attractive and his current relationship less satisfactory. A woman whose mate abuses her does not think to herself, *My reproductive success and that of my children will increase if I leave this cost-inflicting mate.* She thinks instead that she had better get herself and her children to safety. Our mateship dissolution adaptations operate without our awareness of the adaptive problems they solve.

People typically need a clear, socially acceptable justification for leaving a long-term mate, one that explains the breakup to friends, to family, and even to themselves. They need a public rationale that preserves, or minimizes the damage to, their social reputation. Although some simply walk away from a relationship, people rarely use this straightforward solution. One effective tactic for expelling a mate, in evolutionary psychological terms, would be to violate the mate's expectations, so that the mate no longer desired to maintain the relationship. That is, rather than leaving themselves, some people try to drive their partner to take that step. Ancestral men could withhold resources or give signals that investments were being channeled to other women. Women could decrease a man's certainty of paternity by engaging in infidelities or simply withholding sex from him. Cruel, unkind, inconsiderate, malevolent, harmful, or caustic acts would be effective tactics for expelling a mate for both women and men because such acts violate the universal preferences held by both of them for mates who are kind and empathic. These tactics have in common the exploitation of existing psychological mechanisms in the other sex—adaptations that alert people to the possibility that they have chosen a mate unwisely, or that their mate has changed in unwanted ways, and that perhaps they should cut their losses.

The sex differences in benefits from long-term matings in ancestral times, whereby men's benefits came from monopolizing a woman's reproductive capacity and women's from monopolizing a man's investments, have profound implications for the causes of separation and divorce. They imply that men and women evaluate changes in their mates over time by very different standards. As a woman ages from twenty-five to forty, for example, she experiences a rapid decline in her reproductive value, although other components of her mate value may increase and compensate for the loss. During a comparable period a man may elevate himself in status and so enjoy an unanticipated avalanche of mating opportunities. Or he may suffer losses and become desperate to keep his current mate. Ancestral men and women broke up, however, for somewhat different reasons that go to the core of the adaptive problems that each gender must solve to mate successfully.

A major source of evidence on breaking up comes from the most extensive cross-cultural study ever undertaken on the causes of divorce. The evolutionary anthropologist Laura Betzig analyzed information from 160 societies and identified forty-three causes of conjugal dissolution recorded by ethnographers who had lived in the society or by native informants who resided in each culture.[9] Various constraints, such as the lack of a standard method of gathering data and incomplete data, preclude calculation of the absolute frequencies of the causes of divorce. Nonetheless, the relative frequencies are readily available, and as the number of societies revealing a particular cause of divorce increases, the more likely it is that this cause is a universal cause of divorce. Topping the list of causes of divorce are two key events with direct relevance to reproduction—infidelity and infertility.

Infidelity

The most powerful indicator of a man's failure to retain access to a woman's reproductive capacity is her infidelity. The most powerful cue to a woman's failure to retain access to a man's resources is his infidelity. Among the forty-three causes of conjugal dissolution, ranging from the absence of male children to sexual neglect, adultery is the single most pervasive cause, being cited in eighty-eight societies. Among those that highlight adultery, there are strong gender differences in prevalence. Although in twenty-five societies divorce follows from adultery by either partner, fifty-four societies sanction divorce only if the wife is adulterous; in only two societies does divorce occur only following the husband's adultery. Even these two societies can hardly be considered exceptions to the sexual double standard, because an unfaithful wife rarely goes without punishment. In both of these cultures, men are known to thrash their wife upon discovery of her infidelity and occasionally a woman is beaten to death by her husband. Unfaithful wives in these two cultures may not be divorced, but neither do they get off lightly.

The finding that a woman's infidelity is a more prevalent cause of divorce is especially striking because men are more likely to be unfaithful.[10] Alfred Kinsey, for example, found that 50 percent of the husbands but only 26 percent of the wives surveyed had been unfaithful.[11] More recent studies find similar gender differences in infidelity rates.[12] The sexual double standard in reactions to infidelity is not confined to American culture or to Western societies but is observed across the globe. Its pervasiveness stems from three possible sources. First, men have greater power to impose their will, so that women may be forced to tolerate infidelity in their husbands more often than men are forced to tolerate infidelity in their wives. Second, women worldwide may be more forgiving of their husband's sexual indiscretions because sexual infidelity per se has been less costly for women than for men over human evolutionary history, unless also accompanied by the diversion of his resources and commitments. Third, women worldwide may more often be forced to tolerate a husband's infidelity because of the prohibitively high costs of divorce, especially if they have children, who curtail women's value on the mating market. For all these reasons, a wife's unfaithfulness more often causes an irrevocable rift that ends in divorce.

Knowing that infidelity causes conjugal dissolution, some people may use it intentionally to get out of a bad marriage. In a study of the breakup of mates, we asked one hundred men and women which tactics they would use to get out of a bad relationship. Subsequently, a different group of fifty-four individuals evaluated each tactic for its effectiveness in accomplishing the goal.[13] One common method for getting rid of an unwanted mate was to start an affair, perhaps by sleeping around in an obvious manner or arranging to be seen with a member of the other gender in some other questionable situation.

Sometimes an actual affair is not carried out but is merely alluded to or implied. People use the tactics of flirting with others or telling a partner that they are in love with someone else so that the mate will end the relationship. A related tactic is to express a wish to date other people in order to be sure that the two of them are truly right for each other, a means of gracefully exiting from the relationship through a gradual transition out of commitment.

So widely accepted is infidelity as a reason to get rid of a mate that people sometimes exploit it, even if no actual infidelity has occurred. In Truk, for example, if a husband wants to terminate a marriage, he has merely to spread a rumor about his wife's adultery, pretend to believe it, and leave her in indignation.[14] Apparently, people care about justifying a marital dissolution to their social circles. Pretending that an affair has occurred provides this justification because infidelity is so widely regarded as a compelling reason for breaking up.

Infertility

Although ring doves tend to be monogamous—more so than many bird species—they experience a divorce rate of about 25 percent a season. The major cause of breaking a bond is infertility—the failure of the pair to reproduce.[15] Pairs of ring doves that produce chicks in one breeding season are highly likely to mate again the next season; those that fail to reproduce in one season seek out alternative mates the next season.

Failure to produce children is also a leading cause of divorce for humans. Couples with no children divorce far more often than couples with two or more children. According to a United Nations study of millions of people in forty-five societies, 39 percent of divorces occur when there are no children, 26 percent when there is only a single child, 19 percent when there are two, and fewer than 3 percent when there are four or more. The toll on marriage caused by childlessness occurs regardless of the duration of the marriage.[16] Children strengthen marital bonds, reducing the probability of divorce, by creating a powerful commonality of genetic interest between a man and a woman. Failure to produce offspring that transport the genes of both parents into the future deprives a couple of this powerful common bond.

Infertility is exceeded only by infidelity as the most frequently cited cause of divorce across societies. In the cross-cultural study of conjugal dissolution, seventy-five societies reported infertility or sterility as a cause of divorce. Of these, twelve specified the sterility of either the husband or the wife. But sterility, like adultery, appears to be strongly gender-linked. Whereas sterility ascribed exclusively to the man was cited as a cause of divorce in twelve societies, sterility ascribed exclusively to the woman was cited in thirty societies—perhaps reflecting another type of double standard by which women are blamed more than men. In the remaining twenty-one societies, it is impossible to discern whether or not sterility on the part of the man, the woman, or both was a cause.

Not all societies sanction divorce. Where divorce is not authorized, however, provisions are often made for separating a man and woman who do not produce children. In the Andaman Islands off the southern coast of Asia, for example, a marriage is not regarded as consummated unless a child is born.[17] Many villages in Japan hold off recording a marriage until long after a wedding, and frequently the marriage is not entered into the family register in the village office until the first child is born.[18] When marriages are not regarded as legally legitimate until children are born, infertility effectively becomes a cause of marital dissolution.

Old age is linked with lower fertility. This linkage is stronger in women than in men, but even though sperm quality and concentration per ejaculate declines somewhat with age, men in their sixties, seventies, and eighties can still sire children, and they do. Among the Yanomamö, one particularly productive man had children whose ages spanned fifty years. Among the Tiwi of northern Australia, older men frequently monopolize women thirty or more years younger and sire children with them. Although couples in Western culture tend to be more similar in age than those among the Tiwi and Yanomamö, it is not uncommon for a man to divorce a postmenopausal wife and start a new family with a younger woman.[19]

The difference in the reproductive biology of men and women leads to the expectation that older age in a wife will lead to divorce more often than older age in a husband. Although the cross-cultural study on conjugal dissolution did not find old age to be a frequently cited cause of divorce, it was cited in eight societies studied, and in all eight it was the old age of the woman, never the man, that caused divorce.[20] When men divorce, they almost invariably marry younger women.

In evolutionary terms, it makes perfect sense that infertility and infidelity are the most prevalent causes of divorce worldwide. Both represent the strongest and most direct failures to deliver the reproductive resources that provide the evolutionary raison d'être for long-term mating. People do not consciously calculate that their fitness suffers from these events. Rather, infidelity and infertility are adaptive problems that exerted selection pressure on human ancestors for a psychology attuned to reproductive failures. Just as having sex tends to lead to the production of babies even though the people involved may have no awareness of the reproductive logic involved, so anger leads a person to leave an unfaithful or infertile mate, with no conscious articulation of the underlying adaptive logic being required. The fact that couples who are childless by choice are nonetheless devastated by infidelity shows that our psychological mechanisms continue to operate in modern contexts, even those far removed from the selection pressures that gave rise to them.

Sexual Withdrawal

A wife who refuses to have sex with her husband is effectively depriving him of access to her reproductive value, although neither mate necessarily thinks about it in these terms. Since sex throughout human evolutionary history has been necessary for reproduction, depriving a man of sex may eliminate the reproductive dividends on the investment that he has expended in obtaining his wife. It may also signal that she is allocating her sexuality to another man. Men have evolved psychological adaptations that alert them to this form of interference with their sexual strategies.

In the cross-cultural study on conjugal dissolution, twelve societies identified the refusal to have sex as a cause of conjugal dissolution. In all these societies the cause was attributed exclusively to the wives' refusal, not the husbands'.[21] My lab's study of the breakup of mates also found sexual refusal to be a major tactic for getting rid of unwanted mates. Women described their tactics for breaking up variously as refusing to have physical contact with their mate, becoming cold and distant sexually, refusing to let her mate touch her body, and declining sexual requests. These tactics were employed almost exclusively by women.[22]

The success of this tactic is illustrated by one woman's account in the study on the breakup of mates.[23] She complained to a friend that her repeated attempts to break off with her husband had failed. She wanted advice. Further discussion revealed that, although she seriously wanted to get rid of her husband, she never had refused his sexual advances. Her friend suggested that she try it. A week later she reported that her husband had become enraged at her sexual refusal and, after two days, had packed his bags and left. They were divorced shortly thereafter. If women give sex to get love and men give love to get sex, then depriving a man of sex may be a reliable way to stop his love and hasten his departure.

Lack of Economic Support

A man's ability and willingness to provide a woman with resources are central to his mate value, central to her selection of him as a partner, central to the tactics that men use to attract mates, and central to the tactics that men use to retain mates. In evolutionary terms, a man's failure to provide resources to his wife and her children should therefore have been a major gender-linked cause of breakups. Men who are unable or unwilling to supply these resources fail to fulfill a key criterion on which women initially select them.

Provisioning failure by men is a cause of divorce worldwide. In the cross-cultural study on conjugal dissolution, twenty societies cited inadequate economic support as a cause of divorce, four cited inadequate housing, three cited inadequate food, and four cited inadequate clothing. All these causes were ascribed solely and exclusively to men. In no society did a woman's failure to provide resources constitute grounds for divorce.[24]

The seriousness of a man's lack of economic provision is illustrated by the report of a woman in her late twenties who participated in a study of marital separation:

My husband lost a series of jobs and was very depressed. He just couldn't keep a job. He had a job for a couple of years, and that ended, and then he had another for a year, and that ended, and then he had another. And then he was really depressed, and he saw a social worker, but it didn't seem to be helping. And he was sleeping a lot. And I think one day I just came to the end of the line with his sleeping. I think I went out one night and came back and he hadn't even been able to get out of bed to put the children to bed. I left them watching television and there they were when I came back. The next day I asked him to leave. Very forcefully.[25]

In contemporary America, women who make more money than their husbands tend to leave them. One study found that the divorce rate among American couples in which the woman earns more than her husband is 50 percent higher than among couples in which the husband earns more than his wife.[26] Men whose wives' careers blossom sometimes express resentment. In a study on the causes of divorce among women, one woman noted that her husband "hated that I earned more than he did; it made him feel less than a man." Women also resent husbands who lack ambition. Another woman noted: "I worked full-time, while he worked part-time and drank full-time; eventually, I realized I wanted more help getting where I'm going."[27] Women eject men who do not fulfill their preference for a mate who provides resources, especially when they can earn more.

Conflict Among Multiple Wives

Polygyny is a widespread practice across cultures. An analysis of 853 cultures revealed that 83 percent of them permitted polygyny. In some West African societies, 25 percent of all older men have two or more wives simultaneously.[28] Even in cultures in which polygyny is not allowed legally, it sometimes occurs. One study estimated that there are 25,000 to 35,000 polygynous marriages in the United States, mostly in western states.[29] Another study of 437 financially successful American men found that some maintained two separate families, each unknown to the other.[30]

From a woman's perspective, a major drawback of her husband taking additional wives is that resources channeled to another wife and her children are denied to her and her children. Although co-wives may derive significant benefits from one another's presence, such as help with raising children, often one wife's gain is another wife's loss. The cross-cultural study on conjugal dissolution found polygyny to be a cause for divorce in twenty-five societies, largely because of conflict among the man's co-wives.

Conflict among co-wives may have been an adaptive problem that polygynous men in ancestral times had to solve to maintain control over their wives. The problem was how to keep all wives happy so that none left; defection would deprive the man of significant reproductive resources. Some polygynous men adopted strict rules about resource distribution, offering each wife equal attention and equal sex. Among the Kipsigis in Kenya, wives of polygynous husbands have their own plots of land, which are divided equally among them by the husband.[31] Kipsigis men maintain a separate residence apart from their wives, and they alternate the days spent with each wife, carefully allocating time equally. One writer on ancient Islamic cultures in the Middle East concluded: "You should have four wives if your fortune warrants it, and if you can give each one of the four the same attention, like sum for her necessaries, and a separate household."[32] All these tactics tend to minimize conflict among co-wives. Sororal polygyny, in which co-wives are sisters, also tends to minimize conflict, suggesting that genetic relatedness creates a convergence in the interests of women.[33]

Despite men's efforts to keep peace among co-wives, women in societies such as Gambia often leave their husbands when they indicate that they plan to acquire a second wife, even though polygyny is legal.[34] Wives find it difficult to share their husband's time and resources with other women.

Cruelty and Unkindness

Worldwide, one of the most highly valued characteristics in a committed mate is kindness. It signals a willingness to engage in a cooperative alliance, an essential ingredient for success in long-term mating. Disagreeable people make poor mates. Mates who are irritable, violent, abusive, derogatory, beat children, destroy possessions, neglect chores, and alienate friends impose severe costs psychologically, socially, and physically.

Given these costs, cruelty, maltreatment, and ruthlessness rank among the most frequent causes of marital breakup in the cross-cultural study on conjugal dissolution, cited in fifty-four societies. In all cultures these traits are exceeded only by adultery and infertility as causes for splitting up.[35] According to one study of marital dissolution, 63 percent of divorced women reported that their husbands abused them emotionally, and 29 percent reported that their husbands abused them physically.[36]

Unkindness and psychological cruelty may in some cases be related to events that occur during the course of a marriage, particularly adultery and infertility. Infertility, for example, often sparks harsh words between mates in tribal India. One Indian husband said: "We went to each other for seven years till we were weary, and still there was no child; every time my wife's period began she abused me saying, 'Are you a man? Haven't you any strength?' And I used to feel miserable and ashamed."[37] Eventually, the couple divorced.

Adultery also provokes cruelty and unkindness. When a Quiche woman commits adultery, her husband is likely to nag, insult, scold, abuse, and even starve her.[38] Worldwide, adulterous wives are beaten, raped, scorned, verbally abused, and injured by enraged husbands.[39] Thus, some forms of unkindness are evoked by reproductively damaging events that occur within the marriage. Cruelty and unkindness, in other words, may in part be symptoms of other underlying causes of divorce. Psychological adaptations and behavioral strategies become activated to solve these costly problems.

In other cases, unkindness is a personality characteristic of one spouse that is stable over time.[40] In my lab's study of newlywed couples, we examined the links between the personality characteristics of one spouse and the problems they caused their mates. The wives of disagreeable husbands expressed distress because their husbands were condescending, physically abusive, verbally abusive, unfaithful, inconsiderate, moody, insulting, and self-centered.[41] The wives of disagreeable men complain that their husbands treat them as inferiors, demand too much time and attention, and ignore their wives' feelings. They slap their wives, hit them, and call them nasty names. They have sex with other women. They fail to help with the household chores. They abuse alcohol and insult their wives' appearance. Not surprisingly, spouses of disagreeable people tend to be miserable with the marriage, and by the fourth year of marriage many seek separation and divorce.

Given the premium that people place on kindness in a mate, it is not surprising that one of the most effective tactics for getting rid of a bad mate is to act mean, cruel, caustic, and quarrelsome. Men and women say that effective tactics for getting mates to leave include treating them badly, insulting them to others publicly, intentionally hurting their feelings, creating a fight, yelling without explanation, and escalating a trivial disagreement into a fight.

Cruelty and unkindness are used worldwide as a tactic for expelling a mate. Among the Quiche, when a husband wants to get rid of his wife, often because of her infidelities, he makes her position unbearable through a variety of means: "The undesired wife is nagged, insulted, and starved; her husband scolds and abuses her; he is openly unfaithful. He may marry another woman or even outrage his wife's dignity by introducing a prostitute into the house."[42] All these cruel acts reflect the opposite of the kindness that is central to men's and women's universal preferences in a mate.

Mate Ejection Tactics

Extricating oneself from a committed mateship can be diabolically difficult. The rejected partner might not want to let go. Family and friends sometimes apply pressure to stay together. Shared children complicate the disentangling. And in our modern environment, divorce laws and intertwined finances can extend the process of separation from months to years.

Some evolutionary psychologists argue that we have evolved specialized mate ejection adaptations to facilitate breakups.[43] Although the scientific study of mate ejection tactics is in its infancy, it has yielded a few key insights. One tactic is simply to tell the partner straighforwardly that both should start seeing other people. Another is to begin having sex with others and let the partner find out—a tactic judged to be one of the most effective, albeit potentially dangerous. Variants include having sex with a partner's friend, being seen at social gatherings with other potential mates, or leaving evidence of an affair in plain sight so that a partner will discover it.

A third tactic is withdrawal of various kinds of resources. Some mates simply cease showing affection, stop saying "I love you," and stop having sex with the partner. Some stop defending the partner when insulted by others or derogated publicly. Withholding benefits inherent in the mateship sometimes causes the partner to leave for greener mating pastures. Predictably, men are more likely than women to stop giving gifts and other economic resources to the partner as a means of mate expulsion. Women are more likely than men to refuse to have sex with their partner and decline their partner's sexual advances.

The flip side of withholding benefits is inflicting costs. Both men and women become more irritable with their partners and pick fights over small things. When verbal abuse sometimes escalates to physical abuse, such as slapping or hitting, a partner may flee to escape incurring these costs. Because cruelty and unkindness are key causes of dissolution, people sometimes ramp up these unsavory tactics to hasten a breakup.

In the modern environment, a common tactic is "ghosting"— ceasing all communications, such as texting or emailing. Some remove the partner as a "friend" from their Facebook page or change their Facebook status from "in a relationship" to "single." These behaviors send strong rejection signals to the partner and also have the effect of communicating to the broader social network that the relationship is over.

All mate ejection tactics carry potential costs, which range from reputational damage to an ex seeking revenge. The cliché "hell hath no fury like a woman scorned" turns out to apply at least as much to men. Indeed, men are more likely than women to seek revenge using abhorrent tactics such as stalking or posting nude photos of their ex on revenge websites.[44] Consequently, those who initiate breakups often attempt to curtail these costs. Saying, "It's not you, it's me," and "I think we should be 'friends,'" are classic efforts in this direction and are sometimes successful.

Regardless of whether someone is getting ejected or doing the ejecting, both face new adaptive problems after a breakup—problems that require coping strategies.

Tactics for Coping with Breakups

Breaking up a romantic relationship is among the most traumatic life events people experience. In studies of stressful life events, it always ranks in the top five. Only experiences such as the death of a child or the death of a spouse are seen as more stressful. Friendship networks can become strained, and plunging into the mating market anew can be frightening. Breakups can threaten one's social status since our mates are often seen by others as key contributors to the esteem in which we are held. Moreover, breakups often end the flow of benefits to which we have become accustomed, be they economic, sexual, or social.

The scientific study of coping tactics has just broken ground.[45] Women and men alike often try to remain friends with their exes so that the benefits of the relationship do not cease entirely or to minimize the chances of the former partner seeking revenge. Some do the opposite, however, and avoid the ex entirely. Women more than men tap their friendships to discuss the former relationship, hash out its details, mull over what went wrong, and ruminate over future prospects. Both genders sometimes seek sex with others. As one woman we interviewed put it, "The best way to get over a man is to get under another one."[46]

Women are more likely than men to go shopping as a coping tactic.[47] Shopping for new clothes or makeup can enhance a woman's self-esteem and increase her physical attractiveness, paving the way for reentry into the mating market.

Some cope with breakups by seeking solace in alcohol or drugs. Some ruminate endlessly, prolonging their pain by keeping tabs on their former partner's whereabouts or dating activities and monitoring their online presense. And some start stalking their ex in an attempt to remate with them, to interfere with their ex's attempts to remate, or simply to seek revenge.[48]

Eventually, most people move on, reenter the mating market, and begin the process of mate selection, mate attraction, and courtship all over again.

Implications for a Lasting Relationship

The major causes of marital dissolution worldwide are those that historically caused damage to reproductive success by imposing reproductive costs and interfering with preferred mating strategies. The most damaging events and changes are infidelity, which can reduce a husband's confidence in paternity and deprive a wife of some or all of the husband's resources; infertility, which renders a couple childless; sexual withdrawal, which deprives a husband of access to a wife's reproductive value or signals to a wife that he is channeling his resources elsewhere; a man's failure to provide economic support, which deprives a woman of the reproductively relevant resources inherent in her initial choice of a mate; a man's acquisition of additional wives, which diverts resources from a particular spouse; and cruelty and meanness, which involve abuse, defection, affairs, and an unwillingness to continue a cooperative alliance.

The implications of these fundamental trends in human mating psychology for a lasting relationship are profound. To maximize the chances of preserving a long-term bond, couples would do well to remain faithful; produce children together; secure ample economic resources; act kind, generous, and understanding; and attend to their mate's sexual and emotional desires. These actions do not guarantee a successful relationship, but they increase the odds substantially.

Unfortunately, not all damaging events and changes can be prevented. Environments impose hostile forces that no one can control, such as infertility, old age, decreased sexual desire, disease, status loss, social ostracism, and death. These forces can crush a mate's value irrevocably, despite the best intentions. Alternative potential mates sometimes offer to provide what is lacking, so evolution has shaped psychological mechanisms that dispose people to leave their mates under these circumstances— mate-switching adaptations.[49]

Adaptations that function to attend to the shifting circumstances of mating cannot be easily turned off. In ancestral times, it frequently paid reproductive dividends in the event of the loss of a mate to be prepared by maintaining alternative prospects and to trade up when possible. Those who were caught unprepared, who failed to play in the field of possibilities, or who were unwilling to leave a reproductively damaging mate were less likely to produce descendants. Because the costs incurred and the benefits bestowed by a current mate must always be evaluated relative to those available from alternative mates, the psychological mechanisms of mate switching inevitably include comparisons. Unfortunately for lifelong happiness, a current mate sometimes falls short and fails to measure up to attractive available alternatives.

Most of these hostile forces are still with us today. A mate's status can rise or fall, infertility traumatizes otherwise joyful couples, infidelities mount, and the sadness of aging turns the youthful frustration of unrequited love into the despair of unobtainable love. These events activate adaptations that evolved to deal with breakups, causing people to avoid threats to their reproduction. These mechanisms cannot be easily turned off. They cause people to seek new mates and sometimes to break up repeatedly as adaptively significant events emerge over the lifetime.

9

Changes over Time

The world is full of complainers. But the fact is—nothing
comes with a guarantee.

—Detective in the film *Blood Simple*

Among the chimpanzees at the large zoo colony in Arnhem,
the Netherlands, Yeroen reigned as the dominant adult male.[1] He
walked in an exaggeratedly heavy manner, and he looked larger
than he really was. Only occasionally did he need to demonstrate
his dominance, raising his hair on end and running full speed
at the other apes, who scattered in all directions at his charge.
Yeroen's dominance extended to sex. Although there were four
adult males in the troop, Yeroen was responsible for nearly 75
percent of all matings when the females came into estrus.

As Yeroen grew older, however, things began to change.
A younger male, Luit, experienced a sudden growth spurt and
started to challenge Yeroen's status. Luit gradually stopped displaying the submissive greeting to Yeroen, brazenly showing his

293

fearlessness. Once, Luit approached Yeroen and smacked him hard, and another time Luit used his potentially lethal canines to draw blood. Most of the time, however, the battles were more symbolic, with threats and bluffs in the place of bloodshed. Initially, all the females sided with Yeroen, allowing him to maintain his status. One by one they defected to Luit, however, as the tide turned. After two months, the transition was complete. Yeroen was dethroned and began displaying the submissive greeting to Luit. Mating changes followed. While Luit achieved only 25 percent of the matings during Yeroen's reign of power, his sexual access doubled to 50 percent when he took over. Yeroen's sexual access to females dropped to zero.

Although ousted from power and lacking sexual access, Yeroen's life was not over. Gradually, he formed an alliance with an upcoming male named Nikkie. Although neither Yeroen nor Nikkie dared to challenge Luit alone, together they made a formidable coalition. Over several weeks, they grew bolder in challenging Luit. Eventually, a physical fight erupted. Although all the chimpanzees involved sustained injuries, the alliance of Nikkie and Yeroen triumphed. Following this victory, Nikkie secured 50 percent of the matings, and Yeroen, because of his friendship with Nikkie, now enjoyed 25 percent of the matings. His banishment from females had been temporary. Although he never again regained the top alpha position, he had rallied from the setback sufficiently to remain a contender in the troop.

With humans as with chimpanzees, nothing in mating remains static over a lifetime. An individual's value as a mate changes, depending on gender and circumstances. Because many of the changes individuals experience have occurred repeatedly over human evolutionary history, we have evolved psychological adaptations designed to deal with them. A person who steadily ascends a status hierarchy may suddenly be passed by a more talented newcomer. A hunter's promise may be cut suddenly short by a debilitating injury. An older woman's son may become the chief of her tribe. An ignored introvert, long regarded as occupying the bottom rungs of desirability as a mate, may achieve renown through a dazzling invention that is useful to the group. A young married couple bursting with health may tragically discover that one of them is infertile. Ignoring change would have been maladaptive, impeding solutions to critical challenges. We have evolved psychological mechanisms designed to alert us to these changes and motivate us to take problem-solving action.

In a sense, all mating behavior entails changes over time, from the early hormonal stirrings triggered by puberty to grandparents' attempts to influence the mating decisions of their kin. Clarifying one's mating desires takes time. Honing the skills of attraction takes practice. Mating is never static through life. The goal of this chapter is to describe some of the broader changes that occur among men and women over the course of their mating lives—the losses and the triumphs, the uncertainties and the inevitabilities.

Changes in a Woman's Mate Value

Because a woman's desirability as a mate is strongly determined by cues to her reproductivity, that value generally diminishes as she gets older. The woman who attracts a highly desirable husband at age twenty will typically attract a less desirable husband at age forty. This downturn is shown in societies where women are literally purchased by men in return for a bride-price, as occurs among the Kipsigis in Kenya.[2] The bride-price consists of quantities of cows, goats, sheep, and Kenyan shillings that a groom or his family pays to the bride's family in exchange for the bride. A prospective groom's father initiates negotiations with the father of the prospective bride, making an initial offer. The bride's father considers all competing offers. He then counters by demanding a higher bride-price than was offered by any of the suitors.

Negotiations can last several months. A final suitor is selected by the bride's father, and a final price is set, depending on the perceived quality of the bride. The higher the reproductive value of the bride, the greater the bride-price she is able to command. Older women, even if older by only four or five years, command a lower bride-price. Several other factors lower a woman's value to a prospective husband and hence lower her price as a potential bride, such as poor physical condition or a physical handicap, pregnancy, and the prior birth of children by another man.

The Kipsigis' custom of placing a premium on the youth and physical condition of a woman is not unique. In Tanzania, for example, the Turu refund a portion of the bride-price in the event of a divorce, and older wives command less of a refund owing to the physical "depreciation of the wife's body."[3] In Uganda, the Sebei pay more for young widows than for old widows, stating explicitly that an older widow has fewer reproductive years left.[4]

The effect of aging on a woman's mate value shows up in the changing perceptions of attractiveness through life. In one study in Germany, thirty-two photographs were taken of women ranging in age from eighteen to sixty-four.[5] A group of 252 men and women, from sixteen to sixty years of age, then rated each photograph for its attractiveness on a 9-point scale. The age of the subjects of the photographs strongly determined judgments of female attractiveness, regardless of the age or sex of the rater. Young women drew the highest ratings, old women the lowest. These age effects are even more pronounced when men do the ratings. The change in the perceived attractiveness of women as they move through life is not an arbitrary aspect of a particularly sexist culture. Rather, this change in perceptions reflects the universal psychological adaptations in men that equate cues to a woman's youth with her value as a mate.

There are many exceptions, of course. Some women, because of their status, fame, money, personality, or social networks, are able to remain desirable as they age. The American supermodel Cindy Crawford strikes many as looking more desirable at age fifty than most women at age twenty. The averages mask a wide variability in individual circumstances. Ultimately, a person's value as a mate is an individual matter and is determined by the particular needs, values, and circumstances of the individual making the selection. Consider the real-life case of a highly successful fifty-year-old business executive who had six children with his wife. She developed a debilitating disease and died young. He subsequently married a woman three years older than himself, and his new wife devoted a major share of her effort to raising his children. To this man, a younger woman who had less experience in child rearing and who wanted children of her own would have been less valuable and might have interfered with his goal of raising his own children. A fifty-three-year-old woman may be especially valuable to a man with children and less valuable to a man with no children who wants to start a family. To the individual selecting a mate, averages are less important than particular circumstances.

The same woman can have a different value to a man when his circumstances change. In the case of the business executive, after his children reached college age, he divorced the woman who had helped raised them, married a twenty-three-year-old Japanese woman, and started a second family. His behavior may have been ruthless and not very admirable, but his circumstances had changed. From his individual perspective, the value of his second wife decreased precipitously when his children were grown, and the attractiveness of the younger woman as his third wife increased to accompany his new circumstances.

Although averages can obscure individual circumstances, they do give the broad outlines of the lifetime trends of many people. Furthermore, they suggest the adaptive problems that have shaped the human psychology of mating. From the wife's perspective, as her direct reproductive value declines with age, her reproductive success becomes increasingly linked with nurturing her children, the vehicles that transport her genes into the future. From her husband's perspective, her parenting skills constitute a valuable and virtually irreplaceable resource. Women often continue to provide economic resources, domestic labor, social status, and other resources, many of which decline less dramatically with age than her reproductive capacity and some of which increase. Among the Tiwi tribe, for example, older women can become powerful political allies of their mates, offering access to an extended network of social alliances and even helping their husbands acquire additional wives.[6] But from the perspective of other men on the mating market, an older woman's desirability as a prospective mate is generally low, not only because her direct reproductive value has declined but also because her efforts may already be monopolized by the care of her existing children and eventually her grandchildren.

Changes in Sexual Desire

One of the most prominent changes within marriage over time occurs in the realm of sex. Among newlywed couples, with each passing year men increasingly complain that their wives withhold sex. Although only 14 percent of men complain that their newlywed brides have refused to have sex during the first year of marriage, 43 percent express this feeling four years later. Women's complaints that their husbands refuse to have sex with them increase from 4 percent in the first year to 18 percent in the fifth year. Both men and women increasingly charge their partner with refusing sex, although more than twice as many men as women voice this complaint.[7]

One indication of the lower sexual involvement of married people over time is the decline in the frequency of intercourse. When married women are less than nineteen years old, intercourse occurs roughly eleven or twelve times per month.[8] By age thirty, this frequency drops to nine times per month, and by age forty-two to six times per month, or half the frequency of married women half their age. Past age fifty, the average frequency of intercourse among married couples drops to once a week. These results may reflect a lessened interest by women, by men, or most likely by both.

Another indication of reduced sexual involvement with age comes from a Gallup poll that measured the extent of sexual satisfaction and the frequency of sexual intercourse over time among married couples.[9] The percentage of couples having intercourse at least once a week declined from nearly 80 percent at age thirty to roughly 40 percent by age sixty. Sexual satisfaction showed a similar decline. Nearly 40 percent of the couples reported "very great satisfaction" with their sex lives at age thirty, but only 20 percent voiced this level of satisfaction by age sixty.

The arrival of a baby has a significant impact on the frequency of sex. In one study, twenty-one couples kept daily records of the frequency of intercourse over a period of three years, starting with the first day of marriage.[10] The rates of intercourse a year after the marriage were half what they had been during the first month. The arrival of a baby depressed the frequency of sex even more: after the birth, the rate of intercourse averaged about one-third of what it had been during the first month of marriage. Although more extensive studies over longer time periods are needed to confirm this finding, it suggests that the birth of a baby has a long-lasting effect on marital sex, as mating effort shifts to parental effort.

The effect of the length of a marriage on sexual intercourse appears to be influenced by a woman's physical appearance. According to a study of more than 1,500 married individuals, men and women respond differently to the normal changes in physical appearance that accompany aging.[11] As women age, husbands show less sexual interest in them and experience less happiness with their sexual relationship. Men who perceive their wives as quite attractive, however, maintain high frequencies of sex and higher levels of sexual satisfaction. Other research confirms that after the early years of marriage, husbands lose more sexual interest in their wives than wives do in their husbands.[12] Although it is somewhat of a cliché that men want sex more than their partners do, over time this gender difference sometimes flips. These changes may be more a function of the length of the relationship than of age per se. Switching to a new mate typically brings a resurgence of sexual desire.

Changes in Commitment

Women and men become increasingly distressed by their partner's failure to show affection and attention, which suggests a lowered commitment to the relationship. Women are more distressed than men by declining affection. Whereas only 8 percent of newlywed women complain about their partner's failure to express love, 18 percent of women voice this complaint by the time they are four years into the marriage.[13] In comparison, only 4 percent of newlywed men are upset about their wives' failure to express love, which doubles to 8 percent by the fourth year of marriage. Whereas 64 percent of newlywed women complain that their husbands sometimes fail to pay attention when they speak, 80 percent of women are disturbed by this behavior by the fourth and fifth years of marriage. Fewer husbands overall show distress about their partners' inattentiveness, but the increase in this complaint over time parallels that of their wives, rising from 18 percent to 34 percent during the first four years of marriage.

Another indication of the withdrawal of commitment over time is one spouse ignoring the other's feelings. Among newlywed women, 35 percent express distress about having their feelings ignored, whereas four years later this figure has jumped to 57 percent. The comparable figures for complaints by men are 12 percent in the first year and 32 percent in the fourth. These changes signify a gradual diminution of commitment to a spouse over time, which occurs for both sexes but is more upsetting to women than to men.

While women are more disturbed about men's increasing failure to show commitment through affection and attention, men are more distressed by their wives' growing demands for commitment. Whereas 22 percent of newlywed men complain that their wives demand too much of their time, 36 percent of husbands express upset about this demand by the fourth year of marriage. The comparable figures for women are only 2 percent and 7 percent. Similarly, 16 percent of newlywed men express distress over their wives' demands for attention, whereas 29 percent voice this complaint in the fourth marital year. The comparable figures for women are only 3 percent and 8 percent. Thus, although both genders show increasing distress about their partners' demands for commitment, more men than women are troubled by these changes.

These changes are accompanied by a shift in the effort that men allocate to mate guarding—another index of commitment. In evolutionary terms, a man's efforts to guard his mate should be most intense when his mate is youngest and hence most reproductively valuable, because failure to retain a mate carries the most severe reproductive penalties when the woman has the highest value. The age of a husband, however, would not necessarily govern the intensity of a woman's efforts to keep him. The mate value of a man does not necessarily decline from age twenty to forty, as it does for a woman, because his capacity to accrue resources often increases with age. Thus, the intensity of a woman's efforts to retain a mate should be linked less to a man's age than to his effectiveness at providing her with valuable resources.

My lab confirmed these predictions in a study of the tactics that husbands and wives use to retain their mates.[14] Using newly-wed couples ranging in age from twenty to forty, we explored the frequency of nineteen tactics, which ranged from positive induce-ments, such as bestowing gifts and lavishing attention, to negative inducements, such as threats and violence. We then correlated tactics with the age of the tactician, the age of the mate, and the length of the relationship. We found that the frequency and in-tensity of the husbands' efforts were a direct function of the age of their wives. Men guarded wives in their middle to late thir-ties significantly less intensely than wives in their early to middle twenties. Men married to younger wives tended especially to per-form acts that signaled to other men to stay away—telling other men directly that their wives were already taken, showing physi-cal affection when other men were around, and asking their wives to wear rings and other ornaments that signaled their committed status. Husbands of younger women were more likely to glare at other men who paid attention to their wives and sometimes threatened them with bodily harm. In contrast, wives' efforts to keep older husbands were just as frequent as their efforts devoted to keeping younger husbands. Regardless of the husband's age, there was no difference in women's vigilance, monopolization of time, and appearance enhancement tactics. The intensity of women's efforts to guard their mates is unrelated to the age of the man, showing a marked contrast to men's reliance on a woman's age to calibrate the intensity of their guarding.

The most plausible explanation for this sex difference is the decrease in a woman's reproductive capacity with age. If declines in mate guarding were related to the fact that people simply get tired or complacent when they get older, as all of their functions senesce, then the degree of mate guarding would be directly re-lated to the age of the person doing the guarding. But neither the age of the man nor the age of the woman is a good indicator of their efforts to hold on to their mates. And if the intensity of men's guarding zeal were related to the length of the relationship, that zeal would dwindle as the relationship got older. But the study showed instead that the length of the relationship is not related to the intensity of the guarding efforts. In short, the most plausible reason for the effect of a woman's age on the intensity of a man's efforts to guard her is that women of differing ages differ in their overall desirability and men devote less effort to guarding an older wife than a younger wife.

The population of the Caribbean island of Trinidad illustrates this pattern of mate guarding.[15] His observations of 480 individuals at regular intervals showed the anthropologist Mark Flinn that men whose wives are fecund (young and not pregnant at the time) spend more time with their mates and get into more fights with rival men. In contrast, men whose wives are infecund (older, pregnant, or having just given birth) spend less time with their mates and get along better with other men. Flinn concludes that the reproductive potential of a man's mate is the key determinant of the intensity of his mate guarding.

In Middle Eastern societies that encourage the practice of sequestering women, postpubescent women are veiled and concealed most heavily when they are youngest, and these practices relax as women age.[16] Homicidal rages of husbands over real or suspected infidelities occur worldwide and most often if they have young wives, regardless of the age of the husband. Wives who are less than twenty years old are more than twice as likely as women who are more than twenty to be killed by a husband in a jealous rage.[17] These are just a few of the extreme strategies that men use to prevent other men from gaining sexual access to young wives. As their wives get older, men's efforts to control them become less intense.

Changes in Frequency
of Extramarital Affairs

As men's intense mate guarding lessens, women become less constrained by their husbands in their sexual behavior with other men. It has been said in a humorous vein that "monogamy is the Western custom of one wife and hardly any mistresses."[18] Reliable information on extramarital affairs is difficult to come by. The question on this subject caused more people to decline to participate in Alfred Kinsey's study of sex than did any other question, and more of those who did participate refused to answer it than any other question. A shroud of secrecy surrounds extramarital sex, despite the multitude of studies on the subject.

The statistics on the incidence of extramarital sex must therefore be regarded as conservative, in that extramarital affairs tend to be underreported. The Kinsey report suggested that the actual incidence of affairs is probably at least 10 percent higher than reported.[19] Another study of 750 spouses found that the incidence may be even higher. Whereas only 30 percent of these people initially admitted to extramarital affairs, under subsequent intensive questioning an additional 30 percent revealed that they had had extramarital sex, bringing the total to approximately 60 percent.[20]

Women's extramarital affairs change dramatically with age. Affairs are rare among the youngest wives, being acknowledged by only 6 percent of wives at ages sixteen to twenty and about 9 percent at ages twenty-one to twenty-five. The incidence of extramarital affairs goes up to 14 percent of women at ages twenty-six to thirty and hits a peak of 17 percent of women between ages thirty-one and forty. After the late thirties and early forties, extramarital sex by women declines steadily, being acknowledged by 6 percent of women at ages fifty-one to fifty-five and only 4 percent of them at ages fifty-six to sixty. Thus, there is a curvilinear relationship between age and affairs for women: women have few affairs when they are both most and least reproductively valuable, but many more toward the end of their reproductive years.

A similar curvilinear age trend is found for women's orgasms from extramarital affairs. Kinsey tabulated the percentage of women's total sexual activity to orgasm, whatever the source, including marital sex, masturbation, and affairs. Women's orgasms from extramarital affairs represent only 3 percent of women's total orgasms between ages twenty-one and twenty-five, nearly triple to 11 percent toward the end of women's reproductive years at ages thirty-six to forty-five, and drop again to only 4 percent after menopause from ages fifty-six to sixty.

There may be several reasons for why women's extramarital affairs and orgasms peak toward the end of their reproductive years. Women at this time are guarded less intensely by their husbands and thus are better able to take advantage of existing sexual opportunities than more heavily guarded younger women. Older women also suffer fewer costs inflicted at the hands of a jealous husband, and therefore the deterrents to a tempting extramarital involvement might be less powerful.[21] Because the penalties for being caught are lower, older women may feel freer to pursue their extramarital desires. They may also be attempting to produce one last child before their fertility drops to zero—a phenomenon that evolutionary psychologist Judith Easton has called reproduction expediting.[22] Support for the reproduction expediting explanation also comes from the fact that women experience a surge in sexual fantasies and sex drive as they enter their thirties and the proverbial biological clock starts to tick more loudly.

Affairs may also signal an effort by women to switch mates before their own reproductive value has plummeted. Support for this idea comes from a study of 205 married individuals who had affairs. Fully 72 percent of women but only 51 percent of men were motivated by emotional commitment or long-term love rather than sexual desires in their extramarital dalliances.[23]

Another study found that men who had affairs were twice as likely as women to think of the involvement as purely sexual, devoid of emotional attachments.[24] Yet another study found that only 33 percent of women who had affairs believed that their marriages were happy, whereas 56 percent of men who had extramarital sex considered their marriages to be happy.[25] More men than women who are happily married can engage in extramarital sex without emotional involvement and without feeling that their marriages are unsatisfactory. The fact that women who have affairs are more likely to be unhappy in their marriages and more likely to be emotionally involved with the extramarital partner suggests that they may be using their affairs for the purpose of changing mates.

Men's patterns of extramarital sex differ from those of women. Men engage in sex outside marriage both more often and more consistently than women over their lifetime. The desires of married people provide a window on men's greater desire for extramarital sex. In one study, 48 percent of American men expressed a desire to engage in extramarital sex; the comparable figure for women was only 5 percent.[26] In another study of marital happiness among 769 American men and 770 American women, 72 percent of men, but only 27 percent of women, admitted that they sometimes experienced a desire for extramarital intercourse.[27] A study of working-class Germans reveals similar tendencies: 46 percent of married men but only 6 percent of married women acknowledged that they would take advantage of a casual sexual opportunity with someone attractive if it was provided.[28]

These desires often translate into actual affairs. In the Kinsey report on the lifetime incidence of extramarital coitus from age sixteen through age sixty, affairs by husbands surpassed those by wives at every age.[29] Fully 37 percent of married men in the youngest age bracket of sixteen to twenty reported at least one affair, in contrast to a mere 6 percent of comparably aged wives. The incidence of affairs by husbands remained relatively constant over the years, with only a slight downward trend in the later years.

These affairs are not occasional trifles. Instead, affairs make up a significant proportion of men's sexual outlets at every age throughout their life. Extramarital sex comprises about one-fifth of these men's sexual outlets between ages sixteen and thirty-five. It rises steadily to 26 percent at ages thirty-six to forty, 30 percent at ages forty-one to forty-five, and 35 percent at ages forty-six to fifty.[30] For men who engage in extramarital sex with companions and prostitutes, these forms of sex become increasingly important with age and occur at the expense of sex with their wives, which becomes a smaller and smaller fraction of their total. Given our knowledge of men's evolved sexual psychology, these patterns reflect boredom on the part of both spouses at repeating sex with the same person or the decreasing sexual attractiveness of wives to their husbands as a result of their increasing age.

The proportion of men and women who have affairs over their lifetime depends on the culture's mating system. In polygamous cultures, for example, where many men are left mateless and most fertile women are married, the percentages of men and women having affairs would naturally be different from the percentages in presumptively monogamous societies. Bachelors who seek sex have only married women to choose from. Furthermore, it is historically and cross-culturally common for a few high-ranking men to cuckold a large number of low-ranking men, as when Roman emperors such as Julius Caesar were permitted by law to have sex with other men's wives.[31] Under these conditions, the percentage of women having affairs would necessarily be greater than the percentage of men having affairs.

The main point about our evolved sexual strategies is not that men inevitably have more affairs than women or that infidelity is invariably expressed in men's behavior. Rather, men's sexual psychology disposes them to seek sexual variety, and men seek extramarital sex when the costs and risks are low. Some women also seek short-term sex, including extramarital sex, and these affairs may serve reproduction-expediting or mate-switching functions. Nonetheless, it is also true that women's desires, fantasies, and motivations for this form of sex are less intense on average than are men's. Mark Twain observed that "many men are goats and can't help committing adultery when they get a chance; whereas there are numbers of men who, by temperament, can keep their purity and let an opportunity go by if the woman lacks in attractiveness."[32] Extramarital sex remains a larger component of men's desires than women's throughout their lives, although many men refrain from translating that desire into infidelity.

Menopause—The Last Tick of the Biological Clock

A woman's capacity for reproduction reaches zero when menopause is complete. One of the extraordinary facts about women's lifetime development is that menopause occurs so long before life is over. Reproduction completely ends for most women by the time they reach fifty, even though many women live well into their seventies, eighties, or nineties. This situation contrasts sharply with that of all other primate species. Even in long-lived mammals, the post-reproductive phase for females represents only 10 percent or less of their total life span. Only 5 percent of elephants, for example, reach age fifty-five, but female fertility at that age is still 50 percent of the maximum observed at the peak of fertility.[33]

Other female functions decline gradually with age. Heart and lung efficiency, for example, is nearly 100 percent of capacity in the early twenties but declines to only 80 percent by the age of fifty.[34] In contrast, fertility peaks in the midtwenties but is close to 0 percent by the time a woman reaches fifty. The steep decline in women's fertility, in contrast to all other bodily functions, calls out for an explanation.

At one point in history, women themselves were blamed for menopause, owing to "many excesses introduced by luxury, and the irregularities of the passions."[35] Most people today see that as a sexist and antiquated notion. One current theory to account for the puzzling phenomenon of menopause is that women's post-reproductive phase has been artificially lengthened as a result of better nutrition and health care. According to this view, our human ancestors would have rarely lived long past menopause, if they reached it at all. This explanation appears highly unlikely, however, because the increase in the average human life span is due mainly to a decline in infant mortality. Ancestral people who lived to age twenty typically enjoyed a maximum life span close to our own, or roughly seventy to eighty years. Indeed, there is little evidence that medical technology has altered the maximum lifetime of humans at all.[36] The view that menopause is an incidental by-product of longer lives also cannot explain why women's reproductive function declines so sharply, whereas all of women's other vital capacities decline gradually, as if they were designed for a longer lifetime. Selection would be unlikely to favor efficient body functions into the fifties and sixties if ancestral humans did not live beyond fifty. Moreover, the longer-life view cannot explain the differences between the sexes whereby men's fertility fades only gradually, while women's declines precipitously.[37]

A more likely explanation for women's long post-reproductive phase is that menopause is a female adaptation that prompts the shift from mating and direct reproduction to parenting, grand-parenting, and other forms of investing in kin. This explanation, often called the grandmother hypothesis, depends on the assumption that continuing to produce children would actually have interfered with an ancestral woman's reproductive success compared to investing in her existing children, grandchildren, and other genetic relatives. It also assumes that older women would have been particularly valuable to their children and grandchildren. Older women, for example, tend to acquire wisdom and knowledge about health practices, kin relations, and stress management that younger women may lack. They also tend to increase their control over resources and their ability to influence other people. These increased powers and skills can be channeled toward children, grandchildren, and the entire extended network of a woman's genetic clan.[38]

One early test of the grandmother hypothesis among the Ache of Paraguay suggested that, for this group, the reproductive benefits provided by the shift from direct reproduction to grandparental investment may not be great enough to outweigh the reproductive costs to women of their lost capacity to produce children directly.[39] More recent tests show a bit more promising support for the grandmother hypothesis. A study of traditional Gambians found that the presence of maternal grandmothers, but not paternal grandmothers, increased a grandchild's survival for the first two years of life.[40] A study of eighteenth- and nineteenth-century Finnish peoples found that the longer the postmenopausal phase of a woman's life, the higher the probability that her grandchildren would survive.[41]

Another hypothesis for women's menopause is that there is a trade-off between rapid reproduction relatively early in life and more extended reproduction over the life span. Producing many high-quality children early may in effect wear out a woman's reproductive machinery, so that menopause is not in itself an adaptation but rather an incidental by-product of early and rapid breeding.[42] In this view, it becomes critical to identify the conditions that would have allowed ancestral women the opportunity to reproduce early and rapidly.

Early reproduction and births at short intervals, or at three to four years on average, may occur in women because ancestral women could often rely on food and protection offered by an investing mate. The tremendous parental resources that men channel to their children and mates may have created the favorable conditions for early and rapid reproduction. Chimpanzee and gorilla females, in contrast, must do all the provisioning by themselves and so cannot space offspring so closely. In these species, females space out their reproduction over nearly all of their adult lives by having one birth every five or six years. The change in women's lives that produces a cessation of direct reproduction and a shift to investing in genetic relatives may therefore be directly linked to the high levels of parental investment by men. Since men's investment can be traced, in turn, to the active choosing by women of men who show the ability and willingness to invest, the reproductive changes that occur over women's lives are intimately linked with the mating decisions that occur between the sexes.

Changes in Men's Mate Value

While women's desirability as mates declines predictably with age, the same does not apply to men's. The reason is that many of the key qualities that contribute to a man's value are not as closely or as predictably linked with age. These components include a man's intelligence, cooperativeness, parenting proclivities, political alliances, kin networks, coalitions, and, importantly, ability and willingness to provide resources to a woman and her children.

Men's value in supplying resources, indicated by cues such as income and social status, shows markedly different changes with age than women's reproductive value. There are two important differences: men's resources and social status typically peak much later in life than women's reproductive value, and men differ more markedly from one another in the resources and social status they accrue. Men's resources and status sometimes plummet, sometimes remain constant, and sometimes skyrocket with increasing age, whereas women's reproductive value declines steadily and inexorably with age.

For men, a distinction must be drawn between social status and the accrual of resources to understand their lifetime value as mates. In ancestral hunter-gatherer societies, limited hunting capacities and the short shelf life of killed game constrained how much meat men could accumulate. Furthermore, men in current hunter-gatherer societies do not vary widely in the amount of land they hold or the amount of meat they store.[43] Indeed, although men vary in hunting ability, some groups, such as the Ache of Paraguay, share their meat communally, so that individual men do not vary widely in the direct resources they derive from the hunt.

In societies where meat is shared communally, however, skillful hunters do experience a greater reproductive success than poor hunters. This can happen for two reasons. Men who are good hunters are attractive to women and consequently secure more extramarital matings than men who are poor hunters. Women prefer to have sex with the better hunters. The children of good hunters are better nurtured by other members of the group than are the children of poor hunters. Although Ache men do not vary in their meat resources per se, they do vary in their social status derived from hunting, which gives them sexual access to desirable women and better care for their children.[44] Thus, status and resources are somewhat separate qualities.

The advent of agriculture roughly 10,000 to 15,000 years ago and the invention of cash economies permitted the stockpiling of resources far beyond what was possible among our hunter-gatherer ancestors. The differences in tangible resources between someone like Facebook founder Mark Zuckerberg and a homeless person are much greater than those between the highest-ranked head man among the Ache and the lowest-ranked older male who is no longer able to hunt. The same may not be true for social status. Although cash economies have amplified the differences in men's resources, the status differences of contemporary men are not necessarily greater than the status differences among our ancestors.

Although social status is harder to measure than income, contemporary hunter-gatherer societies around the world provide clues to the distribution of social status by age. In no known culture do teenage boys enjoy the highest status. Among the Tiwi tribe, men are typically at least thirty years old—and often middle-aged—before they are in a position of sufficient status to acquire a wife or two.[45] Young Tiwi men lack the political alliances to garner much status.

Among the !Kung, the decade of the twenties is spent refining skills and acquiring knowledge and wisdom about hunting.[46] Not until a !Kung man is in his thirties does he come into his own in taking down large game for the group. Among the Ache of Paraguay, male prestige is also linked to hunting ability, which does not peak until the late twenties or early thirties and carries well into the late forties.[47] Among both the !Kung and Ache, men older than sixty typically become unable to hunt successfully, stop carrying bows and arrows, and show a considerable decline in their political status and ability to attract younger wives. Status among the Ache males may peak somewhere between twenty-five and fifty, corresponding closely with their hunting prowess.[48] Older Ache, Yanomamö, and Tiwi men command respect, status, and awe from younger men because they have survived so many club fights, spear fights, and ax fights. Men maintain status well into middle age if they manage to survive the onslaught of aggression from other men that long.

Similar trends tied to age are observed in contemporary Western societies. One indication of men's resources over their lifetime in contemporary Western society is actual monetary income.

Unfortunately, no worldwide statistics are available on men's and women's resources as a function of age. A particular income distribution by age in the United States, however, has been found repeatedly over the years. The distribution of men's average income in the United States, broken down by age, shows that income tends to be quite low among men in their teens and early twenties. In the decade between the ages of twenty-five and thirty-four, men's income attains only two-thirds of its eventual peak. Not until the decades from ages thirty-five to fifty-four does men's income in the United States achieve its peak. From age fifty-five on, men's income declines, undoubtedly because some men retire, become incapacitated, or lose the ability to command their previous salaries.[49] These income averages conceal great variability, because some men's resources continue to increase throughout their old age, whereas other men remain poor throughout their lives.

Because older men tend to have more status and resources than younger men, men and women of the same age differ on average in their value as mates. In the same decade between the ages of sixteen and twenty-five when women peak in fertility and reproductive value, men's income and status are typically the lowest that they will be in their adult lives. When most women between the ages of thirty-five and forty-four are rapidly approaching the end of their reproductive years, most men in the same decade are just approaching the peak of their earning capacity. To the extent that the central ingredients of desirability are a woman's reproductive value and a man's resource capacity, men and women of comparable age are not typically comparable in desirability.

Greater variability, which is the other critical difference between the value of women and men as mates at different ages, renders age per se a less important factor for men in mating. Men's occupational status in Western societies ranges from janitor or burger flipper to CEO, college president, or successful entrepreneur. Men at the same age vary in income from the nickels and dimes of a homeless person to the billions of a Bill Gates, Mark Zuckerberg, or Warren Buffett. Between the ages of twenty and forty, men diverge dramatically in their ability to accrue resources.

These trends fail, however, to reveal the tremendous variability in the individual circumstances of women who do the choosing. From a woman's perspective, her particular circumstances, not the averages, carry the most weight. Some middle-aged women prefer older men not because of their resources but because they believe that older men value them more than do men their own age. Among the Aka of Africa, for example, men who achieve high status and garner many resources during their lives contribute little to the direct care of their children when they marry. In contrast, Aka men who attain only low status and few resources for a wife and children compensate by spending more time directly caring for the children.[50] One key indicator of a father's investment, for example, is how many minutes a day he spends holding an infant, which is an expensive activity in terms of both calories consumed and other activities forgone. Holding protects an infant from environmental dangers, temperature changes, accidents, and aggression from others. Aka men who maintain positions of status in the group hold their infants an average of thirty minutes per day. Men who lack positions of status, in contrast, hold their infants more than seventy minutes per day. Although women typically prefer men with status and resources, a man's willingness to parent constitutes a valuable resource that can partially compensate for the lack of other qualities.

Some women, because of the tremendous economic resources they command, may not need to select a man based on his external acquisitions. The desirability of men must be evaluated by means of the psychological adaptations of women, and these mechanisms are highly sensitive to circumstances. This is not to

deny the importance of average trends; indeed, selection has produced such trends over thousands of generations of human evolutionary history. Our evolved psychological mechanisms include
not only those that promote mate choices that are specific and
typical of each sex but also adaptations that tailor our choices
over our lifetime to the individual circumstances in which we find
ourselves.

Earlier Death of Men

Human mating mechanisms account for the puzzling finding that
men die faster and earlier than women in all societies. Selection
has been harder on men than on women in this respect. Men
live shorter lives than women and die in greater numbers of more
causes at every point in the life cycle. In the United States, for
example, men die on average four to six years earlier than women.
Men are susceptible to more infections than women and die of a
greater variety of diseases than women. Men have more accidents
than women, including falls, accidental poisonings, drownings,
firearm accidents, car crashes, fires, and explosions. Males suffer a 30 percent higher mortality rate from accidents during the
first four years of life and a 400 percent higher mortality from
accidents by the time they reach adulthood.[51] Men are murdered
nearly three times as often as women. Men die taking risks more
often than women. They also commit suicide roughly three times
more often than women. The ages between sixteen and twenty-
eight, when mate competition reaches a strident pitch, seem
especially bad for men: they suffer a mortality rate nearly 200 percent higher than women at this time in their lives.

The reason for men's higher mortality, like that of males of
many mammalian species, stems directly from their sexual psychology, and in particular from their competition for mates.
The use of risky tactics of competition becomes greater as the

differences in reproductive outcome become greater. Where some males monopolize more than one female, there are tremendous reproductive benefits to being a winner and tremendous reproductive penalties for being a loser. The red deer is a case in point. Male deer who grow larger bodies and larger antlers experience greater mating success on average than their smaller counterparts. They are able to beat their rivals in head-to-head competition. But their success comes at a cost to their survival. Precisely the same traits that give them their mating success lead to a greater likelihood of dying. During a cold winter with scarce resources, for example, the male is more likely to die because of a failure to obtain enough food for his larger body. Larger size may also make the male more susceptible to predation and less agile at escape. To these possibilities must be added the risk of dying directly through intrasexual combat. All these risks follow from the sexual strategies of red deer, which pay off on average in the competition for mates but also generally result in a shorter lifetime.

As a rule, throughout the animal kingdom, the more polygynous the mating system, the greater the differences between the sexes in terms of mortality.[52] Polygynous mating selects for males who take risks—risks in competing with other males, risks in securing the resources desired by females, and risks in exposing themselves to dangers while pursuing and courting females. In a mildly polygynous mating system like our own, some men acquire multiple partners through serial marriage and affairs and others are left mateless. Competition among men and selection by women of men high in status and resources are ultimately responsible for the evolution in males of risk-taking traits that lead to successful mating at the expense of a long life.

Because the reproductive stakes are higher for men than for women, more men than women risk being shut out of mating entirely. Men who are mateless for life are more numerous than similarly mateless women in every society. In the United States in 2015, for example, 67 percent of men but only 54 percent of women in the twenty-five- to twenty-nine-year-old age bracket had never been married.[53] In the thirty- to thirty-four-year-old age bracket, 41 percent of men but only 31 percent of women had never been married. These gender differences reach extremes in highly polygynous cultures such as the Tiwi, where literally all women are married, a few men have as many as twenty-nine wives, and therefore many men are relegated to bachelorhood.[54]

This adaptive logic suggests that the greater risk taking—and hence greater death rate—should occur among men who are at the bottom of the mating pool and who therefore risk getting shut out entirely. Men who are unemployed, unmarried, and young are greatly overrepresented in risky activities, ranging from gambling to lethal fights.[55] Among homicides in Detroit in 1972, for example, 41 percent of adult male offenders were unemployed, compared with an unemployment rate of 11 percent for the whole city. Sixty-nine percent of the male victims and 73 percent of the male perpetrators were unmarried, compared with an unmarried rate of 43 percent in the entire city. These homicides were also disproportionately concentrated between the ages of sixteen and thirty. In short, men low in desirability, as indicated by being unemployed, unmarried, and young, seem especially prone to risk taking, which sometimes becomes lethal. The point is not that killing per se is necessarily an adaptation but rather that men's evolved sexual psychologies are designed to respond to dire mating conditions by increasing the amount of risk they are willing to take.

In ancestral times, the great reproductive gains that risk-taking men generally achieved and the reproductive dead ends that usually awaited more cautious men have favored traits that yield success in competition among males at the expense of success at longevity. In the currency of sheer survival, selection through mate competition has been hard on men.

A Mating Crisis—Especially
for Educated Women

The earlier death of men is one critical factor among several that produces a serious imbalance between the number of men relative to the number of women on the mating market—a disparity that gets more severe with time. This phenomenon is sometimes referred to as "the marriage squeeze," although it occurs whether or not people seek marriage per se. Many factors affect the relative numbers. Rates of infant, childhood, adolescent, and adult mortality differ, with males dying at a faster rate throughout the life span. Men emigrate more often than women, leaving behind a sexual imbalance. Baby booms also cause imbalances because women typically select men older than they are and there are fewer men for the many women born during the boom to choose from the smaller cohort born before the baby boom. From men's perspective, those born prior to the baby boom have a relatively large pool of women to select from, since they tend to choose younger women who were born during the boom period. Far more men than women are imprisoned, creating even more imbalance in the ratio between the sexes on the mating market. And wars end men's lives far more often than women's lives, creating a surplus of women on subsequent mating markets.

Divorce and remarriage patterns over the life span are other key causes of the marriage squeeze. Men who divorce tend to remarry women who are increasingly younger than they are. A 2013 study, for example, found that among first-time married men, only 10 percent married women ten or more years younger than they were and 5 percent married women who were six to nine years younger.[56] Upon remarriage, these figures jumped to 20 percent and 18 percent, so that fully 38 percent of remarried men had brides six or more years younger. It may be a cliché that men marry women increasingly younger as they age and remarry, but in this case the stereotype is verified by the statistics.

These remarriage patterns are not quirks of North American countries but rather emerge in every country for which there is adequate information. In one study of forty-seven countries, age affected women's chances of remarriage more than men's.[57] For the ages of twenty-five to twenty-nine, the differences in remarriage by sex were slight, because young women maintain high desirability at those ages as potential mates. By the ages of fifty to fifty-four, however, the sexes diverge dramatically in their remarriage rates. In that age bracket in Egypt, for example, four times as many men as women remarry; in Ecuador, nine times as many men as women remarry; and in Tunisia, nineteen times as many men as women remarry.

The mating crisis is especially pronounced among educated women. Every year more women than men become college-educated. The disparity is already prevalent across North America and Europe, and the trend is beginning to spread across the world more widely. At the University of Texas at Austin where I teach, the 2016 student body consisted of 54 percent women to 46 percent men. This imbalance may not seem large at first blush. But if you do the math correctly, it translates into a hefty 17 percent more women than men in the local mating pool. A key cause of the broader mating crisis for educated women is that women seek certain qualities in committed mateships. Most women are unwilling to settle for men who are less educated, less intelligent, and less professionally successful than they are. Men are less exacting on precisely these dimensions, choosing to prioritize, for better or worse, other evolved criteria such as youth and appearance. So the initial sex ratio imbalance within the college-educated group gets worse for high-achieving women. They end up being forced to compete for the limited pool of educated men not just with their more numerous educated rivals, but also with less educated women who men find desirable on other dimensions. The good news is that educated women and men who choose each other tend to have happier, more stable, and more affluent marriages.

The sex ratio imbalance as women age is largely an outcome of the sexual psychology of men and women. At the heart of this squeeze is the decline in female reproductive value with age, which caused selection to favor ancestral men who preferred younger women as mates and to favor ancestral women who preferred somewhat older men with status and resources as mates. In the modern environment, intelligence and education predict upward mobility. Young, healthy, and attractive women act on their desires for somewhat older, high-prestige mates, attracting men who might otherwise become mates for older women. Men with status and relative wealth try to fulfill their preferences for youthful, healthy, attractive women. And because ancestral women's preferences for men with resources created a selection pressure for greater male competitiveness and risk taking, men die at a faster rate than women, exacerbating the shortage of men.

Changes in the proportion of men to women throughout life cause predictable changes in their sexual strategies. The degree of selectivity is the first strategy to shift. When there is a surplus of men, fewer men can be highly choosy, and they must settle for a less desirable mate than they would otherwise attract if the sexes were more in balance. A low sex ratio, in contrast, restricts women's selectivity, because there are fewer men from whom to choose. These ratios affect the degree to which both sexes can translate their ideal preferences into actual mateships.

Low proportions of men also cause a destabilization of marriage. A surplus of women makes many of them unable to secure strong commitments. Men with many available women can pursue casual sexual liaisons with aplomb. The current rise of the hookup culture on college campuses can be traced, in part, to the surplus of women. Changes in the ratios of men to women within the United States throughout history support this explanation, because periods of increasing divorce, as between 1970 and 1980, correspond closely to periods when there was a surplus of women on the mating market.[58]

In the late 1980s, in contrast, divorce rates for new marriages were lower than in the previous decade, coinciding with an increase in the sex ratio.[59] At that time American women's marital happiness was also higher than their husbands', whereas it had fallen below their husbands' marital happiness during the preceding fifteen years, when there was a shortage of men.[60] The number of men pursuing business careers doubled between 1973 and the late 1980s, coinciding with the shift from a low to a high ratio of males and suggesting that men were becoming more concerned with their economic success. Men's willingness to invest directly in care for their children can also be expected to increase at such times, though no evidence yet exists on this point. Men may strive to become kinder and gentler to fulfill women's mating preferences when there are relatively few available women.

A shortage of available men also causes women to take greater responsibility for providing resources. One reason is that women are not able to count on provisioning from men. Furthermore, increasing economic assets may represent a woman's strategy to increase her desirability, analogous to the dowry competition in traditional societies. Throughout history, female participation in paid employment has increased during periods of low ratios of men to women. During the 1920s, foreign-born women in the United States outnumbered foreign-born men because of restrictive immigration laws; the participation of these women in the labor force abruptly rose.[61] The existence of fewer investing men causes women to take greater responsibility for securing their own resources.

Women in mating markets of few men also intensify their competition with each other by enhancing their appearance, increasing their health-promoting behavior, and even offering sexual resources to attract men. In the sexual revolution in the United States in the late 1960s and the 1970s, for example, many women abandoned their sexual reserve and engaged in sexual relationships without requiring serious male commitment. This shift in sexual mores coincided with a period of low numbers of optimally older men for women of the baby boom. Increased competition among females with regard to their appearance, as shown by such trends as the rise of the diet industries, the mushrooming of the women's makeup and make-over industries, and the increase in cosmetic plastic surgery—including tummy tucks, liposuction, breast implants, and facelifts—also occurred in this time of a shortage of men.

When there are more men competing for fewer women, the balance of power shifts to women. Women can more easily command what they want from men, and men in turn become more competitive with one another to attract and retain desirable women. Marriages and other long-term committed relationships are more stable, because men are more willing to offer commitment and are less willing to leave. Men have fewer available alternatives and cannot easily pursue casual sexual goals when women are scarce. Men therefore increasingly compete to fulfill women's preferences for a long-term mate, especially by striving for position and showing a willingness to invest parentally.

Not all changes that occur during periods of high ratios of men, however, benefit women. An important drawback is the potential at these times for increasing violence toward women. During periods of male surplus, great numbers of men are excluded from mating because there are not enough women to go around. Furthermore, men who can attract women under these conditions jealously guard them against rivals. Married women in turn have more alternatives, and so the threat of their leaving gains greater credibility. This circumstance may evoke sexual jealousy in husbands, promoting threats and violence to control wives and increased violence against men who threaten to lure a mate away.[62]

The existence of large numbers of men who are unable to attract a mate may also increase sexual aggression and rape. Violence often becomes the strategy of people who lack resources that would otherwise elicit voluntary compliance with their wishes.[63] Rape is sometimes perpetrated by marginal men who lack the status and resources that women seek in long-term mates.[64] Furthermore, the likelihood of war is apparently higher in societies with a high ratio of males than in societies with a low ratio of males, supporting the theory that competition among males intensifies at times of a surplus of males.[65]

Changes in the ratio of men to women throughout life cause corresponding shifts in mating strategies. Adolescent men often live in a world where available women are in scarce supply, because women prefer mature men with position and affluence. Young men's strategies reflect these local conditions of female scarcity, because they engage in highly risky competition strategies, committing the vast majority of violent crimes of sexual coercion, robbery, battery, and murder.[66] In one study, for example, 71 percent of the men arrested for rape were between the ages of fifteen and twenty-nine.[67] These are crimes of coercion against women whom men cannot attract or control through positive incentives.

As men mature into their thirties and forties, the ratio between the sexes typically tilts in their favor, if they have survived the risks and attained positions of reasonable status. They have a wider pool of potential women to choose from, and they enjoy a higher value on the mating market than they did in their youth.

They are better able to attract multiple mates, whether through casual sex, extramarital sex, serial marriage, or polygyny. Men of any age who have little desirability as mates, however, do not enjoy this advantage, and some men are shut out of mating entirely. Women experience an increasingly skewed sex ratio as they age and are more often forced to compromise their mating strategies by lowering their standards, increasing their level of intrasexual competition, securing more resources on their own, or sometimes just opting out of the mating market. These changes over time are all products of our evolved mating strategies.

The Prospects for Lifetime Mating

Human mating changes over a lifetime, from the internal stirrings of puberty through the final bequest of inheritance to a surviving spouse. Both sexes have evolved psychological mechanisms designed to solve the problems posed by change over time—adaptations sensitive to shifts in reproductive value, status and resources, sex ratio, and mating opportunities. The changes affect women and men differently, and some of these changes are unpleasant. Women begin puberty two years earlier than men, but their capacity for reproduction stops two or three decades before men's. The urgency that some childless women feel as their remaining years of potential reproduction wane—the increasingly loud ticking of the biological clock—is not caused by an arbitrary custom dictated by a particular culture, but rather reflects a psychological adaptation attuned to a reproductive reality.

A woman's reproductive value over time affects not only her own sexual strategies but those of the men in her social environment, including her regular mate and other potential mates. When women are young, their partners guard them intensely, clinging tightly to the valuable reproductive resource they have successfully secured. The intense guarding closes off a woman's opportunities for affairs and women see it as a sign of a man's commitment or insecurity depending on circumstances. The sex lives of many couples are initially electrifying, made more so by the presence of interested rivals. With each passing year, however, the frequency of intercourse declines as women's reproductive value declines. Episodes of intense jealousy gradually wane. Men become increasingly dissatisfied, and they show less affection to their wives. Women dislike this diminished attention from their mates and become increasingly irritated and upset about being neglected. Simultaneously, men express mounting distress about the demands of their mates for time and attention.

As women get older, men loosen the grip of guarding, and a higher and higher proportion of women pursue extramarital affairs, reaching a maximum as women approach the end of their reproductive years. Whereas for men affairs are often motivated by the desire for sexual variety, for women affairs are motivated more by emotional goals and may represent an effort to switch mates while they are still reproductively vibrant. Women seem to know that their desirability on the mating market will be higher if they leave their husbands sooner rather than later. After menopause, women shift their effort toward parenting and grandparenting, aiding the survival and reproduction of their descendants rather than continuing to reproduce directly. Women pay for their reproductive strategy of early and rapid reproduction in the currency of a shorter period of fertility.

Changes in men over a lifetime, like those of male chimpanzees, are more variable in the currencies of mating success. Men who increase their status and prestige remain highly desirable over the years. Men who fail to accrue resources and status become increasingly sidelined in the field of mating. Roughly half of all married men pursue some extramarital mating over their lifetime, and for those who do, liaisons occur at the expense of sex with their wives. Some men continue throughout life to compete for new mates, divorcing older wives and marrying younger women. Long attributed by traditional scientists to the fragile male ego, to psychosexual immaturity, to "male menopause," or to a culture of youth, men's effort to mate with younger women as they age instead reflects a universal evolved desire that does not go away.

One startling by-product of the differences in mating strategies of the sexes over the lifetime is that men die at an earlier age than women. This is a predictable consequence of the greater risk taking and intrasexual competition of men as they pursue the status and resources that bring about success in mating. With increasing age, the ratio of men to women becomes increasingly skewed, resulting in a surplus of women, especially among those with higher education. For women who reenter the mating market, the sex ratio imbalance becomes worse with each passing year. Both sexes have evolved mechanisms designed to shift strategies depending on changes in the sex ratio.

Given all the changes that befall men and women over their lifetimes, it is remarkable that in fact 50 percent of them manage to remain together through thick and thin. The lifelong convergence of interests between two genetically unrelated individuals may be the most extraordinary feat in the evolutionary story of human mating. Just as we have evolved mechanisms that draw us into conflict, we have adaptations that enable us to live harmoniously with the other sex. My lab's massive cross-cultural study, for example, found that as men and women age they place less value on physical appearance in a mate and more value on enduring qualities such as dependability and having a pleasing disposition—qualities important for long-term mating success. The adaptations that promote this strategic harmony between the sexes, just as much as the mechanisms that produce strife, stem from the adaptive logic of human mating.

10

Harmony Between
the Sexes

Everything that every individual has ever done in all of
human history and prehistory establishes the minimum
boundary of the possible. The maximum, if any, is completely unknown.

—JEROME BARKOW, LEDA COSMIDES, AND
JOHN TOOBY, *The Adapted Mind*

UNDERSTANDING HUMAN MATING requires recognizing that our
strategies are multiple, flexible, and contingent on context,
culture, and personal condition. Our complex psychological
adaptations, designed by a long history of evolution, give us a
versatile strategic repertoire for coping with the challenges of
mating. With this repertoire, we tailor our mating decisions to
individual and social circumstances in a valiant effort to fulfill
our desires and, ideally, fulfill the desires of special others. In

330 The Evolution of Desire

the mating marketplace, no behavior is inevitable or genetically preordained—neither infidelity nor monogamy, neither sexual violence nor sexual tranquility, neither jealous guarding nor sexual indifference. Men are not doomed to have affairs because of an insatiable lust for sexual variety. Women are not doomed to dismiss men who lack status and prestige. We are not slaves to sex roles dictated by evolution. Knowledge of our multifaceted desires and the costs and benefits of different strategies gives us the possibility of choosing from our wide-ranging mating menu.

Understanding why sexual strategies have evolved and the adaptive problems they were designed to solve provides a powerful fulcrum for changing behavior. Just because humans have physiological adaptations that cause us to grow calluses in response to repeated friction to the skin, for example, it is not inevitable that humans must develop calluses. We can and do create more friction-free environments. Similarly, knowing that jealousy functions to protect paternity for men and the commitment of a mate for women brings into focus the conditions most likely to trigger jealousy, such as cues to sexual and emotional infidelity. In principle, just as we can create environments that minimize friction, we can create jealousy-free relationships. Those who practice polyamory strive to do precisely that, and they sometimes succeed, although it would be naive to think that shutting down such strong emotional circuits is simple or easy.

Throughout this book I have used empirical studies of mating as the building blocks for a theory of human mating psychology. Although I have not hesitated to speculate when warranted, it is anchored in evidence. Now I will go beyond the scientific findings to describe what I see as their broader implications for social interactions in general, and for relations between men and women in particular.

Differences Between the Sexes

Insight into the relations between men and women must penetrate the riddle of gender similarities and differences. Because women and men alike have faced many similar adaptive challenges over evolutionary history, all humans share many psychological solutions. Both sexes sweat and shiver to regulate body temperature. Both sexes place a tremendous value on intelligence and dependability in a lifetime mate. Both seek long-term mates who are cooperative, trustworthy, and loyal. And both desire mates who will not inflict crushing costs on them. We are all of one species from the same planet. Recognition of our shared psychology and shared biology is one step toward producing harmony between the sexes.

Against the backdrop of these shared adaptations, gender differences stand out in stark relief and demand explanation. Men and women differ in their psychology of mating solely and specifically in the domains where they have faced recurrently different adaptive problems over the long course of evolutionary history. Because ancestral women bore the lion's share of responsibility for nourishing their infants, women rather than men have lactating breasts. Because fertilization occurs internally within women, ancestral men confronted the problem of uncertainty over their fatherhood. As a consequence, men have evolved particular mate preferences for sexual loyalty, a psychology of jealousy centered on sexual infidelity, and a proclivity to withdraw commitment when cuckolded, all of which differ in design from the mating psychology of women.[1]

Some of these gender differences may be unpleasant. Many women dislike being treated as sex objects or valued for qualities largely beyond their control, such as youth and beauty, although some exploit these desires for their own ends. Many men dislike being treated as success objects or valued for the size of their investment portfolio and the importance of their status in a competitive world, although they too sometimes exploit these desires for their own ends. It is painful to be the wife of a man whose desire for sexual variety leads him to sexual infidelity. It is painful to be the husband of a woman whose desire for emotional closeness leads her to seek intimacy in the arms of another man. For both genders it is distressing to be regarded as undesirable merely because one does not possess qualities that the other prefers in a mate.

To assume that men and women are psychologically the same, as was generally done in traditional social science and still is in some out-of-date scientific circles, goes against what we now know about our evolved sexual psychology. Given the power of sexual selection, under which each sex competes for access to desirable mates, it would defy scientific logic to find that men and women were psychologically identical in aspects of mating about which they have faced different adaptive challenges for millions of years. At this point in history, we can no longer doubt that men and women differ in their preferences for a mate: primarily for youth and physical attractiveness in one case, and for status, maturity, success, protection, and economic resources in the other. Men and women also differ in their proclivities for casual sex without emotional involvement, in their desire for sexual variety, and in the nature of their sexual fantasies.

Internet dating sites reveal modern expressions of our evolved sexual psychology. Tinder is deluged with more men than women who want casual sex. AshleyMadison.com appeals mostly to married men who seek sexual variety. SeekingArrangement.com caters to men with status and resources and women with youth and beauty who want to parlay their respective assets.

Men and women face different forms of interference with their preferred sexual strategies and so differ in the kinds of events that trigger powerful emotions such as anger and jealousy. Men and women differ in their tactics to attract mates, to keep mates, to eject mates, and to replace mates. These differences are universal features of our evolved strategies. They govern social interactions and fundamental relationships between individual women and men.

Some people complain about these differences, or deny that they exist despite the scientific evidence, or wish that they would cease to exist. But wishes and denials will not make psychological gender differences disappear, any more than they will make men's beard growth or women's breast development disappear. Harmony between men and women will be approached only when these denials are swept away and we squarely confront the differing desires and strategies of each.

The Evolutionary Origins of Patriarchy

The evolution of gender differences has unavoidable implications for feminism, as noted by feminist evolutionists such as Patricia Gowaty, Maryanne Fisher-MacDonnell, Jane Lancaster, Barbara Smuts, and Griet Vandermassen. According to the tenets of many feminists, patriarchy—defined roughly as the control of power and resources by men and the physical, psychological, and sexual subordination of women—is a major cause of the battle between the sexes. Oppression through subordination and the control of resources is said to be motivated by men's desire to control women's sexuality and reproduction. Human sexual strategies bear out major elements of this feminist viewpoint. Men indeed tend to control resources worldwide, although this is changing in many cultures that strive for economic equality. Individual men do oppress individual women not only through their control of resources but sometimes through sexual coercion and violence. Men's efforts to control women do center on women's sexuality and reproduction. And women, as well as men, often participate in perpetuating this oppression.[2]

An evolutionary perspective on sexual strategies provides valuable insights into the origins and maintenance of men's control of resources and men's attempts to control women's sexuality. A startling consequence of sexual strategies, for example, is that men's dominant control of resources worldwide can be traced, in part, to women's preferences in choosing a mate.[3] These preferences, operating repeatedly over thousands of generations, have led women to favor men who possess status and resources and to disfavor men who lack these assets. Ancestral men who failed to acquire such resources failed to attract women as mates.

Women's preferences thus established a critical set of ground rules for men in their competition with one another. Modern men have inherited from their ancestors psychological mechanisms that not only give priority to resources and status but also lead men to make great sacrifices and take great risks to attain resources and status. Men who fail to give these goals a high personal priority fail to attract mates.

One of men's key strategies is to form coalitions with other men. These organized alliances give men the power to triumph over other men in their quest for resources and sexual access. In animals, strong coalitions are seen among baboons, chimpanzees, and dolphins.[4] Male bottlenose dolphins, for example, form coalitions to herd females and thereby gain greater sexual access than would be possible by operating alone.[5] Among chimpanzees, our closest primate relative, males form alliances to increase their chances of victory in physical contests with other chimpanzees, their status in the group hierarchy, and their sexual access to females. Rarely can a male chimpanzee become the dominant member of the troop without the aid of allies. Solitary males without coalition partners are at great risk of being brutally attacked and sometimes killed by males from other groups.[6]

Human males, too, form alliances for gaining resources such as large game, political power within the group, ways to defend against the aggression of other coalitions of men, and sexual access to women.[7] The survival and reproductive benefits derived from these coalitional activities constituted tremendous selection pressure over human evolutionary history for men to form alliances with other men. Since ancestral women did not hunt large game, declare war on other tribes, or attempt to forcibly capture men from neighboring bands, they did not experience equivalent selection pressure to form coalitions.[8] Although women do form coalitions with other women for the care of the young and for protection from sexually aggressive men, these are weakened whenever a woman leaves her kin group to live with her husband and his clan. The combination of strong coalitions among men and somewhat weaker coalitions among women, according to Barbara Smuts, may have contributed historically to men's dominance over women.[9] My view is that women's preferences for a successful, ambitious, and resource-capable mate coevolved with men's competitive mating strategies, which include risk taking, status striving, derogation of competitors, coalition formation, and an array of individual efforts aimed at surpassing other men on the dimensions that women desire. The intertwining of these coevolved mechanisms in men and women created the conditions for men to dominate in the domain of resources.

The origins of men's control over resources is not simply an incidental historical footnote of passing curiosity. Rather, it has a profound bearing on the present, because it reveals some of the primary causes of men's continuing control of resources. Women today continue to want men who have resources, and they continue to reject men who lack resources. These preferences are expressed repeatedly in dozens of studies conducted on tens of thousands of individuals in scores of countries worldwide. They are expressed countless times in everyday life. In any given year, the men whom women marry earn more than men of the same age whom women do not marry. Even professionally successful women who do not really need resources from a man are reluctant to settle for a mate who is less successful than they are. Women who earn more than their husbands seek divorce more often, although this trend appears to be changing, at least within America. Men continue to compete with other men to acquire the status and resources that make them desirable to women. The forces that originally caused the resource inequality between the genders—women's mate preferences and men's competitive strategies—are the same forces that contribute to maintaining resource inequality today.[10]

Feminists' and evolutionists' conclusions converge in their implication that men's efforts to control female sexuality lie at the core of their efforts to control women. Our evolved sexual strategies account for why this occurs, and why control of women's sexuality is a central preoccupation of men.[11] Over the course of human evolutionary history, men who failed to control women's sexuality—for example, by failing to attract a mate, failing to prevent cuckoldry, or failing to retain a mate—experienced lower reproductive success than men who succeeded in controlling women's sexuality. We come from a long and unbroken line of ancestral fathers who succeeded in obtaining mates, preventing their infidelity, and providing enough benefits to keep them from leaving. We also come from a long line of ancestral mothers who granted sexual access to men who provided beneficial resources.

Feminist theory sometimes portrays men as being united with all other men in their common purpose of oppressing women.[12] But the evolution of human mating suggests that this scenario cannot be true, because men and women compete primarily against members of their own gender. Men strive to control resources mainly at the expense of other men. Men deprive other men of their resources, exclude other men from positions of status and power, and derogate other men in order to make them less desirable to women. Indeed, the fact that nearly 70 percent of all homicides are inflicted by men on other men reveals the tip of the iceberg of the cost of competition to men.[13] The fact that men on average die years earlier than women in every culture is further testimony to the penalties men pay for this struggle with other men.

Women do not escape damage inflicted by members of their own sex.[14] Women compete with each other for access to high-status men, have sex with other women's husbands, and lure men away from their wives. Mate poaching is a ubiquitous sexual strategy of our species. Women slander and denigrate their rivals and are especially harsh toward women who pursue short-term sexual strategies. Women and men are both victims of the sexual strategies of their own gender and so can hardly be said to be united with their own gender for some common goal.

Moreover, both men and women benefit from the strategies of the opposite sex. Men lavish resources and protection on certain women, including their wives, their sisters, their daughters, and their mistresses. A woman's father, brothers, and sons all benefit from her selection of a mate who is flush with abundance. Contrary to the view that men or women are united with all members of their own sex for the purpose of oppressing the other sex, each individual shares key interests with particular members of each sex and is in conflict with other members of each sex. Simple-minded views of a same-sex conspiracy have no foundation in reality.

Although today men's sexual strategies contribute to their control over resources, the origins of their strategies cannot be separated from the evolution of women's desires. This analysis does not imply that we should blame women for the fact that men control resources or blame men for their relentless pursuit of them. Rather, if harmony and equality are to be achieved, women and men both must be recognized as linked together in a spiraling causal chain of this coevolutionary process. This process started long ago with the evolution of desire and continues to operate today through our strategies of mating.

Diversity in Mating Strategies

Differences in the desires of men and women represent an important part of the diversity within the human species, but there is tremendous variability within each sex as well. Although more men than women are inclined to pursue purely casual sexual relationships, some men remain exclusively monogamous for life and some women find polyamory, casual sex, or a mixed mating strategy preferable to monogamy. Some men seek women for their economic resources, and some women seek men for their looks, despite average trends to the contrary. Although most men and most women are sexually attracted to the other gender, some are attracted to members of their own gender, some to both, and some to neither. These differences within each gender cannot be dismissed as statistical flukes. They are crucial to understanding the rich repertoire of human mating strategies.

Sexual diversity hinges on the individual circumstances that favor each person's choice of one strategy over another within their repertoire—a choice that may not be consciously articulated. For example, Aka men favor a mating strategy of high parental investment when they lack economic resources.[15] !Kung women favor serial mating in circumstances in which they are sufficiently desirable to continue attracting men who are willing to invest.[16] Our mate value—how desirable we are in the mating market—influences the degree to which we can translate our desires into actual mating outcomes. No mating strategies, however deeply rooted in our evolved psychology, are invariably expressed regardless of social context or regardless of mate value. Knowledge of the contexts that facilitate and impede each sexual strategy aids our understanding of the diversity of mating behaviors within and between the genders.

Knowledge of this diversity leads one to scrutinize certain value judgments for the selfish interests that may be driving them. In Western society, lifelong monogamy is often held up to be the ideal. Anyone who does not conform to this practice is regarded as deviant, immature, sinful, or a failure. Such a judgment may turn out to be a manifestation of the underlying sexual strategies of the person who upholds it. It is often in the best interests of a woman, for example, to convince others of the ideal of lifelong love. Women pursuing a short-term mating strategy pose a threat to monogamous women, siphoning off the resources, attention, and commitment of their long-term mates. It is often in the best interests of a man to convince others to adopt a monogamous strategy, even if he fails to follow it himself. Promiscuous men usurp single men's mating opportunities and threaten to poach already mated women. Our sexual morality, in short, is a key component of our evolved mating strategies.

The short-term sexual strategies of both genders originate deep in human evolutionary history. Evolutionary accounts that emphasize the sexually indiscriminate man and the sexually coy woman grossly overstate the case. Just as men have the capacity for commitment as part of their strategic repertoire, women have the capacity for casual sex within theirs, and they in fact pursue it when they perceive that it is to their advantage to do so.

For a century after Darwin proposed the theory of sexual selection, it was vigorously resisted by male scientists, in part because they presumed that women were passive in the mating process. The proposal that women actively select their mates and that these selections constitute a powerful evolutionary force was thought to be science fiction rather than scientific fact. In the 1970s, scientists gradually came to accept the profound importance of female choice in the animal and insect world, and in the 1980s and

1990s scientists began to document within our own species the active strategies that women pursue in choosing and competing for mates. But in the early decades of the twenty-first century, some stubborn holdouts continue to insist that women have but a single mating strategy—the pursuit of a long-term mate.

Scientific evidence suggests otherwise. The fact that women who are engaged in casual sex as opposed to committed mating shift their mating desires to favor a man's extravagant lifestyle, his physical attractiveness, his masculine body, and even his risk-taking, cocky "bad-boy" qualities tells us that women have specific psychological mechanisms designed for short-term mating. The fact that women who have extramarital affairs often choose men who are higher in status than their husbands and tend to fall in love with their affair partners reveals that women have adaptations for mate switching. The fact that women shift to brief liaisons under predictable circumstances, such as a scarcity of men capable of investing in them or an unfavorable ratio of women to men, tells us that women have specific adaptations designed for shifting from long-term to short-term mating strategies.

People often condemn as immoral the frequent switching of mates and other sexually uninhibited activities. And it often serves their interests to promulgate this view of morality to others. Our sexual morality stems from our evolved sexual strategies. From a scientific point of view, however, there is no moral justification for placing a premium on a single strategy within the collective human repertoire. Our human nature is found in the entire repertoire of our sexual strategies. Recognition of the rich diversity of desires takes us one step closer to harmony.

Cultural Variation in Mating

Cultural variation represents one of the most fascinating and mysterious aspects of human diversity. Members of different societies differ dramatically on some qualities, as in their desire for virginity in a marriage partner. In China in the 1980s, for example, nearly every individual, both male and female, viewed virginity as indispensable in a mate. Nonvirgin Chinese were virtually unmarriageable. Chinese culture has changed, however, over the past thirty years: although virginity is still valued, research from my lab found that its importance in mate preferences has gradually declined.[17] In Scandinavian countries, such as Sweden and Norway, chastity was, and still is, unimportant in a mate. This kind of cultural variability poses a puzzle for all theories of human mating.

Evolutionary psychology focuses on early experiences, parenting practices, and other current social and ecological factors to explain variability in mating strategies. The psychologist Jay Belsky and his colleagues, for example, argue that harsh, rejecting, and inconsistent child-rearing practices, erratically provided resources, and marital discord foster in children a mating strategy of early reproduction and rapid turnover.[18] In contrast, sensitive, supportive, and responsive child rearing, combined with reliable resources and spousal harmony, foster in children a mating strategy of commitment marked by delayed reproduction and stable marital bonds. Children growing up in uncertain and unpredictable environments, in short, learn that they cannot rely on a single mate. They therefore opt for a sexual life that starts early and that inclines them to switch mates frequently. In contrast, children who grow up in stable homes with predictably investing parents opt for a strategy of permanent mating because they expect to attract a stable, high-investing mate. The evidence from children of divorced homes supports this theory. Such children reach puberty earlier, engage in intercourse earlier, and have more numerous sex partners than their peers from intact homes.

The sensitivity of mating strategies to early experiences may help to explain the differences in the value placed on chastity across cultures. In China, for example, marriages historically have been lasting and divorce has been rare, with parents investing heavily in their children over extended periods. In Sweden, many children are born out of wedlock, divorce is common, and fewer fathers invest consistently over time. Chinese and Swedes may select different sexual strategies from the universal human repertoire because of these early developmental experiences. Although the significance of early experiences requires further testing, the evidence so far supports the view that men and women both have casual mating, committed mating, mate poaching, and mate-switching strategies within their repertoires. The particular strategy they choose from this menu depends partly on their early experiences, which vary from culture to culture.

Differences between the relatively promiscuous Ache and the relatively monogamous Hiwi also illuminate the cultural variability of human sexual strategies. The different ratios of males to females in these two cultures may be the critical factor in eliciting a different sexual strategy. Among the Ache, there are approximately one and a half women for every man. Among the Hiwi, there are more men than women, although precise numbers are not available. The prevalence of available Ache women creates sexual opportunities for Ache men not experienced by Hiwi men. Ache men seize these opportunities, as evidenced by the high frequency of mate switching and casual affairs. Ache men can pursue a temporary sexual strategy more successfully than Hiwi men can. Hiwi women are better able than Ache women to secure a high investment from men, who must provide resources to attract and retain a mate.[19] The cultural shifts witnessed today, such as the hookup culture on college campuses and in large urban settings and the rise of casual sex and online dating apps such as Tinder, probably reflect shifts in mating strategies as a function of a perceived or real sex ratio imbalance.

One key cultural variable centers on the presumptive mating system, especially monogamy and polygamy. Some Islamic cultures permit men to marry up to four wives, as specified in the Qur'an. In parts of Utah and Texas in the United States, some fundamentalist Mormon groups place no formal limits on the number of wives a man can marry, and a few marry more than a dozen. Even presumptively monogamous cultures are often effectively polygynous, with some men having multiple mates through serial marriage or affair partners. The more polygynous the culture, the more some men will be inclined to pursue high-risk tactics in an effort to gain status, resources, and mates, either in the current life or in aspirational notions of life after death. Just as mating is a key cause of violence among nonhuman animals from elk to elephant seals, mating and violence are inexorably linked in our own species. Evolved mating strategies are influenced by, and implemented within, these key cultural contexts.

Evolved mating mechanisms are central to understanding differences among cultures in sexual strategies. Cultures differ in the sexual opportunities available, the resources provided by their ecology, the ratio of men to women, and the extent to which they promote long-term versus casual mating. Our evolved psychological mechanisms are attuned to these cultural inputs. Cultural variations in mating reflect differences in the choices made from the whole repertoire of possible human sexual strategies, based in part on cultural input. Every living human has inherited the complete repertoire from successful ancestors.

Competition and Conflict in the Mating Arena

An unpleasant fact of human mating is that desirable people are always outnumbered by the many who desire them. Some men demonstrate a superior ability to accrue resources, have a more appealing body type, or are more highly skilled at ascending status hierarchies. Because women typically desire these men, they compete with each other to attract them. Only women high in mate value, however, succeed. Women of striking beauty are desired by many men, but only a few men prosper in attracting them. The qualities of kindness, intelligence, dependability, athleticism, looks, and economic prospects are all present in the same person only rarely. Most of us must settle for someone who has less than the full complement of desirable qualities.

These stark facts create competition and conflict within each gender that can be avoided only by opting out of the mating game entirely. The fundamental desires of mating, however, are not easily extinguished. The quest to fulfill these desires catapults people headlong into the arena of competition. People do not always recognize competition in its many guises. A man or woman buying the latest facial cream may not construe this attention to skin as competition. A woman or man participating in the latest fitness craze or working late into the night may not construe these actions as competition. But as long as people have mating desires and as long as people differ in the qualities desired, competition will be an inevitable aspect of human mating.

Conflict between the sexes is likewise not easily extinguished. Some men show a thoughtless insensitivity to women's sexual psychology. Men sometimes seek sex sooner, more frequently, more persistently, or more aggressively than women want. Charges of sexual harassment and coercion are almost exclusively levied by women against men because of fundamental differences in the mating strategies of the two sexes. Men's strategies conflict with women's desires, causing anger and distress. Analogously, women spurn men who lack the desired qualities, causing frustration and resentment among the men who are rejected. Women interfere with men's sexual strategies as much as men interfere with women's, although perhaps they do so in less brutal and coercive ways.

Conflict within couples is also impossible to eliminate entirely. Although some couples live harmonious, happy lives together, no couple experiences a complete absence of conflict. The conditions that trigger conflict are often unavoidable. A man who gets fired from his job because of factors beyond his control may find that his wife wants a divorce because he no longer provides the resources on which she partly based her mating decision. A woman with encroaching wrinkles, through no fault of her own, may find that her professionally successful husband desires a younger woman. Some conflict between the sexes is impossible to eliminate because the conditions that foster it cannot be avoided.

The fact that conflicts between men and women originate from our evolved mating psychology is disturbing to some people, partly because it contradicts widely held beliefs. Many of us have learned the traditional view that these conflicts are reflections of a particular culture whose practices perturb the natural harmony of human nature. But the anger that women feel when sexually coerced and the rage that men feel when cuckolded arise from our evolved mating strategies, not from capitalism, culture, patriarchy, or socialization. Evolution operates by the ruthless criterion of reproductive success, no matter how repugnant we may find the strategies produced by that process, and no matter how abhorrent the consequences of those strategies may be.

An especially destructive manifestation of conflict between members of the same gender is warfare, a recurrent activity throughout human history. Given men's tendency to take physical risks in their pursuit of the resources needed for success at mating, it comes as no surprise that warfare is almost exclusively a male activity. Among the Yanomamö, there are two key motives that spur men to declare war on another tribe—a desire to capture the wives of other men and a desire to recapture wives that were lost in previous raids. When the American anthropologist Napoleon Chagnon explained to his Yanomamö informants that the United States waged war for principles such as freedom and democracy, they were astonished. It seemed absurd to them to risk one's life for anything other than capturing or recapturing women.[20]

The frequency of rape during wars throughout the course of human recorded history suggests that the sexual motives of the Yanomamö men may not be atypical.[21] Men worldwide share the same evolved psychology. The fact that there has never in history been a single case of women forming a war party to raid neighboring villages and capture husbands tells us something important about the nature of gender differences—that men's mating strategies are often more violent than women's.[22] The sexual motivation underlying violence also reveals that conflict *within* a sex is closely connected to conflict *between* the sexes. Men wage war to kill other men, but women become sexual victims.

In everyday life in modern society, the battle between the genders occurs between individual men and women interacting with each other socially—in the workplace, at parties, on online dating sites, and at home. The selective exclusion of mates, for example, does not affect all people, only those who lack the desired characteristics. Sexual jealousy is a cost inflicted not by all men on all women but rather by particular men, such as those lower in desirability than their partners, in particular circumstances, such as instances of infidelity, on particular women, such as spouses rather than casual sex partners. Sexual coercion, to take another example, is perpetrated only by some men, notably those with the sociopathic traits of low empathy, high hostility, hypermasculinity, and exploitative predispositions. Most men are not rapists, and most would be unlikely to commit rape even if there were no risk of getting caught.[23]

There is no solidarity among all men or all women that creates conflict between the sexes. Rather, members of each gender generally favor a common set of strategies that differ in some respects from the strategies pursued by members of the other sex. It is possible to speak of conflict between the sexes because the ways in which men and women typically conflict result from the strategies they have in common with their own sex. Still, we must recognize that no man or woman is fundamentally united with his or her own gender, nor fundamentally at odds with members of the other gender.

We are empowered now, more than at any time in human evolutionary history, to shape our future. The fact that deception, coercion, and abuse stem from our mating strategies does not justify their perpetuation. By employing the evolved mechanisms that are sensitive to personal costs, such as our sensitivity to reputational damage and our fear of ostracism, we may be able to curtail the expression of the more damaging aspects of our mating strategies.

Cooperation Between the Sexes

Men and women have always depended on each other for transporting their genes to future generations. Committed mateships are characterized by a complex web of long-term trust and reciprocity that appears to be unparalleled in other species. In this sense, cooperation between the sexes reaches a pinnacle among humans. Our strategies for cooperation in mating define human nature as much as our evolved capacity for language and culture.

Sexual strategies provide us with some of the conditions that facilitate the achievement of lifelong love. Children, the shared vehicles by which genes survive the journey to future generations, align the interests of a man and a woman and foster enduring mating bonds. Parents share in the delights of producing new life and nurturing their children to maturity. They marvel together as the gift of their union partakes of life's reproductive cycle. But children also create new sources of conflict, from disputes about dividing the child care to reduced opportunities for nighttime sexual harmony. No blessing is unmixed.

Sexual fidelity also promotes marital harmony. Any possibility of infidelity opens up a chasm of conflicting interests. Infidelity disrupts mating bonds and leads to breakups. Monogamy encourages prolonged trust between a man and a woman. If a woman is unfaithful, she may benefit by obtaining extra material resources, better genes to pass on to her children, or opportunities to trade up in the mating market. But the benefits that flow to her through infidelity come at a cost to her husband in a reduced certainty of paternity, a destruction of trust, and the potential long-term loss of his mate. A man's infidelity may satisfy his lust for sexual variety or give him a momentary euphoria that mimics that of a polygynous man. But these benefits come at a cost to his wife as a portion of her husband's love and investment is diverted to a rival. Lifelong sexual fidelity promotes harmony between a man and a woman, but it comes at a price for both in sacrificed external mating opportunities.

Fulfilling each other's evolved desires is one key to harmony between a man and woman. A woman's happiness increases when the man brings more economic resources to the union and shows kindness, affection, and commitment. A man's happiness increases when the woman is more physically attractive than he is, and when she shows kindness, affection, and commitment.[24] Those who fulfill each other's desires have happier relationships, especially if there are no interested others in the mating pool who could fulfill them more completely. Our evolved desires, in short, provide the essential ingredients for solving the mystery of mating harmony.

Knowledge of the multiplicity of our desires may be the most powerful tool for promoting harmony. It is a crowning achievement of humankind that two unrelated individuals can bring all of their individual resources into a lifelong alliance characterized by the remarkable emotion of love. This happens because of the tremendous resources that each person brings to the relationship, the bounty of benefits that flow to those who cooperate, and the sophisticated psychological machinery that we have for forming enduringly valuable mateships. Some of these resources tend to be linked to a person's gender, such as a woman's reproductive viability or a man's physical provisioning capacity. But mating resources typically transcend these reproductive essentials to include such capacities as protection from danger, deterrence of enemies, formation of friendships, tutoring of children, loyalty through thin and thick, and nurturance in times of setback. Each of these resources fulfills one of the many special desires that define our human nature.

A profound respect for the other gender should come from the knowledge that we have always depended on each other for the resources required for survival and reproduction. We have always depended on each other for the fulfillment of our desires. These facts may be responsible for the unique feeling of completeness that people experience when they become entwined in the intoxicating grip of love. A lifelong alliance of love is a triumphant achievement of human mating strategies.

Today we are confronted with novel sexual circumstances not encountered by any of our ancestors, including reliable contraception, fertility drugs, artificial insemination, cyber sex, online dating apps, breast implants, tummy tucks, sperm banks, and the capacity to genetically engineer "designer babies." Our ability to control the consequences of our mating behavior is unprecedented in human evolutionary history and matched by no other species on earth. But we confront these modern novelties with an ancient set of mating strategies that worked in ancestral times and in places that are irretrievably lost. Our mating mechanisms are the living fossils that reveal who we are and where we came from.

We are the first species in the known history of three and a half billion years of life on earth with the capacity to control our own destiny. The prospect of designing our destiny remains excellent to the degree that we comprehend our evolutionary past. Only by examining the complex repertoire of human sexual strategies can we know where we came from. Only by understanding why these human strategies have evolved can we control where we are going.

Acknowledgments

THE AUTHOR OF the most important treatise on the evolution of human sexuality in the twentieth century, Don Symons, guided the evolution of this book through his writings, friendship, and insightful commentary on each chapter. Leda Cosmides and John Tooby were fledgling graduate students at Harvard when I first met them in 1981, but they were already developing a grand framework for evolutionary psychology that profoundly influenced my own thinking about human mating strategies. Martin Daly and Margo Wilson had a seminal influence through their work on the evolution of sex and violence. I had the great fortune to collaborate with Martin, Margo, Leda, and John at the Center for Advanced Study in the Behavioral Sciences in Palo Alto, California, on a special project called Foundations of Evolutionary Psychology. That project formed the basis of this book.

I owe a major debt to my superlative research collaborators: Alois Angleitner, Armen Asherian, Mike Barnes, Mike Botwin, Michael Chen, Lisa Chiodo, Ken Craik, Lisa Dedden, Todd DeKay, Jack Demarest, Bruce Ellis, Mary Gomes, Arlette Greer,

Heidi Greiling, Dolly Higgins, Tim Ketelaar, Karen Kleinsmith, Liisa Kyl-Heku, Randy Larsen, Karen Lauterbach, Anne McGuire, David Schmitt, Jennifer Semmelroth, Todd Shackelford, and Drew Westen.

The fifty worldwide collaborators on the international study deserve special thanks: M. Abbott, A. Angleitner, A. Asherian, A. Biaggio, A. Blanco-VillaSeñor, M. Bruchon-Schweitzer, Hai-yuan Ch'u, J. Czapin-ski, B. DeRaad, B. Ekehammar, M. Fioravanti, J. Georgas, P. Gjerde, R. Guttman, F. Hazan, S. Iwawaki, N. Janakiramaiah, F. Khosroshani, S. Kreitler, L. Laehenicht, M. Lee, K. Liik, B. Little, N. Lohamy, S. Makim, S. Mika, M. Moadel-Shahid, G. Moane, M. Montero, A. C. Mundy-Castle, T. Niit, E. Nsenduluka, K. Peltzer, R. Pienkowski, A. Pirtilla-Backman, J. Ponce De Leon, J. Rousseau, M. A. Runco, M. P. Safir, C. Samuels, R. Santioso, R. Serpell, N. Smid, C. Spencer, M. Tadinac, E. N. Todorova, K. Troland, L. Van den Brande, G. Van Heck, L. Van Langenhove, and Kuo-Shu Yang.

Many friends and colleagues read drafts of this book and provided suggestions. Geoffrey Miller offered creative commentary on the entire book for the 1994 edition. John Alcock, Dick Alexander, Laura Betzig, Leda Cosmides, Martin Daly, Bill Durham, Steve Gangestad, Elizabeth Hill, Kim Hill, Doug Jones, Doug Kenrick, Bobbi Low, Neil Malamuth, Kathleen Much, Dan Ozer, Colleen Seifert, Jennifer Semmelroth, Barb Smuts, Valerie Stone, Frank Sulloway, Nancy Thornhill, Randy Thornhill, Peter Todd, John Tooby, Paul Turke, and Margo Wilson provided outstanding help with particular chapters.

My first editor, Susan Arellano, gave encouragement and editorial advice during the early stages. Basic Books executive editor Jo Ann Miller's keen judgment and editorial aplomb marshaled the book to completion. Every writer should have the great fortune to benefit from the intellectual and editorial powers of Virginia

LaPlante, who helped me to transform disorganized scribbles into readable prose and a miscellany of chapters into a coherent book. A bounty of institutional support has blessed me. Harvard University gave me the time and resources to launch the international study. The University of Michigan offered support from the Psychology Department, thanks to Al Cain and Pat Gurin; from the Evolution and Human Behavior Program, thanks to Dick Alexander, Laura Betzig, Kim Hill, Warren Holmes, Bobbi Low, John Mitani, Randy Nesse, Barb Smuts, Nancy Thornhill, and Richard Wrangham; and from the Research Center for Group Dynamics at the Institute for Social Research, thanks to Eugene Burnstein, Nancy Cantor, Phoebe Ellsworth, James Hilton, James Jackson, Neil Malamuth, Hazel Markus, Dick Nisbett, and Bob Zajonc. Grants from the National Institute of Mental Health (MH-41593 and MH-44206) greatly aided the research. A fellowship from the Center for Advanced Study in the Behavioral Sciences, including grants from the Gordon P. Getty Trust and National Science Foundation Grant BNS98-00864, gave me the time and intellectual atmosphere I needed to complete the first draft of this book. The University of Texas at Austin, where I am currently a professor, has continued this wonderful history of institutional support.

For the 2003 edition, Heidi Greiling and I collaborated on a raft of studies on the hidden side of women's sexuality. Work with Martie Haselton revealed some of the cognitive biases that men and women display in making inferences about each other's mating minds. Work with April Bleske exposed an intriguing new answer to the question of whether men and women can be "just friends." Work with David Schmitt provided the first systematic studies of human mate poaching. Work with Todd Shackelford, and also with Kevin Bennett, Bram Buunk, Jae Choe, Mariko Hasegawa, Toshi Hasegawa, Lee Kirkpatrick, and Randy Larsen, explored the defenses against sexual treachery.

Many friends and colleagues, in addition to those already thanked in the acknowledgments to the first edition, helped me in various ways with new material: Rosalind Arden, Mike Bailey, April Bleske, Ruth Buss, Greg Cochran, Josh Duntley, Trish Ellis, Paul Ewald, Steve Gangestad, John Gottschall, Heidi Greiling, Martie Haselton, Kim Hill, Owen Jones, Craig Palmer, David Schmitt, Todd Shackelford, and Randy Thornhill. Steve Pinker and Don Symons deserve special thanks for extraordinary feedback on virtually every aspect of the additional material.

Finally, I owe a heavy thanks to my recent research collaborators and current and former graduate students for some of the discoveries showcased in this revised and updated edition. Special thanks go to Laith Al-Shawaf, Kelly Asao, Mons Bendixen, Kevin Bennett, April Bleske-Rechek, Jaime Cloud, Sean Conlan, Adelia de Miguel, Josh Duntley, Judy Easton, Diana Santos Fleischman, David Frederick, Andrew Galperin, Steve Gangestad, Aaron Goetz, Cari Goetz, Mariko Hasegawa, Toshikazu Hasegawa, Martie Haselton, Patricia Hawley, Sarah Hill, Joonghwan Jeon, Peter Jonason, Farnaz Kaighobadi, Shanmukh Kamble, Leif Kennair, Lee Kirkpatrick, Barry X. Kuhle, Randy Larsen, David Lewis, William McKibben, Cindy Meston, Catherine Moestue, Carin Perilloux, Elizabeth Pillsworth, Steve Pinker, Josh Poore, Ania Raja, Kern Reeve, David Schmitt, Anna Sedlecek, Todd Shackelford, Emily Stone, Bill Tooke, Bill von Hippel, Martin Voracek, Viviana Weekes-Shackelford, Drew Westen, and Joy Wyckoff. Dan Conroy-Beam, now a professor at the University of California, Santa Barbara, gave sage advice throughout and detailed suggestions on many chapters. My superb new editors at Basic Books, Brian Distelberg, Cynthia Buck, and Melissa Veronesi, helped to improve clarity, transition, and tone throughout. Countless conversations with Cristine Legare deepened my understanding of the psychology of human mating.

Notes

Chapter 1: Origins of Mating

1. Jankowiak and Fisher 1992.
2. Beach and Tesser 1988; Sternberg 1988.
3. Darwin 1859, 1871.
4. Major proponents of evolutionary psychology include Cosmides and Tooby 1987; Daly and Wilson 1988; Pinker 1997; Thornhill and Thornhill 1990a; Symons 1979; and Buss 1989a, 1991a.
5. Rozin 1976.
6. Collias and Collias 1970.
7. Le Boeuf 1974.
8. Vandenberg 1972.
9. Smuts 1987; Lindburg 1971; Seyfarth 1976.
10. Thornhill and Alcock 1983.
11. Daly, Wilson, and Weghorst 1982; Symons 1979; Buss et al. 1992.
12. Erickson and Zenone 1976.
13. Betzig 1989.
14. Thornhill 1980a.
15. Buss and Schmitt 1993.

16. Bailey et al. 1994.

17. Bobrow and Bailey 2001.

18. See Rahman and Wilson (2003) for a summary. Although most studies point to moderate heritability of roughly 50 percent, some studies find only 20 to 30 percent concordance for homosexual orientation among monozygotic identical twins, which would suggest a slightly more modest role for heritable influence.

19. For summaries, see Bobrow and Bailey 2001; Muscarella 2000; McKnight 1997.

20. Symons 1987.

21. Low 1989.

22. Guttentag and Secord 1983; Kim Hill, personal communication, May 17, 1991.

23. See Quote Investigator, "Exploring the Origins of Quotations," February 9, 2011 (updated August 17, 2014), http://quoteinvestigator .com/2011/02/09/darwinism-hope-pray/. It should be noted that the quote may be apocryphal.

24. Daly and Wilson 1988.

25. Chagnon 1988.

Chapter 2: What Women Want

1. Trivers 1972; Williams 1975.

2. Trivers 1985.

3. Trivers 1972.

4. Yosef 1991.

5. Draper and Harpending 1982; Belsky, Steinberg, and Draper 1991.

6. Smuts 1995.

7. Hudson and Henze 1969; McGinnis 1958; Hill 1945.

8. Buss 1989a.

9. Buss et al. 2001; Schmitt 2016.

10. Kenrick et al. 1990.

11. Wiederman 1993.

12. Buss 1989a.

13. Conroy-Beam, Buss, et al. 2015.

14. Betzig 1986; Brown and Chai-yun, n.d.

15. Betzig 1986.

16. Hill 1945; Langhorne and Secord 1955; McGinnis 1958; Hudson and Henze 1969; Buss and Barnes 1986.

17. Buss et al. 2001.

18. Langhorne and Secord 1955.

19. Buss and Schmitt 1993.

20. Buss 1989a.

21. Li et al. 2002.

22. Buss 1989a.

23. Jencks 1979.

24. Hart and Pilling 1960.

25. Gurven and Kaplan 2006; Kim Hill, personal communication, May 17, 1991; Don Symons, personal communication, July 10, 1990.

26. McCrae and Costa 1990; Gough 1980.

27. Jankowiak, Hill, and Donovan 1992.

28. Martin Whyte, personal communication, 1990.

29. Townsend 1989; Townsend and Levy 1990; Wiederman and Allgeier 1992; Buss 1989a.

30. Lund et al. 2007.

31. Buss 1989a; Willerman 1979; Kyl-Heku and Buss 1996; Jencks 1979.

32. Langhorne and Secord 1955.

33. Buss and Schmitt 1993; Betzig 1989.

34. Buss 1991b.

35. Jencks 1979.

36. Hermstein 1989; Brown 1991; Brown and Chai-yun, n.d.

37. Barkow 1989.

38. Miller 2000.

39. Hill, Rubin, and Peplau 1976.

40. Buss 1984, 1985, n.d.

41. Buss 1987b; Buss et al. 1990.

42. Buss and Barnes 1986; Kenrick et al. 1993; Thibeau and Kelley 1986.

43. Frank 1988.

44. See Conroy-Beam, Goetz, and Buss (in press), who found that mate value discrepancies predict relationship dissatisfaction within married couples.

45. Trivers 1985.

46. Buss and Schmitt 1993.

47. Jackson 1992.

48. Hughes and Gallup 2003.

49. Brown and Chai-yun, n.d.

50. Ellis 1992, 279–281.

51. Gregor 1985, 35, 96.

52. Buss et al. 1990.

53. Ford and Beach 1951.

54. Hamilton and Zuk 1982.

55. Thornhill and Gangestad 2008.

56. Farrell 1986, 50.

57. Jankowiak and Fisher 1992; Sprecher et al. 1992.

58. Buss 1988c.

59. Sprecher et al. 1992.

60. Thiessen, Young, and Burroughs 1993.

61. Harrison and Saeed 1977.

62. Wiederman 1993.

63. Lukaszewski and Roney 2010.

64. Buss 1991b.

65. Ibid.

66. Lieberman, Tooby, and Cosmides. 2003.

67. Burkett and Kirkpatrick 2006.

68. Buss and Barnes 1986.

69. Secord 1982; Ardener, Ardener, and Warmington 1960.

70. Wiederman and Allgeier 1992; Townsend 1989.

71. Buss 1989a.

72. Gil-Burmann, Peláez, and Sánchez 2002.

73. Khallad 2005; Todosijević, Ljubinković, and Arančić 2003; Moore et al. 2006.

74. Lippa 2007.

75. Singh et al. 1999.
76. Pawlowski and Koziel 2002.
77. Pollet and Nettle 2008.
78. Borgerhoff Mulder 1990.
79. Buss 1989a; Conroy-Beam and Buss, under review.
80. Conroy-Beam, Buss, et al. 2015.

Chapter 3: What Men Want

1. Hill and Hurtado 1996.
2. Apostolou 2014.
3. Symons 1979, 271.
4. Symons 1979; Williams 1975; see also Buss 2015; Buss et al. 2001.
5. Hill 1945; McGinnis 1958; Hudson and Henze 1969; Buss 1989a.
6. Symons 1989, 34–35.
7. Hart and Pilling 1960; see also Buss 1989a.
8. Rudder 2014.
9. Kenrick and Keefe 1992.
10. Kenrick et al. 1996.
11. Guttentag and Secord 1983; Low 1991.
12. Buss 1989a.
13. Hart and Pilling 1960.
14. Orions and Heerwagen 1992; Symons 1979.
15. Ford and Beach 1951.
16. Malinowski 1929, 244.
17. Jackson 1992.
18. Berscheid and Walster 1974; Langlois et al. 1987.
19. Langlois, Roggman, and Reiser-Danner 1990; Cross and Cross 1971.
20. Cunningham et al. 1989.
21. Thakerar and Iwawaki 1979; Morse et al. 1974; Cross and Cross 1971; Jackson 1992.
22. Langlois and Roggman 1990.

23. Gangestad, Thornhill, and Yeo 1994.

24. Ford and Beach 1951.

25. Rosenblatt 1974.

26. Symons 1979.

27. Rozin and Fallon 1988.

28. Singh 1993a, 1993b, 1994.

29. Langhorne and Secord 1955.

30. Hill 1945; McGinnis 1958; Hudson and Henze 1969; Buss 1985, 1989a; Buss and Barnes 1986; Buss et al. 2001.

31. Buss 1987a.

32. Buss, in preparation, a.

33. Lei et al. 2011; Kamble et al. 2014; Souza et al. 2016.

34. Marlow 2004.

35. Low 1979.

36. Buss 1987a.

37. Buss, in preparation, b.

38. Symons 1979.

39. Posner 1992.

40. Wilson 1975, 1978.

41. Jankowiak et al. 1992.

42. Deaux and Hanna 1984.

43. Tripp 1975; Hoffman 1977; Symons 1979, 295.

44. Blumstein and Schwartz 1983.

45. Voland and Engel 1990; Borgerhoff Mulder 1988; Røskraft, Wara, and Viken 1992.

46. Betzig 1992.

47. Elder 1969; Taylor and Glenn 1976; Udry and Eckland 1984.

48. Grammer 1992.

49. Wolf 1991.

50. Kenrick et al. 1994.

51. Kenrick, Gutierres, and Goldberg 1989.

52. Alexander and Noonan 1979; Daniels 1983; Strassman 1981.

53. Alexander and Noonan 1979.

54. Hill 1945; McGinnis 1958; Hudson and Henze 1969; Buss, in preparation, a.

55. Dickemann 1981.

56. Posner 1992.
57. Buss 1989a.
58. Tooby and Cosmides 1989a, 39.
59. Thompson 1983; Weiss and Slosnerick 1981.
60. Buss and Schmitt 1993.
61. Buss 1989b.
62. Greeff et al. 2012; Wolf et al. 2012.
63. Symons 1987.

Chapter 4: Casual Sex

1. Clark and Hatfield 1989.
2. Guéguen 2011.
3. Baranowski and Hecht 2015.
4. Smith 1984.
5. Ibid.
6. Ibid.; Short 1979.
7. Baker and Bellis 1994.
8. Ibid.
9. Ibid.
10. Ibid.
11. Symons 1979, 207.
12. Buss and Schmitt 1993.
13. Schmitt 2003.
14. Kennair et al. 2009.
15. Eagly and Wood 1999.
16. Lippa 2009.
17. Schmitt 2003.
18. Kuhle et al. 2016.
19. Buss and Schmitt 1993.
20. Bermant 1976.
21. Symons 1979.
22. James 1981; Kinsey, Pomeroy, and Martin 1953; quote from Symons 1979, 208.
23. Kinsey, Pomeroy, and Martin 1948, 1953.
24. Hite 2004.

25. Athanasiou, Shaver, and Tavris 1970; Hite 1987; Hunt 1974.

26. Thompson 1983; Lawson 1988.

27. Symons 1979.

28. Elwin 1968, 47.

29. Schapera 1940, 193.

30. Gregor 1985, 84, 72.

31. Flaubert 1950, 203.

32. O'Donohue and Plaud 1991.

33. Kinsey et al. 1948, 589.

34. Ellis and Symons 1990.

35. Hunt 1974.

36. Wilson 1987, 126.

37. Barclay 1973, 209.

38. Ellis and Symons 1990, 544.

39. Barclay 1973, 211.

40. Ellis and Symons 1990.

41. Galperin et al. 2013.

42. Campbell 2008.

43. Gladue and Delaney 1990; Nida and Koon 1983; Pennybaker et al. 1979.

44. Haselton and Buss 2001.

45. Symons 1979.

46. Saghir and Robins 1973.

47. Ruse 1988.

48. Symons 1979, 300.

49. Burley and Symanski 1981; Smith 1984; Symons 1979.

50. Kinsey et al. 1948, 1953.

51. Buss and Schmitt 1993; Small 1992; Smith 1984; Smuts 1985; Barkow 1989; Thornhill 1992; Wilson and Daly 1992.

52. Malinowski 1929, 269.

53. Buss and Schmitt 1993.

54. Burley and Symanski 1981.

55. Janus and Janus 1993.

56. Buss and Schmitt 1993.

57. Ibid.

58. Smuts 1992.

59. Biocca 1970.

60. Smuts 1985.

61. Smith 1984, 614.

62. Colwell and Oring 1989.

63. Glass and Wright 1985.

64. Greiling 1993; Greiling and Buss 2000; see also Spanier and Margolis 1983 and Terman 1938.

65. Symons 1979; Baker and Bellis 1994; see also Gangestad 1989; Gangestad and Simpson 1990.

66. Fisher 1958.

67. Buss and Schmitt 1993; Kenrick et al. 1993.

68. Gildersleeve, Haselton, and Fales 2014.

69. Buss and Shackelford 2008.

70. Symons 1979.

71. Daly and Wilson 1988.

72. Kim Hill, personal communication, May 17, 1991.

73. Muehlenhard and Linton 1987.

74. Hill and Hurtado 1996.

75. Daly and Wilson 1988.

76. Wilson and Daly 1992.

77. Holmes and Sherman 1982.

78. Waynforth, Hurtado, and Hill 1998.

79. Ellis et al. 1999; Surbey and Conohan, 2000.

80. Frayser 1985; Gregor 1985.

81. Guttentag and Secord 1983; Pedersen 1991.

82. Gaulin and Schlegel 1980.

83. Hill and Kaplan 1988; Kim Hill, personal communication, May 17, 1991.

84. Posner 1992.

85. Betzig 1992.

Chapter 5: Attracting a Partner

1. Kevles 1986.

2. Buss 1988a; Schmitt and Buss 1996.

3. Buss and Dedden 1990.

4. Cloyd 1976.

5. Iredale, Van Vugt, and Dunbar 2008.

6. Buss and Schmitt 1993.

7. Hill, Nocks, and Gardner 1987.

8. Townsend and Levy 1990.

9. Holmberg 1950, 58.

10. Ovid 1982, 199.

11. La Cerra, Cosmides, and Tooby 1993.

12. Schmitt and Buss 1996.

13. Tooke and Camire 1991.

14. Buss, in preparation, d.

15. Nancy Jo Sales, "Tinder and the Dawning of the 'Dating Apocalypse,'" *Vanity Fair,* August 6, 2015, http://www.vanityfair.com/culture/2015/08/tinder-hook-up-culture-end-of-dating.

16. Margulis and Sagan 1991, 103; Trivers 1985, 395; Thornhill and Alcock 1983.

17. Allon and Fishel 1979, 150.

18. Chagnon 1988.

19. Barkow 1989.

20. Cloyd 1976, 300.

21. Kiesler and Baral 1970; Stroebe 1977.

22. Cloyd 1976; Nesse 1990. Quote from a man in the bar, told to Buss in 1994.

23. Howard 1981.

24. Schmitt and Buss 1996.

25. Ibid.

26. Dawkins 1976; Symons 1979; Buss and Chiodo 1991.

27. Allon and Fishel 1979, 152.

28. Buss, in preparation, b.

29. Graziano et al. 1993.

30. Wolf 1991, 11.

31. Buss and Dedden 1990.

32. Barth 1987.

33. Buss 1988a; Schmitt and Buss 1996.

34. Hatfield and Rapson 1993.

35. Hatfield et al. 1973.

36. Kim Hill, personal communication, May 17, 1991.
37. Wade and Slemp 2015.
38. Brak-Lamy 2015.
39. Hill et al. 1987.
40. Allon and Fishel 1979, 137, 139.
41. Abbey 1982.
42. Givins 1978.
43. Goetz et al. 2012.
44. Goetz, Easton, and Buss 2014; Goetz, Easton, and Meston 2014.
45. Buss and Barnes 1986; Buss 1988a.
46. Bressler, Martin, and Balshine 2006.
47. Li et al. 2009.
48. Miller 2000.
49. Zahavi 1975.
50. Pinker 1997, 523.
51. Ibid., 534.
52. Buss 2016; Daly and Wilson 1988; Guttentag and Secord 1983; Pedersen 1991.

Chapter 6: Staying Together

1. Thornhill and Alcock 1983.
2. Alcock 1981.
3. Alexander 1962.
4. Thornhill and Alcock 1983.
5. Abele and Gilchrist 1977; Parker 1970.
6. Buss 1988b; Buss and Barnes 1986; Kenrick et al. 1993.
7. Buss and Shackelford 1997.
8. Schmitt and Buss 2001.
9. Schmitt 2001.
10. Arnocky, Sunderani, and Vaillancourt 2013.
11. Ein-Dor et al. 2015.
12. Alexander and Noonan 1979; Daly et al. 1982.
13. Shettel-Neuber, Bryson, and Young 1978; Buss, in preparation, c.
14. Daly and Wilson 1988, 182.
15. Safilios-Rothschild 1969, 78–79.

Notes

17. Buunk and Hupka 1987.
18. Teisman and Mosher 1978.
19. Francis 1977.
20. Buss et al. 1992.
21. Baschnagel and Edlund 2016.
22. Gottschalk 1936.
23. Buunk and Hupka 1987.
24. DeSteno and Salovey 1996.
25. Buss et al. 1999.
26. Scelza 2014.
27. Kuhle 2011.
28. Buss 2013; Sagarin et al. 2012.
29. Bendixen et al. 2015.
30. Takahashi et al. 2006.
31. Ibid., 1299.
32. Buss et al. 2000; Fussell and Stollery 2012.
33. Fussell and Stollery 2012, 155.
34. Ibid., 156–157.
35. Easton, Schipper, and Shackelford 2007.
36. Andrews et al. 2008; Goetz and Causey 2009.
37. Miller and Maner 2009.
38. Buss 1988b.
39. Buss and Shackelford 1997.
40. Lopes et al. 2016.
41. Shettel-Neuber et al. 1978.
42. White 1980.
43. Schmitt and Buss 2001.
44. Dickemann 1981.
45. Betzig, in preparation, 17.
46. Dass 1970, 78.
47. Saletore 1978, 64; Saletore 1974, 61.
48. Van Gulik 1974, 17.
49. Cienza de Leon 1959, 41.
50. Smuts and Smuts 1993.

51. Miner, Starratt, and Shackelford 2009.

52. Daly and Wilson 1988; Russell 1990; Wilson 1989; Margo Wilson, personal communication, June 1993.

53. Buss and Duntley 2011.

54. Daly et al. 1982.

55. Miller 1980.

56. Hosken 1979.

57. Daly et al. 1982; Hosken 1979, 2.

58. Handy 1923, cited in Daly and Wilson 1988, 204.

59. Rasmussen 1931.

60. Wilson and Daly 1992, 311.

61. Chimbos 1978, 54.

62. Daly and Wilson 1988, 196.

63. Miller 1980.

64. Daly et al. 1982.

65. Ibid.

66. Lobban 1972; Tanner 1970; Bohannan 1960.

67. Lobban 1972.

68. Daly et al. 1982.

69. Daly and Wilson 1988.

70. Buss and Shackelford 1997.

Chapter 7: Sexual Conflict

1. Buss 1989b.

2. Byers and Lewis 1988.

3. Haselton and Buss 2000.

4. Saal, Johnson, and Weber 1989; see Abbey 1982 for comparable results.

5. Abbey and Melby 1986.

6. Haselton 2003.

7. Perilloux, Easton, and Buss 2012.

8. Ibid.; Buss and Shackelford 2008.

9. Semmelroth and Buss, unpublished data.

10. Goetz, Easton, and Meston 2014.

11. Ellis and Symons 1990; Hazan 1983.

12. Thornhill and Thornhill 1990a, 1990b.

13. Buss 1989b.

14. Buss, unpublished data from longitudinal study of 107 married couples.

15. Semmelroth and Buss, unpublished data.

16. Buss, unpublished data from longitudinal study of 107 married couples.

17. Zahavi 1977.

18. Buss, unpublished data from longitudinal study of 107 married couples.

19. Ibid.

20. Ibid.

21. Ibid.

22. Blumstein and Schwartz 1983.

23. Conroy-Beam, Goetz, and Buss 2015.

24. Buss, unpublished data from longitudinal study of 107 married couples.

25. Trivers 1985.

26. Semmelroth and Buss, unpublished data.

27. Cassell 1984, 155.

28. Semmelroth and Buss, unpublished data.

29. Ibid.

30. *A Streetcar Named Desire* (1951, Warner Bros.), directed by Elia Kazan, screenplay by Tennessee Williams and Oscar Saul.

31. Daly and Wilson 1988.

32. Wilson 1989; Margo Wilson, personal communication, June 1993.

33. The term "mansplaining," coined by Rebecca Solnit in 2012, refers to a patronizing manner in which a man explains something to a woman; see Rebecca Solnit, "Men Still Explain Things to Me," *The Nation*, August 20, 2012, https://www.thenation.com/article/men-still-explain-things-me/.

34. Whitehurst 1971.

35. Rounsaville 1978.

36. Hilberman and Munson 1978.
37. Daly and Wilson 1988; Russell 1990.
38. Chagnon 1983.
39. Buss, unpublished data from longitudinal study of 107 married couples.
40. Studd and Gattiker 1991, 251.
41. Terpstra and Cook 1985.
42. Studd and Gattiker 1991.
43. Ibid.
44. Ibid.
45. Terpstra and Cook 1985.
46. Ibid.
47. Gutek 1985.
48. Semmelroth and Buss, unpublished data.
49. Studd and Gattiker, in preparation.
50. Semmelroth and Buss, unpublished data.
51. Koss and Oros 1982.
52. Muehlenhard and Linton 1987.
53. Impett and Peplau 2002.
54. Gavey 1991.
55. Russell 1990.
56. Malamuth, Heavey, and Linz 1993; Thornhill and Thornhill 1992.
57. Thornhill 1980a, 1980b.
58. Thornhill and Palmer 2000.
59. Malamuth 1992; Thornhill and Thornhill 1992.
60. Mazur 1992.
61. Thornhill and Thornhill 1983.
62. Freemont 1975, 244–246.
63. Lalumiere et al. 1996.
64. Thornhill and Palmer 2000.
65. Thornhill and Thornhill 1983.
66. Gottschall and Gottschall 2003. Most studies that compare rape-pregnancy rates with pregnancy rates from consensual sex are confounded in various ways. Some collapse across all categories of

rape, such as forced oral sex, anal sex, and penile-vaginal rape, and compare them with penile-vaginal rape resulting from consensual sex. Most fail to factor in the widespread use of emergency contraception given to rape victims, for example, the "morning after pill." The Gottschall study is the first to provide systematic controls for these variables.

67. See Jones 1999, who provided the label for this objection to rape-as-adaptation theories.

68. Malamuth 1981.

69. Young and Thiessen 1992.

70. Malamuth 1986; Malamuth et al. 1991; see also Lalumiere 2005.

71. Russell 1990.

72. Symons 1979, 284.

73. Griffin 1971.

74. S. Mydans, *Austin American Statesman,* March 24, 2002, A25.

75. Buss 1989b.

76. Hartung, n.d.

77. Gilmore 1990.

78. Gregor 1985.

79. Brownmiller 1975.

80. Colin Falconer, "Genghis Khan but You Can't," September 12, 2013, http://colinfalconer.org/genghis-khan-but-you-cant-2/; quoted in slightly different form in Royle 1989.

81. Smuts 1992, 1.

82. Rogel 1976. This finding appears to contradict the Gotschall study, which found a surprisingly high rape-pregnancy rate; future research must resolve the apparent opposition of these two findings.

83. Morgan 1981.

84. Chavanne and Gallup 1998.

85. Ibid.

86. Morris and Udry 1970.

87. Studies summarized by Hickman and Muehlenhard 1997.

88. Ibid.

89. Ibid.

90. Pawson and Banks 1993.

91. Hickman and Muehlenhard 1997.

92. Wilson and Mesnick 1997.

93. Ibid., 507.

94. Ryder et al. 2016.

95. Thornhill and Palmer 2000.

Chapter 8: Breaking Up

1. Battaglia et al. 1998.

2. Howell 1979.

3. Kim Hill, personal communication, 1991.

4. Daly and Wilson 1988; Trinkaus and Zimmerman 1982.

5. Hill and Hurtado 1996.

6. Chagnon 1983.

7. Tooby and DeVore 1987.

8. Conroy-Beam et al., in press.

9. Betzig 1989.

10. Daly and Wilson 1988.

11. Kinsey et al. 1948, 1953.

12. See, for example, Buss 2000; Blow and Hartnett 2005.

13. Conlan 2007.

14. Gladwin and Sarason 1953, 128.

15. Erickson and Zenone 1976.

16. Fisher 1992.

17. Radcliffe-Brown 1922.

18. Beardsley, Hall, and Ward 1959.

19. Chagnon 1983; Hart and Pilling 1960; Buss 1989a.

20. Fisher 1992.

21. Ibid.

22. Buss, unpublished studies.

23. Ibid.

24. Betzig 1989; Fisher 1992.

25. Weiss 1975, 19.

26. Cherlin 1981; Fisher 1992; Whyte 1990.

27. Bowe 1992, 200.

28. Brown 1991; Hartung et al. 1982; Symons 1979.

29. Seiler 1976.
30. Cuber and Harroff 1965.
31. Borgerhoff Mulder 1985, 1988.
32. Stern 1933, 35.
33. Murdock and Wilson 1972.
34. Ames 1953.
35. Betzig 1989.
36. Bowe 1992.
37. Elwin 1949, 70.
38. Bunzel 1952, 132.
39. Daly and Wilson 1988.
40. McCrae and Costa 1990.
41. Buss 1991b.
42. Bunzel 1952, 132.
43. Boutwell, Barnes, and Beaver 2015; Conlan 2007.
44. Duntley and Buss 2012; Perilloux and Buss 2008.
45. Perilloux and Buss 2008.
46. Meston and Buss 2009.
47. Perilloux and Buss 2008.
48. Duntley and Buss 2012.
49. Buss et al. 2017.

Chapter 9: Changes over Time

1. De Waal 1982.
2. Borgerhoff Mulder 1988.
3. Schneider 1964, 53.
4. Goldschmidt 1974.
5. Henss 1992.
6. Hart and Pilling 1960.
7. Buss, unpublished data from longitudinal study of 107 married couples.
8. Udry 1980.
9. Greeley 1991.
10. James 1981.
11. Margolin and White 1987.

12. Pfeiffer and Davis 1972.

13. Buss, unpublished data from longitudinal study of 107 married couples.

14. Buss and Shackelford 1997.

15. Flinn 1988.

16. Dickemann 1979.

17. Daly and Wilson 1988.

18. H. H. Munro (Saki), http://www.quotationspage.com/quote /21852.html; also cited in Byrne 1988.

19. Kinsey et al. 1948, 1953.

20. Green, Lee, and Lustig 1974.

21. Daly and Wilson 1988.

22. Easton et al. 2010.

23. Spanier and Margolis 1983.

24. Thompson 1984.

25. Glass and Wright 1985.

26. Johnson 1970.

27. Terman 1938.

28. Sigusch and Schmidt 1971.

29. Kinsey et al. 1948, 1953.

30. Buss, unpublished data from longitudinal study of 107 married couples.

31. Betzig 1992.

32. Quoted in Symons 1979, 166.

33. Hill and Hurtado 1991; Jones 1975; Croze, Hillman, and Lang 1981.

34. Hill and Hurtado 1991.

35. Utian 1980, cited in Pavelka and Fedigan 1991.

36. Alexander 1990.

37. Hill and Hurtado 1991.

38. Alexander 1990; Dawkins 1976; Hill and Hurtado 1991; Williams 1957.

39. Hill and Hurtado 1991.

40. Shanley et al. 2007.

41. Lahdenperä et al. 2004.

42. Hill and Hurtado 1991.

43. Hill and Hurtado 1996.

44. Kaplan and Hill 1985; Kaplan, Hill, and Hurtado 1984; Hill and Hurtado 1989; Hill and Kaplan 1988.

45. Hart and Pilling 1960.

46. Shostak 1981.

47. Kim Hill, personal communication, 1991.

48. Hill and Hurtado 1996.

49. Jencks 1979.

50. Hewlett 1991.

51. Trivers 1985.

52. Daly and Wilson 1988; Trivers 1985.

53. U.S. Census Bureau, "America's Families and Living Arrangements: 2015: Adults," http://www.census.gov/hhes/families/data/cps 2015A.html.

54. Hart and Pilling 1960.

55. Wilson and Daly 1985.

56. Livingston 2014.

57. Chamie and Nsuly 1981.

58. Pedersen 1991.

59. Ibid.

60. Markman, Stanley, and Storaasili 1991.

61. Gaulin and Boster 1990; Pedersen 1991.

62. Flinn 1988.

63. Wilson 1989, 53.

64. Thornhill and Thornhill 1983.

65. Divale and Harris 1976.

66. Daly and Wilson 1988.

67. Thornhill and Thornhill 1983.

Chapter 10: Harmony Between the Sexes

1. Baker and Bellis 1994; Buss and Schmitt 1993; Betzig 1989.

2. Gowaty 1992; MacKinnon 1987; Smuts 1995; Ortner 1974; Ortner and Whitehead 1981; Daly and Wilson 1988.

3. Buss 1989a.

4. Hall and DeVore 1965; de Waal 1982.

5. Connor, Smolker, and Richards 1992.

6. Goodall 1986.

7. Alexander 1987; Chagnon 1983.

8. Tooby and Cosmides 1989b.

9. Smuts 1995.

10. This analysis of resource inequality, of course, does not deny the existence of other contributing causes, such as the sexist practice of giving women and men unequal pay for the same work.

11. Smuts 1995.

12. Brownmiller 1975.

13. Daly and Wilson 1988; Smuts 1992.

14. Buss and Dedden 1990; Hrdy 1981.

15. Hewlett 1991.

16. Shostak 1981.

17. Lei et al. 2011.

18. Belsky et al. 1991.

19. Kim Hill, personal communication, 1991.

20. Chagnon 1983; Chagnon, personal communication, 1991.

21. Brownmiller 1975.

22. Tooby and Cosmides 1989a.

23. Malamuth 1981; Young and Thiessen 1992.

24. Weisfeld et al. 1992.

Bibliography

Abbey, A. (1982). Sex differences in attributions for friendly behavior: Do males misperceive females' friendliness? *Journal of Personality and Social Psychology, 32,* 830–838.

Abbey, A., & Melby, C. (1986). The effects of nonverbal cues on gender differences in perceptions of sexual intent. *Sex Roles, 15,* 283–298.

Abele, L., & Gilchrist, S. (1977). Homosexual rape and sexual selection in acanthocephalan worms. *Science, 197,* 81–83.

Alcock, J. (1981). Seduction on the wing. *Natural History, 90,* 36–41.

Alexander, R. D. (1962). Evolutionary change in cricket acoustical communication. *Evolution, 16,* 443–467.

———. (1987). *The biology of moral systems.* New York: Aldine de Gruyter.

———. (1990). *How did humans evolve? Reflections on the uniquely unique species.* Special Publication 13. Ann Arbor: University of Michigan, Museum of Zoology.

Alexander, R. D., & Noonan, K. M. (1979). Concealment of ovulation, parental care, and human social evolution. In N. A. Chagnon & W. Irons (Eds.), *Evolutionary biology and human social behavior: An anthropological perspective,* 402–435. North Scituate, MA: Duxbury Press.

Allon, N., & Fishel, D. (1979). Singles bars. In N. Allon (Ed.), *Urban life styles,* 128–179. Dubuque, IA: William C. Brown.

Ames, D. (1953). Plural marriage among the Wolof in Gambia. PhD diss., Northwestern University, Evanston, Illinois.

Andrews, P. W., Gangestad, S. W., Miller, G. F., Haselton, M. G., Thornhill, R., & Neale, M. C. (2008). Sex differences in detecting sexual infidelity. *Human Nature, 19*(4), 347–373.

Apostolou, M. (2014). Parental choice: Exploring in-law preferences and their contingencies in the Greek-Cypriot culture. *Evolutionary Psychology, 12,* 588–620.

Ardener, E. W., Ardener, S. G., & Warmington, W. A. (1960). *Plantation and village in the Cameroons.* London: Oxford University Press.

Arnocky, S., Sunderani, S., & Vaillancourt, T. (2013). Mate-poaching and mating success in humans. *Journal of Evolutionary Psychology, 11*(2), 65–83.

Athanasiou, R., Shaver, P., & Tavris, C. (1970). Sex. *Psychology Today,* July, 37–52.

Bailey, J. M., Gaulin, S., Agyei, Y., & Gladue, B. A. (1994). Effects of gender and sexual orientation on evolutionarily relevant aspects of human mating psychology. *Journal of Personality and Social Psychology, 66*(6), 1081–1093.

Baker, R. R., & Bellis, M. (1994). *Human sperm competition: Copulation, masturbation, and infidelity.* New York: Springer.

Baranowski, A. M., & Hecht, H. (2015). Gender differences and similarities in receptivity to sexual invitations: Effects of location and risk perception. *Archives of Sexual Behavior, 44*(8), 2257–2265.

Barclay, A. M. (1973). Sexual fantasies in men and women. *Medical Aspects of Human Sexuality, 7,* 205–216.

Barkow, J. (1989). *Darwin, sex, and status.* Toronto: University of Toronto Press.

Barkow, J., Cosmides, L., & Tooby, J. (Eds.). (1992). *The adapted mind: Evolutionary psychology and the generation of culture.* New York: Oxford University Press.

Barth, J. (1987). *The sot-weed factor.* Garden City, NY: Anchor Books.

Baschnagel, J. S., & Edlund, J. E. (2016). Affective modification of the startle eyeblink response during sexual and emotional infidelity scripts. *Evolutionary Psychological Science, 2,* 114–122.

Battaglia, D. M., Richard, F. D., Datteri, D. L., & Lord, C. G. (1998). Breaking up is (relatively) easy to do: A script for the dissolution of close relationships. *Journal of Social and Personal Relationships, 15,* 829–845.

Beach, S. T., & Tesser, A. (1988). Love in marriage: A cognitive account. In R. J. Sternberg & M. L. Barnes (Eds.), *The psychology of love,* 330–358. New Haven, CT: Yale University Press.

Beardsley, R. K., Hall, J. W., & Ward, R. E. (1959). *Village Japan.* Chicago: University of Chicago Press.

Belsky, J., Steinberg, L., & Draper, P. (1991). Childhood experience, interpersonal development, and reproductive strategy: An evolutionary theory of socialization. *Child Development, 62,* 647–670.

Bendixen, M., Kennair, L. E. O., Ringheim, H. K., Isaksen, L., Pedersen, L., Svangtun, S., & Hagen, K. (2015). In search of moderators of sex differences in forced-choice jealousy responses: Effects of 2D:4D digit ratio and relationship infidelity experiences. *Nordic Psychology, 67*(4), 272–284.

Bermant, G. (1976). Sexual behavior: Hard times with the Coolidge effect. In M. H. Siegel & H. P. Ziegler (Eds.), *Psychological research: The inside story,* 76–103. New York: Harper & Row.

Berscheid, E., & Walster, E. (1974). Physical attractiveness. In L. Berkowitz (Ed.), *Advances in experimental social psychology,* 157–215. New York: Academic Press.

Betzig, L. (1986). *Despotism and differential reproduction: A Darwinian view of history.* Hawthorne, NY: Aldine de Gruyter.

———. (1989). Causes of conjugal dissolution: A cross-cultural study. *Current Anthropology, 30,* 654–676.

———. (1992). Roman polygyny. *Ethology and Sociobiology, 13,* 309–349.

———. (in preparation). Why monogamy? *Behavioral and Brain Sciences.*

Biocca, E. (1970). *Yanoáma: The narrative of a white girl kidnapped by Amazonian Indians.* New York: E. P. Dutton.

Blow, A. J., & Hartnett, K. (2005). Infidelity in committed relationships II: A substantive review. *Journal of Marital and Family Therapy, 31*(2), 217–233.

Blumstein, P., & Schwartz, P. (1983). *American couples.* New York: Morrow.

Bobrow, D., & Bailey, J. M. (2001). Is male homosexuality maintained via kin selection? *Evolution and Human Behavior, 22,* 361–368.

Bohannan, P. (1960). *African homicide and suicide.* Princeton, NJ: Princeton University Press.

Borgerhoff Mulder, M. (1985). Polygyny threshold: A Kipsigis case study. *National Geographic Research Reports, 21,* 33–39.

———. (1988). Kipsigis bridewealth payments. In L. L. Betzig, M. Borgerhoff Mulder, & P. Turke (Eds.), *Human reproductive behavior,* 65–82. New York: Cambridge University Press.

———. (1990). Kipsigis women's preferences for wealthy men: Evidence for female choice in mammals? *Behavioral Ecology and Sociobiology, 27*(4), 255–264.

Boutwell, B. B., Barnes, J. C., & Beaver, K. M. (2015). When love dies: Further elucidating the existence of a mate ejection module. *Review of General Psychology, 19*(1), 30.

Bowe, C. (1992). Everything we think, feel, and do about divorce. *Cosmopolitan, 212*(2), 199–207.

Brak-Lamy, G. (2015). Heterosexual seduction in the urban night context: Behaviors and meanings. *Journal of Sex Research, 52*(6), 690–699.

Bressler, E. R., Martin, R. A., & Balshine, S. (2006). Production and appreciation of humor as sexually selected traits. *Evolution and Human Behavior, 27*(2), 121–130.

Brown, D. E. (1991). *Human universals.* Philadelphia: Temple University Press.

Brown, D. E., & Chai-yun, Y. (n.d.). "Big Man": Its distribution, meaning and origin. Unpublished paper, Department of Anthropology, University of California, Santa Barbara.

Brownmiller, S. (1975). *Against our will: Men, women, and rape*. New York: Bantam Books.

Bunzel, R. (1952). *Chichicastenango*. New York: J. J. Augustin.

Burkett, B., & Kirkpatrick, L. (2006). What are deal breakers in a mate? Paper presented at the annual meeting of the Human Behavior and Evolution Society, University of Pennsylvania, Philadelphia.

Burley, N., & Symanski, R. (1981). Women without: An evolutionary and cross-cultural perspective on prostitution. In R. Symanski, *The immoral landscape: Female prostitution in Western societies*, 239–274. Toronto: Butterworths.

Buss, D. M. (1984). Toward a psychology of person-environment (PE) correlation: The role of spouse selection. *Journal of Personality and Social Psychology, 47*, 361–377.

———. (1985). Human mate selection. *American Scientist, 73*, 47–51.

———. (1987a). Sex differences in human mate selection criteria: An evolutionary perspective. In C. Crawford, D. Krebs, & M. Smith (Eds.), *Sociobiology and psychology: Ideas, issues, and applications*, 335–352. Hillsdale, NJ: Erlbaum.

———. (1987b). Selection, evocation, and manipulation. *Journal of Personality and Social Psychology, 53*, 1214–1221.

———. (1988a). The evolution of human intrasexual competition. *Journal of Personality and Social Psychology, 54*, 616–628.

———. (1988b). From vigilance to violence: Mate guarding tactics. *Ethology and Sociobiology, 9*, 291–317.

———. (1988c). Love acts: The evolutionary biology of love. In R. J. Sternberg & M. L. Barnes (Eds.), *The psychology of love*, 100–118. New Haven, CT: Yale University Press.

———. (1989a). Sex differences in human mate preferences: Evolutionary hypotheses tested in 37 cultures. *Behavioral and Brain Sciences, 12*, 1–49.

———. (1989b). Conflict between the sexes: Strategic interference and the evocation of anger and upset. *Journal of Personality and Social Psychology, 56*, 735–747.

———. (1991a). Evolutionary personality psychology. *Annual Review of Psychology, 42,* 459–491.

———. (1991b). Conflict in married couples: Personality predictors of anger and upset. *Journal of Personality, 59,* 663–688.

———. (2000). *The dangerous passion.* New York: Free Press.

———. (2013). Sexual jealousy. *Psihologijske teme, 22*(2), 155–182.

———. (2015). *Evolutionary psychology: The new science of the mind.* 5th ed. Philadelphia: Taylor & Francis.

———. (2016). The mating crisis among educated women. *Edge.* http://edge.org/response-detail/26747.

———. (in preparation, a). Cross-generational preferences in mate selection. Department of Psychology, University of Michigan, Ann Arbor.

———. (in preparation, b). Human prestige criteria. Department of Psychology, University of Michigan, Ann Arbor.

———. (in preparation, c). Humiliation, anger, sadness, and abandonment: Emotional reactions to sexual infidelity. Department of Psychology, University of Michigan, Ann Arbor.

———. (in preparation, d). Attraction tactics in single bars. University of Texas, Austin.

———. (n.d.). Contemporary worldviews: Spousal assortment or convergence? Unpublished paper, Department of Psychology, University of Michigan, Ann Arbor.

Buss, D. M., Abbott, M., Angleitner, A., Asherian, A., Biaggio, A., Blanco-VillaSeñor, A., Bruchon-Schweitzer, M., Ch'u, Hai-yuan, Czapinski, J., DeRaad, B., Ekehammar, B., Fioravanti, M., Georgas, J., Gjerde, P., Guttman, R., Hazan, F., Iwawaki, S., Janakiramaiah, N., Khosroshani, F., Kreitler, S., Lachenicht, L., Lee, M., Liik, K., Little, B., Lohamy, N., Makim, S., Mika, S., Moadel-Shahid, M., Moane, G., Montero, M., Mundy-Castle, A. C., Little, B., Niit, T., Nsenduluka, E., Peltzer, K., Pienkowski, R., Pirttila-Backman, A., Ponce De Leon, J., Rousseau, J., Runco, M. A., Safir, M. P., Samuels, C., Sani-tioso, R., Schweitzer, B., Serpell, R., Smid, N., Spencer, C., Tadinac, M., Todorova, E. N., Troland, K., Van den Brande, L., Van Heck, G., Van

Langen-hove, L., & Yang, Kuo-Shu. (1990). International preferences in selecting mates: A study of 37 cultures. *Journal of Cross-Cultural Psychology, 21,* 5–47.

Buss, D. M., & Barnes, M. F. (1986). Preferences in human mate selection. *Journal of Personality and Social Psychology, 50,* 559–570.

Buss, D. M., & Chiodo, L. A. (1991). Narcissistic acts in everyday life. *Journal of Personality, 59,* 179–216.

Buss, D. M., & Dedden, L. A. (1990). Derogation of competitors. *Journal of Social and Personal Relationships, 7,* 395–422.

Buss, D. M., & Duntley, J. D. (2011). The evolution of intimate partner violence. *Aggression and Violent Behavior, 16*(5), 411–419.

Buss, D. M., Goetz, C., Duntley, J. D., Asao, K., & Conroy-Beam, D. (2017). The mate switching hypothesis. *Personality and Individual Differences, 104,* 143–149.

Buss, D. M., Larsen, R. J., Westen, D., & Semmelroth, J. (1992). Sex differences in jealousy: Evolution, physiology, and psychology. *Psychological Science, 3,* 251–255.

Buss, D. M., & Schmitt, D. P. (1993). Sexual strategies theory: An evolutionary perspective on human mating. *Psychological Review, 100,* 204–232.

Buss, D. M., & Shackelford, T. K. (1997). From vigilance to violence: Mate retention tactics in married couples. *Journal of Personality and Social Psychology, 72*(2), 346–361.

———. (2008). Attractive women want it all: Good genes, economic investment, parenting proclivities, and emotional commitment. *Evolutionary Psychology, 6*(1), 134–146.

Buss, D. M., Shackelford, T. K., Choe, J., Buunk, B., & Dijkstra, P. (2000). Distress about rivals: Reactions to intrasexual competitors in Korea, the Netherlands, and America. *Personal Relationships, 7*(3), 235–243.

Buss, D. M., Shackelford, T. K., Kirkpatrick, L. A., Choe, J. C., Lim, H. K., Hasegawa, M., Hasegawa, T., & Bennett, K. (1999). Jealousy and the nature of beliefs about infidelity: Tests of competing hypotheses about sex differences in the United States, Korea, and Japan. *Personal Relationships, 6*(1), 125–150.

Buss, D. M., Shackelford, T. K., Kirkpatrick, L. A., & Larsen, R. J. (2001). A half century of mate preferences: The cultural evolution of values. *Journal of Marriage and Family, 63*(2), 491–503.

Buunk, B., & Hupka, R. B. (1987). Cross-cultural differences in the elicitation of sexual jealousy. *Journal of Sex Research, 23,* 12–22.

Byers, E. S., & Lewis, K. (1988). Dating couples' disagreements over desired level of sexual intimacy. *Journal of Sex Research, 24,* 15–29.

Byrne, R. (1988). *1,911 best things anybody ever said.* New York: Fawcett Columbine.

Campbell, A. (2008). The morning after the night before. *Human Nature, 19*(2), 157–173.

Cassell, C. (1984). *Swept away: Why women confuse love and sex.* New York: Simon & Schuster.

Chagnon, N. (1983). *Yanomamö: The fierce people.* 3rd ed. New York: Holt, Rinehart & Winston.

———. (1988). Life histories, blood revenge, and warfare in a tribal population. *Science, 239,* 985–992.

Chamie, J., & Nsuly, S. (1981). Sex differences in remarriage and spouse selection. *Demography, 18,* 335–348.

Chavanne, T. J., & Gallup, G. G., Jr. (1998). Variation in risk taking behavior among female college students as a function of the menstrual cycle. *Evolution and Human Behavior, 19,* 27–32.

Cherlin, A. J. (1981). *Marriage, divorce, remarriage.* Cambridge, MA: Harvard University Press.

Chimbos, P. D. (1978). *Marital violence: A study of interspouse homicide.* San Francisco: R&E Research Associates.

Cienza de Leon, P. (1959). *The Incas.* Norman: University of Oklahoma Press.

Clark, R. D., & Hatfield, E. (1989). Gender differences in receptivity to sexual offers. *Journal of Psychology and Human Sexuality, 2,* 39–55.

Cloyd, J. W. (1976). The market-place bar: The interrelation between sex, situation, and strategies in the pairing ritual of *Homo Ludens. Urban Life, 5,* 293–312.

Collias, N. E., & Collias, E. C. (1970). The behavior of the West African village weaverbird. *Ibis, 112,* 457–480.

Colwell, M. A., & Oring, L. W. (1989). Extra-pair mating in the spotted sandpiper: A female mate acquisition tactic. *Animal Behavior, 38,* 675–684.

Conlan, S. K. (2007). Romantic relationship termination. PhD diss., Department of Psychology, University of Texas, Austin.

Connor, R. C., Smolker, R. A., & Richards, A. F. (1992). Two levels of alliance formation among male bottlenose dolphins (*Tursiops sp.*). *Proceedings of the National Academy of Sciences, 89,* 987–990.

Conroy-Beam, D., & Buss, D. M. (under review). The importance of age in human mating: Evolved desires and their influence on actual mating behavior. *Evolutionary Behavioral Sciences.*

Conroy-Beam, D., Buss, D. M., Pham, M. N., & Shackelford, T. K. (2015). How sexually dimorphic are human mate preferences? *Personality and Social Psychology Bulletin, 41,* 1082–1093.

Conroy-Beam, D., Goetz, C. D., & Buss, D. M. (2015). Why do humans form long-term mateships? An evolutionary game-theoretic model. *Advances in Experimental Social Psychology, 51,* 1–39.

———. (in press). What predicts romantic relationship satisfaction and mate retention intensity—mate preference fulfillment or mate value discrepancies? *Evolution and Human Behavior.*

Cosmides, L., & Tooby, J. (1987). From evolution to behavior: Evolutionary psychology as the missing link. In J. Dupre (Ed.), *The latest on the best: Essays on evolution and optimality,* 277–306. Cambridge, MA: MIT Press.

Cronin, H. (1993). *The ant and the peacock: Altruism and sexual selection from Darwin to today.* Cambridge: Cambridge University Press.

Cross, J. F., & Cross, J. (1971). Age, sex, race, and the perception of facial beauty. *Developmental Psychology, 5,* 433–439.

Croze, H. A., Hillman, A. K., & Lang, E. M. (1981). Elephants and their habitats: How do they tolerate each other? In C. W. Fowler & T. D. Smith (Eds.), *Dynamics of large mammal populations,* 297–316. New York: Wiley.

Cuber, J. F., & Harroff, P. B. (1965). *Sex and the significant Americans: A study of sexual behavior among the affluent.* New York: Penguin Books.

Cunningham, M. R., Roberts, T., Richards, T., & Wu, C. (1989). The facial-metric prediction of physical attractiveness across races, ethnic groups, and cultures. Unpublished paper, Department of Psychology, University of Louisville, KY.

Daly, M., & Wilson, M. (1988). *Homicide.* Hawthorne, NY: Aldine de Gruyter.

Daly, M., Wilson, M., & Weghorst, S. J. (1982). Male sexual jealousy. *Ethology and Sociobiology, 3,* 11–27.

Daniels, D. (1983). The evolution of concealed ovulation and self-deception. *Ethology and Sociobiology, 4,* 69–87.

Darwin, C. (1859). *On the origin of the species by means of natural selection, or preservation of favoured races in the struggle for life.* London: Murray.

————. (1871). *The descent of man and selection in relation to sex.* London: Murray.

Dass, D. J. (1970). *Maharaja.* Delhi: Hind Pocket Books.

Dawkins, R. (1976). *The selfish gene.* Oxford: Oxford University Press.

Deaux, K., & Hanna, R. (1984). Courtship in the personals column: The influence of gender and sexual orientation. *Sex Roles, 11,* 363–375.

DeSteno, D. A., & Salovey, P. (1996). Evolutionary origins of sex differences in jealousy? Questioning the "fitness" of the model. *Psychological Science, 7*(6), 367–372.

De Waal, F. (1982). *Chimpanzee politics: Power and sex among apes.* Baltimore: John Hopkins University Press.

Dickemann, M. (1979). The ecology of mating systems in hypergynous dowry societies. *Social Science Information, 18,* 163–195.

————. (1981). Paternal confidence and dowry competition: A biocultural analysis of purdah. In R. D. Alexander & D. W. Tinkle (Eds.), *Natural selection and social behavior: Recent research and new theory,* 417–438. New York: Chiron Press.

Divale, W., & Harris, M. (1976). Population, warfare, and the male supremacist complex. *American Anthropologist, 78,* 521–538.

Draper, P., & Harpending, H. (1982). Father absence and reproductive strategy: An evolutionary perspective. *Journal of Anthropological Research, 38,* 255–273.

Duntley, J. D., & Buss, D. M. (2012). The evolution of stalking. *Sex Roles, 66*(5–6), 311–327.

Eagly, A. H., and Wood, W. (1999). The origins of sex differences in human behavior: Evolved dispositions versus social roles. *American Psychologist, 54*(6), 408–423.

Easton, J. A., Confer, J. C., Goetz, C. D., & Buss, D. M. (2010). Reproduction expediting: Sexual motivations, fantasies, and the ticking biological clock. *Personality and Individual Differences, 49,* 516–520.

Easton, J. A., Schipper, L. D., and Shackelford, T. K. (2007). Morbid jealousy from an evolutionary psychological perspective. *Evolution and Human Behavior, 28*(6), 399–402.

Ein-Dor, T., Perry-Paldi, A., Hirschberger, G., Birnbaum, G. E., & Deutsch, D. (2015). Coping with mate poaching: Gender differences in detection of infidelity-related threats. *Evolution and Human Behavior, 36,* 17–24.

Elder, G. H., Jr. (1969). Appearance and education in marriage mobility. *American Sociological Review, 34,* 519–533.

Ellis, B. J. (1992). The evolution of sexual attraction: Evaluative mechanisms in women. In J. Barkow, L. Cosmides, & J. Tooby (Eds.), *The adapted mind: Evolutionary psychology and the generation of culture,* 267–288. New York: Oxford University Press.

Ellis, B. J., McFadyen-Ketchum, S., Dodge, K. A., Pettit, G. S., & Bates, J. E. (1999). Quality of early family relationships and individual differences in the timing of pubertal maturation in girls: A longitudinal test of an evolutionary model. *Journal of Personality and Social Psychology, 77*(2), 387.

Ellis, B. J., & Symons, D. (1990). Sex differences in sexual fantasy: An evolutionary psychological approach. *Journal of Sex Research, 27,* 527–556.

Elwin, V. (1949). *The Muria and their Ghotul.* Bombay: Oxford University Press.

————. (1968). *The kingdom of the young*. London: Oxford University Press.

Erickson, C. J., & Zenone, P. G. (1976). Courtship differences in male ring doves: Avoidance of cuckoldry? *Science, 192*, 1353–1354.

Farrell, W. (1986). *Why men are the way they are*. New York: Berkley Books.

Fisher, H. (1992). *Anatomy of love*. New York: Norton.

Fisher, R. A. (1958). *The genetical theory of natural selection*. 2nd ed. New York: Dover.

Flaubert, G. (1950). *Madam Bovary*. Translated by A. Russell. New York: Penguin.

Flinn, M. (1988). Mate guarding in a Caribbean village. *Ethology and Sociobiology, 9*, 1–28.

Ford, C. S., & Beach, F. A. (1951). *Patterns of sexual behavior*. New York: Harper & Row.

Francis, J. L. (1977). Toward the management of heterosexual jealousy. *Journal of Marriage and the Family, 10*, 61–69.

Frank, R. H. (1988). *Passions within reason: The strategic role of the emotions*. New York: W. W. Norton & Co.

Frayser, S. (1985). *Varieties of sexual experience: An anthropological perspective*. New Haven, CT: HRAF Press.

Freemont, J. (1975). Rapists speak for themselves. In D. E. H. Russell, *The politics of rape: The victim's perspective*, 241–256. New York: Stein and Day.

Fussell, N. J., & Stollery, B. T. (2012). Between-sex differences in romantic jealousy: Substance or spin? A qualitative analysis. *Evolutionary Psychology, 10*(1), 136–172.

Galperin, A., Haselton, M. G., Frederick, D. A., Poore, J., von Hippel, W., Buss, D. M., & Gonzaga, G. C. (2013). Sexual regret: Evidence for evolved sex differences. *Archives of Sexual Behavior, 42*(7), 1145–1161.

Gangestad, S. W. (1989). The evolutionary history of genetic variation: An emerging issue in the behavioral genetic study of personality. In D. M. Buss & N. Cantor (Eds.), *Personality: Recent trends and emerging directions*. New York: Springer.

Gangestad, S. W., & Simpson, J. A. (1990). Toward an evolutionary history of female sociosexual variation. *Journal of Personality,* *58,* 69–96.

Gangestad, S. W., Thornhill, R., & Yeo, R. A. (1994). Facial attractiveness, developmental stability, and fluctuating asymmetry. *Ethology and Sociobiology, 15*(2), 73–85.

Gaulin, S. J. C., & Boster, J. S. (1990). Dowry as female competition. *American Anthropologist, 92,* 994–1005.

Gaulin, S. J. C., & Schlegel, A. (1980). Paternal confidence and paternal investment: A cross-cultural test of a sociobiological hypothesis. *Ethology and Sociobiology, 1,* 301–309.

Gavey, N. (1991). Sexual victimization prevalence among New Zealand university students. *Journal of Consulting and Clinical Psychology, 59,* 464–466.

Gil-Burmann, C., Peláez, F., & Sánchez, S. (2002). Mate choice differences according to sex and age. *Human Nature, 13*(4), 493–508.

Gildersleeve, K., Haselton, M. G., & Fales, M. R. (2014). Do women's mate preferences change across the ovulatory cycle? A meta-analytic review. *Psychological Bulletin, 140*(5), 1205.

Gilmore, D. D. (1990). *Manhood in the making: Cultural concepts of masculinity.* New Haven, CT: Yale University Press.

Givins, D. B. (1978). The nonverbal basis of attraction: Flirtation, courtship, and seduction. *Psychiatry, 41,* 336–359.

Gladue, B. A., & Delaney, J. J. (1990). Gender differences in perception of attractiveness of men and women in bars. *Personality and Social Psychology Bulletin, 16,* 378–391.

Gladwin, T., & Sarason, S. B. (1953). *Truk: Man in paradise.* New York: Wenner-Gren Foundation for Anthropology Research.

Glass, D. P., & Wright, T. L. (1985). Sex differences in type of extramarital involvement and marital dissatisfaction. *Sex Roles, 12,* 1101–1120.

Goetz, A. T., & Causey, K. (2009). Sex differences in perceptions of infidelity: Men often assume the worst. *Evolutionary Psychology, 7*(2), 253–263.

Goetz, C. D., Easton, J. A., & Buss, D. M. (2014). Women's perceptions of sexual exploitability cues and their link to sexual attractiveness. *Archives of Sexual Behavior, 43*(5), 999–1008.

Goetz, C. D., Easton, J. A., Lewis, D. M., & Buss, D. M. (2012). Sexual exploitability: Observable cues and their link to sexual attraction. *Evolution and Human Behavior, 33*(4), 417–426.

Goetz, C. D., Easton, J. A., & Meston, C. M. (2014). The allure of vulnerability: Advertising cues to exploitability as a signal of sexual accessibility. *Personality and Individual Differences, 64,* 121–125.

Goldschmidt, W. (1974). The economics of bridewealth among the Sebei in East Africa. *Ethnology, 13,* 311–333.

Goodall, J. (1986). *The chimpanzees of Gombe: Patterns of behavior.* Cambridge, MA: Harvard University Press.

Gottschalk, H. (1936). *Skinsygens problemer* (Problems of jealousy). Copenhagen: Fremad.

Gottschall, J., & Gottschall, T. (2003). Are per-incident rape-pregnancy rates higher than per-incident consensual pregnancy rates? *Human Nature, 14,* 1–20.

Gough, H. G. (1980). *Manual for the California Psychological Inventory.* Palo Alto, CA: Consulting Psychologists Press.

Gowaty, P. A. (1992). Evolutionary biology and feminism. *Human Nature, 3,* 217–249.

Grammer, K. (1992). Variations on a theme: Age dependent mate selection in humans. *Behavioral and Brain Sciences, 15,* 100–102.

Graziano, W. G., Jensen-Campbell, L. A., Shebilske, L. J., & Lundgren, S. R. (1993). Social influence, sex differences, and judgments of beauty: Putting the interpersonal back in interpersonal attraction. *Journal of Personality and Social Psychology, 65*(3), 522–531.

Greeff, J. M., Greeff, F. A., Greeff, A. S., Rinken, L., Welgemoed, D. J., & Harris, Y. (2012). Low nonpaternity rate in an old Afrikaner family. *Evolution and Human Behavior, 33*(4), 268–273.

Greeley, A. M. (1991). *Faithful attraction: Discovering intimacy, love, and fidelity in American marriage.* New York: Tom Doherty Associates.

Green, B. L., Lee, R. R., & Lustig, N. (1974). Conscious and unconscious factors in marital infidelity. *Medical Aspects of Human Sexuality,* September, 87–91, 97–98, 104–105.

Gregor, T. (1985). *Anxious pleasures: The sexual lives of an Amazonian people.* Chicago: University of Chicago Press.

Greiling, H. (1993). Women's short-term sexual strategies. Paper presented at the Conference on Evolution and the Human Sciences, London School of Economics, Centre for the Philosophy of the Natural and Social Sciences, London (June).

Greiling, H., & Buss, D. M. (2000). Women's sexual strategies: The hidden dimension of extra-pair mating. *Personality and Individual Differences, 28,* 929–963.

Griffin, S. (1971). Rape: The all-American crime. *Ramparts, 10,* 26–36.

Guéguen, N. (2011). Effects of solicitor sex and attractiveness on receptivity to sexual offers: A field study. *Archives of Sexual Behavior, 40*(5), 915–919.

Gurven, M., & Kaplan, H. (2006). Determinants of time allocation across the lifespan. *Human Nature, 17*(1), 1–49.

Gutek, B. A. (1985). *Sex and the workplace: The impact of sexual behavior and harassment on women, men, and the organization.* San Francisco: Jossey-Bass.

Guttentag, M., & Secord, P. (1983). *Too many women?* Beverly Hills, CA: Sage.

Hall, K., & DeVore, I. (1965). Baboon social behavior. In I. DeVore (Ed.), *Primate behavior,* 53–110. New York: Holt.

Hamilton, W. D., & Zuk, M. (1982). Heritable true fitness and bright birds: A role for parasites? *Science, 218,* 384–387.

Handy, E. S. C. (1923). *The native culture in the Marquesas.* Bulletin 9. Honolulu: Bernice A. Bishop Museum.

Harrison, A. A., & Saeed, L. (1977). Let's make a deal: An analysis of revelations and stipulations in lonely hearts' advertisements. *Journal of Personality and Social Psychology, 35,* 257–264.

Hart, C. W., & Pilling, A. R. (1960). *The Tiwi of North Australia.* New York: Holt, Rinehart & Winston.

Hartung, J. (n.d.). Rape: Biblical roots of the long leash on women. Unpublished manuscript.

Hartung, J., Dickemann, M., Melotti, U., Pospisil, L., Scott, E. C., Smith, J. M., & Wilder, W. D. (1982). Polygyny and inheritance of wealth [and comments and replies]. *Current Anthropology,* 1–12.

Haselton, M. G. (2003). The sexual overperception bias: Evidence of a systematic bias in men from a survey of naturally occurring events. *Journal of Research in Personality,* 37(1), 34–47.

Haselton, M. G., & Buss, D. M. (2000). Error management theory: A new perspective on biases in cross-sex mind reading. *Journal of Personality and Social Psychology,* 78(1), 81–91.

———. (2001). The affective shift hypothesis: The functions of emotional changes following sexual intercourse. *Personal Relationships,* 8(4), 357–369.

Hatfield, E., & Rapson, R. L. (1993). *Love, sex, and intimacy: Their psychology, biology, and history.* New York: HarperCollins.

Hatfield, E., Walster, G. W., Piliavin, J., & Schmidt, L. (1973). Playing hard-to-get: Understanding an elusive phenomenon. *Journal of Personality and Social Psychology,* 26, 113–121.

Hazan, H. (1983). *Endless rapture: Rape, romance, and the female imagination.* New York: Scribner's.

Henss, R. (1992). Perceiving age and attractiveness in facial photographs. Unpublished manuscript, Psychologisches Institüt, University of the Saarland, Germany.

Hermstein, R. (1989). IQ and falling birth rates. *Atlantic Monthly,* May, 73–79.

Hewlett, B. S. (1991). *Intimate fathers.* Ann Arbor: University of Michigan Press.

Hickman, S. E., & Muehlenhard, C. L. (1997). College women's fears and precautionary behaviors relating to acquaintance rape and stranger rape. *Psychology of Women Quarterly,* 21, 527–547.

Hilberman, E., & Munson, K. (1978). Sixty battered women. *Victimology,* 2, 460–470.

Hill, C. T., Rubin, Z., & Peplau, L. A. (1976). Breakups before marriage: The end of 103 affairs. *Journal of Social Issues,* 32, 147–168.

Hill, E. M., Nocks, E. S., & Gardner, L. (1987). Physical attractiveness: Manipulation by physique and status displays. *Ethology and Sociobiology,* 8, 143–154.

Hill, K., & Hurtado, A. M. (1989). Hunter-gatherers of the new world. *American Scientist, 77,* 437–443.

———. (1991). The evolution of premature reproductive senescence and menopause in human females. *Human Nature, 2,* 313–350.

———. (1996). *Demographic/life history of Ache foragers.* Hawthorne, NY: Aldine de Gruyter.

Hill, K., & Kaplan, H. (1988). Tradeoffs in male and female reproductive strategies among the Ache (parts 1 and 2). In L. Betzig, M. Borgerhoff Mulder, & P. Turke (Eds.), *Human reproductive behavior,* 277–306. New York: Cambridge University Press.

Hill, R. (1945). Campus values in mate selection. *Journal of Home Economics, 37,* 554–558.

Hite, S. (1987). *Women and love: A cultural revolution in progress.* New York: Knopf.

———. (2004). *The Hite report: A nationwide study of female sexuality.* New York: Seven Stories Press.

Hoffman, M. (1977). Homosexuality. In F. A. Beach (Ed.), *Human sexuality in four perspectives,* 164–169. Baltimore: Johns Hopkins University Press.

Holmberg, A. R. (1950). *Nomads of the long bow: The Siriono of Eastern Bolivia.* Washington, DC: US Government Printing Office.

Holmes, W. G., & Sherman, P. W. (1982). The ontogeny of kin recognition in two species of ground squirrels. *American Zoologist, 22,* 491–517.

Hosken, F. P. (1979). *The Hosken Report: Genital and sexual mutilation of females.* 2nd ed., rev. Lexington, MA: Women's International Network News.

Howard, R. D. (1981). Male age-size distribution and male mating success in bullfrogs. In R. D. Alexander & D. W. Tinkle (Eds.), *Natural selection and social behavior,* 61–77. New York: Chiron Press.

Howell, N. (1979). *Demography of the Dobe !Kung.* New York: Academic Press.

Hrdy, S. B. (1981). *The woman that never evolved.* Cambridge, MA: Harvard University Press.

Hudson, J. W., & Henze, L. F. (1969). Campus values in mate selection: A replication. *Journal of Marriage and the Family, 31,*
772–775.

Hughes, S. M., & Gallup, G. G. (2003). Sex differences in morphological predictors of sexual behavior: Shoulder to hip and waist
to hip ratios. *Evolution and Human Behavior, 24*(3), 173–178.

Hunt, M. (1974). *Sexual behavior in the 70's.* Chicago: Playboy Press.

Impett, E. A., & Peplau, L. A. (2002). Why some women consent to
unwanted sex with a dating partner: Insights from attachment
theory. *Psychology of Women Quarterly, 26,* 360–370.

Iredale, W., Van Vugt, M., & Dunbar, R. (2008). Showing off in humans: Male generosity as a mating signal. *Evolutionary Psychology, 6*(3), 368–392.

Jackson, L. A. (1992). *Physical appearance and gender: Sociobiological and sociocultural perspectives.* Albany: State University of
New York Press.

James, W. H. (1981). The honeymoon effect on marital coitus. *Journal of Sex Research, 17,* 114–123.

Jankowiak, W. R., & Fisher, E. F. (1992). A cross-cultural perspective on romantic love. *Ethnology, 31,* 149–155.

Jankowiak, W. R., Hill, E. M., & Donovan, J. M. (1992). The effects of sex and sexual orientation on attractiveness judgments:
An evolutionary interpretation. *Ethology and Sociobiology, 13,*
73–85.

Janus, S. S., & Janus, C. L. (1993). *The Janus Report on sexual behavior.* New York: Wiley.

Jencks, C. (1979). *Who gets ahead? The determinants of economic
success in America.* New York: Basic Books.

Johnson, R. E. (1970). Some correlates of extramarital coitus. *Journal of Marriage and the Family, 32,* 449–456.

Jones, E. C. (1975). The post-reproductive phase in mammals. In P.
van Keep & C. Lauritzen (Eds.), *Frontiers of hormone research,*
vol. 3, 1–20. Basel: Karger.

Jones, O. D. (1999). Sex, culture, and the biology of rape: Toward explanation and prevention. *California Law Review, 87,* 827–941.

Kamble, S., Shackelford, T. K., Pham, M., & Buss, D. M. (2014). Indian mate preferences: Continuity, sex differences, and cultural change across a quarter of a century. *Personality and Individual Differences, 70,* 150–155.

Kaplan, H., & Hill, K. (1985). Food sharing among Ache foragers: Tests of explanatory hypotheses. *Current Anthropology, 26,* 223–245.

Kaplan, H., Hill, K., & Hurtado, M. (1984). Food sharing among the Ache hunter-gatherers of eastern Paraguay. *Current Anthropology, 25,* 113–115.

Kennair, L. E. O., Schmitt, D., Fjeldavli, Y. L., & Harlem, S. K. (2009). Sex differences in sexual desires and attitudes in Norwegian samples. *Interpersona, 3,* 1–32.

Kenrick, D. T., Groth, G. E., Trost, M. R., & Sadalla, E. K. (1993). Integrating evolutionary and social exchange perspectives on relationships: Effects of gender, self-appraisal, and involvement level on mate selection. *Journal of Personality and Social Psychology, 64,* 951–969.

Kenrick, D. T., Gutierres, S. E., & Goldberg, L. (1989). Influence of erotica on ratings of strangers and mates. *Journal of Experimental Social Psychology, 25,* 159–167.

Kenrick, D. T., & Keefe, R. C. (1992). Age preferences in mates reflect sex differences in reproductive strategies. *Behavioral and Brain Sciences, 15,* 75–133.

Kenrick, D. T., Keefe, R. C., Gabrielidis, C., & Cornelius, J. S. (1996). Adolescents' age preferences for dating partners: Support for an evolutionary model of life-history strategies. *Child Development, 67,* 1499–1511.

Kenrick, D. T., Neuberg, S. L., Zierk, K. L., & Krones, J. M. (1994). Contrast effects as a function of sex, dominance, and physical attractiveness. *Personality and Social Psychology Bulletin, 20,* 210–217.

Kenrick, D. T., Sadalla, E. K., Groth, G., & Trost, M. R. (1990). Evolution, traits, and the stages of human courtship: Qualifying the parental investment model. *Journal of Personality, 58,* 97–116.

Kevles, B. (1986). *Females of the species.* Cambridge, MA: Harvard University Press.

Khallad, Y. (2005). Mate selection in Jordan: Effects of sex, socioeconomic status, and culture. *Journal of Social and Personal Relationships, 22*(2),155–168.

Kiesler, S. B., & Baral, R. L. (1970). The search for a romantic partner: The effects of self-esteem and physical attractiveness on romantic behavior. In K. J. Gergen & D. Marlow (Eds.), *Personality and Social Behavior,* 155–165. Reading, MA: Addison-Wesley.

Kinsey, A. C., Pomeroy, W. B., & Martin, C. E. (1948). *Sexual behavior in the human male.* Philadelphia: Saunders.

———. (1953). *Sexual behavior in the human female.* Philadelphia: Saunders.

Koss, M. P., & Oros, C. J. (1982). Sexual experiences survey: A research instrument investigating sexual aggression and victimization. *Journal of Consulting and Clinical Psychology, 50,* 455–457.

Kuhle, B. X. (2011). Did you have sex with him? Do you love her? An in vivo test of sex differences in jealous interrogations. *Personality and Individual Differences, 51*(8), 1044–1047.

Kuhle, B. X., Beasley, D. O., Beck, W. C., Brezinski, S. M., Cnudde, D., et al. (2016). To swipe left or right: Sex differences in Tinder profiles. Paper presented at the annual meeting of the Human Behavior and Evolution Society, Vancouver, Canada.

Kyl-Heku, L. M., & Buss, D. M. (1996). Tactics as units of analysis in personality psychology: An illustration using tactics of hierarchy negotiation. *Personality and Individual Differences, 21*(4), 497–517.

La Cerra, P., Cosmides, L., and Tooby, J. (1993). Psychological adaptations in women for assessing a man's willingness to invest in offspring. Paper presented at the fifth annual meeting of the Human Behavior and Evolution Society, Binghamton, NY (August).

Lahdenperä, M., Lummaa, V., Helle, S., Tremblay, M., & Russell, A. F. (2004). Fitness benefits of prolonged post-reproductive lifespan in women. *Nature, 428*(6979), 178–181.

Lalumiere, M. L. (2005). *The causes of rape: Understanding individ-ual differences in male propensity for sexual aggression.* Washington, DC: APA.

Lalumiere, M. L., Chalmers, L. J., Quinsey, V. L., & Seto, M. C. (1996). A test of the mate deprivation hypothesis of sexual coercion. *Ethology and Sociobiology, 17,* 299–318.

Langhorne, M. C., & Secord, P. F. (1955). Variations in marital needs with age, sex, marital status, and regional composition. *Journal of Social Psychology, 41,* 19–37.

Langlois, J. H., & Roggman, L. A. (1990). Attractive faces are only average. *Psychological Science, 1,* 115–121.

Langlois, J. H., Roggman, L. A., Casey, R. J., Ritter, J. M., Rieser-Danner, L. A., & Jenkins, V. Y. (1987). Infant preferences for attractive faces: Rudiments of a stereotype. *Developmental Psychology, 23,* 363–369.

Langlois, J. H., Roggman, L. A., & Reiser-Danner, L. A. (1990). Infants' differential social responses to attractive and unattractive faces. *Developmental Psychology, 26,* 153–159.

Lawson, A. (1988). *Adultery: An analysis of love and betrayal.* New York: Basic Books.

Le Boeuf, B. J. (1974). Male-male competition and reproductive success in elephant seals. *American Zoology, 14,* 163–176.

Lei, C., Wang, Y., Shackelford, T. K., & Buss, D. M. (2011). Chinese mate preferences: Cultural evolution and continuity across a quarter century. *Personality and Individual Differences, 50,* 678–683.

Li, N. P., Bailey, J. M., Kenrick, D. T., & Linsenmeier, J. A. (2002). The necessities and luxuries of mate preferences: Testing the tradeoffs. *Journal of Personality and Social Psychology, 82*(6), 947–955.

Li, N. P., Griskevicius, V., Durante, K. M., Jonason, P. K., Pasisz, D. J., & Aumer, K. (2009). An evolutionary perspective on humor: Sexual selection or interest indication? *Personality and Social Psychology Bulletin, 35,* 923–936.

Lieberman, D., Tooby, J., & Cosmides, L. (2003). Does morality have a biological basis? An empirical test of the factors governing moral sentiments relating to incest. *Proceedings of the Royal Society of London B: Biological Sciences, 270*(1517), 819–826.

Lindburg, D. G. (1971). The rhesus monkey in northern India: An ecological and behavioral study. In L. A. Rosenblum (Ed.), *Primate behavior,* vol. 2. New York: Academic Press.

Lippa, R. A. (2007). The preferred traits of mates in a cross-national study of heterosexual and homosexual men and women: An examination of biological and cultural influences. *Archives of Sexual Behavior, 36*(2), 193–208.

———. (2009). Sex differences in sex drive, sociosexuality, and height across 53 nations: Testing evolutionary and social structural theories. *Archives of Sexual Behavior, 38*(5), 631–651.

Livingston, Gretchen. (2014). Four-in-ten couples are saying "I do," again. Washington, DC: Pew Research Center (November 14).

Lobban, C. F. (1972). *Law and anthropology in the Sudan (an analysis of homicide cases in Sudan).* African Studies Seminar Series 13. Sudan Research Unit, University of Khartoum, Khartoum, Sudan.

Lopes, G. S., Shackelford, T. K., Santos, W. S., Farias, M. G., & Segundo, D. S. (2016). Mate Retention Inventory–Short Form (MRI-SF): Adaptation to the Brazilian context. *Personality and Individual Differences, 90,* 36–40.

Low, B. S. (1979). Sexual selection and human ornamentation. In N. A. Chagnon & W. Irons (Eds.), *Evolutionary biology and human social behavior.* Boston: Duxbury Press.

———. (1989). Cross-cultural patterns in the training of children: An evolutionary perspective. *Journal of Comparative Psychology, 103,* 313–319.

———. (1991). Reproductive life in nineteenth century Sweden: An evolutionary perspective on demographic phenomena. *Ethology and Sociobiology, 12,* 411–448.

Lukaszewski, A. W., & Roney, J. R. (2010). Kind toward whom? Mate preferences for personality traits are target specific. *Evolution and Human Behavior, 31*(1), 29–38.

Lund, O. C. H., Tamnes, C. K., Moestue, C., Buss, D. M., & Vollrath, M. (2007). Tactics of hierarchy negotiation. *Journal of Research in Personality, 41*(1), 25–44.

MacKinnon, C. (1987). *Feminism unmodified*. Cambridge, MA: Harvard University Press.

Malamuth, N. M. (1981). Rape proclivity among males. *Journal of Social Issues, 37,* 138–157.

———. (1986). Predictors of naturalistic sexual aggression. *Journal of Personality and Social Psychology, 50,* 953–962.

———. (1992). Evolution and laboratory research on men's sexual arousal: What do the data show and how can we explain them? *Behavioral and Brain Sciences, 15,* 394–396.

Malamuth, N. M., Heavey, C., & Linz, D. (1993). Predicting men's antisocial behavior against women: The "interaction model" of sexual aggression. In N. G. Hall & R. Hirshman (Eds.), *Sexual aggression: Issues in etiology, assessment, treatment, and policy.* New York: Hemisphere.

Malamuth, N. M., Sockloskie, R., Koss, M., & Tanaka, J. (1991). The characteristics of aggressors against women: Testing a model using a national sample of college women. *Journal of Consulting and Clinical Psychology, 59,* 670–681.

Malinowski, B. (1929). *The sexual life of savages in North-Western Melanesia.* London: Routledge.

Margolin, L., & White, L. (1987). The continuing role of physical attractiveness in marriage. *Journal of Marriage and the Family, 49,* 21–27.

Margulis, L., & Sagan, D. (1991). *Mystery dance: On the evolution of human sexuality.* New York: Summit Books.

Markman, H. S., Stanley, S., & Storaasili, R. (1991). Destructive fighting predicts divorce: Results from a 7-year follow-up. Unpublished manuscript, Department of Psychology, University of Denver.

Marlow, F. W. (2004). Is human ovulation concealed? Evidence from conception beliefs in a hunter-gatherer society. *Archives of Sexual Behavior, 33,* 427–432.

Mazur, A. (1992). The evolutionary psychology of rape and food robbery. *Behavioral and Brain Sciences, 15,* 397.

McCrae, R. R., & Costa, P. T., Jr. (1990). *Personality in adulthood.* New York: Guilford Press.

McGinnis, R. (1958). Campus values in mate selection. _Social Forces,_ 35, 368–373.

McKnight, J. (1997). _Straight science: Homosexuality, evolution, and adaptation._ New York: Routledge.

Meston, C. M., & Buss, D. M. (2009). _Why women have sex: Understanding sexual motivations from adventure to revenge (and everything in between)._ New York: Macmillan.

Miller, D. J. (1980). Battered women: Perceptions of their problems and their perception of community response. Master's thesis, University of Windsor, Ontario.

Miller, E. M. (2000). Homosexuality, birth order, and evolution: Toward an equilibrium reproductive economics of homosexuality. _Archives of Sexual Behavior, 29,_ 1–34.

Miller, G. (2000). _The mating mind: How sexual selection shaped the evolution of human nature._ New York: Doubleday.

Miller, S. L., & Maner, J. K. (2009). Sex differences in response to sexual versus emotional infidelity: The moderating role of individual differences. _Personality and Individual Differences, 46_(3), 287–291.

Miner, E. J., Starratt, V. G., & Shackelford, T. K. (2009). It's not all about her: Men's mate value and mate retention. _Personality and Individual Differences, 47_(3), 214–218.

Moore, F. R., Cassidy, C., Smith, M. J. L., & Perrett, D. I. (2006). The effects of female control of resources on sex-differentiated mate preferences. _Evolution and Human Behavior, 27_(3), 193–205.

Morgan, J. B. (1981). Relationship between rape and physical damage during rape and phase of sexual cycle during which rape occurred. PhD diss., University of Texas, Austin.

Morris, N. M., & Udry, J. R. (1970). Variations in pedometer activity during the menstrual cycle. _Obstetrics and Gynecology, 35,_ 199–201.

Morse, S. J., Reis, H. T., Gruzen, J., & Wolff, E. (1974). The "eye of the beholder": Determinants of physical attractiveness judgments in the US and South Africa. _Journal of Personality, 42,_ 528–542.

Muehlenhard, C. L., & Linton, M. A. (1987). Date rape and sexual aggression in dating situations: Incidence and risk factors. *Journal of Counseling Psychology, 2,* 186–196.

Murdock, G. P., & Wilson, S. F. (1972). Settlement patterns and community organization: Cross-cultural codes 3. *Ethnology, 11,* 254–297.

Muscarella, F. (2000). The evolution of homoerotic behavior in humans. *Journal of Homosexuality, 40,* 51–77.

Nesse, R. M. (1990). Evolutionary explanations of emotions. *Human Nature, 1,* 261–289.

Nida, S. A., & Koon, J. (1983). They get better looking at closing time around here, too. *Psychological Reports, 52,* 657–658.

O'Donohue, W., & Plaud, J. J. (1991). The long-term habituation of sexual arousal in the human male. *Journal of Behavior Therapy and Experimental Psychiatry, 22,* 87–96.

Ogas, O., & Gaddam, S. (2011). *A billion wicked thoughts: What the Internet tells us about sexual relationships.* New York: Penguin.

Orions, G. H., & Heerwagen, J. H. (1992). Evolved responses to landscapes. In J. Barkow, L. Cosmides, & J. Tooby (Eds.), *The adapted mind: Evolutionary psychology and the generation of culture,* 555–579. New York: Oxford University Press.

Ortner, S. B. (1974). Is female to male as nature is to culture? In M. Z. Rosaldo & L. Lamphere (Eds.), *Woman, culture, and society,* 67–88. Stanford, CA: Stanford University Press.

Ortner, S. B., & Whitehead, H. (1981). *Sexual meanings: The cultural construction of gender and sexuality.* New York: Cambridge University Press.

Ovid (1982). *The erotic poems.* Translated by P. Green. New York: Penguin Books.

Parker, G. A. (1970). Sperm competition and its evolutionary consequences in the insects. *Biological Reviews, 45,* 525–568.

Pavelka, M. S., & Fedigan, L. M. (1991). Menopause: A comparative life history perspective. *Yearbook of Physical Anthropology, 34,* 13–38.

Pawlowski, B., & Koziel, S. (2002). The impact of traits offered in personal advertisements on response rates. *Evolution and Human Behavior, 23*(2), 139–149.

Pawson, E., & Banks, G. (1993). Rape and fear in a New Zealand city. *Area, 25,* 55–63.

Pedersen, F. A. (1991). Secular trends in human sex ratios: Their influence on individual and family behavior. *Human Nature, 3,* 271–291.

Pennybaker, J. W., Dyer, M. A., Caulkins, R. S., Litowixz, D. L., Ackerman, P. L., & Anderson, D. B. (1979). Don't the girls get prettier at closing time: A country and western application to psychology. *Personality and Social Psychology Bulletin, 5,* 122–125.

Perilloux, C., & Buss, D. M. (2008). Breaking up romantic relationships: Costs experienced and coping strategies deployed. *Evolutionary Psychology, 6,* 164–181.

Perilloux, C., Easton, J. A., & Buss, D. M. (2012). The misperception of sexual interest. *Psychological Science, 23,* 146–151.

Pfeiffer, E., & Davis, G. C. (1972). Determinants of sexual behavior in middle and old age. *Journal of the American Geriatrics Society, 20,* 151–158.

Pinker, S. (1997). *How the mind works.* New York: Norton.

Pollet, T. V., & Nettle, D. (2008). Driving a hard bargain: Sex ratio and male marriage success in a historical US population. *Biology Letters, 4*(1), 31–33.

Posner, R. A. (1992). *Sex and reason.* Cambridge, MA: Harvard University Press.

Radcliffe-Brown, A. R. (1922). *The Andaman Islanders.* Cambridge: Cambridge University Press.

Rahman, Q., & Wilson, G. D. (2003). Born gay? The psychobiology of human sexual orientation. *Personality and Individual Differences, 34,* 1337–1382.

Rasmussen, K. (1931). *The Netsilik Eskimos: Social life and spiritual culture.* Copenhagen: Gyldendalske Boghandel, Nordisk Forlag.

Rogel, M. J. (1976). Biosocial aspects of rape. PhD diss., University of Chicago.

Rosenblatt, P. C. (1974). Cross-cultural perspective on attractiveness. In T. L. Huston (Ed.), *Foundations of interpersonal attraction*, 79–95. New York: Academic Press.

Røskaft, E., Wara, A., & Viken, A. (1992). Reproductive success in relation to resource-access and parental age in a small Norwegian farming parish during the period 1700–1900. *Ethology and Sociobiology, 13,* 443–461.

Rounsaville, B. J. (1978). Theories in marital violence: Evidence from a study of battered women. *Victimology, 3,* 11–31.

Royle, T. (1989). *A dictionary of military quotations.* New York: Simon & Schuster.

Rozin, P. (1976). Psychological and cultural determinants of food choice. In T. Silverstone (Ed.), *Appetite and food intake,* 286–312. Berlin: Dahlem Konferenzen.

Rozin, P., & Fallon, A. (1988). Body image, attitudes to weight, and misperceptions of figure preferences of the opposite sex: A comparison of men and women in two generations. *Journal of Abnormal Psychology, 97,* 342–345.

Rudder, C. (2014). *Dataclysm: Who we are (when we think no one's looking).* Toronto: Random House Canada.

Ruse, M. (1988). *Homosexuality: A philosophical inquiry.* Oxford: Basil Blackwell.

Russell, D. E. H. (1990). *Rape in marriage.* Bloomington: University of Indiana Press.

Ryder, H., Maltby, J., Rai, L., Jones, P., & Flowe, H. D. (2016). Women's fear of crime and preference for formidable mates: How specific are the underlying psychological mechanisms? *Evolution and Human Behavior, 37,* 293–302.

Saal, F. E., Johnson, C. B., & Weber, N. (1989). Friendly or sexy? It may depend on whom you ask. *Psychology of Women Quarterly, 13,* 263–276.

Safilios-Rothschild, C. (1969). Attitudes of Greek spouses toward marital infidelity. In G. Neubeck (Ed.), *Extramarital relations,* 78–79. Englewood Cliffs, NJ: Prentice Hall.

Sagarin, B. J., Martin, A. L., Coutinho, S. A., Edlund, J. E., Patel, L., Skowronski, J. J., & Zengel, B. (2012). Sex differences in jealousy: A meta-analytic examination. *Evolution and Human Behavior,* 33(6), 595–614.

Saghir, M., & Robins, E. (1973). *Male and female homosexuality.* Baltimore: Williams and Wilkins.

Saletore, R. N. (1974). *Sex life under Indian rulers.* Delhi: Hind Pocket Books.

———. (1978). *Sex in Indian harem life.* New Delhi: Orient Paperbacks.

Scelza, B. A. (2014). Jealousy in a small-scale, natural fertility population: The roles of paternity, investment, and love in jealous response. *Evolution and Human Behavior,* 35(2), 103–108.

Schapera, I. (1940). *Married life in an African tribe.* London: Faber & Faber.

Schmitt, D. P. (2001). Desire for sexual variety and mate poaching experiences across multiple languages and cultures. Paper presented at the annual meeting of the Human Behavior and Evolution Society, London (June).

———. (2003). Universal sex differences in the desire for sexual variety: Tests from 52 nations, 6 continents, and 13 islands. *Journal of Personality and Social Psychology,* 85(1), 85–104.

———. (2016). Fundamentals of human mating strategies. In D. M. Buss (Ed.), *The evolutionary psychology handbook,* 2nd ed., 294–316. New York: Wiley.

Schmitt, D. P., & Buss, D. M. (1996). Strategic self-promotion and competitor derogation: Sex and context effects on the perceived effectiveness of mate attraction tactics. *Journal of Personality and Social Psychology,* 70(6), 1185–1204.

———. (2001). Human mate poaching: Tactics and temptations for infiltrating existing mateships. *Journal of Personality and Social Psychology,* 80, 894–917.

Schneider, H. K. (1964). A model of African indigenous economy and society. *Comparative Studies in Society and History,* 7, 37–55.

Secord, P. F. (1982). The origin and maintenance of social roles: The case of sex roles. In W. Ickes & E. S. Knowles (Eds.), *Personality, roles, and social behavior,* 33–53. New York: Springer.

Seiler, M. (1976). Monogamy is "unnatural," man with 9 wives says. *Los Angeles Times,* February 9, pt. 2, p. 1.

Semmelroth, J., & Buss, D. M. (unpublished). Studies on conflict between the sexes. Unpublished data, Department of Psychology, University of Michigan, Ann Arbor, Michigan.

Seyfarth, R. M. (1976). Social relationships among adult female baboons. *Animal Behavior, 24,* 917–938.

Shanley, D. P., Sear, R., Mace, R., & Kirkwood, T. B. (2007). Testing evolutionary theories of menopause. *Proceedings of the Royal Society of London B: Biological Sciences, 274*(1628), 2943–2949.

Shettel-Neuber, J., Bryson, J. B., & Young, C. E. (1978). Physical attractiveness of the "other person" and jealousy. *Personality and Social Psychology Bulletin, 4,* 612–615.

Short, R. V. (1979). Sexual selection and its component parts, somatic and genital selection, as illustrated by man and great apes. *Advances in the Study of Behavior, 9,* 131–158.

Shostak, M. (1981). *Nisa: The life and words of a !Kung woman.* Cambridge, MA: Harvard University Press.

Sigusch, V., & Schmidt, G. (1971). Lower-class sexuality: Some emotional and social aspects in West German males and females. *Archives of Sexual Behavior, 1,* 29–44.

Singh, D. (1993a). Adaptive significance of waist-to-hip ratio and female physical attractiveness. *Journal of Personality and Social Psychology, 65,* 293–307.

———. (1993b). Body shape and female attractiveness: Critical role of waist-to-hip ratio. *Human Nature, 4,* 297–321.

———. (1994). Is thin really beautiful and good? Relationship between waist-to-hip ratio and female attractiveness. *Personality and Individual Differences, 16,* 123–132.

Singh, D., Vidaurri, M., Zambarano, R. J., & Dabbs, J. M. (1999). Lesbian erotic role identification: Behavioral, morphological, and hormonal correlates. *Journal of Personality and Social Psychology, 76*(6), 1035–1049.

Small, M. (1992). The evolution of female sexuality and mate selection in humans. *Human Nature, 3,* 133–156.

Smith, R. L. (1984). Human sperm competition. In R. L. Smith (Ed.), *Sperm competition and the evolution of mating systems,* 601–659. New York: Academic Press.

Smuts, B. B. (1985). *Sex and friendship in baboons.* New York: Aldine de Gruyter.

———. (1987). Sexual competition and mate choice. In B. B. Smuts, D. L. Cheney, R. M. Seyfarth, R. W. Wrangham, & T. T. Struhsaker (Eds.), *Primate societies,* 385–399. Chicago: University of Chicago Press.

———. (1992). Male aggression against women: An evolutionary perspective. *Human Nature, 3,* 1–44.

———. (1995). The origins of patriarchy: An evolutionary perspective. In A. Zagarell (Ed.), *Origins of gender inequality.* Kalamazoo, MI: New Issues Press.

Smuts, B. B., & Smuts, R. W. (1993). Male aggression against female primates: Evidence and theoretical implications. In P. J. B. Slater, J. S. Rosenblatt, M. Milinski, & C. T. Snowden (Eds.), *Advances in the study of behavior.* New York: Academic Press.

Souza, A. L., Conroy-Beam, D., & Buss, D. M. (2016). Mate preferences in Brazil: Evolved desires and cultural evolution over three decades. *Personality and Individual Differences, 95,* 45–49.

Spanier, G. B., & Margolis, R. L. (1983). Marital separation and extramarital sexual behavior. *Journal of Sex Research, 19,* 23–48.

Sprecher, S., Aron, A., Hatfield, E., Cortese, A., Potapova, E., & Levitskaya, A. (1992). Love: American style, Russian style, and Japanese style. Paper presented at the Sixth International Conference on Personal Relationships, Orono, Maine.

Stern, B. (1933). *The scented garden: Anthropology of the sex life in the levant.* New York: American Ethnological Press.

Sternberg, R. J. (1988). *The triangle of love.* New York: Basic Books.

Strassman, B. I. (1981). Sexual selection, parental care, and concealed ovulation in humans. *Ethology and Sociobiology, 2,* 31–40.

Stroebe, W. (1977). Self-esteem and interpersonal attraction. In S. W. Duck (Ed.), *Theory and practice in interpersonal attraction,* 79–104. London: Academic Press.

Studd, M. V., & Gattiker, U. E. (1991). The evolutionary psychology of sexual harassment in organizations. *Ethology and Sociobiology, 12,* 249–290.

———. (in preparation). Evolutionary psychology of sexual harassment: Effect of initiator profile and social context on response of recipients of sexual advances in the workplace. Faculty of Management, University of Lethbridge, Alberta.

Surbey, M. K., & Conohan, C. D. (2000). Willingness to engage in casual sex. *Human Nature, 11*(4), 367–386.

Symons, D. (1979). *The evolution of human sexuality.* New York: Oxford University Press.

———. (1987). If we're all Darwinians, what's the fuss about? In C. B. Crawford, M. F. Smith, and D. L. Krebs (Eds.), *Sociobiology and psychology: Ideas, issues, and applications,* 121–146. Hillsdale, NJ: Erlbaum.

———. (1989). The psychology of human mate preferences. *Behavioral and Brain Sciences, 12,* 34–35.

———. (1992). What do men want. *Behavioral and Brain Sciences, 15*(1), 113–114.

Takahashi, H., Matsuura, M., Yahata, N., Koeda, M., Suhara, T., & Okubo, Y. (2006). Men and women show distinct brain activations during imagery of sexual and emotional infidelity. *NeuroImage, 32*(3), 1299–1307.

Tanner, R. E. S. (1970). *Homicide in Uganda, 1964: Crime in East Africa.* Uppsala, Sweden: Scandinavian Institute of African Studies.

Taylor, P. A., & Glenn, N. D. (1976). The utility of education and attractiveness for females' status attainment through marriage. *American Sociological Review, 41,* 484–498.

Teisman, M. W., & Mosher, D. L. (1978). Jealous conflict in dating couples. *Psychological Reports, 42,* 1211–1216.

Terman, L. M. (1938). *Psychological factors in marital happiness.* New York: McGraw-Hill.

Terpstra, D. E., & Cook, S. E. (1985). Complainant characteristics and reported behaviors and consequences associated with formal sexual harassment charges. *Personnel Psychology, 38,* 559–574.

Thakerar, J. N., & Iwawaki, S. (1979). Cross-cultural comparisons of interpersonal attraction of females toward males. *Journal of Social Psychology, 108,* 121–122.

Thibeau, J. W., & Kelly, H. H. (1986). *The social psychology of groups.* 2nd ed. New Brunswick, NJ: Transaction Books.

Thiessen, D., Young, R. K., & Burroughs, R. (1993). Lonely hearts advertisements reflect sexually dimorphic mating strategies. *Ethology and Sociobiology, 14,* 209–229.

Thompson, A. P. (1983). Extramarital sex: A review of the research literature. *Journal of Sex Research, 19,* 1–22.

———. (1984). Emotional and sexual components of extramarital relations. *Journal of Marriage and the Family, 46,* 35–42.

Thornhill, N. W. (1992). Female short-term sexual strategies: The self-esteem hypothesis. Paper presented at the meeting of the Human Behavior and Evolution Society, Albuquerque, New Mexico (August).

Thornhill, N. W., & Thornhill, R. (1990a). An evolutionary analysis of psychological pain following rape: 1. The effects of victim's age and marital status. *Ethology and Sociobiology, 11,* 155–176.

———. (1990b). An evolutionary analysis of psychological pain following rape: 2. The effects of stranger, friend, and family-member offenders. *Ethology and Sociobiology, 11,* 177–193.

Thornhill, R. (1980a). Mate choice in *Hylobittacus apicalis* (Insecta: Mecoptera) and its relation to some models of female choice. *Evolution, 34,* 519–538.

———. (1980b). Rape in *Panorpa* scorpionflies and a general rape hypothesis. *Animal Behavior, 28,* 52–59.

Thornhill, R., & Alcock, J. (1983). *The evolution of insect mating systems.* Cambridge, MA: Harvard University Press.

Thornhill, R., & Gangestad, S. W. (2008). *The evolutionary biology of human female sexuality.* New York: Oxford University Press.

Thornhill, R., & Palmer, C. (2000). *A natural history of rape: Biological bases of sexual coercion.* Cambridge, MA: MIT Press.

Thornhill, R., & Thornhill, N. (1983). Human rape: An evolutionary analysis. *Ethology and Sociobiology, 4,* 63–99.

————. (1990a). An evolutionary analysis of psychological pain following rape: I. The effects of victim's age and marital status. *Ethology and Sociobiology, 11*(3), 155–176.

————. (1990b). An evolutionary analysis of psychological pain following rape: II. The effects of stranger, friend, and family-member offenders. *Ethology and Sociobiology, 11*(3), 177–193.

————. (1992). The evolutionary psychology of men's coercive sexuality. *Behavioral and Brain Sciences, 15,* 363–421.

Todosijević, B., Ljubinković, S., & Arančić, A. (2003). Mate selection criteria: A trait desirability assessment study of sex differences in Serbia. *Evolutionary Psychology, 1*(1), 116–126.

Tooby, J., & Cosmides, L. (1989a). The innate versus the manifest: How universal does universal have to be? *Behavioral and Brain Sciences, 12,* 36–37.

————. (1989b). Evolutionary psychology and the generation of culture: 1. Theoretical considerations. *Ethology and Sociobiology, 10,* 29–49.

Tooby, J., & DeVore, I. (1987). The reconstruction of hominid behavioral evolution through strategic modeling. In W. G. Kinzey (Ed.), *The evolution of human behavior: Primate models,* 183–237. New York: State University of New York Press.

Tooke, J., & Camire, L. (1991). Patterns of deception in intersexual and intrasexual mating strategies. *Ethology and Sociobiology, 12,* 345–364.

Townsend, J. M. (1989). Mate selection criteria: A pilot study. *Ethology and Sociobiology, 10,* 241–253.

Townsend, J. M., & Levy, G. D. (1990). Effects of potential partners' physical attractiveness and socioeconomic status on sexuality and partner selection. *Archives of Sexual Behavior, 371,* 149–164.

Trinkaus, E., & Zimmerman, M. R. (1982). Trauma among the Shanidar Neanderthals. *American Journal of Physical Anthropology, 57,* 61–76.

Tripp, C. A. (1975). *The homosexual matrix.* New York: Signet.

Trivers, R. (1972). Parental investment and sexual selection. In B. Campbell (Ed.), *Sexual selection and the descent of man,* 136–179. New York: Aldine de Gruyter.

————. (1985). *Social evolution*. Menlo Park, CA: Benjamin/ Cummings.

Udry, J. R. (1980). Changes in the frequency of marital intercourse from panel data. *Archives of Sexual Behavior, 9,* 319–325.

Udry, J. R., & Eckland, B. K. (1984). Benefits of being attractive: Differential payoffs for men and women. *Psychological Reports, 54,* 47–56.

Utian, W. H. (1980). *Menopause in modern perspective: A guide to clinical practice*. New York: Appleton-Century-Crofts.

Vandenberg, S. (1972). Assortative mating, or who marries whom? *Behavior Genetics, 2,* 127–158.

Van Gulik, R. H. (1974). *Sexual life in ancient China*. London: E. J. Brill.

Voland, E., & Engel, C. (1990). Female choice in humans: A conditional mate selection strategy of the Krummerhörn women (Germany 1720–1874). *Ethology, 84,* 144–154.

Wade, T. J., & Slemp, J. (2015). How to flirt best: The perceived effectiveness of flirtation techniques. *Interpersona, 9*(1), 32–43.

Waynforth, D., Hurtado, A. M., & Hill, K. (1998). Environmentally contingent reproductive strategies in Mayan and Ache males. *Evolution and Human Behavior, 19*(6), 369–385.

Weisfeld, G. E., Russell, R. J. H., Weisfeld, C. C., & Wells, P. A. (1992). Correlates of satisfaction in British marriages. *Ethology and Sociobiology, 13,* 125–145.

Weiss, D. L., & Slosnerick, M. (1981). Attitudes toward sexual and nonsexual extramarital involvements among a sample of college students. *Journal of Marriage and the Family, 43,* 349–358.

Weiss, D. S. (1975). *Marital separation*. New York: Basic Books.

Welham, C. V. J. (1990). Incest: An evolutionary model. *Ethology and Sociobiology, 11,* 97–111.

White, G. L. (1980). Inducing jealousy: A power perspective. *Personality and Social Psychology Bulletin, 6,* 222–227.

————. (1981). Some correlates of romantic jealousy. *Journal of Personality, 49,* 129–147.

Whitehurst, R. N. (1971). Violence potential in extramarital sexual responses. *Journal of Marriage and the Family, 33,* 683–691.

Whyte, M. K. (1990). Changes in mate choice in Chengdu. In D. Davis & E. Vogel (Eds.), *China on the eve of Tiananmen.* Cambridge, MA: Harvard University Press.

Wiederman, M. W. (1993). Evolved gender differences in mate preferences: Evidence from personal advertisements. *Ethology and Sociobiology, 14,* 331–351.

Wiederman, M. W., & Allgeier, E. R. (1992). Gender differences in mate selection criteria: Sociobiological or socioeconomic explanation? *Ethology and Sociobiology, 13,* 115–124.

Willerman, L. (1979). *The psychology of individual and group differences.* San Francisco: Freeman.

Williams, G. C. (1957). Pleiotropy, natural selection, and the evolution of senescence. *Evolution, 11,* 398–411.

———. (1975). *Sex and evolution.* Princeton, NJ: Princeton University Press.

Wilson, E. O. (1975). *Sociobiology: The new synthesis.* Cambridge, MA: Harvard University Press.

———. (1978). *On human nature.* Cambridge, MA: Harvard University Press.

Wilson, G. D. (1987). Male-female differences in sexual activity, enjoyment, and fantasies. *Personality and Individual Differences, 8,* 125–126.

Wilson, M. (1989). Conflict and homicide in evolutionary perspective. In R. Bell & N. Bell (Eds.), *Sociobiology and the social sciences,* 45–62. Lubbock: Texas Tech University Press.

Wilson, M., & Daly, M. (1985). Competitiveness, risk taking, and violence: The young male syndrome. *Ethology and Sociobiology, 6,* 59–73.

———. (1992). The man who mistook his wife for a chattel. In J. Barkow, L. Cosmides, & J. Tooby (Eds.), *The adapted mind: Evolutionary psychology and the generation of culture,* 289–322. New York: Oxford University Press.

Wilson, M., & Mesnick, S. L. (1997). An empirical test of the bodyguard hypothesis. In P. A. Gowaty (Ed.), *Feminism and evolutionary biology: Boundaries, intersections, and frontiers.* New York: Chapman & Hall.

Wolf, M., Musch, J., Enczmann, J., & Fischer, J. (2012). Estimating the prevalence of nonpaternity in Germany. *Human Nature,* 23(2), 208–217.

Wolf, N. (1991). *The beauty myth.* New York: Morrow.

Yosef, R. (1991). Females seek males with ready cache. *Natural History,* June, 37.

Young, R. R., & Thiessen, D. (1992). The Texas rape scale. *Ethology and Sociobiology, 13,* 19–33.

Zahavi, A. (1975). Mate selection—a selection for a handicap. *Journal of Theoretical Biology,* 53(1), 205–214.

———. (1977). The testing of a bond. *Animal Behavior, 25,* 246–247.

Index

emotional constrictedness, 234
extramarital sex patterns of, 306
fantasies, sexual, 127–129
income distribution by age, 314
low-commitment sex, 120,
124–130
mate value, 42–44, 74, 311–316,
326, 74
matelessness, 317–318
mortality of, 316–318
patriarchy, 333–338
post-orgasm shift, 131
rape, as perpetrators of, 249–250
regret, sexual, 129–130
resources, changes in, 273,
311–312
risk-taking, 316, 343
sexual orientation, development
of, 21
sexual overperception bias,
227–229, 248
status and resource acquisition
drives of, 71
variety, sexual, 81, 120–129,
132, 146, 250, 307, 332, 348
See also commitment; jealousy;
social status of men
men, mating preferences of
actualization of, 100–101
adolescent males, 85
ancestral men, 82–83, 101, 105,
114, 151, 241
chastity and fidelity, 104–109
commitment, benefits of, 79–83
evolutionary bases of, 109–112
female's physical appearance,
90–95
fertility of mate, 82–83
health, 60–62, 87
homosexuals' preferences,
96–99, 110
low-commitment sex, 120,
124–130

marriage, 79–81
media effects on, 101–104
number of desired sex partners,
120–121
paternity, certainty of, 80,
105–106, 174, 195–196
reproductive potential of women,
86–87, 110
sex drive, 121
sex with strangers, 114, 121–122
sexual variety, 81, 120–129, 132,
146, 250, 307, 332
social status and, 81, 91, 95–96
universal, 110
youth, 83–86, 111, 296, 327
See also extramarital sex
men-to-women ratio. *See* sex ratio
imbalance
Mencken, H. L., 13
menopause
adaptations, 309–310
ancestral people, 309
grandmother hypothesis,
309–310
rapid reproduction and,
310–311, 325–326
Mesnick, Sarah, 263–264
Miller, Geoffrey, 183, 184
monogamy, 24, 40, 339, 348
morality, sexual, 185, 339–340
Muehlenhard, Charlene, 263
mutation loads, 81, 183

naturalistic fallacy, 26–27
non-paternity rates, 109

online dating. *See* Internet dating
orgasm, female
extramarital affairs and, 119, 305
as mating strategy, 120
as selection device, 119
sperm retention and, 118
Oring, Lewis, 139

David M. Buss is professor of psychology at the University of Texas, Austin, and the author of nine books, including *Why Women Have Sex, The Murderer Next Door, The Dangerous Passion,* and the text-book *Evolutionary Psychology,* now in its fifth edition. He lives in Austin, Texas.